MARTIN
GROVE
BRUMBAUGH

MARTIN GROVE BRUMBAUGH

A Pennsylvanian's Odyssey
from Sainted Schoolman
to Bedeviled World War I Governor,
1862–1930

Earl C. Kaylor Jr.

A Juniata College Publication

Madison • Teaneck
Fairleigh Dickinson University Press
London: Associated University Presses

Associated University Presses
440 Forsgate Drive
Cranbury, NJ 08512

Associated University Presses
25 Sicilian Avenue
London WC1A 2QH, England

Associated University Presses
P.O. Box 338, Port Credit
Mississauga, Ontario
Canada L5G 4L8

The paper used in this publication meets the requirements
of the American National Standard for Permanence of Paper
for Printed Library Materials Z39.48-1984.

Library of Congress Cataloging-in-Publication Data

Kaylor, Earl C.
    Martin Grove Brumbaugh : a Pennsylvanian's odyssey from sainted schoolman to bedeviled World War I governor, 1862–1930 / Earl C. Kaylor, Jr.
      p. cm.
    Includes bibliographical references and index.
    ISBN 0-8386-3689-6 (alk. paper)
    1. Brumbaugh, Martin Grove, 1862–1930. 2. Governors-
-Pennsylvania—Biography. 3. Educators—Pennsylvania—Biography.
4. College presidents—Pennsylvania—Biography. 5. Pennsylvania-
-Biography. 6. Juniata College (Huntingdon, Pa.)—Presidents-
Biography. I. Title.
F154.B8935 1996
940.2'8—dc20   95-31882
                                        CIP

PRINTED IN THE UNITED STATES OF AMERICA

To
Masters Jordan, Nicholas, Tyson,
and little Miss Quincy—
you are a grandfather's joy

Contents

Foreword

CLAUDE FLORY

This is the book that for a long time I dreamed of writing. I can assure you that it is here better done than if my dream had materialized. Dr. Kaylor has previously published the history of Juniata College and of the Dunkard Church in central Pennsylvania. His scholarship has delved deeply into the educational and social history of Pennsylvania and the nation. His research techniques are skillful and conscientious.

It is out of this highly pertinent background of preparation that Dr. Kaylor has written this biography of Martin Grove Brumbaugh. In reading it I have learned a great deal—with pleasure.

Since no one still living shared as much of Dr. Brumbaugh's comings and goings as I did during the last four-plus years of his life, Dr. Kaylor has invited me to record some of my impressions and relate some of my memories.

I was Dr. Brumbaugh's chauffeur during my four years of college. By his own account he drove a car only once.

One of the perquisites of the governorship in 1915 was an elegant Packard—glass-enclosed passenger area, two outside attendants, chauffeur, and footman. The Brumbaughs had returned to their Germantown home for the weekend. It was a hot, sunny afternoon. M. G. decided the car would be better off in the garage. He had no trouble starting it—he had watched Chauffeur Snyder several times. But as he passed through the garage door he realized he did not know how to stop it. There was a big shelf above the door with a load of bricks stored on it. The bump of the car against the back wall dislodged the shelf. The bricks came tumbling down in a huge pile behind the car. The governor crawled out over the mound of bricks and never touched a steering wheel again. He also asked Mrs. Brumbaugh to cancel the plans she was making with Chauffeur Snyder for a series of lessons. Driving was too dangerous for anyone but experts.

I was his oarsman and fishing companion during the summer months on the beautiful glacier-carved lakes of Maine. I was his golf caddie and in my senior year his occasional partner. I now and then knelt down before him and pulled on and buckled his galoshes in snowy weather. Ann Groninger, his college secretary, and I were the witnesses to his will.

9

From the day of my arrival in Huntingdon the Brumbaughs treated me almost like a member of the family. The fact that he had been governor of Pennsylvania and, in 1916, prominent among those seeking nomination as the Republican candidate for president, did not make M. G. the least bit haughty in his attitude toward a plain, simple college freshman. In fact, I never saw him exhibit an attitude of self-superiority toward anyone. On one occasion we were virtually two kids together. We were in a fishing camp deep in the woods of northeast Maine. Our cabin had two bedrooms, thanks to a six-feet-high wall of boards. M. G. had gone to bed in their room, I in mine. Mrs. Brumbaugh was reading aloud to us. She stopped. There was a noise on the porch. M. G. and I rushed to the door. A full moon revealed a cow moose pushing a tin pail around. Hearing us, she stalked off in a dignified moose manner. We followed her, M. G. in his nightshirt, I in my pajamas, in and out among the other cabins, until she disappeared into the forest.

What was the essence of Martin Grove Brumbaugh from the perception of an unsophisticated college boy who had known nothing but the strenuous life of a dairy farm?

He was a great teacher: a teacher of students; a teacher of teachers. In the long run I probably learned more from him out of class than I did from my formal teachers in class.

Dr. Felix E. Schelling, eminent Elizabethan scholar at the University of Pennsylvania and one of the greatest influences in M. G.'s graduate study (and in mine, forty years later) had a memorable educational pronouncement: "Teaching is like pugilism—you have to hit several times in the same spot if you want to make a lasting impression. Only a very few are gifted with knock-out power." That is something we ordinary teachers need to constantly remember. Not so pugilist Brumbaugh. He could tell you once and it was forever.

Early in my association with him we were on an overnight train trip. I had never before been on a Pullman sleeper. In the morning, despite having the upper berth, I arrived at the washroom several minutes before M. G. I stopped at the first sink. The car was swaying. A veneer of overnight dust covered the basins. There is no doubt that I splashed about considerably. Having finished washing I realized that my sink did not have a mirror. I walked across the room to one that did, and proceeded to tie my necktie. As I was doing this Dr. Brumbaugh came, and went straight to the sink I had left. In a tone of regretful disapproval he exclaimed: "I wonder what hog washed here!" I am sure he supposed that I had from the beginning been at the sink at which he saw me. I never told him otherwise. This was probably sixty-six years ago, and I have never (at least almost never) used a sink, either at home or in an international airport washroom, without tidying it up a bit before I left. This of course is trivial, but I can assure you that when Dr. M. G. taught you, you stayed taught.

Despite his distinguished study at Juniata and Harvard, his Ph.D. diploma and later a Phi Beta Kappa key at Penn and his seven honorary degrees from various colleges, there was one field of knowledge for which he was given inaccurate credit in his obituary: engineering. A reporter for a major Philadelphia paper interpreted his B.E. (Bachelor of English) degree from Juniata in 1881, as "Bachelor of Engineering."

Dr. Kaylor has described inclusively and effectively the Brumbaugh impact on American education.

Martin Grove Brumbaugh was well liked. I do not recall encountering anyone who did not like him. Men and women, equally, seemed to enjoy being in his company. In the fall of 1925 the whole Juniata campus was calling him "Prexy"— a term of enthusiastic affection. We also were singing a modified version of a Sunday-school song: "M. G. wants me for a sunbeam. . . . I'll be a sunbeam for him." The devotion of teachers throughout the state was perhaps the core of his strength in his successful campaign for the governorship.

One of M. G.'s favorite family stories on the topic of how firmly he impressed people had its setting in the delightful village of Wayne, Maine, site of his summer holiday home. The scene, Sunday morning at the little Methodist church; a guest preacher—his first time in Wayne. After the service the Brumbaughs went as usual to the Maureda Inn for dinner. A short time later the preacher came. The Maureda proprietor introduced him to the governor. The preacher said: "I spotted you in the congregation. I said to myself, 'Now there is an intelligent farmer.'"

On request "Prexy" could recall a few stories of being disliked—at least temporarily. President Wilson had invited Governor Brumbaugh and his honorary staff to ride horseback in the 1916 inaugural parade. Colonel Kolb, staff member, M. G.'s near neighbor, financial advisor, and close friend, was completely inexperienced in horseback riding. He feared mounting would be especially embarrassing. Before it was time to start, he led his horse around a nearby corner, found someone to help him, and came back gracefully established in his saddle. A moment later an assistant marshal made him dismount, explaining that no one was permitted to mount before his superior officer. The marshal reported that he left Colonel Kolb saying over and over in a low but emphatic voice: "Damn Martin, *damn* Martin."

My favorite M. G. story of dislike took place after the United States had entered World War I. The hero was Mrs. Brumbaugh's Tibetan spaniel. A very intelligent dog, Fritz apparently concurred in family opinions and attitudes. In response to the national food challenge of the time, the Governor had converted a part of the lawn of their Germantown home into a victory garden. One of the major Philadelphia papers, which had supported the Brumbaugh campaign, had become caustically critical of him in recent months. The governor felt that the criticisms were unjustified, unfair. But what could he do about it?

Fritz to the rescue! Despite its recent faultfinding the paper had sent a photographer to picture the governor working his victory garden. The photographer studied his angles and backgrounds, placed his camera on the ground, and came around the garden to pose the governor just as he wanted him. Meanwhile Fritz went around the garden on the other side, sniffed the camera with great hostility, and urinated copiously upon it.

Martin Brumbaugh was a man of placid and kindly temperament. I cannot recall ever hearing him fuss at Mrs. Brumbaugh. Nor did he ever fuss at me. The most emphatic thing he ever said to me was brought on by a fish. He wanted to cast for pickerel. For bait he needed the bellies of baby sun perch. We were in shallow water, six or eight feet deep, some two hundred yards from the dock. M. G. was fishing for the baby perch with one of his prized possessions—a five-ounce, nine-foot-long, forty-dollar rod that someone had given him for brook trout in the Poconos. Suddenly an explosion: a "whale" leaped high out of the water about ten feet from the boat, trying to shake the little hook from his throat. He couldn't. M. G. "played" him for fifteen to twenty minutes. He told me that the fish was gradually tiring and that the next time he succeeded in getting the big bass close to the boat, I should carefully put the landing net under him and lift him in. I looked around. I had forgotten the landing net!

The master fisherman played his catch for another ten minutes. Then he explained to me that we must lean to the right in unison and dip a great deal of water into the boat and he would try to float the fish in on the water pouring in over the gunwale. It worked! If you have ever tried to land an eleven pound bass with a five-ounce bamboo rod and no net, you may think this is a "fish story." It isn't.

When M. G. had recovered a bit from his half-hour fight with the fish, he said to me in the most emphatic tone of voice he ever used to me: "Don't you ever, *ever*, go out in this boat again without the landing net!" I didn't.

Martin Brumbaugh truly enjoyed his fishing; he was virtually a piscatorial addict. In the spring berry season even his most frequent quotation was from the bible of fishing, Izaak Walton's *Compleat Angler*: "Doubtless God could have made a better berry than the strawberry, but doubtless God never did."

When a neighbor from Maine visited the Brumbaughs once in Huntingdon she was so impressed with the scenic Pennsylvania mountains that she said to M. G.: "It is so beautiful here, I am surprised that you take the trouble to come to Maine." His reply was: "My front yard here is not full of bass."

President Brumbaugh and "Prof." Rowland, Juniata's popular vocal teacher and choral director of my college days, shared the same sense of humor. Frequently when Brumbaugh in Maine caught a really big bass he would cut off the tail, put it in a plain envelope and mail it to Rowland in Huntingdon. This was in pre-airmail days. Naturally by the time the fish tail arrived in Huntingdon it was outrageously stinky. "Prof." thought it was good fun. I doubt if either Rowland or Brumbaugh ever asked the post office people what they thought.

During the years I knew him Dr. Brumbaugh greatly enjoyed golf and bridge. He kept a deck of cards on his library desk at home and frequently let his hands play mechanical solitaire while his brain worked on serious problems for the college.

It is well known that he loved his cigars. Having finished dinner he would push back from the table, cross one leg over the other and light up his Blackstone. He looked majestic, regal. He could blow the most perfect smoke rings I have ever seen, clusters of them.

Whenever he sent me to buy cigars he always gave me money to pay cash for them—even though I was buying them at a store at which he had a long-standing monthly account. He apparently did not want to keep a record of his smoking, even for himself.

A non-negotiable event on the Brumbaugh spring calendar was to spend a Sunday afternoon looking for the first arbutus of the season in one or another of the nearby state parks. I was always quite cooperative on the arbutus expedition, as the Brumbaughs let me take a girl classmate along to help me look.

Martin Brumbaugh was a lover of nature. Probably the first poem I ever learned from him was a glorification of the great out-of-doors.

> And I have loved the woods, the boundless woods
> In all their glory and their majesty;
> Magnificent—the forest solitudes
> Eloquent of God and liberty.
> Yes, loved them ever since I was a child . . .
> When nature as a mother on me smiled
> And in her love a lofty language taught . . .

When you know the story of his early youth the poem seems almost autobiographical.

Martin Brumbaugh had an almost unlimited memory for poetry. I have no doubt that it was a part of the foundation for his superior skill in both speaking and writing. Poetry for him, as for George Saintsbury, was the recording of "the best that has been known and thought in the world," something that deserves to be learned by heart—a very different experience from mere memorization.

Dr. M. G. had an impressive command of language, especially oral. He was undoubtedly one of the great extemporaneous speakers of his time. He started as a lecturer at teachers' institutes in his mid-twenties and followed his governorship with two seasons of national Chautauqua alongside William Jennings Bryan, the most famous "silver-tongued orator" of the early twentieth century. I never heard who received the more applause.

M. G. told me that as a young man he trained himself to be comfortable with extemporaneous speaking by accepting engagements, and then deliberately refraining from any formal preparation until he arrived at the site of the meeting. He must have had an awesome confidence in the scope of his knowledge and in the constant availability of his vocabulary. Indeed he told me that of all the men in political life when he was, he felt that only Woodrow Wilson had an active vocabulary equal or superior to his own.

I well remember a chapel talk of Dr. M. G. in old Founders. It was on the Renaissance, for many speakers a subject so colossal as to be boring. On this occasion, it was spellbinding. The living transformation of one world into another. I left the chapel promptly and waited in the president's outer office for whatever directions he had for me for that afternoon and evening. He soon came, followed by one of my schoolmates, who expected to pursue a career in law or the ministry. He obviously envisioned himself as making great speeches on short notice. There must be a magic formula! "Dr. Brumbaugh," he said, "would you mind telling me how long it took you to prepare that speech?" "Young man," said the president, "the preparation of that speech took me just five minutes—and forty years."

Many of Dr. M. G.'s chapel prayers closed with a petition for resolution and strength for each of us to follow God's plan for us. And then, nearly always came the unusual phrase: "And save us from sudden death, if it be Thy will."

Only some fifteen years ago did I discover, in perusing a directory of saints, that there is a St. Martin, whose special function is to intercede for those who wish to avoid sudden death. I have often wondered since, did Martin Brumbaugh know of St. Martin? Or did he, in spite of clear health reports from his doctor, mystically anticipate the sudden, fatal event on the golf course at Pinehurst?

Martin Brumbaugh's sensitivity to "the best that has been known and thought in the world" is reflected in much of his own superb writing. The closing paragraph from his baccalaureate address to the Class of 1929 is a memorable example:

> Have no fear of the black night of failure. Look up and remember that the supremest guidance of us all is the Holy Son of the Holy God. . . . Companion with him. . . . Let him be Guardian of your career, and you will go hence to serve and to sweeten the life of your kind. . . . In the June-time of your soul may you grow beautiful for Him.

Surely this is as lovely a challenge as any group of graduating students ever heard.

These are some of the unforgettable memories in my association with a great and good man.

Preface

Biographies have always seduced me, both as a reader and a historian. A good biographer is ipso facto a good storyteller, and therein lies the seduction for me. So I have no serious problem with Emerson's famous dictum: "There is properly no history; only biography." This biography-is-history formula quite rightly makes the study of human beings, no less than of nations or wars, the legitimate end of scholarly activity. Martin Brumbaugh appreciated Emersonian historiography, authoring a couple biographies of his own. But he gave the genre sharper focus. In the introduction to his cousin Gaius's epical *Genealogy of the Brumbach Families*, he wrote, "The understanding of a life is the understanding of an age."

That was certainly true of Brumbaugh's life story. His public career stretched from Reconstruction times to the Great Depression. In that span of history the United States entered the world stage, became an empire, fought in "The Great War." On the home scene the first decade of the 1900s brought on the Progressive Era, a brief but dynamic period of social, economic, and political reform everywhere in the country. The last decade of Brumbaugh's life, a decade Americans remember as the "Roaring Twenties," had little of the "normalcy" President Warren Harding urged upon a nation bloodied by war and disillusioned by the peace.

But most important for this book, Brumbaugh's lifetime coincided with spectacular educational progress in the United States; the idea of a tax-supported school system, from first grade through high school, was becoming fixed in American law. The nation's profound faith in formal education also caused a scramble to the halls of ivy, with new colleges and universities—public and private (most of them open to both sexes)—blossoming forth in profusion. This expanding mass of educated persons, with public school or college diplomas, had no precedent in all of history.

The extraordinary life of Martin Grove Brumbaugh, a man dazzling in intellect and full of charm, gives us a superb glimpse into those bygone times of national transformation. His vocational odyssey—as country schoolmaster, then county superintendent, then joint university professor and small-college president, then Puerto Rico's first commissioner of education, then top man of Philadelphia's school system, then Pennsylvania's World War I governor, then reborn college president—provides a singular story of ability, ambition, accomplishment, and of public affection.

His was a name once familiar to every Pennsylvanian and many other Americans. It was his fame and popularity as a Keystone State educator—Woodrow Wilson reportedly ranked him among America's three most eminent schoolmen of the Progressive Era—that led to his excursion into politics. The only career educator to be elected governor of Pennsylvania, his administration was marked—and hampered—by a perennial tug-of-war with political boss rule. Meanwhile, he had long been hailed as one of the nation's marquee names on the teachers' institute circuit and had come to enjoy a national and international reputation as a forerunner in the turn-of-the-century Sunday-school and public-playground movements.

No biography of one of America's greatest schoolmen of the past, however, can be considered complete that ignores his unflagging fidelity to a church (Brethren) or the seldom-seen symbiosis between a man and a college (Juniata). Both institutions combined to indelibly shape his character, his personal ideals and values, his career choice—and both, especially Juniata, would benefit immensely from his institutional loyalty.

As governor, the second and last minister of the Gospel to hold that high state office, he proudly professed being a birthright "Dunkard," as the Brethren were once commonly known. What makes this fact an oddity is that the Brethren share a plain-people tradition with the Mennonites and Quakers, a triad of small religious groups that identify themselves collectively as the historic peace churches. Thus Pennsylvania's "War Governor" of 1915–19 brought to Harrisburg's Capitol Hill, in one of history's ironies, a heritage of biblical pacifism. It was doctrinal baggage the church's pioneer historian—and only member ever elected to the governorship—refused to renounce but which he would unavoidably compromise.

As for Juniata College, founded by Brethren-born Brumbaugh relatives when Martin was fourteen years old, it became an inextricable part of its famous graduate's life, no matter where his career was to take him. Juniata was the first permanent institution of higher learning established by the Brethren, and, like many of the denominational colleges of the late nineteenth century, it gradually grew from humble beginnings into a strong citadel of knowledge. All during his adult years the small, maturing, liberal arts school—nestled among the mountains of south-central Pennsylvania—leaned heavily upon his guidance. It would come of age under his mentorship, both in his roles as two-time president and perennial trustee. At times the college's demands became a burden to him, but he never stinted with time or tithe in its cycles of need, even when governor. As a result, for all Juniatians and many progressive Brethren of his era, Martin Brumbaugh became an institutional icon. That story is so interlaced with his larger career that it must be told, and cannot be dismissed as only of parochial importance.

Unfortunately, the private thoughts of Juniata's "Saint Martin" at those times when his Brethren-based values conflicted with the kinds of pragmatic decisions he had to make as a public servant are too often nowhere recorded. For me, the biographer of a man in perpetual motion, this only gives credence to Mark Twain's quip: "Biographies are but clothes and buttons of the man—the biography of the man himself cannot be written."

Brumbaugh kept no diary, only a little, shirt pocket-size date book that tracked his movements. Only rarely do his letters catch him in moments of introspection. Thus in my research I turned up a lot about his "clothes" and "buttons" but too little about the inner man: his fears, his loves, his hatreds, his worries, his temptations, his motives, his regrets.

Much as it would have helped the narration, I have not "created" his thoughts, although I sometimes do "suggest" what might have been going through his mind. Nor do I embroider scenes, going beyond sources and events to offer moods or invent dialogue, thus warping historical evidence to make this biography a better read. Instead, I allow the public records, letters, family members, and others to speak for themselves. Also, I do not trifle with the language used in quotations to make it less quaint to the modern ear. This makes for stilted, dated speech, but I have avoided combining fact and fiction.

My interest in Martin Brumbaugh dates from the mid-1970s, when I wrote *Truth Sets Free*, the centennial history of Juniata College. I discovered at that time that the only in-depth studies of his life were a doctor's dissertation and a couple of master's theses. All three primarily dealt with his career in education, or some aspect of it, and relied almost exclusively upon public sources. By their very nature and literary style, none of them could be called a biography in the strict sense of the word or could be expected to attract a broad readership. Also, because of circumstances, they left untold much of Brumbaugh's private life as well as his wider work outside education.

But, after reading these academic exercises, I never entertained any thought of myself becoming a Brumbaugh biographer. Then I got a letter from Dr. Claude Flory, after *Truth Sets Free* had come out. In it he proposed that I do a proper biography of the hero he once chauffeured, and offered to give me possession of his bonanza of Brumbaugh papers. I flew to Tallahassee, Florida, one April day to look it over and was excited by what I saw. The retired Florida State University professor revealed that there were other boxes of Brumbaughana at his summer home in Highlands, North Carolina. I did not realize it at the time, but my weekend visit fell on Brumbaugh's birthday, a rather fitting coincidence, I think.

Several months later I arranged for Mr. Rex Hershberger, a friend, strong Juniata booster, and then-college trustee, to accompany me on a minivan trip south to load up the several dozen boxes of my scholarly haul. The logical place for it was in the archives of Juniata's Beeghly Library, and that is where it can now be found, organized and cataloged.

It was the custom among Brethren of an earlier age, especially with men, to address each other by the initials of their two given names. Thus in church circles and by Juniatians Brumbaugh was called "M. G.," usually with a prefixed title such as Dr. M. G. I use his initials in referring to him from time to time when I place him in the company of Brethren or Juniatians, not to affect a breezy familiarity but because that was the name he went by among family, relatives, and acquaintances.

These last ten years, as a college professor and more recently as a retired one, I have spent a lot of hours thinking about this remarkable man, who did much good in yesteryears and rightly won much glory for it as a result. Thomas Carlyle said, "A well-written life is almost as rare as a well-spent one." Pretty cynical words these. But whatever the literary merits of this biography of Martin G. Brumbaugh, nobody can deny his was a life "well spent."

Acknowledgments

Several years ago there was a *New Yorker* cartoon in which a publisher is telling a would-be author, "Well, it's good, but people just don't write books all by themselves anymore." The publisher spoke the truth, figuratively if not literally. Thus my lone name on the title page, implying a solo act, is preposterously misleading. Many people aided in the preparation of this biographical study.

Nobody lent more of a helping hand than Dr. Claude Flory, who, as I mentioned in the preface, turned over to me the entirety of his vast collection of Martin G. Brumbaugh's papers. Without this documental windfall it would have been impossible to write the kind of biography I had in mind—one that was narrational, amply anecdotal, and carefully researched. Then, too, Dr. Flory himself was a crucial resource. He is, today, the only person qualified—more than six decades after Brumbaugh's death—to impart inside-the-family impressions of Martin G. Brumbaugh the *man*. The two of them, for a few years in the late 1920s, enjoyed a veritable father-son rapport. Finally, he was literary godfather to this project at every stage of composition as well as constant encourager.

Another very present helper was Iralene Jackson Neary. For five years—with a one-year hiatus—she was my long-suffering typist, co-researcher, and therapist during spells of writer's block. Her heirs at the word processor during her absence, Jane Croyle and Kristie Morrison, each in turn, proved Iralene-like in efficiency and patience. And always there, from start to finish, was Verna Horne, who cheerfully assumed other clerical tasks. My daughter Susan, a computer whiz, helped out in many ways and took over as indexer-in-chief in the end.

In very personal ways, I am deeply indebted to Harold Brumbaugh, Daisy Parker Flory, Rex and Dorothy Hershberger, Clemens Rosenberger, and his mother, my late dear friend Pauline Rosenberger, and F. Samuel Brumbaugh. Their supportive gestures—quiet, diverse, and most generous—were truly authorial blessings.

As in my past endeavors at writing history, the staff of Beeghly Library at Juniata College freely put their services at my every beck and call. So, manifold thanks to Donna Grove, John Mumford, Vernon Schlotzhauer, and Donald and Hedda Durnbaugh. Library Circulation Supervisor Lynn Jones, bless her heart, never hesitated to give my requests priority attention. And a special tip of the hat to former head librarian Peter Kupersmith, who greatly facilitated my research by giving me uncommon liberties in his domain.

Former faculty colleagues, Bernice Heller and Jose Nieto, now and then played linguistic rescuers when my college-level Spanish failed to meet the test.

Valuable assistance over the years also came from students of mine, usually through independent, credit-carrying studies. The list includes Wayne Bevan, Brian Geiger, Craig Miller, Linda Mumaw, and Timothy Phelps. But, in addition, I must spotlight Joan Gosnell, today a professional archivist, who first put the Brumbaugh papers into some semblance of order and sleuthed two summers for me while a college intern at Harrisburg, Pennsylvania, and Washington, D.C. For the two maps I am beholden to Brian Hack, a 1994 Juniata alumnus and aspiring art historian who also advised me in the selection of photographs for this publication.

The promotion and marketing of this book got skillful attention from Donald Moyer, vice-president for college development, and from David Gildea, director of college communications. All the while, President Robert Neff proved a bulwark of encouragement.

Off campus among non-Juniatians, I invariably encountered a similar brand of gracious cooperation. Down at Louisiana State University, graduate student Jeff Hale dug up a treasure trove of historical information, which he passed on to me. People in various university offices—at Harvard, Penn, Drexel—and Harriet Callahan at LSU and Christine Seetoo of the Philadelphia Marine Museum responded promptly, courteously, and with intrigued curiosity to my phoned or mailed inquiries.

My ultimate thank-you goes to Harriet, who never allowed my much too long preoccupation with another age and another person's life to endanger our marriage of four and a half decades.

MARTIN
GROVE
BRUMBAUGH

1

Family Heritage

THE Civil War had reached its one-year mark, almost to the day, when Martin Grove Brumbaugh was born, on 14 April 1862. In the East there had been a months-long lull in the fighting. Just outside the nation's capital the popular but pompous George B. McClellan drilled his soldiers diligently. Dubbed "Young Napoleon," the brilliant West Pointer faced the urgent task of rebuilding a new Army of the Potomac. The president had given him command of the Union's major force in the eastern theater soon after the Bull Run fiasco of the past summer. A superb organizer and drillmaster, he was just what a demoralized army needed. But much to Lincoln's disgust, McClellan was not yet ready, after the better part of a year, to begin a march on Richmond.

Out West the story was different. There the Yankees were on the move in a full-scale campaign. While McClellan readied his army for action, another general, Ulysses S. Grant, had lately made his name a household word among Northerners. His victories in Tennessee—at places like Fort Henry, Fort Donelson, and Shiloh—produced headline news between February and April. It was that spring of Martin's birth that the press gave the cigar-chomping conqueror his famous nickname: "Unconditional Surrender" Grant.

Brumbaugh's birthplace, deep in what was then the wilds of Huntingdon County, Pennsylvania, was far removed from any combat zones. His nativity took place in an old log farmhouse that stood in the vicinity of what was known as Fink's Bridge, overlooking the Raystown Branch of the Juniata River. This was one of the county's most isolated spots, fringed by vast forested land and high ridges. The log cabin would not be his home for long; however, its ambient Raystown watershed would geographically frame the story of his boyhood years. He would grow up close by—in Woodcock Valley, then dotted from end to end with barns built by his blood relations. Here in these farm-and-forest environs of Penn Township he learned to love his native state, its history, and its great outdoors.

In Brumbaugh's day the Raystown Branch snaked its sluggish way north from its source in the mountains just west of Bedford, the locale of a famous frontier fort. "The Branch," as it was called, flowed some fifty miles through the countryside before pouring into the Juniata River near Huntingdon, the county seat and

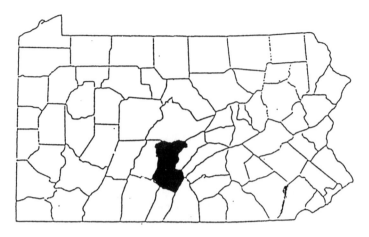

Shaded area indicates Huntingdon County.

once an Indian fort itself. Its narrow, mountain-pinched watercourse through the county left it without a single streamside community. There would be a period of time in Martin's life when he came to know every twist and shoal of the "Branch" in the last several miles before its confluence with the Juniata. As a young lumberjack he floated logs down that stretch while cutting timber for his father. Since the early 1970s the northernmost thirty miles of the tributary form Raystown Lake, one of the largest man-made dams in the Northeast. The territory that comprised much of Martin's childhood Eden has lost none of its natural beauty. Still, to the historian's dismay, the new lake has consigned the old farmstead and other Brumbaugh-era landmarks to watery oblivion.

Martin's parents had set up housekeeping in the Fink's Bridge log cabin when they married in November 1855. They farmed a piece of land rich in Indian lore, in an area that had long been crisscrossed by a network of trails. Since time immemorial, the Kittanning Path—the main route for warrior bands traveling between the Susquehanna and Allegheny Rivers—passed along the nearby banks of the Juniata. Off this warpath the Raystown Branch, downstream a short way from Fink's Bridge, took a sharp bend. There the Indians, in their migrations and on their hunts, made regular use of a sheltered campsite at the base of a high cliff. (Archaeological diggings took place at the rock shelter up to the last days before it was flooded by Raystown Lake.) So it was, Martin learned as a boy, that his natal terrain once fell athwart a north-south pathway much traveled by the red man since prehistoric times.

Indeed, other telltale signs of past Indian activity were closer at hand, easily seen from the Brumbaugh farmhouse. Not far from the kitchen door lay a huge, partially buried boulder whose well-worn concave top unmistakably indicated its age-old use as a grinding stone. The Fink's Bridge property also marked the place of grisly violence during the American Revolution. Somewhere on the farmland a settler had built a cabin for his family. All of them were massacred and their crude home burned to the ground by a marauding band of Indians, incited by the British. A little cemetery, close by the Brumbaugh dwelling, stood as mute testimony to this backwoods tragedy.

Such stories and the many Indian legends of the Juniata Valley fascinated Brumbaugh as a youngster. The passing of time never abated his curiosity about Native Americans—their virtues, their customs, and their history. As a popular lecturer he often charmed audiences by pronouncing the Iroquois word Onayutta (anglicized into Juniata by the white man) without moving his jaw—as he said the Indians did. In late life Brumbaugh reportedly talked of getting the state to mark the historic Indian places of his boyhood purlieus, especially the Kittanning Trail. But he died before he could do anything about this project.

The Fink's Bridge sojourn of the Brumbaughs ended when Martin was three years old. The family—he had an older sister and a baby brother by then—hauled their household goods in farm wagons across two ridges on the west and back into Woodcock Valley, a short distance away and the home base of both parents. In and around this area Martin would spend the rest of his growing-up years.

Woodcock Valley, whose name folklore ascribes to the small game bird that once abounded there, stretches southwest of Huntingdon a dozen miles or so. Elongated, it is squeezed between Tussey Mountain on the west and Piney Ridge on the east. Overlooking Piney Ridge, beyond what is now Raystown Lake, ranges Terrace Mountain, along whose base the Branch runs its torturous course. The Valley is also cut up by knolls and low ridges and many creeks. Because of its topography, Woodcock Valley became a patchwork quilt of hillside fields, its rolling acres deep with limestone soil. This is what, presumably, attracted Martin's great-great-grandfather, Jacob Brumbaugh, to the area in the early 1790s.

The Brumbaughs came of an ancestry traceable to early medieval times. Over the centuries their lineage had scattered all along the Upper Rhine—in France, Germany, and Switzerland. The family name is derived from "Brombach," which means noisy or humming brook. Martin Brumbaugh, aware of his own gift for ready talk, often facetiously said it meant "babbling brook." There is a still-thriving village today named Brombach, just over the German border north of Basel, Switzerland. Brumbaugh genealogists have speculated that their family tree had its roots there. Whether or not patriarch Jacob himself came from Brombach, or from anywhere in that part of Bavaria's Black Forest, is not known.

What can be verified, however, is that he, at age nineteen, emigrated to Pennsylvania with his parents in 1754, arriving on the ship *Nancy*. The immigrants took up land in Montgomery County near Norristown but did not tarry long in the Quaker colony. They moved on and by 1760 were frontier farmers, whose land neighbored that of other Brumbaugh newcomers at a German settlement in western Maryland, near what would become Hagerstown. "Jockel"—Jacob's lifelong nickname—had already married. His first wife died, perhaps at childbirth, just before the American Revolution; she bore him six children. Before long, the widower, who never learned to read or write, remarried.

At this point Jacob Brumbaugh's story becomes unclear. But apparently by 1770, he, three younger brothers, and his father had bought large farm tracts in south-central Pennsylvania—in Morrisons Cove, a score or more miles northeast of Fort Bedford. The Brumbaugh families made the 150-mile trek over a forest road in oxen-drawn Conestoga wagons. Indian troubles during the Revolution, however, forced the pioneering settlers to flee back to Maryland several times. Soon after the War for Independence ended they all returned to Morrisons Cove—Jacob to his 198 acres—not to be harassed again.

But Jacob must have been afflicted with wanderlust. About 1794, a few months shy of his sixtieth birthday, he uprooted his ménage to relocate once more. This time it was to Woodcock Valley, only a few miles to the east of Morrisons Cove, on the other side of Tussey Mountain. The next year, the sexagenarian, a hardy soul who lived into his eighties, fathered his fifteenth—and last—child. All fifteen children, in a kind of actuarial wonder for that time, lived to adulthood and married. Nine of them spent all or part of their minority at Timothy Meadows, the name the family gave their new 219-acre farm.

Years earlier, before leaving Maryland, Jacob had become a Dunker.* One of his wives—which one is unknown—is said to have been the first convert west of the Blue Ridge Mountains. The Dunkers, who in 1708 began as a persecuted sect in Germany, had adopted a lifestyle similar to that of the Mennonites, a much older religious body. To many outsiders in America the two communions were all but indistinguishable. Along with the Amish, an even more reactionary sect, they came to be known as the "plain people." Like the Mennonites and Amish, the Dunkers were nonconformists and absolute pacifists; they opposed learning and forbade seeking or accepting public office. The "plain people" were nonliturgical and noncreedal in their theology. None of the three groups, in rejecting many values of colonial America, took offense at being labeled "peculiar." Their historical base was eastern Pennsylvania, especially Lancaster County.

Unlike the Mennonites, however, the Dunkers—almost to the last devotee—had abandoned Europe for America by the 1730s. They came, for the most part, in two large multifamily removals, lured to William Penn's "holy experiment" for religious and economic reasons. They initially settled in Germantown (later a famous residential district of Philadelphia) in 1719. Here the Dunker immigrants established their mother congregation four years later.

This wholesale exodus to Penn's colony found the order, which never won a large following in the New World, with no official name. Even in Jacob Brumbaugh's

---

*Dunker, or Dunkard, was a nickname, an English corruption of the German word *tunken,* meaning "to dip." The Dunkers used it of themselves, though for outsiders it often had a derisive connotation. A basic tenet of theirs in the past was baptism by trine immersion, forward.

time they identified themselves as Dunkers or simply as "brethren," using a familiar New Testament term. For decades they conducted services in German. And when they finally did get around to coining a formal name for themselves, they purposely flaunted their Old World roots and sectarian devotion. They first decided upon Fraternity of German Baptists in 1837, and then in 1871, German Baptist Brethren. However, soon after the century's turn—in 1908—the group denominated itself Church of the Brethren, the first of many halting steps toward eventual identification with mainstream American Protestantism.

As it turned out, no family bloodline in the denomination's history seemed to chafe more at Dunker hideboundness than that of Jacob Brumbaugh's. Dozens of his descendants—most notably his great-great-grandson Martin—would choose to play the rebel. Yet, curiously, none of them reflected the rebel's sense of alienation. As progressives, the Brumbaughs transformed their Pennsylvania bailiwick into a tiltyard of various reforms, doggedly but tactfully protesting Dunker obscurantism and provincialism. Yet, through it all, none of the Woodcock Valley Brumbaughs turned out to be a deserter.

Until the reforms finally came, and all the while Martin was growing up, the clannish Brethren preferred farm life or lived in rural villages. They were distrustful of the "wicked" city and regarded higher learning as destructive of spiritual values. Some became shopkeepers, like Martin's father, or learned a trade, or taught school, like several of his relatives. But no one entered the trained professions, the earliest exception being one of his uncles.

A Brethren boy like Martin would have heard grown-ups, uneasy with distinctions of rank and title, address each other as "brother" or "sister." The dress code for Dunker men in his youth was a black frock coat, plainly tailored with standing collar (no lapel) and buttoned close to the neck, broad-brim black hat, cropped hair, and full beard. A mustache was forbidden; it suggested the military. For women it was long hair (rolled into a bun), a bonnet, and a dark-colored one- or two-piece dress. At worship services they wore a lace headpiece called a "prayer covering."

Every generation of Brumbaughs produced preachers, including Martin himself and his father. But Brethren fear of theological learning meant, until the 1900s, the absence of a trained clergy—and, for a long time, church buildings. The Brethren in the 1800s operated under a system called the "free ministry." Preachers were "called" from among the church membership, receiving no pay. The highest ordained authoritarian office was that of elder; there was usually one elder to a congregation, attained by progressing through two probationary degrees. Nothing more than rudimentary schooling was needed to qualify Dunker menfolk to preach or govern. Either office, preacher or elder, gave honored standing in a German Baptist community.

George Brumbaugh, Jockel's son and Martin's great-grandfather, became the first resident elder of the Woodcock Valley flock in the late 1830s. He had been called to the ministry about 1820. Before that time elders and preachers from outlying areas, notably Morrisons Cove, provided the spiritual care. Beginning in 1804 the Brumbaugh's Timothy Meadows stone home served as the Dunker "house church." George had helped his father build it that year to replace the family's original dwelling. A stone structure was something of a rarity along the frontier of south-central Pennsylvania. The building stood—boarded up and in partial ruin after Raystown Lake went in—until December 1988, when a fire of mysterious origin gutted the interior. The only intact homestead of the half-dozen or so pioneer families that opened Woodcock Valley, it had been held by a Brumbaugh for 178 years.

Typical of some Brethren backcountry homes after log cabins were outgrown and before there were churches, it was fitted with hinged, swing-back partitions on the first floor. When necessary the partitions could be opened to make a large room for worship services. Here George preached in German and conducted the Love Feast: a common meal (called the Lord's Supper), followed by the foot-washing rite and the Communion of bread and wine. In making ministerial visits George always rode horseback, on "Possum," wild as a colt for children and strangers but gentle as a kitten for its owner.

Ever the model Dunker, he paid a twenty-dollar fine in 1822 rather than take his unpaid turn as collector of township taxes. His religious scruples against holding political office left him no alternative.

In the early 1830s George, a tall, heavyset, broad-chested man, divided Timothy Meadows between the two eldest of his five sons. By then the farm, which boasted one of the first "up-and-down" water-powered sawmills in a wide area, was locally known for its fine orchards. Martin's grandfather, also named Jacob, inherited the stone house (shared with his parents until their death) with his apportioned acreage. He was a devout man—but no minister—with a long patriarchal beard who lived to be eighty-four. Though a layman, Jacob always sat up front with the preachers, facing the congregation, at Sunday worship. He was bilingual, but grandson Martin would have heard him habitually use German at family worship and in saying grace at meals. Into this pious household Martin's father, George, was born in 1834, the second of ten children.

George, like his father and grandfather, grew up to be a strapping six-footer, with a thick head of hair and the distinctive Brumbaugh facial feature: bushy eyebrows. His early years, however, are a blank. There is evidence he was among those of his generation who first began to defy Dunkerism's opposition to civic duty. By the time he was born, all twenty-four states had some kind of public school system. To many farm-weary Dunker lads, teaching came to offer—at least for several months each year—a ticket for escape. George must have thought so, too.

In 1849, at age fifteen, he decided to give teaching a try, among the very first of the Woodcock Valley Dunkers to do so. He stuck by it for several years, helping to work Timothy Meadows spring through fall and spending the winter months as a teacher. In all, he taught at four different schoolhouses in his part of the Valley (it was common those days for teachers to rotate among schools). His meager schooling little prepared him to teach. Neighbors told of seeing him in the spring months sometimes studying a textbook tied to a plow handle while tilling in the fields.

In 1855 George, by then properly bearded, married a neighbor, a farm girl named Martha Grove, who was two years younger to the very month. Martha's lineage, like that of her husband, boasted eighteenth-century Woodcock Valley settlers. A pretty, delicate-looking woman, she stood barely five-feet tall. Martha—everybody called her Mattie—was said to have been a lifelong Dunker, although there is no proof of this. Curiously, the Martin Brumbaugh papers and memorabilia include next to nothing about his mother or his Grove relatives. However, once when governor he said, "I owe a great deal to my mother, to her fine Christian spirit, and to her steadfast teaching concerning the right things." He also mentioned fond memories of her singing to him—probably hymns—when he was a child. Both parents, he one time mentioned, learned to read as first-graders from the Bible. Although George and Martha grew up on farms not far apart, the lay of the land—a series of lateral ridges—relegated them to different schoolhouses.

The newlyweds, as we saw earlier, began their married life on a farm along the Branch. When they moved there is unknown, but courthouse records indicate the 140-acre farm, bought by George's father in May 1858, was still owned by him. Children soon came along: a son who died at childbirth (unnamed), and Amanda, born in June 1858.* Four years later they had Martin, followed by Frank in 1864. Irvin, the last of the Brumbaugh brood, came along in 1867. (All three boys were given the middle name of Grove.)

By Irvin's time, Valley Brethren had come to see in the young father a potential Dunker preacher. In 1863, a year after Martin was born, George, at age twenty-nine, accepted their call to the free ministry. He joined the exclusive company of an all-Brumbaugh preaching quintet. He turned into a good "exhorter" and was dubbed "Talking George"—to distinguish him from a namesake cousin of lesser sermonizing talent.

Soon after he was licensed, however, the Timothy Meadows "house church" was outgrown. In 1864 the members put up a plain brick structure close by on Brumbaugh farm land along the James Creek. On the outside it looked like a country schoolhouse without a belfry (early Brethren meetinghouses avoided steeples). Typically, it had two entrances, one for "brothers" and one for "sisters" and children—all the better to keep men and women segregated inside.

Here in the James Creek Church, as it was called, George Brumbaugh took his turn at preaching duties for many years, never aspiring, it seems, to be an elder.

---

*There are no records that give the birth date of the unnamed baby boy—only a small cemetery stone that reads, "Infant son of G. B. and Martha," in the ancestral Brumbaugh family graveyard on the homestead farm. It could have been either before or after that of Amanda but most likely not after Martin's.

Here, too, son Martin attended church regularly and heard expounded the simple virtues that shaped his character and gave him a lasting set of values. He would unabashedly tell a reporter in 1915, as Pennsylvania's newly elected governor: "I was born among the Dunkards and I have lived among them most of my life. . . . While I respect all other Christian denominations, I am very proud and very glad of my connections with the Dunkard church."

In the spring of 1865, a year or so after he took to the pulpit, Talking George made the permanent move back into Woodcock Valley. For some time now his physician brother, Andrew, had been coaxing him to do this. The Civil War had just ended. But northerners were still in a state of shock, mourning the death of Abraham Lincoln, the nation's first assassinated president. George and Martha, being Dunker abolitionists, no doubt privately shared in the North's grief and gloom. The Brumbaughs and their three children took up village life at Marklesburg, Penn Township's main settlement.

The hamlet, laid out in the summer of 1844, was situated about two miles south of Timothy Meadows. It developed along the Huntingdon-Everett road, which cut the valley into almost equal halves. Tracks of the Huntingdon and Broad Top Railroad, then in operation for a decade, ran parallel to the road a half-mile to the east. The HBTRR served the coal, iron ore, and lumber industries that sowed the surrounding ridges and valleys with mines, forges, and sawmills. The railroad also furnished passenger service between Huntingdon and Cumberland, Maryland. One of its flag stops was called Brumbaugh's Crossing, located at Timothy Meadows, a stone's throw from the homestead.

At first George rented a large two-story, weatherboarded house near the cross-roads center of Marklesburg and opened a general store. It is not clear what he ultimately had in mind for a livelihood: farming or village merchantry. Over the next two years he engaged in a bewildering series of land and property transactions. How he, for the past several years a hillside, hardscrabble farmer, was able to bankroll all of it is hard to say. In November 1865 he paid $850 for 137 acres along Tussey Mountain, on the southern fringe of Marklesburg. Then a year later he bought two lots in Grantsville, a nearby cluster of homes along the Huntingdon and Broad Top Railroad line. Meanwhile, he had picked up the adjacent lot to the south of the house he was renting. Finally, in May of 1867 George decided to purchase the rented dwelling itself—for $950. To raise some cash ($450) he sold off half his Tussey Mountain acreage, apparently to his oldest brother, Henry.

These would not be the last of Talking George's real estate transactions. Within the next half-dozen years he acquired enough land to make him Penn Township's most propertied citizen. But in achieving that status he ruinously overextended himself, much to the future complication of his son Martin's young life.

2

A Village Boyhood

MARKLESBURG, when the Brumbaughs moved there, was a growing village. Within a decade its population increased by more than a third—to slightly more than three hundred. By the time Martin finished public school, two churches—Methodist and Lutheran—anchored opposite ends of the community. At the south edge stood a frame one-room schoolhouse. Along the dusty main street, were deployed the usual array of village shops: harness, shoe, cabinet, cooper, gunsmith. There was a resident doctor but, after 1866, not George's brother, Andrew. He left Marklesburg that spring to open an office in Huntingdon.

The villagers already had a general store, but that did not keep Martin's father from opening another one: the George B. Brumbaugh Mercantile House. He set it up in the south end of the family domicile. This left a kitchen, a parlor, and two upstairs bedrooms for living quarters. Separate doorways provided entrances to either side of the building. Later, after buying the rental home, George would add a brick storeroom to the rear of the business half. It was built with bricks he had burnt at the Fink's Bridge farm. The frame structure, like all houses along mainstreet Marklesburg, fronted hard by the Huntingdon-Everett road. There was space enough, however, for several hitching posts along the highway berm.

The George B. Brumbaugh Mercantile House grew to be a veritable country emporium. It carried everything from groceries to dry goods, paints to medicines, notions to hardware. Above the dress goods counter glared a stuffed panther. It had stalked Martin as a toddler when the family lived at Fink's Bridge, lurking around the farm until an uncle shot it. Years later, Brumbaugh took to sporting one of the panther's claws as a good-luck charm. When he was governor it could be seen dangling from his vest chain—along with his Phi Beta Kappa key.

Martin's father ran his store on a barter system social historians have termed "cracker-barrel bargaining." The practice, common in rural communities those days, allowed people to pay in kind as well as in cash. Farmers usually bartered, while villagers and the families of ore-mine workers paid with money. Talking George, however, proved too much the trusting soul; he readily extended credit to any strapped customer. This would be his undoing as a businessman in the depression of the 1870s.

31

George, guided by Dunker values, never actively sought public office, yet, heretically, he never shunned it when called upon. Respected and well-liked in the valley, he soon became the local postmaster. For eighteen years, from 1866 to 1884, the James Creek Post Office—Pennsylvania had another Marklesburg—operated out of his store. All the while he took on other civic duties: borough engineer and burgess, council member, school-board director. George the popular preacher and prominent merchant had indeed become the proverbial community pillar by the time Martin finished his boyhood schooling. The son never said so, but his father's career, modest as it was, must have helped him see that a man could be both civic-minded and a good Dunker.

"Mart" or "Marty," as the home folks called Talking George's oldest boy, grew up a virtual fixture in the Brumbaugh country store and post office. There, he often boasted, he got his "real education" and some understanding of human nature. "I talked and did business with farmers and their families," he once said, "and heard their opinions and experiences." He measured the farm products the men and women brought in, counted the eggs, and weighed the butter. In this way, he would recall, "I grew to know the wholesome country life of the people." Besides helping in the store, the "deputy postmaster" made twice-a-day treks to the railroad station at Grantsville, two miles away, to pick up mail bags. Sometimes it was by horseback, sometimes by buggy. For a long time, though, his father balked at letting him take the horse he really hankered to use: the spirited one. Despite all his wheedling, Brumbaugh once wrote, remembering his boyhood disappointment, it had to be "an old family horse so docile that he never did shy, buck, kick, or run."

While clerking he became the "local gossip," as he later drolly described himself. From Martin women shoppers got "a morning edition of the [Woodcock Valley] daily news." At day's end the men, lounging on the counter or nail kegs, heard the "evening edition." Sometimes the juvenile newsmonger's father lent him out as a field hand when farmers needed extra help haying or harvesting. Decades later, when he ran for governor, the press often profiled him as a farm boy. It was a description he never discouraged, even though he knew it to be overdrawn. During the campaign he kept reminding the voters of his down-home past. He made much of the practical lessons he learned in the store and out in the fields, living and working with common people.

Tied down at the store and post office, Martin seldom, if ever, got a full week of schooling. His chronic absenteeism was not unusual in an age before compulsory attendance laws, especially in rural areas. The rhythm of agricultural seasons got priority. When he became a fifth grader—in 1872—the state lengthened the school year from four to five months. Country schools, like the one in Marklesburg, opened each fall anytime between September and November. There are hints that not all of Martin's teachers were males, though certainly most were. He one time paid public honor to the woman, unnamed, who taught him to read "in a little green primer."

The daily routine and the facilities varied very little in one-room country schools of that era. The ages of pupils might range from six to twenty. For the tallest and the shortest of them, the standard unadjustable desk exacted a daily torture. Overcrowding was another nuisance. Every year of Martin's schooling, for example, nearly one hundred youngsters packed Marklesburg's lone classroom.

Such conditions restricted the curriculum to basics—the three "R's"—in the primary grades. In the upper grades the pupils would also study spelling, grammar, the history of the United States, and geography. Instruction was textbook-centered and built upon memorization and recitation. The set form was to summon each grade up front—to stand in groups of two, three, or four—and "say the lessons." Then they were sent back to their seats. Meanwhile, the nonreciters, until their turn, had to sit quietly for hours with little to do. Brumbaugh once told how he was introduced to history:

> I remember . . . the day our teacher told us we would begin history. . . . 'You may take the first ten pages in your books for tomorrow'. . . . We learned and recited these word for word. Then we learned the next ten, and the next, until we knew that book by heart.

Woe to the lazy boy or girl who did not memorize the day's lesson: Out came the paddle!

Blessed with a steel-trap mind, he did well in his studies under the rote-learning system, facilely committing to memory choice passages in English and American literature. His ability to memorize was evident early on. In those days, it was a custom in rural Protestant America for Sunday schools to conduct Bible memory contests. When just seven years old, Brumbaugh won such an event at the local Methodist church. Unlike Tom Sawyer, who cheated to win as a Sabbath-day contestant, the Marklesburg Sunday schooler took his prize honestly—by reciting word for word 144 Bible verses in a row.

The boy Martin was fascinated by oratory. He once said, when musing on his past, that he dreamed of growing up to be an eloquent speaker. In his preteen years he sometimes gave vent to this aspiration by playing the preacher. He would coax Frank and Irvin—one or both of them—into the family's backyard stable and subject them to ad lib homilies.* The inspiration for these fraternal calls to worship might come after Martin heard what he thought was a good sermon by Talking George or one of the other Brumbaughs at the James Creek Church. Other times reading a Bible story seemed to give him the fancy.

Later, as a teenager, he would seek out the solitude of his father's Trough Creek sawmill and there, by Copperas Rocks (a familiar landmark still today), give memorized declamations. The gigantic, overhanging rocks functioned like a

---

*Martin's sister, Amanda, when eleven years old, died in 1869, the cause of death unreported in her obituary.

sounding board, amplifying his voice. Brumbaugh's Demosthenic dreams did, in fact, come true. Though never exactly hailed as silver-tongued, he found himself, in his prime years, often sharing the platform with lionized Chautauqua spellbinders like William Jennings Bryan.

One time, when he was about thirteen, Martin decided to put his budding speechcraft to a test. Soapbox debates were popular in Marklesburg during his youth, so he volunteered to take part in one. But, as luck would have it, the opponent he drew that debate night turned out to be his schoolteacher. This understandably made the seventh-grader the underdog in the opinion of the audience. What subject they argued—the forum was probably the schoolhouse—nobody remembered. But the practice he got at Copperas Rocks did not fail the teenaged debater that night. It was the schoolboy, not the teacher, who reaped the laurels. The teacher, as Frank would recount the incident, did not take too kindly to the defeat. And Martin, teasingly, would never let him forget it, said Frank.

Brumbaugh the villager not only liked to talk, he was also an omnivorous reader. As a boy, he fell into the mildly annoying habit of reading at meals. His literary passion, by the time he was eight, included dime novels. Many dime novels were nineteenth-century versions of today's westerns and first appeared in the 1860s. These lurid booklets told of adventures and heroic feats taking place out in the exciting "Wild West." The Hollywood-like cast of sagebrush characters were all there: hunters, prospectors, outlaws, gamblers, dance-hall girls, cattle thieves, and, of course, gun-toting cowboys and war-whooping Indians. Certainly not fit company, even in the world of imagination, for a Dunker preacher's son.

Dime novels were commonly sold in country stores, but it is hard to think that pulp magazines of this kind would turn up among Talking George's merchandise. So how or where the store owner's son got hold of them is something of a mystery. But, as Frank once said in reminiscing about his brother's boyhood taste in literature: "At that time the reading of dime novels was considered a sin, and Martin sinned a great deal." According to Frank, from time to time his big brother would furtively call his buddies together for a "book review." Huddled in hiding, the gang sat enthralled while M. G. narrated for them the latest frontier-life fiction he had read.

His growing-up years as a clerk and mail boy were not, to be sure, all work and no play. Marbles was one of his favorite summertime games. He had happy memories of going, as a little shaver, on huckleberry-picking excursions to nearby mountainsides in the company of his mother and other village women. One of his boyhood chums was Charles M. Schwab of Williamsburg, the future founder of the Bethlehem Steel Company and World War I shipbuilder. Schwab would often ride along with his father on his peddling route, which included the Brumbaugh store. Both boys would relish memories of being treated to big slabs of pie, freshly baked by Martin's mother. Summer days allowed leisure time enough for him to dangle a line in the pools and riffles of Trough Creek, angling for brook trout. He would remain a rod-and-reel addict the rest of his life. Winter months, foxhunting on Tussey Mountain became another of his alfresco pastimes, although he lost the hunter instinct as a man.

Nor was he above pulling off a few high jinks as a boy—some that bordered on vandalism. There was the time, for example, when the three Brumbaugh brothers decided to stage a circus. Martin, so the story goes, took it upon himself to "borrow" a neighbor's prize white horse from its pasture and, needing a zebra for the "big top," began painting black stripes on it. The neighbor, who took great pride in the horse, washing and currying it frequently, was away for the day. But toward dark he came home, before the paint job was finished. When the Brumbaugh trio saw the owner approaching they scurried for cover. Martin hid in an apple tree. Whatever his age, the prankster apparently already had the reputation of a mischief-maker, because when the bedaubed animal's owner saw what had been done to it, he called out into the dusk: "I know who's at the bottom of this; it's that darned Mart Brumbaugh."

Another of Brumbaugh's favorite stories about himself told of the time he and one of his pals heard the state was offering a two-dollar bounty on hawks, which were ravaging chicken yards. The two of them devised a trap and caught one of the birds of prey. They took it to the local justice of the peace, a very gentle man who was also a Methodist elder, and asked for their money. The justice said, "Boys, I don't want the hawk. You are supposed to bring me just the head and swear that you killed the hawk."

The boys retired. They had no handy hatchet, but they had seen chickens killed by wringing their necks. Martin, the larger of the two trappers, grabbed the hawk by the head and swung it around furiously. Finally the body tore loose at the neck, leaving both the hawk's head and the hawk's executioner a gory mess. The lads returned to the magistrate's home. Martin thrust the bloody head at him and said in a loud voice: "I'll be goddammed if I didn't kill this hawk." The two bounty hunters got their money *and*, needless to say, an earnest explanation of what legal swearing means.

About the time Martin became a teenager, he probably overheard villagers discussing lurid newspaper stories about the moral state of the union. Breaches of public morality abounded at all political levels. By the time in 1873 when William "Boss" Tweed was convicted, the Democratic Tweed Ring had already defrauded New York City of as much as two hundred million dollars. The Republican "Gas Ring" in Philadelphia was also milking the taxpayers, although less profitably. One Louisiana carpetbag governor, who left office in late Reconstruction years an enriched boodler, boldly bragged that "down here . . . corruption is the fashion." In Washington, D.C., President Ulysses Grant's administration became a carnival of cupidity, full of grafters and incompetents.

The scandal-scarred Grant presidency suffered further ill repute from the paralyzing depression that followed close upon public disgrace. The Panic of 1873 burst out with startling rapidity and lasted for six years. It would be the longest and severest recession Americans had yet experienced, bringing widespread bankruptcies, unemployment, and violent strikes.

Marklesburg, too, felt the hard times. Out-of-work customers, short of money, became something of a problem for the Brumbaugh store. So Talking George, in August of 1874, decided to buy some forest land, partly as an investment but also to give his delinquent patrons a chance to work off their debts cutting timber for him. From J. Simpson Africa, a prominent Huntingdon businessman and banker and currently a state legislator, he bought 1,870 mountainous acres comprising six different tracts spread over three adjoining townships. The purchase price was three thousand dollars, a cost Talking George seemingly could ill afford. Apparently, however, the deal involved little money down. Completely forested, the purchased territory was one of rugged beauty, with ravines so deep sunshine never reached their depth, picturesque waterfalls, cold caves, and streams teeming with fish.

When George Brumbaugh bought this wild wonderland, vestiges of the charcoal-iron industry that had once flourished there before the Civil War could be seen everywhere. The forge, which had served the nearby ore mines, was gone but

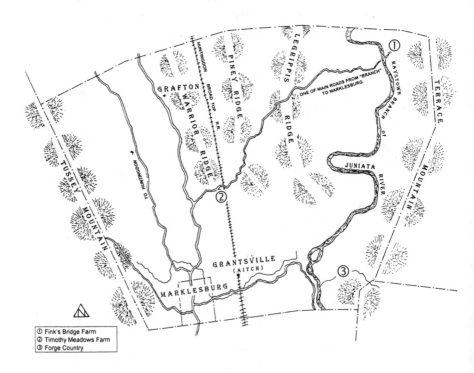

Penn Township in the 1870s and Brumbaugh landmarks.

not the sawmill. Martin's father was able to repair it and put it into use. Still standing were twenty-six old houses, once homes for workmen. A couple of them were two-storied, but most were log cabins. In addition, a stone "mansion," where the superintendents had lived, stood a short distance away; it was in better condition.* To the local people the site was known as the "Forge," despite the absence of its identifying landmark.

Two years later, George got hold of more real estate: a couple of lots in Marklesburg and one in West Huntingdon along the railroad tracks. This cost him a little over seven hundred dollars. Landowning, it seems, had come to be an obsession of the merchant-preacher, despite a serious cash-flow problem. His reckless behavior, before very long, would shame the family, especially its eldest son.

But the 1870s brought other, happier developments that would change the whole course of Martin's young life. For more than a decade now, Dunkers had been engaged in a serious dialogue, at Annual Meeting and through their religious papers, over two interrelated questions. One was, Is learning a good thing? The other was, If so, should there be private Brethren schools beyond the eighth grade? Since before the Civil War several efforts had been made—in Pennsylvania, Virginia, and Indiana—to start secondary schools. All were short-lived; the idea was still too radical for most Dunkers. Conservatives among the faithful had come to tolerate, since the 1830s, a basic common-school education for their children. But any further schooling they deemed spiritually unsafe, a threat to the simple life and a Bible-based faith. Just as worrisome was the fear of losing bookish, more sophisticated offspring to mainline-Protestant churches. Some diehards linked learning and schools with the coming of a paid ministry, a prospect just as frightful.

Still, teaching proved a powerful attraction to Dunker farm boys even by the time of the Civil War. By the Reconstruction decade some of them had found their way into private academies. Such schools, many of them denominational in origin, had been long-popular teacher-training institutions. Others began showing up at state normal schools, of more recent origin in preparing teachers. (High schools, as part of the nation's public tax-supported system, experienced rather slow growth until the late nineteenth century.) As Dunker hard-liners rightly feared, secondary education did take its toll in the form of apostasy among their young people— especially those who had attended church-related academies. That only stiffened opposition to prolonged schooling.

The more liberal faction within Dunkerdom was no less troubled by the defection of young blood (the German Baptist Brethren then numbered probably no more than fifty thousand). But their solution to the problem of attrition called for Dunker-owned or operated schools. As a result the school movement, dormant for

---

*Today the Brumbaugh tracts make up practically all of Trough Creek State Park. When governor, Martin Brumbaugh restored the superintendent's mansion, but it was later demolished to make way for Raystown Lake.

a time after Appomattox, took on new life in the early 1870s. Most likely Martin Brumbaugh, even after he became a teenager, went about his village existence little aware, if at all, of the school crusade. But at the very thick of it were three of his close relatives.

Martin's reformer kinfolk had each followed a similar path as Dunker liberals. All three were ex-Penn Township farmers, academy alumni, and onetime school-teachers who had forsaken a rural life for that of the "big" town—Huntingdon. The county seat in the 1870s, with a population of about four thousand, was located along the main line of the Pennsylvania Railroad and was the northern terminal of the Huntingdon and Broad Top Railroad. Not a single member of the German Baptist Brethren lived there until Martin's relatives came with their families.

The first Huntingdonian among them was Dr. Andrew B. Brumbaugh, Talking George's younger brother and the one responsible for the store owner's setting up business at Marklesburg. He became a favorite of Martin's, who affectionately called him "Uncle Andy," or more often "Uncle Doctor." As noted in the previous chapter, Dr. Brumbaugh hung out his shingle in the railroad town soon after the Civil War. He was the first Dunker to earn a medical-school degree, having obtained one at the University of Pennsylvania in 1866. He became the family physician of the town's leading citizens and the local surgeon for the Pennsylvania Railroad. A compassionate man like his brother George, he did a lot of charity doctoring; some said he did more of that kind of healing than for fees. Hence he was remembered as "a good doctor but a poor collector."

By the early 1870s he had made it his personal mission to start a Brethren school in Huntingdon. One of its selling points, he thought, was the town's railroad passenger service. When talking about his pet project he sometimes smacked his right fist into his left palm to punctuate a point. He conducted a private letter campaign, directed at Brethren leaders, stating his case. He even took leases on several lots as possible school sites. Brethren house guests, especially those with some authority, were treated to buggy tours of these lots and other choice locations. All the while his captive audiences had to ride along listening to the doctor's steady spiel about the need for a school and Huntingdon as the rightful place for it.

For allies in the Huntingdon cause the railroad surgeon called upon a pair of Brumbaugh cousins, Henry and John. In 1870, leaving their Branch farm—Henry was married and a dozen years older than John, a twenty-year-old bachelor—the two of them had moved to Marklesburg. They rented a house and converted part of it into an office and press room. Here they began putting out a weekly Brethren paper, the *Pilgrim*. They worked long hours, setting type by day and writing editorials and business letters or running off *Pilgrim* copies after dark. No doubt Martin on many a summer night heard through his open bedroom window the clicking of their old Washington handpress long past his bedtime.

Almost from its first issue the *Pilgrim* became a mouthpiece for "a good liberal education" and Brethren schools. By "liberal" the Brumbaugh brothers meant an education in a religious milieu, like the kind they themselves had received at a Methodist-backed academy in Huntingdon County's little community of Cassville. Good as their academy experiences were, one *Pilgrim* editorial argued, they would have preferred being taught by Brethren.

The opposition they encountered was sincere, if reactionary. One gray-haired elder, with typical Dunker candor, once told Henry and other proschool cohorts, "Well, Brethren, I love you, but I don't love your cause." Such disdain for schools failed to reckon, however, with willful sons hungry to learn. One standby of the Brumbaugh trio told how he had outwitted parental restraints upon his boyhood education: "My father considered it his religious duty to raise me in ignorance, and so did not permit me to have a light to study by. This did not daunt my courage, for I would crawl out on the porch roof at night and read by the friendly light of the moon."

Then there was Abraham Harley Cassel, whose celebrated private library would one day be the link between the Dunker antiquarian bookman and Martin Grove Brumbaugh the Brethren historian. As a small boy in the early 1830s, however, he too got around home pressures against education. According to Cassel, one time a storekeeper gave him a few candles so he could secretly read in his bedroom before falling asleep. But when his father caught him in this nighttime practice he was denied a light when he went upstairs to bed. But Cassel resorted to modern technology in disobeying this paternal interdict. Matches had just been invented and from a peddler he intrigued to buy seventy-five of them for twenty-five cents each. That was a terrible expense for a poor farm boy, but for a time at least the matches enabled him covertly—and defiantly—to read on. To protect himself from discovery, he used the family's heavy black umbrella (stored in his room) as a kind of tent. He opened it on the floor, crawled under, lighted his candle, and proceeded to read.

Because the Brumbaugh printers knew all too well the antieducationist element within Dunkerdom, they did not push for brotherhood-owned schools. Rather, as they editorialized in one 1872 edition, "Let the schools be gotten up as a private enterprise, similar to our periodicals. . . . Place everything on a clear and independent basis and then have Brethren for teachers and officers." In other words, they were proposing joint-stock enterprises. Moreover, the brothers insisted, it was presumptuous to use the word "college" for these institutions just yet. They suggested calling them Brethren high schools.

Meanwhile, Henry—after several visits to Huntingdon and being escorted about by his doctor relative—had a dream one night. He dreamt, as he later told a friend, of seeing in his cousin's adopted town "a school full-fledged and a large body of students marching down one of the main streets." So Henry and John bought a lot in West Huntingdon, at Fourteenth and Washington Streets, from another Brumbaugh cousin, on which they put up a three-story brick building in 1873. Henry and his family made their home in one half of it—John took rooms a few doors away—and the other half housed the business.

Eighteen months later Huntingdon Brethren still numbered fewer than a dozen. The little band had been worshipping in homes or out at James Creek. Then in June 1875 they busied themselves renovating a first-floor room of the *Pilgrim* building for midweek and Sunday services. The Huntingdon school dream had not been forgotten, but all proschoolers agreed, none more so than the Brumbaughs, that a school and a strong congregation must go hand-in-hand. This was imperative, they knew, to allay any misgivings naysayers might have about an unnurtured student body. Now at last, that summer of 1875, the local Brethren did have a conventicled congregation, though hardly a thriving one. It would technically exist as a mission point of the James Creek Church until 1878. Nonetheless, the Brumbaughs thought it solid enough to qualify Huntingdon as a tenable school town.

Thus early in 1876, convinced the time and place were right, the Brumbaughs—the doctor and Henry and John—moved fast. *Pilgrim* readers got only a few weeks advance notice about their plans to start the Huntingdon Normal Select School—the first in a series of subsequent names—in mid-April. Theirs would be a private "experiment," the blurbs emphasized, nonsectarian, and—like the state normal schools and a dozen or so Pennsylvania church-related colleges—coeducational. The Brumbaughs purposely refrained from using the word Brethren in the name of their school.

The Huntingdon "experiment" made its beginning on 17 April 1876. Only three students showed up—one of them the doctor's fourteen-year-old son, Gaius, the other two, girls. Classes were held in a cramped, second-story room in the *Pilgrim* printing plant. The teacher was twenty-nine-year-old Jacob Zuck, a grammar-school principal from Maryland and a friend of John. The two had met at Millersville State Normal School in the spring term of 1873 and had become boon companions. They were introduced by the principal, Edward Brooks, an up-and-coming educator and textbook writer. As fate would have it, Brooks would later be the teacher and then the admiring colleague of Martin Brumbaugh.

In the interval since 1873 Zuck had authored articles for the *Pilgrim* championing the need for Brethren schools. A frail man, he walked with a limp, the result of a childhood accident. He arrived in Huntingdon with no promise of a regular income. But John Brumbaugh did offer board for whatever he could pay until, if ever, things got better for him.

As they all knew, the nation's centennial was hardly a propitious time to start a pilot school, quite apart from Dunker opposition. The Panic of 1873 had not yet run its course. As Henry Brumbaugh lamented in a *Pilgrim* piece, the country was mired "in a financial depression that it has been our lot seldom to experience." He could see sad evidence of it all around him in Huntingdon. Tall stacks of silent factories told the everywhere-familiar story of industrial arrest. Car works, closed down, had put scores of men out of work. All over town signboards read: "This lot for sale," a signal that people were pulling out or needed ready cash. Coal-oil lamps at street corners went unlighted; wooden sidewalks rotted away, leaving ankle-twisting spaces. Even Jacob Zuck, the school's loudest rooter, had qualms under the circumstances. The day before classes began he confessed to John Brumbaugh, "I can't see the way to success in this enterprise." Then, ashamed of his doubts, the pious Zuck added prayerfully, "[But] God will show us the way as we go onward."

Zuck drove himself hard the first year, living on a dollar a week. Henry Brumbaugh marveled at the educator's grit and put the *Pilgrim* at his disposal to promote the school. Gradually the teacher's tireless work and the *Pilgrim's* stepped-up publicity began to produce encouraging results. By the spring of 1877 the rolls carried forty-five names, which included a few from out of state. That February the school vacated its print-shop quarters for a three-story brick house a block away. The upstairs rooms were utilized as dormitory space for a few single students and Zuck—accommodations until then unavailable. The rest of the students continued to rent rooms in private homes.

Everything looking upbeat, Zuck and the Brumbaughs began making bolder plans. They organized the school that spring as a joint-stock company, a share worth one hundred dollars. One of the earliest names listed on the books as a shareholder was that of George B. Brumbaugh. (It was at this time that George bought a lot in Huntingdon near the *Pilgrim* building.) At the same time, defying Brethren right-wingers, the Huntingdon junta changed the name of their "experiment" to Brethren's Normal School. They even talked of erecting an all-purpose building somewhere in town—on a plot of ground they hoped the townspeople would donate.

Beginning with the summer session of 1877, yet another Brumbaugh appeared on the school scene: Martin's twenty-five-year-old Uncle Jacob. Unmarried, Jacob Brumbaugh was the youngest of Talking George's three surviving brothers and an 1874 graduate of Millersville State Normal School. By signing on with Zuck's tiny faculty—Zuck plus a young woman—the new instructor had to leave a principalship at a small community north of Harrisburg. For him this career change meant forfeiting a monthly salary of $120. It also meant going five payless months before Zuck could ante up a little cash for him—the grand sum of fifty-five dollars. It helped, of course, that his room and board came free at his doctor brother's downtown home.

In December a citizen's group finally began to take seriously the appeal for land. But before anything definite could be worked out, the year 1877 ended under ominous circumstances, both for Huntingdon and for the Brethren's Normal School. The twisted chain of events that ensued would link an institutional crisis with a major turning point in Martin Brumbaugh's life.

The year-end trouble started Christmas week when a smallpox epidemic swept the town. The Normal School students had already gone home for the holidays. It was while returning by train, soon after New Year's, that some of them first got word of Huntingdon's plight. Passengers heard rumors of death and widespread quarantine.

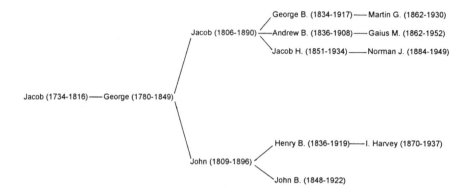

Paternal lineage of Martin G. Brumbaugh and his Juniata College relatives.

Upon their arrival they were met with the odor of disinfectant (carbolic acid) everywhere. Then in quick order came a death at the school and in mid-January a town council ban—for an indeterminate time—against all public gatherings.

What followed seemed to doom the far-from-established Normal School to a prompt demise. Woebegone students and teachers scattered, most to distant homes. Tentative plans called for resuming classes soon after Valentine's Day, but the big question in everybody's mind was, Who would come back?

Three students, all Ohioans, presented a special kind of problem when the School shut down. They refused to go home, fearful this would mean they would never return. They hoped to find temporary asylum with a farm family or two outside of town and wait out the public-health crisis. But farmers were boycotting Huntingdon and did not welcome the company of anyone exposed to the disease.

It was Jacob Brumbaugh, under these inhospitable circumstances, who proposed the solution for the trio's predicament. He suggested they take refuge at the Forge, where some of the "woodchoppers" hired by his brother, George, stayed in one of the old houses on weekdays. Here then, about five miles from Marklesburg, the Ohio "Orphans" (they belonged to a boarding club called the Seven Orphans) would live out a six-week exile. The three boys settled themselves upstairs in the superintendent's old crumbling "mansion," afraid to spend wilderness nights on the ground level.

At first the Forge work hands stayed their distance, suspecting the intruders to be smallpox carriers. Time soon allayed such worries. George Brumbaugh, as postmaster, saw to it that the boys got mail two or three times a week, which helped lessen their sense of isolation. This made them privileged persons in that time before free rural delivery. Eagerly awaited, too, were the frequent visits by Martin. Every few days his mother would fill a pair of saddlebags with food and other supplies and see him off, on horseback, to the Trough Creek hideaway.

Sometimes when the weather turned bad or very cold, Martin stayed over with the "Orphans." On such occasions all four of them slept in one bed, the disquieting cry of the wildcat providing a nocturnal serenade. More than once the Forge exiles, led by their newfound friend, spent the day exploring the natural wonders of the Trough Creek wilds.

On one visit the matter of Martin's future education somehow came up. The "Orphans" invited him to go back to the Normal School with them after the smallpox panic was over. Brumbaugh never chose to say, when telling of the incident years later, how he replied to the proposal—or whether he had given previous thought to college-going. There is family testimony, however, that he had for some time been mulling over the idea of more schooling. (Jacob Brumbaugh always took credit for being the one who talked his nephew into furthering his education.) In any event, when the Ohioans returned to Huntingdon in late February, the epidemic having at last run its course, they did indeed have their fifteen-year-old Forge companion in tow.

So it came about that Martin Brumbaugh found himself identified with what would prove to be the first permanent college founded by the Brethren. He still looked every bit a Dunker country boy that spring of 1878. Little did he know his name, for many years, would be synonymous with the institution: he would give it, in its first half-century, the kind of guidance, in one capacity or another, that made possible its evolution into a liberal arts college with a national reputation.

On the other hand, no one at the Normal School could have guessed that the gangling youth who had just joined them, his baggy trousers stuffed down into high-top boots, would become one of the most eminent graduates in its history.

3

Making of a
Schoolman

ONLY the average story of a poor boy," was the way Martin Brumbaugh liked to characterize his rise from Dunker rustic to urbane governor of Pennsylvania. All during the 1914 gubernatorial campaign he played up this "poor boy" image—both from the hustings and in newspaper interviews. Usually with a dismissive gesture he would then pooh-pooh such talk, saying, "It was good for me," or "I only did as many other boys." Some reporters, following up on this theme, found good press copy in telling of the hardships Brumbaugh had faced in getting a college education.

The future of the Brethren's Normal School, of course, seemed most problematical when young Martin showed up as a student in February 1878. The smallpox scare had passed, but the teaching staff faced a major challenge: regrouping the scattered student body. As it turned out, this was done quicker than thought possible; the three-term academic year for 1877–78 had a total enrollment of 172: 119 men and 53 women.

Meanwhile, Martin, as a new Normal Schooler, took lodging with relatives at what came to be called the Reservoir Farm on the outskirts of Smithfield, across the Juniata River. It was then owned by Talking George's oldest brother, Henry, who had bought it for one of his daughters and her husband. (Later, in 1889, the state built the Huntingdon Reformatory close by; the farm's springs fed the reservoir that for a time supplied water to the prison inmates—hence the farm's name.) For at least his first term, then, Martin probably did odd jobs around his older cousin's place to help pay the cost of his keep. But it was a four-mile round-trip to and from the school, where he boarded with a club of boys.

To a reporter in 1914, describing what he did to defray his school costs, Brumbaugh said:

> I started at first by sweeping out the halls and the rooms. Afterwards I got a kind of promotion. I was assigned to ring the bell at college which summoned the students to class, and I also had the work of opening and shutting down windows. If a storm arose in the night it was my duty to get up and close the windows.

This telescoped summary is difficult to break down into specific time periods. The janitorial duties, of course, could have begun at once, even though he commuted. The other jobs—window-watching and bell-ringing—imply dormitory life and a position of responsibility. In Martin's case these came much later, but precisely when is purely speculative.

Martin, his report card shows, got off to a good start in higher education. For the term, he ranked first in two classes—United States History and Constitution (100 percent) and Mental Arithmetic (100 percent), second in Political Geography (85 percent), and third in two other classes—Physical Geography (94 percent) and Written Arithmetic (94 percent).

Almost every weekend he walked the ten miles home to attend the James Creek Church. Sometimes he hitched a wagon ride. He returned on Sunday nights, again either on foot or as a hitchhiker. He must have felt he could not afford to travel by way of the railroad, even though the one-way fare was only a few pennies.

Brumbaugh once observed that he had gone off to school with no idea of being anything but a clerk in his father's store. His good grades, therefore, did not reflect the success of a student spurred by some lofty goal. Jacob Zuck must have detected this lack of focused ambition in the youngster. So one day, toward the close of the first term, as Brumbaugh later recounted, the principal called him aside. He asked, "Martin, what are you going to make of yourself?" "I don't know, sir," was the answer. Then Zuck said, "Well, I believe that if you'd try real hard you might become a schoolteacher." He advised Martin to take the "peripatetic test," so called because every summer the county superintendent of schools traveled around conducting them at different places. If passed, these examinations—part oral, part written, and often attended by school board members —gave teachers with limited education provisional employment for one year. Until permanently certified by the superintendent, a teacher had to be tested annually. Martin agreed to take the qualifying test but was warned by Zuck that he would have "to study hard" to pass the ten "branches" covered in it.

He did study hard and he did pass, finding the event, as he later put it, a "memorable struggle." He said getting the provisory certificate was the "proudest moment" of his life. When he came home that evening his mother, greeting him anxiously, asked: "Well, did you get one?" Martin answered with a jubilant yes. As he recollected the happy occasion, she said, "Well, I'm glad of it, my boy," and cooked a chicken supper to celebrate.

The next obstacle the sixteen-year-old would-be teacher faced was finding a school. The first school directors he contacted, probably near Marklesburg, turned a deaf ear to him because of his inexperience. Then his Uncle Doctor stepped in, having heard of a vacancy in one of Oneida Township's three schools, north of Huntingdon a few miles. So, wasting little time, he rounded up Martin and the two of them set out in the doctor's buggy. They took the Stone Creek Road (now Route 26) and headed for the home of a township school director named Adolphus White.

It must have been in September or early October, because the director, a farmer, was out in a field cutting corn when they rode up.

Uncle and nephew tramped out to the stubble-studded field. They even pitched in to help shock the corn while explaining the purpose of their visit. To Martin's delight, he was hired on the spot. The salary promised him would be twenty-six dollars a month, which was about two-thirds the county average for males. Mr. White went on to caution that the school was rather large for an applicant so young and that some of the pupils would be older than the teacher.

Obviously, hiring practices in the county had not changed much since Martin's father taught school. It was still very common to recruit teachers as young—and as poorly prepared—as Talking George had been when he became an antebellum schoolmaster. And the way Martin himself was hired—summarily and only days before school opened—further illustrated the lackadaisical attitude of too many of the county's school directors.

Martin Brumbaugh began his long career in education, that fall of 1878, at Center Union, about six miles north of Huntingdon. He took over a one-room frame schoolhouse with a little roofed porch. It nestled against a hillside overlooking two or three houses, a little Baptist church, and a brooklet. He dubbed the locality of his school "Hard Jack Hollow." Sawmills still dotted the surrounding dells, although the lumber business had long since declined.

Center Union's school enrolled forty pupils his first year. The basic curriculum he followed, by state mandate, had changed little since Martin's own student days at Marklesburg. But now, however, there was general uniformity in what textbooks Huntingdon County teachers used. Daily absenteeism, a major problem for the nation's schools of that era, was all too evident at "Hard Jack Hollow"; there it averaged upward of 25 percent. Still, his earliest letters home were, for the most part, in good humor. Printed at the top of one of his earliest missives appeared the words: "No trouble Yet."

Brumbaugh lived with a family by the name of Shoff. They ran a country store along Stone Creek Road about a half-mile south of Center Union. For years the Shoffs boarded whoever the local schoolteacher happened to be. One of their grandsons remembered Martin's being "as poor as the proverbial Job's turkey." He still managed to buy an inexpensive Christmas present for each of his pupils. Mrs. Shoff also got something—a small saltcellar in the shape of a Christmas star. It cost a nickel. He liked his landlady but not her cooking; in one letter he snidely mentioned "those beans [she is now] using without mercy."

In some ways, Martin's correspondence with his parents reveals a man-child mature beyond his years. He worried about his father's logging business and the way it was dragging the family deeper and deeper into debt. He volunteered advice on how to handle creditors and what wages to pay the loggers.

The Center Union letters further disclosed the expanding intellectual curiosity of a new-generation Dunker. The young teacher soon recognized his academic deficiencies. He decided he needed to go back to the Normal School for more training. But, in the meantime, he ordered six volumes of a self-study program called "Fourteen Weeks in the Sciences"—a series on physiology, physics, chemistry, botany, zoology, and astronomy published by A. S. Barnes and Company. Huddled in his cold room on winter nights, bundled up and reading by the light of a kerosene lamp, he waded through all six books. His favorite study guide was the one titled *Descriptive Astronomy*. Stargazing fascinated him; he thrilled at being able to "trace all the Constellations that are visible now," he wrote home. Often thereafter, on a clear night, the teaching tyro could be found sitting on an old rail fence studying the heavens. There is no evidence, however, his science studies made him question his religious faith.

His letters also told of debates held every two weeks, probably in the Center Union schoolhouse. He came close to flat-out bragging about his forensic ability and knowledge of history. One letter described an oratorical matchup on who was a better man: William Penn or Captain John Smith. He alone sided with Penn; three or four other speakers, including the Methodist minister from the nearby hamlet of Donation, stood with Smith. Martin spoke for a whole hour. "As I am well posted in history," he wrote, "I silenced all of them." In fact, he added, "Men here tell me that I told them more history since I have been here than they ever knew before." He said he was good at public speaking because "I always watch [not to] get into a sleepy way of Talking."

He reported, too, the weekend treks to Huntingdon and worshipping there with the Brethren in their print-shop sanctuary. Saturday nights he often spent at his Uncle Doctor's.

As the weeks passed Martin grew restless and began counting the days left in the term. The problem was not so much the school as the absence of a social life. He once mockingly referred to "this Partly civilized district." Another letter said, "I hope that [next time] I will get to a place better suited for a person who always was used to good living," meaning better cuisine as well as company.

When the school year ended, he was asked to return in the fall. His correspondence indicates Adolphus White liked him and sometimes invited him over to a family meal. At the same time, however, the directors of a school closer to Marklesburg had begun to feel him out. A visit to the Normal School one March Saturday to attend a debate reinforced his yen, and sense of need, for further study. All his friends there urged him on. His mind made up, he wrote home that wherever he taught in the fall, it was *"best"* he take more course work in the summer.

The five months at Center Union earned its teacher $110. In those days coal miners averaged four times as much a year, postal and clerical workers eight times that, and utilities employees nearly seven times more. The national average for public-school teachers added up to double what he got. But, being frugal, Martin made his money go a long way. He not only paid his rent but bought several articles of clothing, some books, and a variety of trifles. He still managed to save fifty-seven dollars—just enough to cover the fifty-five dollar fee for the spring term at the Normal.

During his brief absence the Normal School had taken a more solid hold—enough so that the Brethren in other states began to talk about starting schools of their own. Also, hometown Huntingdon by now had put community support behind the Brumbaugh-Zuck project. In the spring of 1878 a group of townspeople had raised sufficient funds to buy a three-acre plot of ground on the West End's undeveloped heights. This included the lots owned by Martin's Uncle Doctor, most of which had been a potato patch the year before. A four-story T-shaped brick building, with a tower entrance facing toward town, was now fast nearing completion (it still stands, as Founders Hall, the present-day administration building). Since the past November the school had been chartered with the more upscale name of Brethren's Normal College. When Martin Brumbaugh came back in April 1879 for further study, the student body numbered more than one hundred for the spring term alone.

Euphoria was everywhere evident on the Hill that April as the students and professors moved into the new building. Since space was very limited, an unmarried professor had to share a room with a student. Because of this arrangement, Martin and his uncle Jacob, a bachelor, became roommates. They quartered on the top floor, which housed the men. This was the setting of one of Brumbaugh's favorite personal tales.

Like other dormitory rooms, theirs was furnished with a two-tiered bed. Martin naturally got assigned the top bunk. His uncle Jacob at this time was courting Rachel Jodon, a young student from Dauphin County (whom he later married). One night he stayed out quite late and his nephew, with puckish intent, arranged his own pillow and bedclothing to give the impression he was asleep with his face to the wall. Then he hid under the lower bunk.

His uncle, always something of a spoilsport, finally came in. He quietly undressed, donned his night shirt, extinguished the faint kerosene light and, probably still thinking romantic thoughts of Rachel, stepped to his bed. At this moment the nephew emitted a low growl, and reaching from under the bed grabbed Jacob by both ankles. The uncle let out a yell of fright. The prank, Brumbaugh would conclude in telling the story, led to one of the severest tongue-lashings he ever got.

By this time the Normal was promoting itself among the Brethren as "A HOME, A SCHOOL, AND A CHURCH." Accordingly, the chapel in the new multipurpose building was designed to do double duty as a sanctuary. It was outfitted with pews, and every Sunday the congregation, which would not have a church of its own until 1910, usurped the chancel. The Huntingdon elders and preachers, for decades, were either professors or administrators. All students not only had to attend weekly chapel, but also to attend worship services twice on Sunday, morning and evening.

In early May the Hilltop community, still caught up in celebrating its recent good fortune, was dealt a stunning blow by the sudden death of Jacob Zuck. Only thirty-three years old, he died of pneumonia. The dampness of still-drying plaster in his dormitory room had been too much for the sickly educator, people said. The college confronted its second crisis in little more than a year. People wondered, even despaired about, who could take the place of the one person upon whom the success of the college had seemed most to hinge. Martin Brumbaugh took the principal's death especially hard. He had been looking forward to doing a special favor for Zuck. Back in February the founding teacher had asked him to give part of his summer to traveling around the county recruiting students. Now he had no heart for it, although he did talk three of his Center Union pupils into following him to the Normal for the spring term.

On the evening of Zuck's funeral the Huntingdon Brethren gathered on the banks of the Juniata River to perform the rite of baptism. Among a foursome of baptismal candidates was Martin himself, who had become a seventeen-year-old a couple of weeks before. The mother of David Emmert, the art teacher, witnessed the scene. She watched Martin wade a short distance into the river, to where the current flowed waist-deep. Henry Brumbaugh, the officiant, stood there, ready to immerse him three times. Upon reaching his cousin's side, Martin knelt on the river's pebbly bottom. In a voice loud enough for the riverside onlookers to hear, the trustee chairman asked him several questions. The purpose of this brief, pre-liminary ritual was to assure the congregation that the applicant had made a volun-tary, sincere, informed decision—the criteria of believer's baptism as taught by the Dunkers. Martin answered all the questions with a yes, as he was supposed to, and the baptismal act followed.

In dripping clothes he made his way back to the riverbank. As he did so, Mrs. Emmert turned to her son and said, more prophetically than she knew, "That boy may someday fill Professor Zuck's place." William J. Swigart, one of the non-Brumbaughs closely identified with the Normal College's first half-century, showed similar prescience. He was present both at Zuck's burial and Martin's baptism, and the entry in his diary for that day reads: "A star has set—a new star has risen." Martin would have liked the way some people were linking his name and destiny to that of his onetime mentor, had he known what they were thinking about him the day he joined the church. For as he always avowed, Zuck was his earliest model and the man most responsible for guiding him into teaching. The Normal's first headmaster, Brumbaugh once said, "shook a lot of nonsense out of my head and put a few guidances [sic] into it."

With Zuck gone, the trustees, at their annual stockholders' meeting in July, gave considerable attention to academic leadership. They created a new position of president, to which they named James Quinter, publishing partner of Henry and John Brumbaugh and a major stockholder of the college. Since before the Civil

War, Quinter's name had been linked with the agitation for a Brethren school. The dean of Dunker printers, he had hounded the Brumbaugh brothers into a publishing merger in the fall of 1876, as much to be identified with their "experiment" at Huntingdon as to profit from pooled resources.

Because of Quinter's age (sixty-three) the presidency was meant to be a titular post. But choosing him was a calculated action. No churchman stood higher in the brotherhood's esteem; the trustees counted on the prestige of his name to help ensure the college's post-Zuck survival. By then two out-of-state sister schools were vying for students.

The de facto head of the Normal remained the principal. The trustees gave that position to Martin's uncle Jacob, who had been filling in since Zuck's death. (Like Harry S Truman's middle initial, Jacob's apparently stood for nothing and variously was signed or printed H, H., or H__.) Jacob, who would marry the next year, did duty as the Normal's principal until 1893. Stern and somber, he turned into the campus snoop, sniffing out tobacco-odored clothes and outgoing mail and rounding up after-dark curfew violators. Behind his back, resentful students tagged him with the nickname "Jakie."

July 1879 also brought, under terms of a new charter, the formal creation of a permanent board of trustees (fifteen members). From then on—until well into the next century—the Brumbaugh clan kept a controlling grip on the affairs of their institution. Henry would be trustee chairman forty years; Jacob, vice-chairman a similar span; Dr. Andrew, secretary nearly three decades; and John, chief fund-raiser in the Normal's formative period. Rookie schoolteacher Martin was blithely unknowing that July, but within a half-dozen years—at age twenty-two—he, too, would come on the board. In every case only death removed these Brumbaughs; they collectively amassed over two hundred years of service as trustees.

All that summer, after spring term's July close, Martin lived at home, working in the store or out at the sawmill. One day his father was seriously injured in a tree-felling accident out at the Forge. Struck a glancing blow on the head by a limb, George lay unconscious in bed for days. The burden of running the family businesses—the store, the post office, and the sawmill—fell upon Martin's shoulders the rest of the summer while his father recuperated.

Meanwhile, the harried son brushed up for the annual teacher's test, passed it, and got a position at a school two miles from Marklesburg. It was located at Grantsville, a community of sixteen houses and some shops along the Huntingdon and Broad Top Railroad (there was also a station and a telegraph and express office). This meant he could live at home, saving room-and-board costs.

The Grantsville school represented a step up in size (sixty-five pupils) and pay ($35 a month). Unlike Martin's first teaching position, very little is known about the second one. He once spoke, however, of fond memories of the 1879–80 school year. He said it was happily devoid of nagging discipline problems. The classes not only went well but six of his charges were inspired to become teachers because of him. Still, at many a day's end he would set out for home, dinner pail in hand, utterly exhausted. "There were times," wrote Brumbaugh years later about his Grantsville months, "when I could have thrown myself in a fence corner on the roadside and counted it sweet rest." At the local teachers' institute, conducted in Marklesburg in November, he spoke twice—in the morning on teaching the alphabet and spelling and in the evening on object lessons.

Being the son of Talking George, one of the area's leading citizens, must have enhanced the seventeen-year-old's standing among the Grantsville people, young and old. Perhaps that would account for how he got involved in teaching a Bible class. From one of his local aunts he learned that a number of adults in that neighborhood wanted to study the Holy Book. They had in mind, she said, a midweek meeting night. Whether he volunteered to be the teacher, or was asked to be, is not clear. At any rate, he organized a study group composed mostly of the parents of his pupils. It met on Wednesday evenings in different homes.

Martin's biblical knowledge could not have been very extensive. As a boy, he had sometimes attended Sunday school, probably at the Methodist church, since it is not certain the Dunkers at James Creek as yet had one. But he admittedly found it boring. He would have learned a little about the Bible at family worship, at preaching services, and more recently at Zuck's mandatory Sunday Bible class at the Normal. There is no evidence that in his personal use of the Scriptures he had proceeded in a systematic or studious way. It is true, however, that during the late Seventies he contributed a number of quite thoughtful biblically based articles to the *Primitive Christian,* the *Pilgrim's* new name after the Brumbaugh-Quinter merger. That year at Grantsville, nevertheless, gave birth to a Bible buff whose lectures on the Old and New Testaments, after he became president of his alma mater, were popular events on campus.

Gratifying as Brumbaugh remembered his Grantsville months to be as a teacher and debuting biblicist, the school year 1879–80 started out for him with very upsetting family news. One day that fall his uncle Henry Brumbaugh,* a prosperous Woodcock Valley farmer, came to him with the grim word his father was bankrupt. All the family property—home, store, timberland—would have to be auctioned off at a sheriff's sale. The problem was that the village merchant, like a good Dunker, refused to take legal action and force his country-store customers to pay up. Martin, as his letters reveal, knew his father was in financial trouble and was being dunned about the Forge debt. But he was hardly prepared, at age seventeen, to hear that J. Simpson Africa and the bank planned to foreclose.

As mentioned, a prime reason George Brumbaugh had invested in the Forge

---

*Not to be confused with trustee-chairman Henry, who was Martin's first cousin once removed.

timberland was to give work to unemployed men so that they could settle store bills. In recent years he had been paying nine dollars a week for their labor. But, as so often happens, their charges at the store—for groceries, over-the-counter medicines, dry goods, clothing—always exceeded their pay. And so, as Martin himself once summed up the situation: "The great financial coup of my father, therefore, came to nothing and bankruptcy stared him in the face."

Talking George had not paid a penny on the Forge property, either toward the principal or for interest for a couple of years. As of late November 1878 he owed $2,520, the $520 being accumulated interest. J. Simpson Africa had been very lenient toward Martin's father; no pressure had been put on him to meet his debt until now.

Martin's uncle Henry not only bore the baleful message that Africa was calling in his note; he also offered a way out, a deal. The James Creek Brethren, he reported, had met to discuss Talking George's financial plight. As a result, they were willing to raise the amount of the defaulted mortgage—which would be the equivalent today of about a $22,000 debt—from within the congregation and from among relatives. Henry would then use the money to buy the imperiled estate at the public sale, holding it in trust until the lien was cleared.

But there was a catch: Martin had to agree to make himself jointly responsible with his father for paying off the debt by the time he reached twenty-one, and preferably sooner. "Will you do it?" Henry Brumbaugh asked, knowing his under-age nephew could legally do nothing more than give his word.

His father's crisis came at a bad time for Martin. He had worries of his own trying to prepare himself for the future, now that he had some idea of what he wanted to do with his life: teach. Helping to bail out the family's holdings would only complicate getting started on a career. But what other options did a loyal Dunker son have but to promise to do what the Woodcock Valley people asked? So he solemnly plighted his honor. Uncle Henry then gave notes to a supportive group of kith and kin and paid off George Brumbaugh's mortgage.* The loans ranged from ten dollars to $550. The property, held as security, was to be deeded back, according to the pact, when all the notes were paid off. Meanwhile, the George Brumbaugh family operated the store, post office, and logging business as if they were still the owners.

For the time being, Martin put his pledge and family money matters out of mind. By the spring of 1880, having twice given teaching a whirl and generally pleased with the way things had gone, he felt certain he had found his lifework. He once said:

> My only ambition then and later was to be a school teacher. I thought school teachers were well paid and that they were happy, useful and independent men. Perhaps I might have aspired to be a lawyer had I been a Methodist or a Baptist instead of a

---

*At first George's property was divided up and held in trust by three people, including Henry, but eventually everything ended up in Henry's hands.

Dunkard. The members of my church never go to law with one another, nor with persons outside the church unless in defense of their property or their honor.*

So it was back to the Normal College for Martin that April—to finish out the two-year bachelor of English curriculum and get its coveted diploma. To cut costs he probably again did custodial chores of various kinds, including washing blackboards and cleaning out chalk troughs.

Prior to this time Martin had met his college expenses in another way. Ever since his teaching year at Center Union, he had sold textbooks for his uncle Jacob, who moonlighted as an agent for a Philadelphia publishing company. Pennsylvania did not have a compulsory free textbook law until 1893, so at Center Union and Grantsville Martin had a built-in market. Some school districts at that time, especially those in cities, did provide books. Others bought them wholesale and then sold them to children at cost. It is not clear what the practice was in Huntingdon County, or whether Martin peddled textbooks to school directors or to pupils. This source of extra money dried up after 1880, however, since he no longer would have classroom contacts.

Martin seems to have taken up where he had left off the previous year—as a stellar student. The evidence, though fragmentary, indicates high grades in all his subjects. (The college did not begin to keep a registry of final grades until 1883.) One month, however, he was docked in deportment (graded down to 95 percent)— for "rushing up the stairway." The Normal's total yearly enrollment by now surpassed three hundred, taught by a faculty of eleven.

Not surprisingly, Martin shone as a debater. In the early years of the Normal, the only extracurricular activity was the Literary Society. The society met each Friday evening and was a major cultural event; its membership comprised teachers, students, and townspeople. Some of its programs centered around impromptu debates. On those occasions each member placed in a box a slip of paper on which was written a controversial topic to be debated pro and con. Then one of the group would be called upon, go to the rostrum, draw a topic, and take one side of it.

Martin took part in every debate held while he was a collegian. "I talked whether they wanted me to talk or not," he once wisecracked of himself. Already people were saying of him, as he admitted years afterward, that his mouth was "like a railroad drug store, 'open day and night.'" He amazed audiences, according to eyewitness reports, by first arguing one side of a question and then the other— convincingly making his case either way. He practiced at debating in a way reminiscent of his Copperas Rocks declamations at the Forge. Some of the boys in his

---

*Some newspaper articles, when Brumbaugh was elected governor, mentioned that he had "read law" with a Huntingdon County judge for a short time. The reference was to Judge Thomas M. Bailey, but when this was or how long it lasted is unknown. The governor-elect only said it was for a brief period. George Brumbaugh, however, stubbornly opposed his son's studying law for any length of time.

class would join him on a hike out to a nearby farm. There, he once recalled, they "would tie [their] watches to the fence stakes and debate to the frogs, and learn how to make a certain number of points in three minutes." He found it good discipline.

This self-description of an outgoing, garrulous teenager contradicts George Brumbaugh's memory of his son's personality as a collegian. In 1914, during Martin's gubernatorial campaign, the father, then in his early eighties, told reporters:

> When Martin was a boy, he was bashful as a student at Juniata College. . . . I told him to keep in touch with his teachers, to be at hand when someone was needed quickly, and then I said, "You will be at the hub of the wheel. You will be on the spot." That is what Martin did.

As George recalled, "I did not burden him with too much advice. One day I said, 'Be yourself, Martin, even if you are not bigger than a thumb; David was himself, and he counted for more than Goliath.'"

Martin graduated in June 1881, with distinction, in a class of seven—the Normal's third commencement—receiving a bachelor of English degree.

Much of his time the summers of 1880 and 1881 he spent out at the Forge, living in the old stone "mansion." The logging and sawmill business offered the best way to make quick money for the bankrupt Brumbaughs. They were able to win bids on some good contracts. Martin swung an ax alongside the lumbermen, paired up on a crosscut saw, and put in long hours at the sawmill while his father and brothers looked after the store.

Over the next several years, Brumbaugh remembered, "When I had ten dollars or one hundred dollars I would go to one of the men who held Uncle Henry's note and pay the principal in full, together with six per cent interest." Thirty years later the one-time lumberjack would parlay his sawmill summers into political capital when campaigning for governor among the woodsmen of northern Pennsylvania. He drew cheers talking their jargon and flashing a saw-scarred finger.

Perhaps it was during this period of his youth that Brumbaugh did something he always enjoyed telling about. As a student trying to get by on a very low food budget, he became so hungry one day that he started nibbling on raisins. He never stopped until he had eaten a whole pound of them. In a short time he felt rather bloated. Thinking to relieve the feeling, he drank a couple of glasses of water. This made him feel worse. He went to the phone—the college installed one in 1881— and called Dr. Andrew Brumbaugh. He said, "Uncle Doctor, I feel very bad. I think I'm going to die." His uncle asked, "Do you have a fever?" Martin said, "I don't think so." "Have you eaten some spoiled food?" the doctor then inquired. "No," answered Martin, "I've only eaten a pound of raisins." "And?" the doctor questioned. Replied the nephew, "I drank two glasses of water." Whereupon his uncle snapped, "You ought to die, you fool," then prescribed an emetic and hung up in disgust.

Martin returned to College Hill the fall of 1881, this time to start the two-year bachelor of science course. Then, in March of 1882, he left for Millersville State Normal School to study calculus and advanced mathematics. Part of the time he also did supervised teaching at the Millersville Model School. (A student-teacher in those days did not get classroom experience in the public schools under a mentor.) One of his teachers that spring and the man who critiqued his practice teaching was Edward Brooks, the principal. He was the author of a series of arithmetic textbooks widely used in the public schools of the Middle Atlantic states. In fact, Martin himself had learned how to cipher from Brooks textbooks as a schoolboy at Marklesburg. The future professional paths of Brooks and Brumbaugh would cross many times, deepening a friendship born of mutual admiration.

Shortly before he departed the Hilltop for Millersville, however, Martin found himself a substitute teacher for the college Bible class. Bible study, although not a regular academic course, was obligatory for all students every Sunday. Who asked him to be a Sunday morning backup, and why, is unknown. Perhaps his Grantsville reputation had something to do with it. At any rate, he agreed to fill in when needed, a decision of no small consequence.

One Sunday the Normal's Henry Brumbaugh happened to sit in on a lesson taught by Martin. He liked what he saw and heard. After the study hour ended, Henry sought out a couple of the trustee-professors. He told them that he had found just the right person for a faculty position opening up in the fall. When asked who it was, he answered, "M. G."* Apparently the idea had not occurred to any of them, perhaps because of his age. But, it seems, no one objected.

Martin knew nothing about this hallway parley until he returned from Millersville and dropped in on graduation exercises in July. As soon as the program was over, his cousin Henry sought him out in the audience. The head trustee explained what he had in mind, which Martin, just turned twenty, no doubt found flattering. The job offer was too good to turn down, even though taking it would detour degree plans. So Martin accepted on the spot. No member of the college's faculty would ever be so young when hired.

He spent the rest of that summer out in the mountains cutting timber. Sometimes, to supplement the family income, he must have worked on lumber jobs other than the ones contracted by his father. That seems to have been the case in 1882, since most of his time was put in along Sugar Camp Run. This was south of the Forge by several miles and near the coal-mining town of Broad Top City.

Here, as Martin remembered, he helped fell giant white pines, cut breast-high as the practice was in those days. This became the custom because most of the cutting was done in the deep snows of winter. But even when the snow was gone, the trees were cut high in case the butts were shaky. Once down, the tree trunks were barked, lopped into sixteen-foot logs, and dragged to a loading site. The logs

---

*It is difficult to pinpoint how old Martin was when the Brumbaughs began calling him by his initials. The Bible-class story seems to be the earliest anecdotal use of them.

would be hauled on the Huntingdon and Broad Top Railroad to Huntingdon, re-loaded by crane on Pennsylvania Railroad cars, and shipped down the Juniata Valley to Dauphin. There the logs would be sawed into boards and sold for one hundred dollars a thousand feet.

One day the young M. G. approached the crew boss at Sugar Camp Run, a lapsed Dunker, with an unusual proposal. He, the youngest of a work gang in their early twenties, wanted to form a camp club. It would foster social, mental, and spiritual growth, he explained, and promote a love of the out-of-doors. The outfit's boss, though probably dumbfounded, gave his okay to the idea.

Each man, according to Martin's plan, was supposed to take an hour's walk in the woods one day a week, without gun or knife, picking no wildflowers. In the evening, then, sitting around a campfire, the clubbers would take turns describing in detail what they had seen. The club had a wholesome effect, according to its organizer. He claimed it ended all drinking bouts in camp as well as carousing at the area saloons. The fellows gave all their spare time to "intellectual enjoyments." Out of that club at Sugar Camp Run, said Martin, came a banker, three preachers, three attorneys, and, of course, a governor.

The young lumberjacks also mixed sport with hard work and nature hikes. The timber-cutting crew that summer held a contest with a Mann's "Major Axe" as first prize. It went to that pair who sawed down, peeled, and skidded the most logs in a day. Martin and his partner tallied twenty-one logs, quite a day's work but not good enough to win the ax. In the Dunker logger's memories, the months at Sugar Camp Run were among the happiest of his life.

From the fall of 1882 through the spring of 1884, the better part of two years, Brumbaugh, as "Professor M. G.," taught literature, grammar, rhetoric, and natural sciences. He also held the title of librarian for one year (1882–83), which mainly involved checking books in and out on Saturday mornings.

Another duty fell upon him in March of 1883: proctoring the third floor, the level on which he roomed. Each hall had a "disciplinarian," usually one of the single professors. He once recalled that, at curfew each night, he would go down the hall shouting, "Lights out! Lights out!" Perhaps the bell-ringing "promotion" he once alluded to came at this time. It involved summoning to classes, meals, and Sunday services—probably by jangling a hand bell—the residents on his floor. (The tower bell, which is still rung on special occasions today, would not be installed until the fall of 1884.)

Somehow, along with preparing for classes he taught, the greenhorn professor managed to sandwich in a course or two toward the B.S. degree.

Having come of age in 1883, the professor began to take more seriously his lien-lifting promise to Uncle Henry Brumbaugh. His letters home that spring revealed more than a trace of impatience with his father's slipshod bookkeeping system and his failure to get a good day's work out of the woodsmen. They also fretted about some of the James Creek people who had begun pestering him by mail for quicker action on their short-term loans. Once he bluntly directed his father to send him—posthaste—"a *full list* of *all* your *indebtedness*." In chiding language he urged getting squared with the James Creek IOUs first and only after that begin wiping off more recently incurred debts. It was "wonderfully annoying" to him, as the son once quaintly put it, how his father had adopted a repayment schedule exactly the reverse.

The story most widely told about Martin's part in clearing the mortgage took place the summer of 1883. He and his father had won an order for 1137 chestnut telegraph poles from the Pennsylvania Railroad that spring. The poles were to be thirty-five feet in length and fourteen inches in diameter at the butt. Whenever the father-son team could, especially on Saturdays and holidays, they worked the logs down the Raystown Branch and over its shoals. This was not always an easy task, because by July low water gave them trouble. Sometimes they had a logjam on their hands. Then the surefooted son would run out over the tumbled logs with a stick of dynamite in hand, drop his charge, and scamper back to the bank by clambering over the moving mass after the explosion. At Ardenheim, where the Branch empties into the Juniata, the Brumbaughs had erected a barrier to hold the poles until they could be hoisted onto flatcars and shipped off. The railroad tracks there ran, as now, close to the riverbank.

On the night before summer commencement, a violent storm hit the Huntingdon area. The swollen river current broke the boom holding the latest supply of logs and swept them downstream—as far as Harrisburg, one hundred miles away. Undaunted, George and Martin set out the very next morning to recover the lost poles. Fortunately, all of them were marked, like branded cattle. The Brumbaughs, using cant hooks, moved slowly down the river, rolling the logs in and floating them to the nearest railroad station to be loaded.

It was a herculean task that lasted for weeks. Searching the riverbanks meant aching bodies, sleepless nights, wet clothes, and torn hands. Some poles, identified by their markings, were found hidden under haystacks. The two loggers slept in barns and lived on milk and what they bought from farmers. But the search was not given up until all the poles had been retrieved.

The whole railroad deal paid off profitably; the Brumbaughs cleared $2100 on the contract—two-thirds of the Forge indebtedness. And the scattered-poles ordeal would reward Martin in another, unexpected way before a year's passing.

By late fall 1883, after a four-year wait, mortgage-burning day finally came. All notes had been met. Martin—alone, unescorted by his father—carried them one day to his uncle Henry's house, which stood on a farm adjacent to the Brumbaugh homestead. As the nephew liked to tell the story, "We sat down at a table, tore the notes in little pieces, and put the pieces into the fire." "To us," he always chuckled when describing the occasion, "it was a very impressive ceremony."

Martin had every reason to be pleased with himself at the time of the farmhouse ritual. He had indeed upheld *his* end of the bargain that made his father a debt-free man, helping to raise more than three thousand dollars, counting interest costs. Several weeks after the note-burning kitchen scene, uncle and nephew got together again on family business matters. It was a few days before Christmas. The Yuletide conclave had a very curious outcome: Henry redeeded all of the family properties to his nephew, not to his brother. Martin never talked about this holiday outcome. Whether or not Talking George, only forty-nine years old, was consulted beforehand or ever gave consent to being divested of his holdings, his son never said. Nor do we know if the nephew had foreknowledge of what his uncle intended to do. The Brumbaugh kindred, however, obviously thought the son had a far better head for business than the father. The George B. Brumbaugh Mercantile House closed its doors, and soon after its former owner resigned as postmaster.*

Martin Brumbaugh, unexpectedly a man of land and property at age twenty-one, was still very much a country bumpkin. But he was obviously bright, a warm and outgoing person, and hardworking. Already he exhibited the habits and instincts of a born teacher. The next decade would see him largely purged of naïveté, his reputation as an educator grow rapidly, and his name become known beyond his native county.

---

*Thereafter the Marklesburg tax records list him as a laborer, until 1891. That year he, his son Irvin, and a cousin opened the Brumbaugh Company General Store at a different Marklesburg location from the original family business (which was razed several decades later).

4

County Superintendent

THE spring and summer of 1884 produced a presidential campaign in the United States that, by election time, degenerated into one of the most scurrilous in the nation's political history. Huntingdon's three newspapers, like the press everywhere in the country, titillatingly reported all the scandal-mongering. The Democrats charged that Senator James Blaine, the most popular Republican of his generation, had been guilty of corrupt railroad dealing when he had been a congressman. The Republicans in turn accused Grover Cleveland, New York's bachelor governor, of having fathered an illegitimate child. Blaine denied everything; Cleveland did not and won—by less than twenty-six thousand votes.

Martin Brumbaugh himself became an office seeker that mudslinging year of the Blaine-Cleveland presidential race. Sometime in the spring he decided to run for county superintendent of schools, talked into it by his uncle Jacob. No other Dunker, so far as we know, had ever sought an elective office of this importance. In 1884 the superintendency attracted more than the usual number of candidates— five in all—since the incumbent was not seeking reelection. Martin, his twenty-second birthday just passed, quite rightly saw his age as a possible handicap. So did other Brumbaughs. His uncle Henry, the farmer, told him to go after the job anyway, even though sure to lose. The experience would be good for him next time around. Three years older then, he would have a better chance.

Another person young Brumbaugh talked to was George B. Orlady, then the county's thirty-year-old district attorney, who would be a judge on the Superior Court of Pennsylvania when Brumbaugh became governor. According to Orlady, "One day a long-legged country boy came into my law office and said that he would like to be county superintendent. He asked me if I were in favor of his election, and what I thought his chances would be." The lawyer looked the visitor over carefully, shook his head, and said quite frankly that he was too young. Without political influence, Orlady advised, he could not hope to win. Nevertheless, he wished the aspiring public servant good luck.

Brumbaugh was undaunted. To help disguise his pubescent looks he sprouted chin whiskers and coaxed out a mustache. He took a leave of absence during the Normal College's spring term and trudged all over Huntingdon County for two months. He canvassed every single school director—all two hundred or so of them.

Not long into the contest Martin got his first lesson in dirty politics—small-time, of course, by 1884 national standards. He was victimized by smear tactics, Huntingdon County style. Someone began circulating a leaflet that forewarned:

> [I]t will be well for the directors to consider the consequences if the *Dunkard* is elected. His headquarters are at the Dunkard Normal School and will likely remain so, even if he had declared to the contrary in the *Local*. If he is elected Huntingdon County will be supplied by Dunkard teachers, even if they are brought in from Va., Mo., Ohio, etc. The main idea is to make Dunkardism popular. They want to make this county the Dunkard centre of a large radius. They are the most sectarian church in the U.S., except the Catholic. Why, in their estimation to be a Dunkard is greater than a king! Therefore, vote for any one in preference to the Dunkard, even if he does come around with his deceitful smiles.

Brumbaugh's backers at the Normal College put out a rather sophisticated four-page brochure that they sent to each school director. It highlighted his quali-fications, abilities, and training. It also included newspaper endorsements and glow-ing testimonials by school directors at Center Union and Grantsville, by Jacob Brumbaugh, and by professors at the Millersville State Normal School.

Nowhere in this campaign pamphlet was there reference to his age, an inten-tional omission. To his brother Frank, who must have had something to do with its preparation, he wrote: "Do *not print my age*." And to his folks, who perhaps looked askance at his politicking, he pleaded, "[I] trust you won't harm me any."

Brumbaugh spent the last days of the campaign electioneering in Shirley Town-ship, a flourishing center of Dunkerism. All the township directors there, however, were known to be backing a candidate from their own area. But that did not stop the young political hopeful. So, late one evening he called at the home of a director by the name of James Harper, a non-Dunker. Harper was a sturdy, plain-spoken, Scots-Irish farmer who right off said his vote was pledged to another candidate. But he invited Brumbaugh to come in for a bite to eat and even stay overnight if he wanted to.

The weary campaigner promptly accepted the gracious invitation. In the course of their over-the-supper-table chitchat, Brumbaugh's host asked him, "Are you any relative of that boy who helped his father with the telegraph poles last summer?" No, the candidate said, he was not a relative; *he was* "that boy." This got Mr. Harper to rethinking his vote. Next morning the overnight guest departed after breakfast with a handshake and, much to his delight, another director on his bandwagon.

That vote change not only helped, but may have been decisive. When the directors met in the courthouse on Tuesday afternoon, 6 May, college trustee chairman Henry Brumbaugh was there as an observer. It took two pollings before Martin, who netted 111 of the 221 ballots cast, finally eked out a one-vote majority; the next highest vote-getter both times was the Shirley Township candidate. Some directors angrily demanded a bigger victory margin. But the outvoted rivals themselves conceded defeat and, like good sportsmen, urged a unanimous vote for the winner. That was done, and the county had a superintendent-elect, Pennsylvania's youngest ever.

His well-wishers among the Huntingdon and Woodcock Valley Brethren heard about the election outcome with elation. Henry Brumbaugh made it the main entry in his diary for that day. As Martin once noted, the superintendency "was a rich and honorable office in the view of the Dunkards and all the rest of the rural inhabitants." His annual salary of $1,048.50 seemed a princely sum to them. They were even more impressed when, reelected in 1887, he got a raise to twelve hundred dollars a year.

In the month of June the new superintendent presided over his first county teachers' institute. That summer he also held his first superintendent's "peripatetic" examination. There before him, among the other test-takers, sat "Uncle" Mike Kiper, as children had long affectionately called him. An old-timer, he had begun teaching in the 1830s, fifty-one years before. It was Uncle Mike Kiper, his textbook the Bible, who taught first-grader Martha Grove to read and later had George Brumbaugh in the upper grades as a pupil. He had been a family friend for a generation since then. When Martin attended his first teachers' institute in 1878, he sat at Uncle Mike's side every session.

Now, six years later, he was the county superintendent, the supervisor of his parents' beloved teacher. And as he looked into the faces of the examinees, Brumbaugh one time recalled, he thought to himself, "Well, old Uncle Mike, you have slipped along for a good many years, but you are not up to . . . modern things." But to the superintendent's surprise, the "absolutely" best speller of all the teachers he ever tested proved to be Uncle Mike Kiper. His point in telling this story, decades later, was that the "three R school" and its limited curriculum, although by then outmoded, did excel in teaching the basics: how to "make boys write and cipher and read." And, as Brumbaugh said, Uncle Mike "was the very three R's . . . incarnate."

The biggest postelection event for the superintendent, however, was his late-summer marriage. His intended was Anna—"Annie" to most people—Konigmacher, a student at the Brethren's Normal College and a year older than he was. Curiously, the couple's courtship is a total blank in the Martin Brumbaugh story.

Anna's family history was linked to one of the most notable religious and cultural experiments in colonial America. Her paternal ancestors, early-eighteenth-century German immigrants, belonged to the Ephrata Society in Lancaster County. The majority of the original Ephrataites were ex-Dunkers at the time —the 1730s; they organized into a kind of Protestant monastic commune. Sabbatarians, they called themselves Seventh-Day Baptists. The Konigmacher progenitors were not celibates but "householders," living on Zion Hill in their own home. Thus, though in full fellowship, they never resided in the Ephrata Cloister itself. Monastery life died out after a few decades, but a small congregation continued on. Anna's grandfather, William, served for almost four decades—until he died—as a trustee, and in his last years as the trustees' secretary and treasurer.

Her father, Edwin, a retired Ephrata pharmacist since 1882, was also a trustee until he became a Dunker, around 1855, when in his mid-thirties. One of the organizers of the Ephrata National Bank, he had served for many years as a director. He had also been a director of the Ephrata Water Company. At the time of Anna's marriage, he had just completed a three-year term as a Normal College trustee. He married late in life, at age thirty-nine. His first wife died in 1866, and Anna, his only surviving child, was raised from early girlhood by a stepmother. Her baptism took place at Huntingdon the same year as Martin's and, like his, in the Juniata River.

Their nuptials took place in the Konigmacher's Ephrata home at nine o'clock on Thursday morning, 28 August. It was a pleasant day with twenty-five guests present, including the college's Henry Brumbaugh. Anna had roomed her first year as a Normal student in Henry Brumbaugh's home. Daughterless, he and his wife grew very fond of her. College-era photographs show the bride to have been a petite, buxom young woman with big, deep-set, doleful eyes and thin, compressed lips.

The summer of Martin's marriage also saw him co-opted as a trustee of his alma mater—and made vice-chairman! This dual honor—board member and officer—seems premature, callow and unmoneyed (although well-propertied) as Brumbaugh then was. County superintendent of schools was, admittedly, probably the highest political office yet held by a Dunker. But that triumph alone hardly fitted him for this sort of nepotistic institutional station. The motive behind the board's decision, therefore, was obviously more pragmatic than honorific. As public education's top man in the county, the trustees' vice chairman was ideally situated to recruit, from among schoolteachers and pupils, future students for the Normal College. That is, in fact, what he did, and with immediate success.

While the hyperenergetic Brumbaugh attended to the duties of superintendent, both newlyweds finished up course work at the Normal College. In June 1885 Anna got her B.E. diploma and Martin, the first to do so there, his B.S. Where they lived the initial year of their marriage is not known. But in late fall they moved into a new brick house on the corner of Moore and Seventeenth Streets, directly across from the Normal's campus (today it is the college guest house). The lot they built on was bought from his uncle Jacob, who at the time lived next door on Moore Street. Edwin Konigmacher put up some of the wherewithal that enabled his daughter and son-in-law to become homeowners so soon after marrying. And, of course, Martin Brumbaugh's credit standing was unassailable since, with all the land and property he owned, he posed little security risk.

Martin, photographic evidence indicates, continued to sport whiskers for several years after taking up the superintendency, probably to make himself look more mature. He could not have meant them to be a badge of his Dunkerism because, mustached as well as bearded, he was in violation of the facial-hair code. He also ignored prescribed Dunker habiliment, outfitting himself in the secular style of that era. The Huntingdon Brethren—and their college—would in the near future be judged, in the eyes of many, heretics on the question of clothes. All the early photographs show the male students in ties and lapeled coats; coeds tended to dress more conservatively. Huntingdon "sisters," however, were among the first to switch bonnets for fashionable hats. Dress reform among the Brethren would not officially come until the early twentieth century. And even until then, the Huntingdon congregation, although liberal on attire, saw fit to honor the brotherhood taboo against such modish things as gay colors, high-heeled shoes, silk hose, tight skirts, canes, spats, and jewelry.

The young superintendent worked out of an office in the courthouse. He oversaw a system that embraced about 9000 school-aged children, 235 teachers (whose ages averaged twenty-five), and a few more than 200 school buildings. His bailiwick, of course, was almost wholly an aggregation of country and village schools, only 47 of which were graded. There were no separate high schools and scarcely any secondary students. Huntingdon, its population plateaued at 4000 or so, was the biggest town; Mount Union, twelve miles east, was second in size, with 760-some residents, three times more than any other community.

Brumbaugh's duties required him to make annual visits to all the schools under his care. A dog-lover, he often shared the buggy seat on these rounds with Spot, a fox terrier and the household pet at the time. Some people playfully referred to his canine companion as the "assistant superintendent."

More than once in making the circuit Martin stayed overnight in homes with schoolable youngsters. He turned these stopovers into occasions to preach—for the benefit of parents and pupils alike—against habitual absenteeism. He pleaded with youngsters to finish the grades. One wonders whether Brumbaugh, in his exhortations, ever owned up to his own erratic attendance as a schoolboy.

As a county superintendent, he faced two attendance problems every superintendent, urban or rural, then faced: a high drop-out rate and truancy. He had phenomenal success concerning the first. In 1884, when he took office, the number of children "not in school" was 1,540. By 1887 that figure had fallen to 267, an amazing decline in so short a period of time. This was especially remarkable because Pennsylvania did not have a compulsory attendance law until 1895. Brumbaugh frequently lamented the absence of such legislation when he was a young school official.

He had far less success in dealing with truancy (irregular attendance). As he knew from his own schoolteaching days, daily absenteeism in Huntingdon County averaged over 20 percent—which was a little higher than the state average of 17 percent. But despite his preachments and much to his disappointment, this remained the pattern during his six years in office. Absence, he would have known from personal experience, did not necessarily imply indifference. Schoolboy labor was greatly needed on nineteenth-century farms, especially during spring and fall. And in cities immigrant families needed the extra income from child labor. In 1887, Pennsylvania mandated a school year of at least six months, which only exacerbated the truancy problem.

Brumbaugh garnered quite a repertory of amusing stories about his experiences with children while a county superintendent. One of them he could never tell without a big laugh. The way he told it:

> I was superintendent of Huntingdon County schools as a young man. One cold day while driving *my* two-horse team [that was a mark of position] to a country school, I stopped to pick up a little mite of a girl on her way to that schoolhouse. Sharing the buffalo robe with her, I asked, "How is school going?" She turned her little face up toward me and with an extremely serious, sober look, she said, "We learn dumber everyday."

Besides nonattendance, another of Brumbaugh's concerns, like that of his predecessors, was the physical condition of the county's schoolhouses. All but a few were frame structures, the rest brick. Three-fourths of them he found "unfit." They lacked suitable furniture, equipment, and privies, according to his reports. He complained about substandard conditions of light, heat, ventilation, and playgrounds. As for interior decor, he later recalled:

> I saw school rooms decorated—if at all—with cheap patent medicine posters, cigarette pictures, and glaring announcements of the best brands of soap, beer, and whiskey.

Needless to say, decorative tastes of this sort offended Martin's Dunker sensibilities. Under his architectural guidance many "unfit" schoolhouses were renovated, many others better equipped, and more than two-score new ones built. This six-year record, by statewide comparisons, rated as no mean feat.

By the late 1880s Huntingdon County had come to be a microcosm of what was happening everywhere in the United States: increasing numbers of women entering the teaching ranks. In 1884 the county employed eighty-one females, a little over 32 percent of the instructional force. A half-dozen years later the figures stood at ninety-nine and 40 percent, respectively. In Pennsylvania overall at that time, the spread was even greater, with women making up about two-thirds of the public-school teachers employed. To Brumbaugh and other educators throughout the nation, this trend held no mystery: The answer was underpaid male teachers. In Huntingdon County men averaged $33.63 a month during "Superintendent M. G.'s" last year. The state average was not much higher.

The exodus of men from the classroom, serious enough for Brumbaugh to mention, did not seem to trouble him overly much. In fact, he was something of an equal-opportunity advocate. He was outraged by the sexism reflected in the taken-for-granted pay differential for men and women teachers. "This is wrong," he tersely wrote in his first annual report to the state superintendent of public instruction.

Little good his protest did, either in Harrisburg or his home area. He was bucking the Victorian times. All during his two terms, in spite of his pitch for equal compensation, Huntingdon County school directors kept upping the wages of men and freezing those of women. By 1890 a woman's monthly check added up to six and a half dollars less than a man's. This amounted to a substantial disparity, taking into account the value of the 1890s' dollar.

Brumbaugh achieved a better record in his efforts to raise standards for teacher certification and to promote professional growth. There was obvious need for this. His rural school system, typical of the times in bucolic districts, was plagued by woefully undertrained and inexperienced teachers. Only one among his classroom force in 1884 was a college graduate; ten held two-year normal-school diplomas. Twenty-two others had done some studying either at a college or a normal school. Nearly 20 percent had never taught before, while about 31 percent had five years or less experience.

Few of the county's teachers, therefore, could be considered true professionals. Indeed, that held true practically everywhere in the nation, except perhaps in some of the major cities. For Brumbaugh, nonetheless, teaching was a high calling. He even defined it as "holy work" in one of his annual reports. He minced no words in criticizing directors who, disregarding competence, played politics or showed favoritism in hiring teachers.

To weed out unfit applicants he devised rigorous qualifying tests and was gratified by the quick results. There were failures each year, to be sure (one year at a 50% rate), but increasingly the candidates came better prepared when examined. Each year he was able to grant a few permanent certificates. One area in which aspiring teachers were tested was "theory of education," but year after year their pedagogical ignorance greatly troubled him. He wrote in 1889: "Scholastic attainments have advanced, but there is a lack of knowledge *how to teach*."

To remedy the problem of amateurish pedagogy, Brumbaugh made effective use of the teachers' institute. Institutes had been adopted in most states by the end of the Civil War as a way of providing special assistance to inexperienced or poorly trained teachers. Organized at the county level (large cities held their own), they were short (four to five days), intensive in-service training sessions for teachers of all grades. Guest instructors were brought in, some of state and national note, from all sectors of public education. Frequently, speakers of Chautauqua caliber lectured on inspirational topics.

Pennsylvania ranked as a leading state in institute work, but none of its county superintendents had ever put more stock in the idea than did Huntingdon's Brumbaugh. He had attended his first one the year he taught at Center Union. Now, as superintendent, he threw himself lustily into promoting in-service development of this kind. He got the general public involved, including civic leaders as well as teachers. So successful was he that within a couple of years he could tell Harrisburg about "the almost phenomenal growth of our county institute."

The facts justified tooting his own horn. For example, the institute for 1885, his first to plan, counted several no-show teachers and about three hundred interested citizens. His next-to-last one, in 1889, was minus only two teachers while attracting over fourteen hundred noneducators. By then Brumbaugh had been able to bring to his institutes such dignitaries as Pennsylvania's governor and its superintendent of public instruction, out-of-state big-city administrators, and platform favorites like Philadelphia's Russell Conwell, of Temple University and "Acres of Diamonds" fame.

Superintendent Brumbaugh resorted to other motivational and remedial strategies, also with good results for his classroom staff—and for his reputation in Harrisburg. Thus it soon became evident that Pennsylvania had a county superintendent of schools with seemingly boundless energy and a suasive administrative style. Just as obvious was his commitment to "new education" ideas. "New education" was current academese for those theories of the late nineteenth century that collectively fermented a wide range of pedagogical reforms—reforms that took a more scientific and experimental approach to what today is called educational psychology, child development, and teaching methods. By 1885 these various philosophies were being discussed everywhere in educational circles, by kindergarten teachers no less than by college professors.

In this respect Martin Brumbaugh was not at all ill served by his schooling at the hands of Dunkers. At the Brethren's College he had taken two courses from his straitlaced but pedagogically enlightened uncle Jacob: "Mental Science" and "The Art and the Science of Teaching." Then, too, at Millersville State Normal School he had studied under Edward Brooks, one of the biggest names among new-education enthusiasts. (The professors at his Huntingdon alma mater often whimsically referred to their college as a branch of Millersville because so many of them, including his uncle Jacob, were its alumni.)

As superintendent, Brumbaugh never ceased to advocate educational reform. In his annual report for 1890, he referred to the "violent agitation of the 'new' and the 'old'," and the dilemma educators faced. Should they endorse the "'new' whose principles are yet crude and indefinite?" he asked. Or should they continue in the "old," to be dubbed "fogies"? In a Lutheran "Here I Stand" type of manifesto, the twenty-eight-year-old schoolman proclaimed: "I oppose no 'new.' I placate no 'old.' Education that is traditional is doomed. Education must be prophetic."

Though often at odds in their theories, progressive educators were unanimous on one point: they did not romanticize the one-room school with its reliance upon rote learning from a book. The chief evil of the rote-and-recitation method, they argued, was that it deterred pupils from grasping the ideas behind the words they hurriedly mouthed. It allowed no chance for explanation or for discussion.

This also bothered Brumbaugh. As he put it, "Have you the power, by your presence, movements, and words to challenge and awaken and direct thought . . . in your pupils? If so, *you are a teacher.*" It would be interesting to know what classroom tack the superintendent himself had taken a decade earlier as a lowly, but apparently popular, teacher at Center Union and Grantsville. Was it a reprise of the one inflicted on him as a boy, or was it the teacher-actuator mode he now lauded?

According to end-of-the-century reformers, traditional teaching, especially in its one-room guise, focused too much on subject matter. It completely ignored the differing needs, interests, and abilities of each learner. New-education proponents, therefore, made much of child psychology and the child-centered curriculum. Brumbaugh was not able to do much about curricular changes in Huntingdon County, filled as it was with overcrowded one-room schools. But, from the start, he did preach to his teachers "their need more than anything else to study *child nature.* . . ." This would help the less seasoned among them to better understand and cope with the stages of emotional, intellectual, and cognitive growth public schoolers go through.

In his thinking, however, all this had to be put into the perspective of teaching as "holy work." He first used this term in his report for 1886, and it was the leitmotif of his pedagogy ever after. This hallowed status of teaching meant several things to Martin Brumbaugh. First of all, it denoted taking a more affectionate and empathetic attitude toward schoolchildren as opposed to the classroom authoritarianism of the times. Once, when county superintendent, Brumbaugh was lecturing in Louisiana, and in one speech made the point: "Put this down in your heart of hearts: you will never make a boy do the right thing by telling him not to do the wrong thing. Let me say that plainly. If there is one word that will not count in your discipline it is the word don't." Not everyone in the audience agreed. As he recalled,

When the talk was over a large manly woman, weighing about two hundred and sixty, came up and looked me in the face and said: "Mr. Brumbaugh," I said, "Yes, ma'am." She said, "I just heard your address and I am a great deal concerned about that talk on the word don't." I said, "I am glad you heard it." She said, "I am not so sure I understand you. Do you mean to say that we should never say don't to these children?" I said, "Yes, ma'am. Something like that was my thought." She said, "Do you read your Bible?" You can answer a woman's question if you know what she is getting at, but when you don't you always halt. I said, "When I was a child I used to read my Testament." She said, "Do you read the Old Testament?" I said, "I have." She said, "Do you remember the ten commandments?" I said, "I have heard of them." She said, "How do they begin?" Two hundred and sixty pounds of woman and the Bible against a man two thousand miles from home. What would you say? It looked like a gone case, didn't it? As I ran over these commandments in my mind there before her I thought

Thou shalt not, Thou shalt not, Thou shalt not. And then I remembered to say to her what I want you to write on your heart: There was one that spoke as no man ever spoke, who said in a moment of inspiration, "It has been written thou shalt not, but I say unto you love your neighbor, do good." And if you want the spirit of Christ instead of the spirit of law in your teaching, you must tell the boys and girls constantly what they shall do, not what they shall not do.

"Holy work" was also his rhetorical way of saying that teachers—he included school directors, too—are not only answerable to each child and to society for how they carry out their educational duties, but ultimately to God. Therefore teaching, as he saw it, involved the sacred obligation to treat each pupil as a child of God. Twenty years hence, this would be the underlying assumption of his best-known book, *The Making of a Teacher.* But his most graphic utterance on the spiritual nature of the teacher-pupil relationship came *after* he was out of public education. As governor he was once asked to speak at an educational conference. At one point in his address, conflating parts of two familiar oracles by Jesus—one from the sheep-goat parable about the Last Judgment (Matt. 25:31–46) and the other against all forms of child abuse (Matt. 18:6)—Brumbaugh warned: "[W]hatever we do to these little ones we also do to Him, who loved them . . . and who died that they might live and live abundantly."

Although Brumbaugh engineered no major curricular reforms as superintendent, he did work at adding "drawing" and music as core subjects. Child-centered proponents ascribed great value to the creative arts and to self-expression. Many Americans in those days considered such activities trivial, stealing time from the "three R's." Some Pennsylvania schools, however, had begun to include instruction in vocal music and drawing soon after the Civil War. In Huntingdon County Brumbaugh used his educational post as a "bully pulpit" for what he called "an all-sided preparation for complete living." He wrote:

It is not true that time spent in studying that which has no direct bearing upon the probable business pursuits of the child is wasted time. . . . Let it not be forgotten that cultured minds . . . will adapt themselves to any ordinary business more readily than those minds to which only utilitarian instruction has been given. . . .

Therefore, his argument went, any curriculum so imbalanced as to exclude aesthetic appreciation should be written off as "false reform." He rested his case with a biblical fillip: "No man liveth by bread alone." That said, he proudly announced that 63 schools introduced art his first year in office, bringing the total number to 79; by the end of the third it was taught in 145. Music, too, took "rapid hold," he reported, and by 1887 there were 86 schools with singing classes.

As an administrator, Brumbaugh meanwhile found himself championing a curricular reform not of his own instigation but one he heartily endorsed. Early in the 1880s the Woman's Christian Temperance Union (WCTU), soon after Frances

Willard became its president, set in motion a national effort to infiltrate the public schoolrooms with what it called "Scientific Temperance Instruction." In 1885, after a two-year crusade, the Pennsylvania WCTU successfully lobbied the General Assembly into passing a compulsory law of this kind, one of the first in the country. It provided for Drys-generated lessons, which made use of graphic materials, on the physiological and social evils of drinking.

Brumbaugh, a confessed finger-shaking teetotaler his whole life, often spoke of the Dunkers as the "oldest temperance society in the country." It was a disappointment to him, then, when the law went neglected in many school districts throughout the state. To what extent Huntingdon's superintendent incorporated WCTU lessons into the classrooms of his own schools cannot be ascertained. But teachers' institutes, the records show, did feature lectures on such topics as "Physiology, Hygiene, and Narcotics."

The antiliquor cause also enlisted Brumbaugh in a more personal, volunteer role. His superintendency coincided, shortly after the WCTU victory, with a follow-up drive to outlaw alcoholic drink in Pennsylvania by a constitutional amendment. Similar struggles took place in three-fourths of the states in the decade of the Eighties. To take prohibition out of partisan politics, the strategy adopted by Drys in most parts of the country was to agitate for special statewide referendums. This would put the decision in the hands of the people and not of their legislators. Prohibition amendment committees sprang up all over the Keystone State when Governor James Beaver, in late January 1889, signed into law a bill calling for a popular vote in June.

Huntingdon County came up with a Prohibition Amendment Committee of its own early that year. The superintendent of schools became its secretary and chief press agent. He, more than the president, J. Randolph Simpson, a prominent Huntingdon attorney, did most of the tub-thumping. He spoke at scores of rallies and penned numerous newspaper articles during the five-months-long crusade.

Long afterward, during his gubernatorial contest, the question of prohibition would again stir up the state. Brumbaugh did not hesitate to remind the electorate of his part in the no-drink campaign of 1889. He took pride in telling the public that, while the amendment lost overwhelmingly statewide, in Huntingdon County it carried by a hefty margin.

All things considered, the county seems to have had a very visible public figure in its energetic superintendent. His alma mater, as a result, may very well have gained a direct institutional fallout from his popularity. When its trustee vice-chairman took over the local school system in 1884, the names of 52 county citizens appeared in the college catalog. Four years later the catalog listed the names of 104 area residents. Quite plausibly, the explanation for this enrollment surge from the home front is that teachers were simply heeding their leader's call to upgrade classroom aptitude. Moreover, the Brethren's Normal College was conveniently located to serve that purpose. So in late March, after the public school year ended, its ranks would swell with the influx of teachers he had influenced. This set a trend that would endure long into the future.

The last years of the 1880s, meanwhile, had brought the first administrative change at the Brethren's Normal College since Jacob Zuck's death a decade before. James Quinter, at seventy-two, was closing out his ninth year as president in 1888 when he died under dramatic circumstances. He was in North Manchester, Indiana, attending the denomination's annual meeting. He had just begun a public prayer, kneeling on the stage of the tabernacle tent, when a heart attack struck him down. Three thousand shocked conference-goers witnessed the revered churchman's public death that mid-May Saturday afternoon.

The following month the trustees debated at length whether or not to retain the position of president. They first voted it out; then the Huntingdon contingent—a majority on the board—reconsidered three weeks later and reinstated it, still as a titular post. Martin's fifty-two-year-old cousin, Henry Brumbaugh, the trustee chairman, reluctantly accepted the title. His uncle Jacob stayed on as principal to run the day-to-day affairs on the campus. With Quinter gone, however, the college had as its head a churchman who lacked the late president's stature among the Brethren, and even more his pulpit flair.

By the time of the college's first presidential change of guard, Martin Brumbaugh had already become, with meteoric rush, a teachers' institute catch all over Pennsylvania and several of its adjacent states. The Brumbaugh reputation, before long, would reach as far away as Louisiana. His income as an institute lecturer, at age twenty-eight, was annually enriching him by more than $4600. He was so popular that he was forced to reject many more engagements than he booked.

His institute fees plus his superintendent's salary made him relatively prosperous for a Huntingdonian of that era. So he began to look for ways to invest the surplus. In February 1889 he bought the old Baptist church, at the northwest corner of Seventh and Washington Streets, in downtown Huntingdon. He had it torn down and, at about the time of the disastrous Johnstown flood, saw to the erection of a large three-story brick building (81 x 100 feet). The first floor was designed as a store, the upper levels as commercial rental space and apartments. The huge timbers used in the construction of the edifice came from the "barrens," a desolate section of the Forge property. A frame house, a stable, and a couple of sheds were left standing on the lot. Rent from the house, apartments, and the store space made this a very profitable investment.

The architecture of the Brumbaugh building marked a welcome departure from the plain boxlike exteriors of previous downtown business places and set a trend in more pleasing facades. Brumbaugh also had a part in another advance of local historical interest: the end of the "Gaslight Era" in the borough and the introduction of electric lighting. In September 1889 he got the contract to supply 175 poles to carry the power lines for street and domestic electrical service, which became a reality the next year. For a long time, however, electricity was a nighttime convenience; street lights went out at midnight, while homes had current only from dusk until dawn.

At the time electricity came to Huntingdon, Brumbaugh's second term as county superintendent was about to expire. He decided against a third-term bid, even though the school directors assured him reelection was a mere formality. Teaching, not supervising, was his true love. He found a position waiting for him at his alma mater—in the natural sciences and pedagogy. But not until he met one condition: he had to "stop smoking absolutely," according to trustee minutes. Sometime as superintendent he had fallen victim to nicotine, presumably in the form of cigars, the vice of his later years. College rules outlawed use of tobacco by anyone on campus, students and professors alike. Two trustees—President Henry Brumbaugh, the chairman, and voice instructor William Beery, one of the fabled "Three Orphans"—were deputed to meet with M. G. Apparently, he knuckled under to the ultimatum, gave up tobacco for the time being, and spent the year 1890–91 at the college. His salary of eight hundred dollars was supplemented by his sizable institute income.

It was during the second teaching stint at the Normal that a red-faced M. G. once again found Uncle Doctor the "soul of frankness." He woke up one morning with a sore throat, so he called Dr. Brumbaugh and told him his troubles. The uncle said, "Gargle with a solution of sodium chloride." The nephew said, "Can I get that in the laboratory?" Came back the reply, "Salt, smarty!" "I hung up the receiver quickly," Brumbaugh said, telling of this telephonic exchange years later. "The joke was on me because I was then teaching chemistry."

In the summer of 1890, Brumbaugh became a father for the second and last time. George Edwin, named for the two grandfathers, was born on 27 August; Mabel Amanda had made her advent three years earlier, on 18 November 1887. Mabel seems not to have been a namesake, but her middle name no doubt honored her father's deceased sister. Neither son nor daughter would remember being very close to their workaholic father. Over the years a hectic public schedule, frequent and prolonged absences from home, and the hours spent in teaching, studying, researching, writing, and administering left him little time or energy to be a parent.

It is probably a mistake, therefore, to think that M. G.'s professorial return to the Brethren's Normal College was anything more than a transient commitment. Teachers' institutes all over Pennsylvania and adjacent states were giving him wider exposure and putting him on the platform with educators he not long ago had only read about. This experience no doubt fed his ego but also gave rise to strong feelings of inferiority. He could see he needed more advanced degrees to help promote his educational career. So he was probably honest with his Brumbaugh superiors on the Hill, who were always forwarders of his ambitions. Quite likely, they were told he had no intention of staying beyond the academic year 1890–91.

The Gay Nineties, as destiny would have it, turned out to be a decade of dynamic consequence for Martin Brumbaugh—as it was for the American people.

For him, personally, it would be a ten-year span marked by high-geared professional growth. The 1890s saw him reap scholarly honors and, as an educator, win a national reputation unprecedented for a Dunker. And all this well before he had reached his fortieth birthday, a remarkable record for an academician of whatever religious faith.

Brumbaugh's log-cabin birthplace.

The Timothy Meadows homestead, as it was in 1969. The brick addition was made in 1860, while a plank wing (not shown) was attached on the rear of the stone half sometime later. For several decades, a trio of Brumbaugh families lived in the three-unit complex.

Stern-looking Brumbaugh relatives in Dunker garb.

The only known photograph of
George B. Brumbaugh, *right,*
as a young man. His companion is Theobald Fouse, a Woodcock Valley friend.

The one extant picture of Martin's mother, probably
taken in her thirties, wearing—most un-Dunkerlike—
forbidden jewelry and a stylish blouse.

A tintype of Martin as a lad. His Marklesburg boyhood home would be razed decades later.

The Huntingdon Normal College, circa 1880. Its earliest brochure vaunted the school as staffed with "Live Teachers."

Martin's beloved "Uncle Doctor" Andrew B. Brumbaugh.

Uncle Jacob Brumbaugh, Martin's college prof. and one-time dormitory roommate.

The Normal College graduate, 1881.

Anna Konigmacher's graduation class, 1885. She is standing at the far right.

The tall skinny schoolmaster, looking untypically sobersided.

Martin strikes a lofty pose—perhaps while a student at Millersville Normal School.

The bewhiskered superintendent.

Martin and Anna at the time of his Harvard stay, with baby son Edwin and daughter Mabel.

The Brumbaughs, soon after M. G. became a college president and a Penn professor.

Dapper-looking M. G. as Penn's popular professor of education.

5

Bayous and
Graduate Degrees

AMERICAN historians commonly refer to the last quarter of the nineteenth century as the Gilded Age, a derogatory term borrowed from a satirical novel by Mark Twain and Charles Dudley Warner. The label aptly captures the moral degeneracy of the times: seamy public scandals of all sorts, unscrupulous manipulation of the stock market, political corruption at all levels of government, and lavish living by the newly rich. The period also saw the beginning of a major population shift, a trend that would build up momentum and carry over well into the 1900s. Millions of people, the bulk of them young, began to take leave of farms and small towns. In search of a more exciting life they flocked to the city, which—like the factory—had become a symbol of the new America.

For Brethren teenage mavericks, few of whom as yet were swept up in this demographic phenomenon, the Gilded Age proved momentous for other reasons. First of all, their denomination was twice rent by major divisions between 1881 and 1883. These splits grew out of multiple social and theological differences: over foreign missions, dress and the simple life, Sunday schools, education, governance, and rural-urban tensions. Many Dunker youth, like Martin Brumbaugh, chose to side with the more forward-looking faction. The future of the church's leadership, as it turned out, would be theirs to claim.

Second, when the air of controversy had cleared, higher education was no longer anathema within the main communion. Whereas in 1876 an intact church body had but a solitary school, minuscule and on trial, a postschism denomination could claim, halfway into the Gay Nineties, five of its present-day colleges, including one in California. And, in 1900, it would add a sixth, the last of them, giving Pennsylvania two.* For the Brethren, then, the nation's notorious Gilded Age became, in their cultural history, the golden age of college founding. (Between the

---

*There are six Brethren colleges today, all founded between 1876 and 1900: Juniata (1876) and Elizabethtown (1900) in Pennsylvania; Bridgewater (1880) in Virginia; Manchester (1889) in Indiana; McPherson (1887) in Kansas; and LaVerne (1891) in California.

Civil War and World War II, to put higher education into historical context, more than eight hundred colleges and universities were founded in the United States.)

By the end of that liberatory quarter-century, no Dunker name was so widely known among public school educators, especially east of the Mississippi River, as that of Martin G. Brumbaugh. His county superintendency had not gone unnoticed by bureaucrats in Harrisburg. What he was able to get done in revamping a backward rural school system intrigued State Superintendent of Instruction E. Elisha Higbee. That was one reason Higbee agreed to be a highlighted speaker at one of Huntingdon County's annual teachers' institutes. Moreover, as mentioned in the previous chapter, Brumbaugh himself had already become, by the late 1880s, something of an institute headliner in many parts of Pennsylvania and bordering states. When Higbee had the chance, then, in 1889, he did not hesitate to give Brumbaugh's career a boost.

In early spring of that year Dr. Higbee got an inquiry from Colonel Thomas D. Boyd of Louisiana. The letter asked him to nominate someone to come down to that part of the Deep South, during summers, to help with teachers' institutes. Presumably, Boyd, a transplanted Virginian who did more than any other man after the Civil War to establish public education in Louisiana, wrote to other state superintendents in the North asking for names. From Pennsylvania, the lone name Higbee sent off was that of Brumbaugh's, apparently without telling him.

Brumbaugh later recalled that Boyd's subsequent invitation came in the form of a telegram. He said he flatly turned it down. But the colonel, who the previous year had become the second president of the Louisiana State Normal School at Natchitoches, very much wanted the young county superintendent to come. So he dispatched a letter, saying: "I have received several applications for the position tendered you, but you have been recommended to me in such high terms, and your experience corresponds so exactly with the requirements of the case, that I hope we shall not fail to secure your services." In that letter of 14 April, he proposed a salary of twenty-five dollars a week plus travel expenses, which doubled the telegraphed offer. Brumbaugh, the letter said, was to give institute work a month's time, 10 May to 13 June. As a cultural bonus, promised Boyd, "[Y]ou will have an opportunity to observe nearly all spheres of Louisiana life." The colonel's importunity finally brought Brumbaugh around, and so began the Louisiana chapter of his career in education.

The public schools of that state in the late 1880s were still in post-Civil War shambles. The elementary grades there received minimal state funding. Only Shreveport and New Orleans had accredited high schools; all other secondary institutions were private or parochial. As for teacher training, not until 1884 did Louisiana get its first normal school. The state's total illiterate population ten years of age and over in the mid-1880s exceeded 49 percent of the populace. And even as late as 1889 less than half of the public-school population still had not enrolled for a free education.

Brumbaugh had run into some bad conditions in Huntingdon County, but he was shocked by the deplorable state of schools in Louisiana. He once told of speaking to the teachers of Natchitoches parish on one of his early institute trips. Among other things, he tried to impress upon them the value of what he called "illustrative teaching"—using a blackboard to make little sketches and pictures. Pictorialization helps children better understand, he argued. After his talk a "very beautiful girl" came up to him. She asked, "What do you mean by a blackboard?" Dumbfounded, Brumbaugh said, "Why, my dear, don't you know what a blackboard is?" She said, "I never heard of such a thing." Then she went on:

> You ought to see my schoolhouse. It never was finished. It has no windows; just holes where windows were to be. No doors; just a hole where the door is to go. It has no floor but the earth. And when I began the school there was no furniture in it, and the children and I sawed off blocks from the logs lying about and made seats. We all sit on seats made that way.

Louisiana's postbellum educational problems dated back to Reconstruction times when the "Carpetbag" constitution of 1868 stipulated a single, integrated school in each parish for children from six to twenty-one years of age. Native white people of that former slave state rejected any kind of enforced integration, and so their children attended, if at all, privately financed all-white schools. Many "charity schools," attended mostly by blacks and a few poor white children, were partially supported by the Peabody Education Fund. The first of its kind in America, the endowment was established in 1867 by the famous merchant-banker, George Peabody. The philanthropist's gift was the sum of two million dollars, to be used to educate "the young of the more destitute portions" of the South and Southwest.

Reconstruction ended in 1877, and two years later Louisiana adopted a new constitution restoring white supremacy and segregation. Colonel Boyd and others now began to rebuild statewide support for public education. But most Louisianians attached a certain stigma to educating children out of the people's purse. Sentiment favored free schools for indigent children but not for children of middle-class and well-to-do families. This viewpoint, deep fixed, proved a problem to reformers. The public schools were usually taught by poorly trained teachers, whereas private schools got the superior ones. Naturally, private-school teachers enjoyed a better standing in public esteem.

The most immediate need in the 1880s, then, with only one, newly started normal school in the whole state, was to uplift the quality of instruction. The solution seemed to be, as in other states at the time, teachers' institutes. In 1886 the state legislature sanctioned the idea of institutes but voted no money. The Peabody Fund came to the rescue, enabling Boyd to begin sponsoring first-rate institutes, centrally planned and organized through his office.

Quite possibly some citizens of the Pelican State looked upon Brumbaugh during his first institute summer as a "damn Yankee," if not a Johnny-come-lately carpetbagger. The Civil War and the Radical Republican rule that followed were still fresh memories for many an ex-Confederate. But Colonel Boyd always said the Pennsylvania county superintendent had been an instant hit among Louisiana educators. "He had not been in our state ten days," the colonel once remarked, "when the choice of several honorable and lucrative positions was offered him."

For five summers, then, Brumbaugh went south, peregrinating all over Louisiana. His travels between 1889 and 1893 opened up a whole new world to him—a world of bayous, swamplands, cotton fields, canebrakes, and levees.* These summertime trips also took him to the glamorous Crescent City itself, New Orleans, which must have been an unforgettable sight to him, only yesterday a Woodcock Valley villager.

Brumbaugh liked to refer to himself, in years to come, as "conductor of teachers' institutes" when speaking of his Louisiana experience. He also styled himself that way in self-profiles he prepared after becoming a public figure. Sometimes he put the word "first" before the title. Actually, there is nothing in Colonel Boyd's correspondence with him that gave his work an official name. It is clear, however, that Boyd looked upon him as his right-hand man, sought his counsel on personnel, on topics to be covered in the institutes, on assignments, and on logistics, and gave him pretty much a free hand in how he went about his business. Brumbaugh, in other words, seems to have been the colonel's institute field commander, though untitled.

His first summer he traveled to widely scattered points in the state, some very rural. For the next three years Boyd divided the instituters into two teams, one to operate in southern districts, the other in the northern parishes. Brumbaugh would do duty with one team or the other during that time. His last summer, 1893, like his first one, was spent canvassing a wide area, unattached to a team. Each team was made up of practicing teachers, faculty from Boyd's normal school, and a leader. The teachers and normal school faculty, for the most part, handled the lectures on instructional methods and practices in the various "branches of learning," both at elementary and secondary levels.

Brumbaugh's role, as the colonel defined it, was to be an exhorter—to propagandize Louisianans about the urgency of "building up the public school system." He was to talk about the "necessity for professional training of teachers," about the "free school system . . . in Europe and America," and "how they [public schools] are maintained." The "felt want" of his by-then Jim Crow state, Boyd told

---

*It seems that Brumbaugh's memory later betrayed him when he came to date the period of his Louisiana work. In vitae he prepared for biographical dictionaries and directories, including *Who's Who in America,* and even in personal interviews he erroneously gave the years 1886 to 1891 for it. A master's thesis in 1937 and a doctoral dissertation in 1966 perpetuated this error. Letters from Colonel Boyd to Brumbaugh clearly indicate the years were 1889 to 1893.

Brumbaugh, was twofold: the need to convince the "upper class of our people to . . . [rise above their] ante-bellum prejudice against public schools" and to enlighten the "lower class[, which] has not yet learned their value." The problem, he claimed, was that "in the minds of both classes there exists a vague dread that in some way free public education will bring about an undue elevation of the black race. More-over, both segments of society resented, Boyd said, "that this elevation is paid for by the excessive taxation of the whites."

If Colonel Boyd, eight years Brumbaugh's senior, wanted a propagandist in his out-of-state prolocutor, then he got one of the first order. The colonel once described the Yankee schoolman as "one of the ablest institute conductors in the United States, [who] has been wonderfully successful not only in instructing and inspiring teachers but in entertaining and stirring up the general public." Many Louisianians—judges, educators, and other leading citizens—would remember how he went about his institute work with evangelical zeal. Some even spoke of him as a "popular evangelist" because of the way he translated teaching and public schools into a kind of religious obligation in a democratic society. Dr. Edwin L. Stephens, when president of Louisiana Industrial Institute at Lafayette, once recalled ap-provingly how a typical Brumbaugh oration hearkened back to "real old camp meeting times." In 1908 Stephens, in an editorial for the *Louisiana School Review*, wrote of his first impressions of Brumbaugh:

> When the Editor of the *Review* launched out into the educational sea of our State in the year 1892, the first great ship he espied on that sea was the T.D.B. [Boyd]—which has ever continued to be the Flagship of the Fleet. And the next one was this "foreign bottom"—the M.G.B., which had been imported from Pennsylvania during several summers to assist and instruct our fleet in the major evolutions and in modern, im-proved firing.

During Brumbaugh's 1893 visit Boyd scheduled him for several lectures at the Chautauqua in Ruston, a town in north-central Louisiana. The Louisiana Chautauqua, modeled after the most famous one in New York State, was organized in 1890 and dedicated to the improvement of teachers and the raising of educa-tional standards in the state. The Peabody Educational Fund bore most of its costs for the nearly two decades it existed. Brumbaugh was a natural choice to be a Chautauqua speaker, and one of his 1893 lectures was slated for Friday, 7 July, immediately before the Reverend Sam Jones, a pulpit-pounding itinerant Method-ist preacher from Georgia. Jones enjoyed unbounded popularity as a regular at-traction at the Ruston Chautauqua. In drawing great crowds—they were known as "Sam Jones crowds"—he was the Billy Graham of his day in the South. Nearly two thousand people had turned out, filling the auditorium, but to hear the man of God, not the teacher.

At the appointed hour Brumbaugh took his place on the spacious rostrum, which was always adorned with greenery and flowers. Bunting and portraits hung above the stage. He waited patiently for silence. Not getting it, he started off in an innocent sort of way, unheard by the audience. The crowd, restless to hear Jones, buzzed on. Then, according to an eyewitness:

[A]ll of a sudden Brumbaugh stamped his foot (13"—same as the big guns of a battleship) and stunned that crowd into attention as by a clap of thunder: "Hear!" he shouted, "I am a teacher, and a schoolteacher must have order."

The audience hushed. With perfect timing he broke the tense silence. He said, "I'm also a Dutchman—I say it before somebody else says it about me." A roar of laughter swept over the tabernacle, whereupon he jumped head-on into a compelling oration on a seemingly dull subject: "Civil Government." But the Chautauquans, seduced by the speaker, promptly and completely forgot Sam Jones, it was said.

As an orator, Brumbaugh already excelled as a storyteller. He was blessed with a low-pitched, resonant, mellifluous voice that projected well. He once said, self-deprecatingly, that he spoke in a "jerky" cadence. But that is not how people remembered his delivery, nor do his printed speeches bear this out. The evidence suggests he was no demagogue, no tub-thumper, but a speaker who moved audiences by eloquence, anecdotes, humor, feeling—all conveyed in a more or less conversational tone of voice.

Even newspapermen found his art of public speaking impressive. In 1893 Brumbaugh addressed the Louisiana Educational Association, which met in annual session that year at Baton Rouge. The reporter who covered the conference for the *Baton Rouge Advocate* wrote that Brumbaugh's evening lecture, larded with witticisms, held the audience in rapt attention even after the delegates had put in a long day. At the end of the talk, he said, "cries of 'go on' 'go on' came from all parts of the hall."

Colonel Boyd more than once told Brumbaugh—and others—how much he valued all that his northern friend had done to further the struggle to modernize public education in Louisiana. The colonel himself, one educator has written, was "retiring and bashful to the point of timidity. He planned and advanced others to execute, keeping himself in the background, and claiming and expecting credit for none of the achievements." But in bringing Martin Brumbaugh to Louisiana, Boyd thought he did deserve some personal thanks. As he wrote to the Pennsylvanian in 1893:

I have been working for the public for 20 years with little benefit to myself except the approval of a clear conscience, and I count it among the most signal services ever rendered to the people of Louisiana that I brought you among them. They owe me a debt of gratitude for that if for nothing else.

The year before, when Brumbaugh set out for Harvard, Boyd, as a character reference, wrote to the faculty admissions committee:

[Brumbaugh] impressed me as a man of unusual natural ability, of wide and varied reading, of extensive general knowledge, and of great versatility of talent. Pleasing in address, fluent in speech, . . . he never failed to win the close attention and the unstinted applause of his audience. He came among us a stranger from a distant section, holding opinions widely at variance with our views upon current topics, yet such was his tact . . . that he never uttered a word that gave offense. . . .

The colonel tried hard to keep the Yankee Dunker close to the Louisiana scene. When he learned, early in 1891, that Brumbaugh intended to give up the Huntingdon County school superintendency, he wrote: "I think I can prevail upon Dr. Curry [the Peabody Fund agent] to give us the means to offer you eight months of work in La." By 1893 he had upped his deputy's summer salary to fifty dollars a week and expenses. Then, in 1894, the Louisiana legislature passed a law, drafted by Boyd, creating a state-salaried officer with the title Institute Conductor. The colonel's first choice for the new position was Brumbaugh, who, by then engaged with other academic responsibilities, declined it. However, the conductorship would eventually be filled, at one time or another, by two Brumbaugh disciples.

Many of Brumbaugh's admirers in the land of bayous, it should be noted, thought his single, most spellbinding performance among them took place in the political arena, not on the institute platform. This happened in 1890, when the governor and the legislature fell into gridlock over renewing the charter of the Louisiana Lottery Company. Opposition to charter renewal came from the Anti-Lottery League and Governor Francis T. Nicholls, an ex-Confederate general who had literally given an arm and a leg to the South's lost cause. Nicholls had been elected in 1888 in what was perhaps the most bitter gubernatorial campaign of Louisiana history until that of 1991 and the David Duke candidacy. The Civil War hero, in running for the state's highest office, had pledged to destroy the lottery, which he said made "Louisiana the acknowledged headquarters of gambling" in the United States.

The stalemate at Baton Rouge developed in June 1890 when Governor Nicholls vetoed a law that gave the lottery new life. The standoff tied up all state business and appropriations for months—even the pay of teachers was held up. That summer Brumbaugh had been scheduled to direct the institute team working the southernmost parishes. Prior to his arrival, the Anti-Lottery League finagled lawmakers into holding a special session where lottery opponents could argue their case. Curiously, the League chose Colonel Boyd's articulate twenty-eight-year-old alter ego, an out-of-stater, to be one of their principal spokesmen. Unfortunately for the historian, his antilottery speech never made it into public print. But one high-court judge who spoke of it years afterward said, "The young man appeared before the legislature and poured forth his eloquence in a most impressive way." In July, when the legislature dealt with the veto, the lower house overruled the governor, but the senate fell short of the necessary two-thirds vote. Brumbaugh's nongambling compeers credited him with making a major contribution to their victory.

Never again but once, following his five summers spent in the South, did Brumbaugh return to Louisiana—in 1922, to speak in New Orleans. Many times after 1893 Colonel Boyd and other Louisianians invited him to come back to the Chautauqua, either as a "platform attraction" or as one of the faculty for the four-week summer normal institute held there each year. But year after year the "MGB" date books consistently recorded, "No to Ruston."

But Martin Brumbaugh's influence would linger on long after through the work of surrogates from his alma mater. These were promising young men, all recent alumni, who came to be known as the "Brumbaugh Infusion" or the "Pennsylvania Invasion." He recruited them when Colonel Boyd asked him to scout out normal-school graduates from up North who could come down and help man classrooms, be principals and superintendents, or teach in his normal school.

More than a dozen Brethren schoolroom missioners journeyed to that part of the Sunny South, some to stay. Two Brumbaugh conscripts in particular enjoyed long and distinguished careers in Louisiana: Robert L. Himes ('88) and John E. Keeny ('82). Both Himes and Keeny, popular institute lecturers themselves, were key figures in the development of Louisiana's school system in post-Brumbaugh decades.

Robert Himes was the first of the Brethren's Normal College alumni to be recruited by Brumbaugh. In 1890 he began teaching for Colonel Boyd at the Natchitoches Normal College. In the summer of 1891 Brumbaugh took him on as an institute team member, and before long Himes became a favorite of Boyd's. In 1896 the colonel was elected president of Louisiana State University; two years later, after waging a salary war, he lured Himes to Baton Rouge to teach psychology. Someone at the time of this appointment described Himes as "one of the ablest, most versatile, and most enthusiastic teachers in Louisiana." Colonel Boyd also made Himes, who would serve as state conductor of teachers' institutes for a couple of years in the mid-1890s, superintendent of instruction at the Louisiana Chautauqua. Himes would later become business manager of LSU. There is a building on the university campus today named in his honor.

By the same token, John Keeny's thirty-five-year educational career in Louisiana embraced a variety of positions: principal of three different high schools; mathematics professor at Natchitoches and then acting president there (1901–4); organizer and, for fifteen years, director of the summer normal school at Lake Charles; state institute conductor (1904–7);* president of the Louisiana Polytechnic Institute (1907–26). He also put in a term on the state education board, beginning in 1905. As a result, the former Huntingdonian won widespread acclaim among state educators that was equal to that of Brumbaugh and Himes. "I do not think," said a southern contemporary of his, "that any one person did more to promote education in Louisiana than did J. E. Keeny." The mustachioed "Professor," as LPI

---

*This position became full-time in 1905, second in rank to the state superintendent of education. It would eventually be phased out.

alumni called him even during his presidency, built the state's polytechnic school from preparatory and junior college status into that of a four-year college. Present-day Keeny Hall is a memorial to him on the LPI campus.

Himes and Keeny, and others of the "Invasion," were not involved in founding the Louisiana Educational Association (1883), membership of which was open to all who were interested in the cause of education in the state, not just teachers. But they quickly moved into top posts in the Louisiana Teachers' Association, organized in 1891. The "Invasion" was instrumental in starting and editing its publication, the *Louisiana School Review* (1894), forerunner of today's *L.A.E. News.*

Some Louisianians came to feel, as time went on, that perhaps they owed an institutional debt for their state's late-nineteenth-century educational renaissance as well as individual debts to those who made up the "Invasion" troupe. One appreciative educator was Dr. Edwin L. Stephens, the man who thought so highly of Martin Brumbaugh's camp-meeting-like teachers' institute pep talks. As for the "Invasion" and its college, he said in 1914, looking back over the past quarter-century: "Of all the schools of the North that have contributed to the growth and development of our public schoolwork in this state none has done so much" as the "Invasion's" alma mater.

Brumbaugh, in September of 1891, meanwhile, had begun his climb up the graduate-degree ladder. He had come to realize, as he once remarked, that "in order to make a place for [him]self in the world of teaching," he needed better credentials. At that time only three Dunkers had earned the master of arts degree through graduate study (some had honorary M.A.s); none had done it at a university or prestigious college. Brumbaugh would change that, having quietly set his sights on Harvard University.

So, early that fall month—and institute lecturing almost to the day of departure—he gathered up his family, took a train to Boston, and enrolled as a special student at the Ivy League school.

A fellow passenger in the Brumbaugh coach—as far as Philadelphia—was another Huntingdonian, John C. Blair. Blair was a small-town entrepreneur who had risen overnight from struggling stationer to global industrialist. His story was right out of Horatio Alger books, then so popular. Like Ragged Dick and all the other Alger heroes, Blair had made the most of his "main chance" in life.

He was a rich man, thanks to an idea borrowed from a friend, David Emmert, in 1877. (They were about the same age then—mid-twenties.) Emmert, who would later be Brumbaugh's art teacher at the Brethren's Normal College, paid a visit to Blair's little stationery shop one day that fall. While chatting with the owner he idly fashioned a crude tablet out of newsprint and carpet tacks. He intended to use it as a notebook. The young shopkeeper, on the lookout for a more lucrative business venture, took close notice. Emmert had unwittingly given him the idea he needed. From that casual creation sprang, virtually overnight, a whole new stationery line: the paper tablet.

The Blair Handy Tablet found an instant world market. At the same time, America's public-school system began to adopt it to replace the cumbersome slates. Writers seem to have found the tablet a godsend too. From Hartford, Connecticut, Mark Twain dashed off a chit to Blair in 1884 saying, "Your packets are an unspeakable convenience. They make authorship a pastime!"

Brumbaugh and Blair were well acquainted. They had been pivotal founders of the Huntingdon County Historical Society back in October of 1887. Moreover, the industrialist's personal physician was Martin's Uncle Doctor. The two struck up a conversation soon after boarding the train. As the miles clattered by, Brumbaugh spoke of his personal dreams and of the challenges educators faced in that day of enormous economic and social change. Apparently, he revealed an ambitious side of his character the tablet maker had never seen before. He came across as a go-getter of Blair's stamp. When the self-made, small-town tycoon returned to Huntingdon, it was reported, he was full of talk about the county's former school superintendent. He predicted for him a destined role as a future leader in American education.

The Brumbaughs rented an apartment at 22 East Brookline Street in Cambridge, within easy walking distance of the university.

Martin was attracted to Harvard because William James was there, but he never said why he took no courses from the great philosopher. One other Dunker, a Midwesterner, had preceded him to the university, but as an undergraduate. Brumbaugh's application blank was filled out in exquisite longhand. Included with his application was a page of "testimonials" from eleven men, printed by hand press on a legal-size sheet. Special students were required to furnish character and competence references, which were then reviewed by a faculty committee. This took the place of an admissions examination. Most of Martin's supporters were educators from Pennsylvania and Louisiana. Among those quoted were Colonel Thomas Boyd and Henry Houck, then Pennsylvania's deputy superintendent of education. The latter would soon become one of the applicant's dearest and most trusted friends.

Harvard, in 1891, had 189 graduate students and a total student body of 2,658. Brumbaugh took only two courses all year, probably one each semester. He studied "English Literature of the Seventeenth Century" under LeBaron R. Briggs, professor of English and dean of Harvard College, and took "Shakespeare" with Professor Francis J. Child. These courses were designed for both graduate and undergraduate students. Harvard transcripts from that era have not survived, so there is no record of his grades.

In Briggs and Child, Brumbaugh came under the tutelage of two academic giants then on the Harvard faculty. An alumnus, LeBaron Briggs that fall of 1891 had just been named to a newly created post, dean of the college, to handle student relations. "To the end of his life," wrote Samuel Eliot Morison in his "unofficial" history of the university (1936), "he was the students' friend, beloved by all for his humanity, perception, and kindly humor." It was said men deliberately got into trouble just so they could visit the dean's office to talk to him. In 1902 Briggs would become dean of the faculty of arts and sciences, a position he held for the next twenty-three years.

Also at the forefront of world scholarship was Francis Child, another alumnus. Morison, in an earlier "official" Harvard history, wrote of Child: "None who knew him can recall without tenderness his curly hair, his fine brow, his concentrated, expressive features, his short, sturdy figure, his heedless gait." Nicknamed "Stubby," he was, like Briggs, rated a professorial darling by students. His colleagues also considered him a person of rare qualities. William James was moved to write to his brother Henry that in Child he discerned a man of "moral delicacy and richness of heart that [he] never saw and never expect to be equaled."

Brumbaugh would always speak of Child in particular as one of the most stimulating teachers he ever had. But there was one Harvard instructor he wrote off even before taking any of his courses. His unfavorable opinion of the man, whom he never identified, came about quite by chance. One day Brumbaugh was seated in a streetcar and happened to eavesdrop on a conversation between this particular faculty member and a young woman. He had already given some thought to enrolling in one of the professor's literature classes. So he decided to size up this "prospective tutor" of his by listening more carefully to what the two passengers were talking about. Recalled Brumbaugh, when telling of the incident a few years later:

> Among other things [the professor's] conversation drifted to his home. He said: "I had good honest parents. My mother was an honest woman. My father was gentlemanly enough, as such things go. But, you know, they were not the kind of people you would care to meet."

"I never went into his class," the eavesdropper said. The reason? Because, he warned, "Beware of those that speak slightingly of the mother that nursed them through sickness and pain and distress; of the father who provided for them when they were little and helpless. Beware of the ingratitude that is stamped upon every expression of disrespect to father and mother."

While in Massachusetts, Brumbaugh still kept a crammed calendar on the institute beat back in the Keystone State. It got to be too much for him. "I found out at Harvard," he once said, reflecting on his Cambridge days, "that I would have to be nearer Pennsylvania. I was earning my living lecturing and the trip from Boston to Pennsylvania was too long to fill lecture engagements."

Before his leave-taking, however, he met with a cycling accident. It happened on an icy street, causing him to fall off his bicycle and break his left arm. This injury left him with a chronically aching forearm the rest of his life. The only way he could get relief was to keep the arm elevated on a pillow.

Early in Brumbaugh's Harvard sojourn, the Huntingdon Brethren had seen fit to give him a ministerial call. This took place at a special congregational meeting on Saturday, 14 November 1891, in his absence but not without his nod. Normal College president H. B. Brumbaugh, the senior elder, presided at the election. The licentiate, probably in the salt-and-pepper wool suit he often then wore, preached his first sermon in the chapel/sanctuary a couple of months later—on 19 January, a raw zero-degree Tuesday evening. According to a special diary of his (1890–1900) that listed all sermon titles and their texts and the dates and places given, the topic was *Hitherto Hath the Lord Helped Us*, from 1 Sam. 7:12. This must have been his "Sermon of the Year," because he preached the same sermon over the next thirteen months (in eight other churches), and then never again. As time would show, Martin was content, like his father, to remain a lay preacher; he had no aspirations to rise to the rank of elder. But he did allow himself to be advanced to second degree (1893), which entitled him to conduct baptisms and perform marriages.

For several years he ruled out routine pulpit work to concentrate on institute lecturing and getting a graduate degree. Having rejected Harvard as too far out of his institute orbit, he decided that the University of Pennsylvania would better allow him to combine speaking to teachers and studying for a doctorate. And so he matriculated there in September 1892, renting a room in an attractive home at 3715 Spruce Street in West Philadelphia, near the campus. On weekends he would return to Huntingdon and his family.

One time the Penn graduate student came back to his rooming house late at night after studying at the university library. Hearing a noise, he discovered a stranger in his quarters. With his enormous size and strength he probably could easily have overpowered the thief. But, a pacifist, he confronted the intruder instead with stern words, not bare fists. He reportedly said, "If you will drop what you have taken I will say nothing more; just get out quietly. That's what I order you to do." Whereupon the housebreaker quickly departed.

Commuting to and from Philadelphia by the Pennsylvania Railroad in those years he regularly fell into the company of William O. Smith, then an assemblyman (later, a congressman) from Jefferson County. Smith passed through Huntingdon on Monday afternoons on his way to Harrisburg. A score of years later, as editor of the *Punxsutawney Spirit*, he wrote a laudatory column about Brumbaugh, then a candidate for governor. The former lawmaker recalled that back in the early 1890s

a tall, gaunt young man used to board the train at Huntingdon and ride down the road. Somehow or other we became acquainted. The young man's conversation soon impressed the writer that he was a big, wholesome fellow with lofty ideals. He . . . talked about his work with charming frankness, a sort of ingenuousness that was refreshing. We liked him so much that after a while, when the train passed Huntingdon and the big, rawboned farmer-looking schoolman didn't get aboard, we felt disappointed.

He went on to say:

> We remember distinctly having formed the impression of him that he was going to be one of the really big men of the country some day, because he was so devoted to his work and so apparently unconscious of his personality.

The editorial concluded with a chance remark by Brumbaugh on one of the train trips. As quoted, his words sound almost cocky, but for Smith they were oracular:

> We asked him one day why he didn't run for the Legislature, thinking he was the kind of material needed there. He replied that he had no doubt his people would send him there if he wanted to go, but he thought his field of usefulness was along educational lines, and he intended to stick to his present work.

When Brumbaugh went off to Penn he gave no hint—at least in public—that his goal was a Ph.D. Nor did he ever say who, if anybody, urged him to go for a doctor's degree. There is reason to think, however, a doctorate might well have been a secret goal of his since his college days. The clue is found in his senior thesis. In it he lamented that teaching, because it suffered from low professional standing, held no vocational lure for the "brightest minds." He declared: "The world needs not lawyers, doctors, and theologians, but earnest, thorough teachers. Young men aspire to the title M.D., or D.D., but how few labor for A.M., Ph.D.!"

It took him less than three years to get one (1894), picking up an M.A. (1893) along the way. While working on his doctor's dissertation, he garnered a rather novel academic award: the Michael E. Sadler Scholarship for University Extension Work in the United States. As the Sadler Scholar for 1893, he found himself caught up by a new movement in higher education recently imported from Great Britain.

The idea of making university courses accessible to the masses in evening, weekend, or summer classes had its origin in Cambridge, England, in 1871. Before long, "university extension" became an integral part of the English educational system. The movement, through British academic missionaries, especially Michael Sadler of Oxford, spread to the United States. His efforts led, in June 1890, to the organizing of the American Society for the Extension of University Teaching at Philadelphia (ASEUT), which became its national headquarters.

The body had no organic connection with the University of Pennsylvania, but Dr. Edmund James of the Wharton School, one of the society's founders, was its first president (1891–95). Universities and colleges located in major cities throughout the United States, using Penn and Philadelphia as a model, began to initiate courses geared to nondegree adult students. It was Brumbaugh's task, as the Sadler Scholar, to promote the society's mission on a nationwide scale. As a Penn-approved lecturer and one of ASEUT's fifteen directors, he would continue to be actively involved with extension work after his scholarship expired.

The Ph.D. program at Penn was relatively new when Brumbaugh began his studies there; the university did not introduce it until 1882. At that time the various disciplines were all lumped under one degree-granting department: philosophy. Little progress was made the first decade, but by 1892 the university had about a hundred doctoral students, hailing from thirty-five different undergraduate schools.

Among Brumbaugh's professors were some of the university's best of that day, and some of the very youngest; not all of them held an earned doctorate. One of his instructors was Josiah H. Penniman, Brumbaugh's junior by a half-dozen years, who taught the English novel. A Penn graduate and the valedictorian of the class of 1890, Penniman, although of lowly academic rank (instructor in English) when Brumbaugh was there, would become the president in 1923. In a rare reversal of professor-student roles, he got his Ph.D. at his alma mater the year after Martin, who sat on Penniman's examining board. Penniman later took pedagogy courses under his former student at Penn when the Huntingdonian came back to teach.

Another of his teachers was George S. Fullerton, born of Episcopalian missionary parents in India. Three years younger than Brumbaugh, Fullerton, who had been educated at Penn and had a divinity degree from Yale and an honorary LL.D. from Muhlenberg College (1892), was the Adam Seybert Professor of Intellectual and Moral Philosophy. One of the creators of the graduate school, he would later distinguish himself first as dean of the college and then as vice provost. Fullerton's brilliance was recognized by Penn in 1887 when he was made, at the age of twenty-seven, a full professor. Dr. Edward P. Cheyney, in his history of the university, wrote that Fullerton's use of the Socratic teaching method and of hypnotism variously "perplexed, awakened, and delighted his . . . students." A winsome person of great influence at Penn, he wrote on Kant and Spinoza and published a widely acclaimed book titled, *A Plain Argument for God*. Brumbaugh took Fullerton's course in psychology ("Metaphysics") and one in the history of ancient and medieval philosophy. The two men, in a few years, would tour Europe together and strike up a close friendship. In 1904 Fullerton left Penn and went to Columbia to teach philosophy, but they kept in touch through letters. Fullerton's suicide in 1925 would come as sad news to his longtime friend.

Under Simon N. Patten, an Illinoisan with a Ph.D. from the University of Halle, Brumbaugh studied economics. Patten helped to establish the Wharton School in 1883 and, a prolific writer, became a national expert on protectionism. According to Cheyney, Professor Patten was "an economist of much originality and distinction, a natural-born teacher and intellectual leader. . . . [He] raised a whole generation of disciples who became men of influence." He was one of a group of scholars with German university Ph.D.s who helped found two still-prestigious professional societies in the 1880s: the American Economic Association and the American Academy of Political and Social Science.

Quite likely Brumbaugh also took course work under two other men (there is

no record of his Penn transcript): Edward Potts Cheyney and Morton W. Easton.*
He would have studied English history under Cheyney, then in the early stages of
what would become a brilliant career teaching and writing about European history.
And for "English Philology," required of those majoring in English literature, he
would have had Easton. Easton was in his fifties and the oldest of Martin's professors
by a dozen years; he held a Columbia M.D. and a Yale Ph.D. in ancient languages.

The man who directed Brumbaugh's doctoral dissertation was Felix E.
Schelling, the John Welsh Centennial Professor of History and English. A native
of the Hoosier State, Schelling was another Penn alumnus who stayed on to take a
master's and a law degree from the university. He practiced at the Philadelphia bar
for three years before joining the faculty in 1886. He was older than Brumbaugh
by barely four years but already a noted Elizabethan scholar by the early 1890s. He
taught three courses Martin enrolled in: "Theory and History of English Versifi-
cation," "Modes of Nineteenth Century Poetic Thought and Expression," and "Origin
and History of the English Drama." During his academic career Schelling edited
and authored several literary works. His book titles included, among others, *Poetic
and Verse Criticism of the Reign of Elizabeth, The Discoveries of Ben Jonson,* and
The English Chronicle Play. In 1898 Franklin and Marshall College gave him a
Ph.D.

Brumbaugh had a high regard for Schelling, both as a teacher and as a scholar.
Once, soon after getting his doctorate, he commented in a speech at a National
Education Association conference: "The real awakening to an understanding of
what literature is and how it is to be studied came to me under [two] great teach-
ers—the late Dr. Child, of Harvard University, and Professor Schelling, of the
University of Pennsylvania."

Guided by Schelling, Brumbaugh, who in 1893 was now living at 3615 Lo-
cust Street, wrote his dissertation, entitled "A Study of the Poetry of John Donne."
There was a strong romantic streak in the Dunker graduate student, so it is something of a curiosity that his academic interest was piqued by a poet characterized
by down-to-earth imagery and language. Probably it was his dissertation advisor,
as so often is the case for a doctoral candidate, who directed his research attention
to Donne. Then, too, it could be speculated Izaak Walton had something to do with
the choice of subject. His *Compleat Angler* had been a second bible to Brumbaugh
since youth. Walton, the doctoral candidate perhaps knew, had written the first
biography of Donne (1640).

John Donne (1572-1631), English poet and Anglican priest, was a convert
from Catholicism who rose to be dean of St. Paul's in London. As a clergyman, he
earned the reputation of being the greatest preacher of his day. As a poet, he won
praise and many disciples. But he also roused criticism for what Brumbaugh called

---

*Although Brumbaugh's transcript is not on record, his memorabilia include packets
of class notes taken during his Penn graduate-school days.

his "rugged verse." Donne's poetry, much of it dwelling on sexual themes and written in the idiom of a rake, marked a repudiation of Petrarchan-Elizabethan saccharinity. For example, Ben Jonson, a contemporary, penned the familiar verses that begin: "Drink to me only with thine eyes / And I will pledge with mine." John Donne the unsentimentalist, by contrast, wrote in a love song of his own: "For God's sake, hold your tongue and let me love."

Donne's total poetic output was actually rather meager. After his ordination—in 1615 at age forty-three—he wrote very little poetry. His popularity as verse maker, therefore, was based largely on his work as Jack Donne, the roué, rather than as Dr. Donne, the dean of St. Paul's. By the late seventeenth century the poet's reputation had gone into decline. Not until almost three centuries later—in the 1920s—did his versecraft again attract popular attention.

Martin Brumbaugh's dissertation, it can be argued, anticipated this revival by more than thirty years, although today it is a study totally ignored by Donne scholars. His was the first Ph.D. thesis on the poet written in America. Between 1894 and 1982, interestingly, 223 more were churned out, many of them at Ivy League universities. Moreover, it has been estimated that in the seventy years since World War I well over two thousand books, monographs, essays, and notes have also appeared on Donne by literary critics. Though viewed as a ridiculed rhymester by academics when Brumbaugh did his dissertation, Donne since 1918 has "engaged some of the best minds of the scholarly world," as one authority put it. "Nearly all serious students of literature," this writer points out, "now agree Donne occupied a significant and permanent position in our understanding of the development of English poetry."

In his doctoral research, Brumbaugh set out to recover "some of the positive and dominant characteristics of [Donne's] genius" largely lost over the centuries as a result of "unfair" and "inadequate" criticism leveled at his technical weaknesses and stylistic peculiarities. Therefore, he concentrated on the bard's "divine" poems and verse letters instead of on his witty love prosody.

Brumbaugh enjoyed quoting poetry and often dazzled audiences by spouting chief passages from Shakespearean plays. But very little of Donne ever cropped up in his repertoire or in his writings. "Death" and "A Hymn to God the Father," which was later set to the music of a Bach melody, did, however, become a part of his personal poetic treasury. His favorite Donne lines were the final four stanzas of "A Valediction Forbidding Mourning." The poet wrote "A Valediction" as a good-bye poem for his wife when he left on a visit to the Continent in 1611. The Brumbaugh-cherished stanzas read:

> Our two souls therefore, which are one,
> Though I must go, endure not yet
> A breach, but an expansion,
> Like gold to airy thinness beat.

If they be two, they are two so
As stiff twin compasses are two
Thy soul, the fixed foot, makes no show
To move, but doth, if th' other do.

And though it in the centre sit,
Yet when the other far doth roam,
It leans and hearkens after it,
And grows erect as that comes home.

Such wilt thou be to me, who must
Like th' other foot, obliquely run,
Thy firmness makes my circle just,
And makes me end where I begun.

Psychohistory, although frequently practiced, is still a suspect tool to many historians these days. But one has to wonder if "A Valediction" was as autobiographical for Martin Brumbaugh as it was for John Donne. Both were immersed in their professional positions and pressured by urgent requests for their services as spokesmen for their times. Conscientious men, both must have felt guilty ministering to a larger family of mankind to the neglect of their own little nests. Both, perhaps, tried to reconcile their frequent absences by the concept presented in "A Valediction": two souls, husband and wife, psychically one even "when the other far doth roam."

By today's standards, Brumbaugh's ninety-nine-page study, sparsely footnoted and lacking an annotated bibliography, does not appear to be a scholarly product of exceptional merit. But some European academicians, notably Professor Alois Brandl at Strasbourg, praised it for dealing with phases of English literature never examined before. And in this country the Modern Language Association (MLA) invited him to present a paper on Donne at its annual meeting at Yale during Christmas week of 1895. Probably Felix Schelling had something to do with arranging this, since he belonged to the MLA and personally had a high regard for Brumbaugh's thesis. For some reason, Martin did not attend the meeting and give his paper.

A decade later, in 1906, Wrightman F. Melton wrote—and published—a doctoral thesis at Johns Hopkins University entitled "The Rhetoric of John Donne's Verse." His was the second Ph.D. thesis on Donne in the United States. Melton, a Southerner who later taught at Emory University and in 1943 was named poet laureate of Georgia, gave careful study to Brumbaugh's dissertation. Several times he either cited it or quoted from it. In drawing upon it at one point, Melton noted, "Professor Brumbaugh comes thrillingly near to our subject"—that is, anticipating a peculiar rhetorical-metrical characteristic of Donne's more in Melton's realm of inquiry than Brumbaugh's. He found the country's first authority on Donne to be gracious and helpful to him and expressed, at several places, "gratitude" for the "kindly sympathy and generous encouragement" he got when interviewing Brumbaugh or corresponding with him.

Schelling, it seems, grew annoyed that the dissertation was never published. At his prodding Brumbaugh finally agreed—in 1905—to publish it if someone could be found to provide a needed bibliography. Apparently, Melton heard of these plans, because twice his Johns Hopkins thesis mentioned Brumbaugh's "interesting work . . . soon to be published." Schelling took it upon himself to find a professional bibliographer and hired Dr. John L. Haney to carry out the task. The assignment was completed within a few months. But Brumbaugh, caught up by his election as Philadelphia's head schoolman, never got around to printing his work on Donne, much to Schelling's and Haney's disappointment. Thus Haney's *Bibliography of John Donne*, as the compiler once dryly lamented, "remains among the substantial collection of my unpublished works."

As noted earlier, Brumbaugh did not actually blaze the brotherhood trail that led to postgraduate academic degrees. By 1893 when Brumbaugh got his master's degree, a half-dozen Brethren young men had earned M.A.s. Interestingly, fourteen Brethren had by the mid-Nineties obtained the M.D. degree at a medical school. Martin's Ph.D., however, was a Dunker first by a half-dozen years.

The rest of the Gay Nineties would see Brumbaugh suddenly propelled to the forefront of public education throughout the East—as college president, university professor, textbook writer, acclaimed institute lecturer. Amazingly, he was all of these things at the same time. And by the century's close he would be sharing the platform at educational conferences with the nation's best-known names, his own being one of the drawing cards.

6

Rise to
Public-School Fame

MONTHS before his Ph.D. was in hand, Martin Brumbaugh had already been handpicked to head his alma mater. H. B. Brumbaugh's diary for Friday, 12 May 1893, reads simply: "Resigned as President of Normal in favor of M.G.B." Unfortunately, the trustee minutes for that Friday meeting are lost. Until the late 1890s, the Huntingdon clique on the board, which made all administrative and academic decisions, kept the minutes of their meetings on little scraps of paper. A number of these fragmentary jottings are missing, so there is no way of knowing whether or not it had been prearranged for M. G., the board's vice-chairman, to take over the Normal College once he completed his graduate education. It does appear, however, that he was expected to come back in some capacity. The whole time he was at Harvard and Penn, the college catalog carried his name on the faculty page as "On leave of absence."

At any rate, he demurred for two months before making up his mind to accept the presidency. Something Colonel Thomas Boyd said that July, before a public audience, provides a clue as to why Brumbaugh deliberated so long. It was during the Keystone Stater's last institute summer in Louisiana. He was at Ruston to speak to a gathering of teachers. The colonel, in introducing him, announced that his second-in-command "now stands hesitating whether to accept the chair of pedagogy in one of the largest institutions in the country or one of two chairs as president of colleges offered him at the same time."

The faculty position Boyd alluded to was at the University of Pennsylvania; the two presidencies were at the Brethren's Normal College and at Louisiana State University. Brumbaugh expressed absolutely no interest in becoming LSU's top man, an honor that rather fittingly then went to the colonel. He also said no to Penn. His decision to stay in Huntingdon meant, it was later revealed, that his income would be a third or less of what it would have been at the other places. Since his dissertation was as yet only in the middle stages of completion, the incoming leader asked to delay taking up his new Hilltop duties until January 1894. Grateful trustees eagerly granted his request.

101

The main reason his predecessor, his cousin Henry, had stepped aside was because the trustees hoped to begin moving the college more purposefully in a liberal arts direction, away from being solely a normal school. Already they had a four-year optional "classical" course on the books designed to do that. Then, too, competition within the brotherhood was getting stiffer; three other Brethren colleges had earlier made such a shift.

There was no public announcement of the presidential switch until the November 1893 issue of the *Juniata Echo*, the name of the campus paper at that time. The *Echo* article described him as one "who brings energy, talent, and ability to take up the work." It promised that "Under his guidance the College will take rank with the best." His presidency put an immediate end to the office of principal, long held by his uncle Jacob. This made administrative sense. The Normal College was still relatively small: at that time there were 293 students (total for all three academic terms) taught by 13 faculty members and 4 "student-teachers." Total expenditures for 1892–93 had been $18,576.06. Of that amount $4,986.89 went toward teachers' salaries. Since the presumption was that Martin would be the first actual CEO in the school's eighteen-year history—a president-dean in one person—there was no longer a need for another academic administrator. Jacob Brumbaugh, of course, continued on as a professor.

Martin Brumbaugh took up his work at the Normal College—there was no inaugural ceremony—under circumstances reminiscent of those encountered by the institution's founders in the mid-1870s: a national depression. This latest one would linger on until 1897. The hard times began in May 1893 when the stock market crashed a few months after Democrat Grover Cleveland—the only president to serve two nonsuccessive terms—entered the White House for the second time. The economic wreckage and social pain turned out to be even worse than during the slump of the Seventies.

Unemployment had shot up from 3 percent in 1892 to 18 percent in 1894 (compared to the high point of 13 percent in the depression of the 1870s). Hundreds of banks failed; scores of railroads went bankrupt; over sixteen thousand businesses folded. In Pennsylvania, the slowdown triggered strikes all over the state—fifty-three in 1893 and twenty-seven in 1894. Economic distress and mass unemployment provoked, in the spring of 1894, a national protest march upon Washington. Dubbed "Coxey's Army," it enlisted jobless men who delivered to Congress their demands for relief and New Deal-like work projects.

The hard times passed virtually ignored by the campus paper, except for a couple of indirect references. Blithely defying the financial state of the country, the college broke ground in October 1894 for a four-story brick building, the first since Founders Hall went up in 1878. To be used for classrooms, it would be called Students Hall. Brumbaugh thus got his first taste of fund-raising the maiden year of his presidency, although capital campaigns in those days at the Brethren's College relied more on key trustees making the alumni rounds than the president. And outsiders rarely, if ever, got any kind of money-raising visit. Even so, Brumbaugh's leadership inspired the *Juniata Echo* to make the boast in July 1895: "No College in this country has increased so rapidly during this financial depression as ours."

A year earlier, in June, the campus had seen the name Juniata College in public print for the first time in the *Echo*. It had been adopted officially at the January meeting of the trustees, who made plans to legalize it later by amending the charter. The name-changing decisions came about in deference to a brotherhood ruling against the use of "Brethren" in denominating a college. Place names—such as that of a town—were recommended. (Of the six extant Brethren-founded colleges, all are so-named except for the one in Huntingdon.)

It was President "M. G.," as everybody soon familiarly called him, who suggested the new appellation. The word Juniata is of Indian origin; it is a corruption of Onayutta, which means "Standing Stone," referring to a local historical marker. This sacred relic (14 feet high and 6 inches square) stood on the right bank of the Stone Creek near where it flows into the Juniata River, just east of downtown Huntingdon. On its smooth sides were carved the holy records of the Oneida tribe. In 1754 the Oneidas migrated out of the area and disappeared; tradition says they carried it with them, but there is no evidence that was what happened. Some years later a second stone, very much like the first one, was erected on the same spot, but it was subsequently destroyed. Brumbaugh, in 1897, obtained a fragment of it, embedded in the walls of an old bake oven, to be showcased in the college library. Today the two-foot-long chunk is housed in the campus museum.

But it was Indian lore and physical geography, not etymology, that inspired the young president to choose the name Juniata for his college. In the 1890s the grandeur of the local river valley, set amidst a panorama of mountains and hills, was more visible from Founders Bell Tower than it is today. As M. G. knew, the natural beauty of the area had not gone unappreciated in the legends of its Indians. One romantic folktale has it that the river is the namesake of a comely Indian lass—thus showing, as trustee-chairman Henry Brumbaugh wrote about the name change, "that nature's children love and admire that which God has made so beautiful." For M. G. and his cousin Henry at least, Juniata was self-evidently the most appropriate new name—leavened as it was with the rich cultural and historical heritage of south-central Pennsylvania and its river-riven mountainous splendor. The college's rechristening, made legal by a new charter, took place in September 1896.

The year 1896 was an important milestone in Juniata's history for another reason: that was when it gained state accreditation as a liberal arts college. A recent Pennsylvania law, passed in 1895, established a certifying board called the College and University Council. The statute also set minimum standards in terms of assets, facilities, and teaching personnel. There is some question whether Juniata technically qualified for accreditation under certain provisions of the act. But apparently Brumbaugh's magical influence with the twelve council members—three of whom, including Edward Brooks, were bosom friends—did the trick. President M. G. handed out the institution's first B.A. diploma in 1897 to the one graduate, a male. A year later (1898) the United States commissioner of education also elevated Juniata to the status of "College."

For the school year 1895-96, full-time resident Juniatians paid about $196 (basic charges) for three terms. It cost their counterparts at Ivy League colleges considerably more, of course: at Harvard, from $372 to $1000 (basic charges plus general expenses); at Princeton, from $311 to $645; at Cornell, from $350 to $500. At the University of Michigan and Oberlin, however, some students got by on less than two hundred dollars a year, while at the University of Kansas it could be done for as little as $175. Other normal and small liberal arts colleges in Pennsylvania were competitive with Juniata's costs.

Juniata's president recruited students as actively as any member of the faculty in those days long before the college had an admissions office. His appearances at teachers' institutes often provided an excellent marketplace to do so. That is how he won over Emma (Nyce) Ellis—at an 1894 institute in Norristown, Pennsylvania. She would become the wife, mother, and grandmother, respectively, of three Keystone State college presidents; her husband and son, in tandem succession, would pilot Juniata, their alma mater, for thirty-eight years (1930-68). Brumbaugh made her future spouse, Charles C. Ellis, his special protégé as a teachers' institute phenomenon, especially in Louisiana, and one day his vice president on College Hill.

Said Emma Ellis about that day in 1894, "I was all set to go to West Chester Normal until I heard M. G. No man in my mind could use language like Dr. Brumbaugh. After I heard him at Norristown, I came here." But, she went on, Huntingdon seemed so far away from Waynesboro, her home. She was frightened and lonely at Juniata—until M. G. put his arm around her (this would be a trademark of his two presidencies with female students) and said comfortingly, "Don't worry, Emma, we'll take care of you." "He was like a father to us all," she fondly remembered. "He knew and called every student, even years later, by their first names."

During Emma Ellis's sophomore year (1895-96), the University of Pennsylvania dealt Juniata a severe blow. The Quaker City school snatched Juniata's leader away—at first only partially, but later altogether. Actually, Brumbaugh himself brought on this sudden turn of events, albeit unintentionally. Teaching, by the 1890s, was becoming more a profession than a craft. Increasingly, there were educators who advocated that teacher preparation no longer be the special academic sphere of normal schools. They urged that America's colleges and universities begin to offer courses in this field.

The principal stimulus for this movement grew out of the demand for better-trained high-school teachers. In 1873 the University of Iowa had led the way, creating the first permanent university chair of education. The University of Michigan followed suit in 1879. After 1890 the number of such chairs mushroomed, and by the turn of the century there were around 250.

The debate about pedagogy's justifiable place in the traditional liberal arts curriculum of American higher education did not escape the faculty of the University of Pennsylvania. Others had made the case for it before Martin Brumbaugh set foot on campus as a graduate student. But where they had failed he succeeded, once Charles C. Harrison became provost in the early 1890s (the office of provost was then the highest academic office). Brumbaugh convinced Harrison that Penn ought to introduce pedagogics, even if on a limited scale at first. The provost gave him the green light to take his case to the university's governing board. His persuasive powers worked with them, too. Now the problem was to find the right man to inaugurate the new discipline.

Brumbaugh, when asked for names, touted Dr. Oscar T. Corson, Ohio's commissioner of common schools. He had come to know Corson on his many teachers' institute trips to the Buckeye State. Provost Harrison took Brumbaugh's advice, but the Ohio educator had no interest in the professorship. Turning the tables, he argued that Penn could do no better than to invite the same man who had nominated *him* to fill the post. Martin Brumbaugh, said Corson in lauding his friend, commanded a wide popularity in the field of pedagogy despite his relatively young age. When Edward Brooks, then superintendent of Philadelphia schools and a published pleader for university pedagogy courses, heard of his former student's nomination, he promptly voiced a loud amen to Harrison. Brooks often boasted that it was his recommendation that got Brumbaugh the Penn job.

At any rate, Harrison decided to look no further. He went after Brumbaugh at the very time the Penn nominee was pondering the presidency of his alma mater. Apparently, the provost did not give up, even after Brumbaugh had said yes to his fellow Hilltop trustees. Perhaps, in Harrison's defense, he thought the presidency of a small, isolated college like Juniata could not keep its headman busy enough. Perhaps, too, Brumbaugh encouraged that idea. The terms Harrison offered specified a one year, renewable appointment, beginning October 1, 1894, at a salary of $750 for nine months plus weekly travel expenses between Huntingdon and Philadelphia. Brumbaugh was expected to teach a graduate course on Friday evenings and, for undergraduates, a Saturday morning class.

A teaching load this light, if the deal did go through, would put Brumbaugh's appointment on a part-time basis, thus allowing him to stay on as Juniata's president. But, as he certainly realized, to accept the Penn contract was bound to raise serious questions on College Hill about his commitment as Juniata's leader and what a split-time president would mean for the college's long-range plans. That did not stop him from finally giving an affirmative answer. Still, the decision undoubtedly gave him some sleepless nights, torn as he must have been by the quandary he found himself in.

The Penn turn of affairs was quietly announced in the February issue of the

Juniata Echo, tucked unobtrusively into a column of news trivia titled "Notes." The terse notice began, "The readers of the *Echo* will be glad to learn that Prest. [*sic*] Brumbaugh has been elected to the chair of Pedagogy in the University of Pennsylvania." It concluded: "Linking the College here with the University spirit will be most helpful and valuable to all our students." Just how this arrangement would benefit Juniata was not explained; the *Echo's* statement was probably a case of institutional whistling in the dark. At this time Brumbaugh stepped aside as the board's vice-chairman, the office going to his uncle Jacob, but he stayed on as a regular member.

In spite of holding down two academic positions concurrently at distant places, Brumbaugh, driven and energetic as ever, felt no need to cut back on his teachers' institute calendar. For example, during the week before Christmas in 1896 he attended seven institutes and spoke nineteen times, traveling 1836 miles and spending five nights on a train. The pace never slackened with the new year. His 1897 date book gives the following summary for the months of August through December: "174 lectures to 830 each of 144,226 people. Also about eight sermons and six S.S. talks." As a platform attraction, he continued to be as popular out of state as he was in Pennsylvania. His going fee for institute work by 1897 was twenty-five dollars a day plus travel expenses, up five dollars from 1896.

This hustling way of life left him even less time at home with his family than when, more than a decade before, he first began meriting his work-like-a-Trojan reputation. Anna Brumbaugh must have been a lonely wife from the day she married him. And now, as Juniata's "first lady," she was forced into a bind, her duties complicated by the demands of taking care of two little ones, ages six and three, in 1894. But she got very little parenting help from an absentee husband and father. Martin's frequent absences from home caused some people to worry about the couple's marital stability. Perhaps that is why—to reassure worrywarts—the *Echo* carried an enigmatic M. G. quote in one of its issues of that time. It was simply a one-liner, saying he and Anna were yoked by "a good solid knot."

Domestic necessity, it would thus seem, was what brought Flora Belle Parks into the president's home, first as nanny and then as one of the family. Flora Belle, through her mother's Brumbaugh paternal line, was a fifth cousin of Martin's. Born on 24 March 1875, she was of the same generation as him, although thirteen years younger. Her parents, George and Mary Ann, lived at Entriken, several miles south of Marklesburg, where a number of Brumbaugh families had congregated. Her father made his living as a house painter.

She was nineteen, and thus regarded a ward, when taken into the Brumbaugh home to be live-in maid and babysitter. But this arrangement was intended to be mutually beneficial: it would enable Flora Belle to take classes at Juniata, something she had set her heart on for quite a while. Unfortunately, fate would soon intervene and prevent her from ever becoming a Juniatian, a story later to be told.

Flora Belle, however, a statuesque beauty with light brown hair, silkaline skin, and long, shapely fingers, stayed on as one of the Brumbaugh household even after Mabel and Edwin had grown up and gone off to college. Eminently nubile as a young woman, she would spurn matrimony until her early forties when—in 1916— she became the bride of her onetime guardian, by then a widower.

Anna's maternal lot being somewhat eased by Flora Belle's timely succor, Brumbaugh could now attend to his weekend Penn professorship with a clearer conscience. There was still the question of how much he would be compromising his small-college presidency. But he nonetheless took on the Philadelphia obliga- tion with typical zeal. For two years he endured the ordeal of a commuter's long- distance ride, by rail, between Huntingdon and the Quaker City. He bade Hilltoppers his good-byes early each Friday afternoon and returned on Sunday. Edward Cheyney, once his teacher and now his colleague, would write forty-five years later that Penn's first professor of pedagogy was a man of "great energy and competence" and of "much influence" with his students. In short order, noted Cheyney, "women and men alike came trooping to [his] classes."

As his contract called for, Brumbaugh taught both at the undergraduate and graduate levels. Working teachers took his Saturday-morning classes, while the classes on Friday evening enrolled those with college degrees and engaged in master's or doctoral programs. For the most part, the Saturday "Courses for Teach- ers"—their rubric in the university catalog—provided practical and technical train- ing. Today these noncredit courses would be designated continuing-education units. They had no departmental niche and, at first, were not applicable toward a degree. A person satisfactorily completing one of them was issued a "Certificate of Study." By 1896, however, certain Brumbaugh-taught pedagogical courses did count toward a baccalaureate degree in any of several established disciplines. This concession so soon by the faculty suggests that from the start the first professor of pedagogy brought academic respectability to teacher preparation. The ready acceptance of the "Courses for Teachers" program by his professorial peers, Provost Harrison reported to the Penn trustees, "filled [Brumbaugh] with enthusiasm and pleasure."

His emphasis in Friday-evening advanced courses was largely historical and philosophical and not so much that of in-service training, his objective on Satur- day mornings. Because he taught graduate students, he was ipso facto a member of the philosophy faculty. That department, as noted earlier, alone granted all Ph.D.s, no matter what discipline. It had been divided, for administrative reasons, into a number of groupings. One group included four fields: philosophy, ethics, psychol- ogy, and pedagogy. Within a half-decade Brumbaugh was made chairman of this disciplinary cluster—Group VIII.

The rest of the week, back at Juniata, he taught literature, philosophy, and pedagogy and looked after presidential doings. His occasional chapel talks, far more interesting that the usual homiletic fare, unfailingly turned an attendance requirement into a memorable event. And, of course, teachers' institutes, especially in the summer and fall months, poached upon what little free time was left over from all his academic commitments.

Professionally, the highlight of the year 1895 for him was his grand tour of Europe and England. The purpose was to study higher education in Western Europe, a project that would take him to famous university cities. Perhaps another reason, although unstated, had to do with collecting material for a book on Brethren historical origins. He went in the company of two men from Penn: George Fullerton, his former professor and now dean of the college and vice-provost of the university; and Samuel M. Lindsay, a twenty-six-year-old sociologist with a doctorate from Halle.

The three academic tourists on 26 June took passage on the *Friesland*, a modern Dutch steamer operated by the Red Star Line. This clipper bow liner, which carried more than nine hundred passengers, plied the Atlantic between Antwerp and New York. The threesome's itinerary took them to most of Europe's oldest and loveliest cities: Dresden, Paris, Cologne, Berlin, Leipzig, Nuremberg, Venice, Florence, Rome, Naples, Milan, Bern, Geneva, Basel. From these points they journeyed to other historic centers of learning: Halle, Jena, Heidelberg, Zurich, Padua, Salerno, Strasbourg. At Strasbourg they met and dined with Professor Brandl, the forty-year-old German scholar whose books on Coleridge, the romantics, and Shakespeare had only recently appeared. Brandl was the European professor who had praised so highly Brumbaugh's thesis on Donne.

While in Italy, the sight-seeing professors were tormented by fleas. Brumbaugh oftentimes would good-naturedly grumble to his flea-bitten companions about their misery. Then he would bring smiles to their faces by a comforting refrain: How nice it would be when they got back to "God's Country"—Pennsylvania!

On the return trip the travelers stopped off in England. They went sight-seeing in London, and toured nearby historic countryside points. One excursion, at Brumbaugh's request, took them to Thomas Gray's birthplace and Stoke Poges Church near Windsor, thought to be the scene of the poet's most celebrated poem, "Elegy Written in a Country Churchyard" (1750). Brumbaugh brought back a bundle of cuttings from the church's "ivy-mantled tow'r" mentioned in the poem's second stanza. Soon after arriving stateside, in late August, he scheduled himself to speak to Juniatians on the scholarly bachelor poet. At the end of the talk he handed out a leaf of ivy from the vines on the towered church to everyone present.

In early summer 1896, Brumbaugh dropped another governance bombshell, the second in two years. That June he stunned the Juniata trustees with the news he planned to make Philadelphia his place of primary residence—at least on a trial basis. On Monday the 22nd, according to H. B. Brumbaugh's diary, he met with local board members and "defined his future relations to the College." A special bulletin spelled out publicly what these "relations" would be. He would live in Philadelphia from October 1896 to May 1897, the announcement said, but would remain President of Juniata College, organize the work in September, frequently visit the College to give a regular course of lectures to the students on the latest and best in literary and pedagogical development and to preach in the Chapel, attend the special Bible Session and participate in its work as usual, [and] regularly be at the College to teach and lecture to students during May and June of the Spring Term.

The trustee minutes do not record what kind of salary adjustment, if any, was made as a result of these new conditions.

Martin's second cousin, Harvey Brumbaugh, the son of the trustee chairman and a classicist, was named vice-president to give on-campus academic oversight. As might be expected, the idea of their headman off living at the far end of the state left everybody on campus wondering and uneasy. To bolster morale, Dr. A. B. Brumbaugh stressed in an *Echo* editorial: "The success of the work and the prosperity of the school will not depend on the presence or absence of any one member of the devoted workers as long as there is a united purpose."

That summer Martin bought a house at 311 Fortieth Street in West Philadelphia, a couple of blocks from the Penn campus. Anna, the children, and Flora Belle were settled in by early fall. For a couple of years Martin would rent the Huntingdon house to his brother Frank and his family. But he reserved one of the bedrooms for himself—to use when back visiting the Hill on college business. It must have been evident to Huntingdon people that the Martin Brumbaughs now considered themselves adopted Philadelphians and would never move back.

Now that he was Philadelphia-based and teaching full-time at Penn, Brumbaugh was able to expand his course offerings in pedagogy. Students were attracted to his classes in droves—public-school teachers, undergraduates, and graduates alike. His mail, by now, included a steady flow of fan letters. A number of them were penned by single women who obviously had a crush on the young professor. Among his admirers was Anne Heygate-Hall of the Philadelphia Normal School, who would team up with him five years later in preparing a primer. She wrote: "I can truly say [you have] helped me more in my profession than any other person has, and I say this without forgetting John Ruskin."

Other adulatory letters began coming from professional colleagues. Among them, for example, was a little missive from Edward Brooks. After listening to Brumbaugh speak one time, under the auspices of Penn's public lecture series, he wrote:

I was proud of you last night. Yours was the brightest and best speech of the evening. . . . It afforded me pleasure to say to my friends that you were formerly one of my pupils. With such a start as you have made . . . there is a splendid career for you.

Brumbaughana of those years also include an appreciative note in 1897 from Nathan C. Schaeffer, Pennsylvania's superintendent of instruction—this one a testimony to Martin's already apparent deft political touch. Schaeffer thanked him for influencing Governor Daniel Hastings and the state's college presidents to reappoint him to office—with a raise—when there was reluctance upon the part of some, including the governor, to do so. Wrote Schaeffer, who would go on to hold the post of state superintendent until 1919, "I owe it all to your efforts in molding public sentiment." Hastings, who for several years as a young man taught school before studying law, had wanted Brumbaugh, not Schaeffer (a Democrat), but his first choice turned him down.

And there were warm letters from Henry Houck, who for nearly forty years would be the state's influential deputy superintendent of instruction. He always addressed Brumbaugh as "Marty." The two of them, proud Pennsylvania Dutchmen, developed an undying friendship. Later, when "Marty" enjoyed a national reputation, Houck, twenty-five years older, would affectionately refer to him in public as "my boy."

Adulation also came his way after he spoke at the annual convention of the National Education Association in Buffalo, New York, held in July 1896. Others on the program included such notables as David Starr Jordan, the famous naturalist and first president of Stanford University, and William T. Harris, United States commissioner of education, perhaps the premier educational figure of his day. Brumbaugh was scheduled for a morning address on the 9th. Even before his speech, according to the *Buffalo Express*, "It had been noised abroad . . . that a new genius had been discovered" in the field of education. The speaker, as a result, faced a "hall that was filled quicker and more solidly than at any previous session," reported the paper.

Indeed, the news story summarizing the convention's program for the day of his address had started out by making a special point of Brumbaugh's impressive performance. It began:

> A bright star, long obscured behind the clouds of Central Pennsylvania existence, burst on the educational firmament at the general session of the convention at Music Hall yesterday morning. This new genius is Dr. Martin G. Brumbaugh. . . . He is a man of magnificent appearance, tall, erect, smooth shaven, with a clean, clear-cut, strong, intelligent face. . . . His address was profound in thought, polished in form and splendidly delivered.

In the judgment of the reporter, who took it upon himself to meter audibly the fervor of clapping after each speech: "Such applause as he received at the close of his address was second only to that accorded Dr. William T. Harris." The newsman added in a gratuitous postscript, "And mark you, Dr. Brumbaugh is comparatively a beginner when placed alongside Dr. Harris."

Another reporter—this one for the *Pennsylvania School Journal*—also had laudatory things to say about Penn's pedagogy professor. The writer sat in on one of Brumbaugh's morning classes, which met in Room 205 in College Hall, the administration building. The topic of that day's lesson was, "The Importance of

Word Enrichment as a Child's Equipment for Life." There were fifty-some teachers in the class. The lesson went especially well, prompting the visitor to describe Brumbaugh as "a born teacher, magnetic, forceful, spontaneous, and a master of his subject."

Meanwhile, in the spring of 1897 Brumbaugh turned down the principalship of the Philadelphia High School for Girls. It would have paid four thousand dollars a year, a salary, Nathan Schaeffer wrote him, few men would have spurned. Edward Brooks dropped him a line, agreeing, "You decided wisely." Explained Brooks, the Penn professor was destined for greater things; his audience already embraced the university, the state, and "a large part of the country." "How I wish," the Quaker City superintendent concluded, "I could [live] to see you and your record some twenty-five years hence."

About the time of the Girls' High School offer, the two older Brumbaugh brothers fell into some kind of misunderstanding.* What sparked the squabble, or when it began, never came out in the letters of theirs that survive. Perhaps it grew out of certain arrangements the two men had made between themselves. Frank's family was then living in the frame tenant house on Martin's downtown Huntingdon property. This conveniently enabled Frank, a railroad mail clerk, to look after the maintenance of the corner store building for Martin and collect the rent. Also, he was engaged in selling off some of his brother's furniture and other household goods at the Seventeenth Street home near the college. Apparently, Frank got blamed for something; in one letter he said, "You hold me responsible for doing you a great wrong." Another letter made reference to having "lost the confidence" of his brother, who had put him "in a humiliating position." These are cryptic plaints, leaving little to be deduced about the origin of their spat.

Possibly the cause of the brothers' tiff may be found elsewhere. Among the Martin Brumbaugh papers is an anonymous poison-pen clipping—actually a cartoon page torn out of a book. Pictured in a nineteenth-century parlor are three demons, winged and horned, on each of which appears, reading from left to right, one of the following words: WORLD, DEVIL, FLESH. The pointed-eared demonic spirits hover over a closed casket lavishly topped with floral wreaths. On the fringed velour draped over the casket's base are the words REV•DEMUS•HYPOC-RISY. Between the three evenly spaced handles on the coffin's front someone had boldly printed, in red ink, the initials MGB. Against the fringed bottom of the velour leaned a row of more wreaths, two of them much larger than the rest. Superimposed across one is the inscription WORLDLY FAME, and across the other WORLDLY AMBITION.

Was this devilish tableau Frank's way of accusing his brother of an un-Dunker-like lifestyle, of saying that early success had made him too self-centered, too ambitious and materialistic? What gives credence to the notion that

---

*Brumbaugh, neither as boy nor adult, was as intimate with his other brother, Irwin, as he was with Frank, closer in age to him.

Frank was the cartoon-sending culprit is a passing remark of his in another letter during this period of disaffection. In it he enigmatically referred to the "danger you were drifting into (and the history of two years only confirms what I told you) makes the burden harder to bear." Did Martin think his younger brother a busybody, making unfair charges? We do not know, nor are we sure what "danger" alarmed Frank. But it is curious that Martin never discarded the fiendish picture-page.

Martha Brumbaugh no doubt was pained to see her two sons scrapping, but, for a certainty, she very much missed the older one. In May of 1897 she wrote a particularly soulful letter—utterly ungrammatical and with misspellings and colloquialisms dispersed throughout—telling of her desire and need to see more of him and the grandchildren. Near the beginning of it, she said:

> I went up to your place the first time I was [in Huntingdon] since youns are gone it was a sad visit for me no one was there I sat on the poarch and cried when I seen your trees and plants and flowers . . . your yard is so nice some roses have buds when I thought about the children how glad they would be to play under the cherry trees they are so full of cherries but the garden looks so hard that I couldn't look at it the worms are eating your currants bushes that good ground ought to be planted and the grass kept down

After further comments about the run-down condition of the grounds around his Seventeenth Street house, she went on:

> I always liked your home but when I seen it this time it made my heart ache will youns come back or are you going to stay I hear so may stories I am ancious to no I never asked you before . . . you have the nicest home up there don't let a stranger have it yet keep it awile yet bring the children back to play in the yard awile.

Toward the end of her letter Martha made the only known reference by a family member to the death of her daughter, Amanda, in 1869:

> is Mabel well again take good care of her she is all most the age my little girl was when she left me oh how hard it is to give up our children I feel it yet I get lonely here.

About the time of his mother's letter, Brumbaugh had succeeded in putting pedagogy at Penn on firmer academic footing. He made it possible for students in his field to qualify for a prestigious scholarship. It so happened that Provost Harrison had, in 1895, established a half-million dollar endowment in the graduate school memorializing his father: the George L. Harrison Foundation for the Encouragement of Liberal Studies and the Advancement of Knowledge. The idea for this act of filial remembrance had first come from George Fullerton, the vice provost and

Martin's personal friend. So he probably had Fullerton's backing when he went to the provost and asked that the division of pedagogy be eligible for Harrison fellowships. He got his way, and throughout the twelve years he was identified with Penn a number of his students won the award. In fact, Provost Harrison's annual report for 1903 pointed out that "one of the major preferences in choice of major subject for those who hold Fellowships under the George L. Harrison Foundation is that of Pedagogy."

The provost, from the start, liked his pedagogy professor as a person and appreciated the popularity he enjoyed. But he must have begun to think, after a few years, that Brumbaugh's alma mater was claiming too much time from his Penn post. For, on New Year's Day 1898, he sent him a memo that read: "Do you not think it time that your name should cease to be officially connected with Juniata College? . . . Please consider this matter, and will you let me hear from you at your earliest convenience." Then, on the 11th, came a one-sentence handwritten note from Vice-Provost Fullerton: "The Provost is quite satisfied with your suggestions as to Juniata College."

Like so many decisive moments in Brumbaugh's life, there is nothing on record explicating what these "suggestions" were. Thus the nature of this understanding between him and Harrison escapes the frustrated biographer. But operatively nothing much seems to have changed; the Juniata catalog still listed him as president and a trustee. He continued to make periodic trips to the campus, never missed stockholders' meetings, and he was made privy to all important administrative decisions.

In mid-February of 1898 newspaper captions blazoned the sinking of the battleship *Maine* in the harbor of Havana, heralding the coming of the Spanish-American War. A few days later, with the nation in an uproar, Brumbaugh left for Chattanooga, Tennessee, where he was scheduled to be a headline speaker at a national convention of school superintendents. His friend Nathan Schaeffer, an officer of the National Education Association, the sponsoring organization, had helped plan the conference. John Dewey, who in another year or two would emerge as America's foremost twentieth-century voice in progressive education, first at the University of Chicago and then at Columbia, sat in the audience. After one of the sessions a Southern superintendent came up to Schaeffer and asked, "How did you find so many brilliant fellows?" He specifically had Brumbaugh in mind.

That spring of 1898 his surging reputation generated more than thirty invitations to be a high school commencement speaker. For years to come this kind of mail, often copious, would mark for him the onset of springtide as surely as the vernal equinox.

In early July he presided, as incoming president, at the three-day forty-third annual session of the Pennsylvania State Teachers' Association (PSTA). At that time the PSTA—which Brumbaugh had joined in 1885 and of which he later became a life member—was hardly more than an interest group. As a professional society, it was still pitifully small, with but 221 members.* The educators met in the courthouse of Centre County's old historic town of Bellefonte. Brumbaugh had been preceded as PSTA president by some of his closest professional peers: Edward Brooks (1868); Henry Houck (1872); Nathan Schaeffer (1883); Elisha Higbee (1889).

His inaugural address on the night of 5 July was titled "An Educational Struggle in Colonial Pennsylvania." The thesis he propounded—and his credo ever after—was that "Pennsylvania was unquestionably . . . the foremost colony of America." He prefaced his address by saying of his native state: "We should welcome every effort to make our people familiar with a history so rich and pure and sweet and good, that the world may know and love Pennsylvania as we do." After a round of applause, he went on to note that his "own work at the University would be largely directed to bringing to light the unwritten history of Pennsylvania on educational lines." Some of this sounds like cloying rhetoric, but there is every reason to believe Brumbaugh was utterly sincere about his love for the Keystone State. That is why he chose never to relocate beyond its borders despite many tempting career opportunities.

In telling the teachers a story familiar today but up to then largely untold, Brumbaugh extolled William Penn both as a man and as a colonial proprietor. He detailed Penn's heroic life, his Quaker beliefs, his hatred of slavery, his respect for the Indian, his Frame of Government, his dictums on education. Because Penn's "holy experiment" was based on religious freedom, emphasized Brumbaugh, "Pennsylvania became the refuge of all nationalities, all conditions, all creeds." By implication, of course, he meant to discommend the intolerance and societal homogeneity that had characterized Puritan New England.

Of Pennsylvania's diverse colonial population—English, Welsh, Scotch-Irish, German—it was the Pennsylvania Germans (or "Dutch"), argued Brumbaugh, who emerged as the saviors of the "holy experiment" after the days of Penn had passed. The bulk of his speech, after these contextual observations, dealt with the "educational struggle" referred to in its title: the cause, the contestants, the outcome. The dispute began in the 1750s, about the time of the French and Indian War. It pitted two prominent colonial intellectuals—William Smith, rector of Christ Church in Philadelphia (Anglican) and provost of the College of Philadelphia (later the University of Pennsylvania), and Benjamin Franklin—against the Germans. The Smith-Franklin ploy, the Germans felt, meant to deprive them of their language and religion by setting up charity schools, largely financed by the mother country, and make English citizens of them. While some unsuspecting Germans obligingly fell in with the plan, Brumbaugh said, there was one man who immediately read cultural chauvinism into it: Christopher Sauer I, of Germantown.

---

*Today the PSTA's successor, the Pennsylvania State Education Association, is a powerful professional union whose membership hovers around 108,000.

At the time he delivered his Bellefonte paper, the PSTA president, among all his other current literary activity, was close to completing his book-length pioneering study of Brethren origins. He had been working on it ever since his European trip in 1895. His research had introduced him to Sauer, an immigrant from Wittgenstein, Germany, who, although never baptized a Dunker, believed like one.* A multitalented man who practiced several trades, Sauer won his fame through his print shop. The Sauer Bible, published in 1743, was the first Bible in a European language to be printed in America. It could be found in every German home in the colonies, Brumbaugh said. Every German family had at hand, he went on at some length, sundry other products of the Sauer print shop and press: a family almanac, a secular newspaper *(Der Hoch-Deutsch Pennsylvanische Geschichts-Schreiber),* the ink and paper used for stationery purposes, and most of the books and pamphlets the household read. As a result, Christopher Sauer exercised a powerful influence upon German voters.

Thus in the political controversy over the charity-school proposal, as the PSTA speaker grandiloquently put it, "This Christopher Saur [*sic*] raised his voice, and through his newspaper his voice became many-tongued, and sounded round every German hearthstone in the country." He rose up to be the "knight of these Germans." Therefore, declared the president-elect, because of Sauer's defiant editorial opposition together with the friction that grew up between the colonies and England, which had provided heavy funding and political aid, the scheming of Smith and Franklin failed. The Germans continued to hold to their own schools, stressing religious education and teaching in their own tongue.

Brumbaugh's speech ended with the accusation that historians seriously erred in the way they heretofore wrote about the Pennsylvania Germans. He charged: "It is little less than criminal to say that the early Germans of Pennsylvania were either ignorant or opposed to education. They were among the most learned men that crossed the Atlantic." Many, said Brumbaugh, including Sauer (this is debatable), could boast "college diplomas." Thus "the great ignorance imputed to them by writers of history belongs more justly to the writers themselves." The political battle Sauer led and helped win, however, had an unfortunate sequel for the province's one hundred thousand German citizens, lamented the speaker. Their "lines of life"—as rural people—deprived them of the need for higher education. As a result, after the American revolution they forfeited to the English their once "high position" in founding schools.

Brumbaugh's inaugural speech marked the beginning of his abiding scholarly interest in the Pennsylvania Germans. In another talk to the teachers the last day of the meeting, he said that "while it is time we told the world about the growth of the system of education we have built up among ourselves," he himself, in researching and writing on Pennsylvania's educational history, would focus on the colony's

---

*His namesake son, however, would become a leader of the sect by the time of the Revolutionary War.

early German-speaking immigrants. No doubt his own heritage, both familial and religious, largely dictated this academic pursuit. Already his "Uncle Doctor" and cousin Gaius had begun to collect data on the family genealogy, and from time to time he filled in some gaps as a favor. The result would be the monumental *Genealogy of the Brumbach Families*, published in 1913. Then, too, his research in Europe and at home opened up for him a whole new understanding of how the Dunkers, once a voice for learning, fell silent, and even became obscurantist.

Intrigued by his cultural roots, Brumbaugh had joined the Pennsylvania German Society in the fall of 1895. Just recently organized (in 1891), the society specified that a regular member must be "a descendant of early German or Swiss emigrants to Pennsylvania." Those who started it deplored how historians, too long, were guilty of inaccuracies about or studied indifference to the productive place these early immigrants and their progeny had and continued to have in the life of their host state and the nation. Early on, the society began to promote research and monographic studies in an effort to give historical credit wherever the Pennsylvania Germans were due it. Much of Brumbaugh's sideline writing was inspired by this kind of pride in his Teutonic ancestry. Eventually, in 1927, he would be elected the society's fortieth president.

Perhaps, then, being a proud Pennsylvania Dutchman was what sustained his unembarrassed loyalty to the little, rural-oriented denomination he belonged to, despite his having become something of a cosmopolite. In 1897 he delivered a series of Bible lectures on the Book of Ruth and the Gospel of John at Juniata. They later appeared, by popular demand, as a book, which he dedicated "To the Church of the Brethren and Juniata College—the Church and School I love." Though an aberrant Dunker—he would have said "Dunkard"—Brumbaugh was not shamming when he wrote this inscription. He gave no evidence, his whole life, that he was ever anything but loyal to the two institutions that shaped and dominated his early years.

When exactly he began to research the European and colonial origins of the Brethren cannot be pinpointed. But in 1895 the denomination had called for "some brother" to publish a history of the "Brethren Church." The book was to give particular attention to the historical conditions that made its "inception . . . a necessity." His European trip in 1895 was partly spent in searching out and collecting materials on the subject during his travels along the Rhine in Germany. He spoke at several annual conferences about his project and what he had found. It was said these talks were always greeted with overflowing audiences. Many who heard them urged him to put them into book form. In 1899, then, he published *A History of the German Baptist Brethren in Europe and America*. This groundbreaking study stands even today as a commendable work of scholarship.

Like a true-blue member of the Pennsylvania German Society, he wrote, "Perhaps no religious sect is so little understood and so persistently misrepresented as the German Baptist Brethren." But, he argued in the preface, the Brethren, little concerned about record keeping or narrative history, must bear much of the blame for being misunderstood. Over the years they had lost, for the most part, all interest in their past. Their history was not only unwritten but largely forgotten. As Brumbaugh wrote, "Our past is to us a sealed record." He lamented that in preparing his book no member of his religious order, with one exception, aided him in any way, despite repeated pleas for source materials.

A History of the German Baptist Brethren took a revisionist look at Dunker origins, both in Europe and in colonial America, and this later appealed mightily to brotherhood progressives. Brumbaugh, and other writers who followed in the early twentieth century, according to *The Brethren Encyclopedia,*

> wanted to correct the impression that the Brethren were withdrawn and backward. They were eager to justify Brethren existence and sought to portray the Brethren as having generally been in the forefront of cultural, educational, and religious advance.

Brumbaugh's book, expanding on the thesis he set forth in his Bellefonte State Teachers' Association address, called attention to the vigorous literary and intellectual activity of Brethren colonial ancestors. He contended that before the church was a score of years old it had made a strong and permanent impress upon the life and thought of colonial America. He emphasized the fact that no press before the Revolution exerted so great a cultural force as that of the Sauer family, not even Franklin's as historians mistakenly said. He noted that the early Dunker leaders were men of scholarship and learning, much involved in the founding of the Germantown Academy. What he sought to do, in a word, was to give back to the Brethren their lost educational consciousness.

The book raised a paradox, however: how did a church nurtured into being by literate men fall into educational decline to the extent that its fathers were on record as opposed to schooling? Brumbaugh's answer did not come in the book but in later articles and talks; it too had been anticipated in his Bellefonte address. His research convinced him that the Smith-Franklin maneuver to anglicize the German churches through English schools aroused such intense opposition among the Pennsylvania Germans—no group more so than the Dunkers—that the next generation interpreted this dissent to mean rejection of education as such. *A History of the German Baptist Brethren*, therefore, came from his pen as a challenge. As he once said a few years after it appeared: "We began [as] an educated and powerful church. Let us try with all our energies to restore the church to its early and its splendid history."

The only Dunker to come to Brumbaugh's aid in researching his history, the man the author said exemplified the "true spirit of the scholar and philanthropist," was Abraham H. Cassel. Cassel's mother was a great-granddaughter of the Germantown printer, Christopher Sauer, and the great-great-granddaughter of Peter Becker, the first colonial Dunker preacher. His father was opposed to formal education, but, with some help from a sister, Cassel taught himself to read and write. (Cassel was the farm boy mentioned in chapter 2 who defied his father, buying matches and reading by candlelight under an umbrella in his bedroom at night.) His public schooling, which totaled a mere six weeks, came wholly the year he turned eleven. When the Brumbaughs started the Brethren school at Huntingdon, he became a stockholder, and his daughter, Hannah, put in a year of study there in 1877–78, a classmate of Martin Brumbaugh's.

Cassel was a farmer from near Harleysville in eastern Pennsylvania and a book collector who had assembled a valuable store of materials, mainly by and about the Pennsylvania Germans. His was one of the largest private collections in the country—over fifty thousand items: books, magazines, newspapers, tracts, pamphlets. It dwarfed most public and college libraries and was visited by historians, authors, professors, and editors, often from great distances.

When Cassel died in 1908 a newspaper obituary described him as "the foremost Pennsylvania bibliophile and a widely known authority on the Germans in America." Brumbaugh, in eulogizing the eighty-six-year-old antiquarian at his funeral, said of him: "No man ever lived or will live who will do for the Dunkard Church what Bro. Cassel has done. Our history was engraved and preserved on the shelves of his library. He kept safe our records as a denomination." Brumbaugh had relied extensively on Cassel's knowledge and collection in writing his church history, which he dedicated to the remarkable book-lover "as a Token of Love and Gratitude."

The year before Brumbaugh's *History* came out, Cassel, his eyesight failing and his wife having just died, decided to sell off his library. The book's author, with covetous urgency, at once began deluging his aged friend with letters, pleading that the Brethren materials in it, if nothing else, be kept intact. Juniata College, he insisted, was the perfect place for them; the new brick fireproof transept of Students Hall would ensure safekeeping.

Cassel agreed, but there followed months of haggling before he finally settled on a price of twenty-five hundred dollars. The college, now with the mortgage of a new dormitory, Oneida Hall, on its hands, was in no position to bear the expense. So Brumbaugh had no choice but to go it alone, on a demand note (which he made good in less than two years). The date of purchase was 1 February 1899. Later, Cassel rebated five hundred dollars to the college.

Juniata got about a third of the collection, some eleven thousand books and four thousand pamphlets, much of it selected Americana.* It included a stock of rare foreign works, valuable colonial imprints, and scores of almanacs. Thrown in as a bonus was the Cassel correspondence—three boxes full, in themselves a treasure-trove for historians. Building upon the Cassel collection, Brumbaugh hoped

---

*Cassel had already disposed of a large part of his library by 1881. What little was left over, mostly books, after Brumbaugh made his purchase was given away to other colleges. But Martin always said Juniata got the "cream" of the collection.

to make Juniata the chief repository for Brethren sources and writings, past and future. In 1900 he sent out circulars to a thousand ministers in the eastern part of the United States soliciting historical miscellanies of all sorts having to do with the Brethren denomination; but the project never panned out. The Cassel materials, however, preserved partly in the Juniata College archives and partly in the Treasure Room, remain to this day a veritable gold mine for social and cultural historians. As Brumbaugh once commented, "[N]o man who attempts to write a history of the German population of America can do so without coming to Huntingdon."

Meanwhile, another publication had put the Brumbaugh name, as coauthor, on a grammar-school reader: *Stories of Pennsylvania*, printed by the American Book Publishing Company in New York City. It was one in a series of state *Stories* put out by the publishers. Other writers in the series included famous men like William Dean Howells of Ohio (editor of the series), Joel Chandler Harris of Georgia, and Frank R. Stockton of New Jersey. The man who collaborated with Brumbaugh on the volume was Joseph Walton, then professor of history at the West Chester Normal School. The *Journal of Education*, a weekly national periodical, introduced *Stories* with a laudatory comparative sketch of the two authors. It noted:

> Messrs. Walton and Brumbaugh are rare men. Both are of good Pennsylvania stock, both have a comfortable financial inheritance, both have taught successfully, both won educational honors as county superintendents, both retired in hours of professional triumph for earnest university study along modern lines, both have historical and literary taste and talent, [and] both are skilled talkers and writers. . . .

Stories, subtitled "School Readings from Pennsylvania History," came off the press in November 1897. The three hundred-page book contained sixty-seven short stories on the history of Pennsylvania, beginning before Penn and coming down to Lincoln at Gettysburg. As Brumbaugh had pledged himself to do before Pennsylvania's schoolteachers at Bellefonte, he attempted to counteract the predominant attention historians had heretofore customarily paid to New England and Puritanism. Pennsylvania, for example, had its own Paul Revere (Caesar Rodney) and its own Tea Party (in Philadelphia, three weeks before Boston's). Penn's colony, the young reader was told, was the home of the Declaration of Independence and the Constitution, and on its famous Civil War battlefield, Gettysburg, the hopes of the Confederacy were buried. So the purported mission of the authors, drawing upon Pennsylvania's "unwritten history," was to show schoolchildren why their native state, and not New England, deserved to be honored as Mother of the Republic. Hopefully, the preface states, readings would inspire them to "prize all the more [their] own rich social, political, educational, and religious environment after becoming familiar with the struggles of an ancestry not so highly favored."

While written with the charm of romance, each story, including Indian tales, was thoroughly researched and rendered in a historically accurate and trustworthy way. The authors based their sketches on colonial accounts and on original sources found in the state archives or preserved by the Pennsylvania Historical Society. Direct fictitious conversation was only sparingly used.

Overall, *Stories*, which sold for sixty cents, elicited very favorable reviews. Professional periodicals gave it high marks. The *Journal of Education* declared it "made a positive contribution to American history and to the world's knowledge" and claimed that "There is no other book so indispensable to a Pennsylvania school-house." The *Teacher*, organ of the Educational Club of Philadelphia, touted *Stories* as the obvious substitute for present reading books with their "pointless poems, spiritless tales, and morbid soliloquies." The *Ohio Educational Monthly* raved that *Stories* made the past "alive" for pupils through its real-life accounts of history-making people. Said the reviewer, "The merit of the book is being recognized in all sections of the country—even in New England, which, up to the time of its publication, was supposed to have a monopoly on colonial history." County and city school superintendents—some from out of state—also raised cheers for the debut of *Stories*. The Pottstown superintendent, for example, wrote: "My boy of 12 picked up *Stories of Pennsylvania* and began to turn over the leaves. Soon he said: 'This book is full of good stories; I must read it.' We will, without doubt, soon place some of the books in our schools."

By May 1898 *Stories*, having been only five months on the market, was in its third edition. The book, which many schools used as a supplemental reader in classes on United States history, apparently evoked a public interest in translations and reprints from original historical documents in the teaching of both American and European history. So Brumbaugh and Walton teamed up once again, beginning soon after *Stories* went into print. Over the next couple of years, through the Christopher Sower Printing Company in Philadelphia, they edited and issued six "Liberty Bell Leaflets."* These pamphlets, usually eighteen to nineteen pages, included certain records and letters related to the influence of the early Quakers on Pennsylvania and New Jersey.

The late Gay Nineties were hectic years for Brumbaugh. Deadlines and pressures were coming at him from all sides: his cooperative literary activities with Dr. Walton; his *History of the German Baptist Brethren*; his grueling teachers' institute schedule; his teaching duties; his trips to Huntingdon; and the feverish rush during the summer of 1899 to get out the five volumes of his *Standard Readers*. He wrote to Abraham Cassel that February, when the two were dickering over the octogenarian's library, "I am a very busy man. My time is my money. . . . I am at work on my books—the source of my bread and butter." He fretted about any

---

*Charles G. Sower was the great-great-grandson of Christopher Sauer I, the famous colonial printer. Brumbaugh bought five thousand dollars' worth of stock in the Christopher Sower Printing Company in January 1898. Charles Sower would publish a number of Brumbaugh's books.

disruption of his writing routine, like having to lobby lawmakers. In a March letter to Cassel, he complained, "I am sent to Harrisburg to the Legislature nearly every spare hour I have to see after some legislation for schools."

A member of the Pennsylvania German Society once described Brumbaugh as a man who "early became accustomed to doing several things at once." Indeed, it was evident by the 1890s that the secret of his success and power lay not only in his natural endowments but also in his genius for hard work. Dr. Edgar Fahs Smith, who was vice-provost eight of the years Brumbaugh taught at Penn, said of the professor of pedagogy, "He does more after the time that the average man lays aside his labor than is ordinarily done in a whole day."

Frank Brumbaugh had similar memories of his brother's night-owl work habits. He liked to tell of the time when Martin had come back to the Juniata campus on one of his flying, squeezed-in trips. He gave an evening talk in the chapel. When he finished, choosing not to mingle with the audience, he went directly to his home across the street. He at once set to work on some kind of academic task. The dispersing crowd could see the yellow glow of a kerosene lamp through a window in his second-floor bedroom.

Frank, whose family was renting the absentee president's house at the time, was an early riser. The next morning, just as the first faint streakings of dawn began to show over Lion's Back—a low, wooded ridge just east of College Hill— he got up and dressed. He noticed a light in the upstairs room (the one always reserved for Martin during his presidential visits). At first he thought his brother had forgotten to turn down the wick. But when he opened the door he saw Martin sitting in a chair deep in thought, an open book on the desk before him. He had spent the night hours alternately catnapping and working.

Sooner or later, family and friends worried, overwork and stress would take a toll. As it happened, in March 1898 Brumbaugh had a "nervous collapse" (the term he used in a letter to Abraham Cassel), and so the doctor ordered him to bed for several days. Over the next year and a half he often mentioned, in corresponding with the Dunker book collector, his chronic run-down condition.

Despite overfatigue, Brumbaugh barely broke his hustling stride. His 1899 calendar lists him making, on top of everything else, thirty public appearances between January and August. True, he begged off more than seventy other invitations, but the engagements he scheduled, both in and out of state, were a diverse lot involving a great deal of preparation time: from Sunday-school gatherings to civic clubs to a variety of educational conferences and teachers' institutes. He gave a major speech at the Indiana State Teachers' Association, which met at Fort Wayne in early spring, and shared the platform spotlight with G. Stanley Hall, the world-famous child psychologist and president of Clark University in Massachusetts. Ill health sent him to bed again in September.

No doubt, that last summer of the 1890s, the strain his publisher put him under to deliver, in final copy, the manuscripts of his five-volume *Brumbaugh Standard*

Readers added to his lingering health problems. He had been working on the *Readers* for a year, but Charles Sower had set the first of September as the target date for setting print. To meet the deadline, Brumbaugh found solitude for the summer in a house at Valley Forge that had become a favorite retreat of his. Even so, he took time during those months to preach Juniata's baccalaureate sermon in July as well as to lecture in Gettysburg, Harrisburg, and Wilmington, Delaware.

It would be interesting to know how it came about that Brumbaugh took on the basal readers project. Nationwide, the Gay Nineties brought an avalanche of new textbooks for public-school subjects, set loose by all the "New Education" debate. Especially outdated were readers that reflected a preindustrial culture. For example, the long-popular McGuffey readers, of which Americans bought one million copies between 1850 and 1900, stressed the values of an agrarian and classless society. As a rule, their stories ignored urban life, except to show how cities were corrupt compared to village and country living.

The Christopher Sower Company had been in the textbook business for some time. Among its current best-selling titles were those of Edward Brooks in arithmetic and higher mathematics. So perhaps it was Charles Sower, getting up in years (seventy-eight) and ailing, who took the initiative and turned to Brumbaugh in a move to enter the highly competitive reading-textbook market. Such speculation makes sense: Brumbaugh's name was well known to school administrators and teachers in the East; the two had collaborated to bring out *Stories of Pennsylvania* with great success; and Martin was a stockholder in the company.

In putting together his graded *Readers*, Brumbaugh shied away from any McGuffey-like didactic scheme to transmit values, stock attitudes, and tag lines. Nor did he try to redress the urban-rural imbalance in story content. Rather, he followed a clearly defined pedagogical plan. His primary purpose in the first three *Readers*—he wrote practically all the stories himself, but not the poems—was to teach children to read, then to lead them to read with interest. The design of *Four* and *Five* was to get them to use good language but, above all else, to appreciate the best in English literature.

Each story or selection was preceded by new words to be used in that section, with diacritical marks for the teacher's aid. The *First Reader* provided a phonetics approach to vocabulary drill, although sight analysis of words (or, in today's parlance, "look-say" or "sight-word") could also be used if any teacher preferred that learning technique. The illustrations for the first three *Readers* were done by Maria L. Kirk of Philadelphia, who was trained in drawing childhood scenes.

The *Fourth* and *Fifth* books were made up of a variety of literary models, from Shakespeare to Lincoln to one of his own published speeches (on nature study, a favorite topic of his).* In these two volumes he included brief annotations of philological, historical, or literary import, as well as biographies and an occasional full-

---

*Brumbaugh, as the owner of hundreds of acres of forested land on and at the foot of Terrace Mountain in his native county, had early come to advocate the place of nature study

page portrait of an author. He included more poetry in them than in the lower-level *Readers*. He purposely juxtaposed a poem, or poems, after a prose passage. Poems, Brumbaugh wrote, "create a love for the highest forms of literature, and . . . impart an ethical sequel to prose selections." A prose exercise "unfolds a fact," he went on. "The poem that follows lifts the fact to the threshold of the emotional life." The author argued that when that happens (i.e., when "the emotional life is touched"), the pupil can identify with the "spirit of the selection" and hence its "ethical significance." Both prose and poetry, but especially the latter, train the imagination, and this is the "greatest intellectual training" reading can give. He even recommended eyes-closed exercises to stimulate mental images while someone, a teacher or a pupil, read a paragraph or a stanza.

The two upper-level editions were not, of course, entirely devoid of moralizing. But it was done subtly, not in a McGuffey-preachy way. All his teaching days Brumbaugh steadfastly held the belief that there was one virtue the public school system of America should, without fail, impart to every child: patriotism. As he put it in the preface to the *Fifth Reader*:

> Among the many virtues made prominent in the selections here given none is more fully, more carefully, more eloquently set forth than the love of country. Ample material is given to inculcate love of our history and, through it, love of our country. Emphasis is placed especially upon those attributes of a free people so essential to a right appreciation of free institutions. In this way it is believed this reader will be an effective means of setting high and just ideals in the minds of the young.

Sower's letters over the next couple of years to Brumbaugh, who left for Puerto Rico shortly after the *Readers* came out, suggest that sales at first were slow, especially for the *Third Reader*. But Philadelphia's the *Teacher* predicted that any "educational books from [Brumbaugh's] pen should be received with more than usual interest." And, indeed, in time the marketing picture improved, although statistics are hard to come by. Orders gradually began coming in from surrounding states;

---

in the curriculum of the public schools. But it should first take an "artistic" bent in the elementary grades, not a "scientific" one, he insisted. "A child should be encouraged to love a tree," he often said in talks and articles. In this "emotional" way, the child learns about nature, its beauty, its processes, its many lessons about the "wonderful world of God." The scientific method in the primary school kills this "spiritual" identificaiton with the out-of-doors. Brumbaugh, therefore, saw great educational value in Arbor Day, which began in 1872 and was observed, at various times in the spring, by many states. On that day the pupils of public schools planted trees and took nature hikes in the effort to foster interest in the preservation of forests. In 1898 Brumbaugh joined the Pennsylvania Forestry Association and for many years was a close friend of Dr. Joseph T. Rothrock, a physician, from McVeytown, Pennsylvania. A professor of botany at Penn since 1877 and after 1893 the first commissioner of forestry for the state, Rothrock would later be acclaimed as the state's father of forest conservation.

New York sales, wrote Sower in February 1901, were as good as Philadelphia's. By that year New Jersey schools (Atlantic City and Trenton) had also adopted the *Readers*. Boston schools began placing orders, too. As for outlying areas of Pennsylvania, another Sower letter two months later reported that one of the company's book agents had introduced the *Readers* into many rural schools. A Sower Publishing Company blurb in the *Teacher* as late as June 1908 declared that the books "are always used in large quantities in the Philadelphia schools." By Brumbaugh's estimate, between eight to ten thousand copies were sold in Puerto Rico during his year-and-a-half stay on that island.

Years later, in 1925, John H. McCracken, president of Lafayette College, said he thought the *Readers* explained, in a big way, why the name of Brumbaugh was "interwoven in" and "almost synonymous" with Pennsylvania education. A New Yorker, he told how, after moving to Easton in 1915, he first heard of the *Readers*:

> I remember how startled I was one day when my boy of six or seven years, running down the stairs, said, "Where is my Brumbaugh, where is my Brumbaugh?" I was somewhat at loss to know to what he referred, and it was only after inquiry that I learned the reader which he was using in school was affectionately known as his "Brumbaugh."

The *Readers* were not long on the market, however, when the author's integrity came under attack by certain school directors and teachers in New York City. An anonymous pamphlet circulated there insinuating that the Penn professor did not write all five volumes. The evidence cited was "a want of symmetry in the series." According to the allegations, the *First Reader* was written by a "former lady teacher," who expected to do all five but gave up. The *Second* and *Third Readers* were done, it was said, by a "book agent"; only the *Fourth* and *Fifth* were authentic Brumbaugh creations. The Sower Publishing Company ran disclaimers in the *Pennsylvania School Journal* and in New York City's educational periodicals. By early 1901 the issue was a past event. But the textbooks, unfortunately, would embroil their creator in another controversy three years later.

In May 1899, however, when the author of the *Readers* was frantically trying to meet their publication deadline, a letter arrived (dated the 9th) and written in Dr. A. B. Brumbaugh's exquisite penmanship. In it was buried some trustee news: "You have been unanimously elected to [your] present position in Juniata College." A postscript explained, "Your present position means President of the College." The nephew responded on the 13th, saying he definitely wanted to resign. On 3 June his uncle, as trustee secretary, wrote to thank him for donating the Cassel materials to Juniata. But again, via a postscript, the doctor declared, "Your offer to resign will not be considered, as the Trustees could not accept your resignation under any consideration." Understandably, board members probably hoped to continue capitalizing on M. G.'s name—for the prestige they thought it bestowed upon the college and for the boost it gave to capital campaigns. One can only guess to what extent his presidency, especially on only a nominal basis, directly contributed to Juniata's steady growth. But by 1900 the college, with a three-term total enrollment of 359, ranked first in size among the half-dozen Brethren institutions.

It is clear at this stage of Brumbaugh's career that he meant to dissolve all close administrative ties to Juniata, though still carrying on as trustee. Because of the board's beseeching, he did, for the time being, acquiesce in keeping the title of president but saw himself as a nonfunctional president rather than an absentee president. The trustees, facing up to the obvious implications of his will and pleasure, promoted twenty-nine-year-old Harvey Brumbaugh, now with a recent Harvard M.A. after his name, to acting president. Harvey, a kindly, self-effacing young man still two years shy of marriage, knew all too well his place in the pecking order. There was no escaping M. G.'s charismatic sway over the campus, even in his absence. It was *his* counsel, not Harvey's, the trustees inevitably first solicited on troublesome academic and financial matters.

Early in the fall of 1899, a change of location bid came from President Andrew S. Draper of the University of Illinois. The letter of invitation informed Brumbaugh that he was Draper's first choice to fill a recently vacated position in pedagogy on his faculty, a position carrying a salary of two thousand dollars. As with all other out-of-state academic proposals that would show up in his mail, he unhesitatingly said no to the Midwest opportunity.

His reputation by this time—he was now thirty-seven—could easily have turned his head. Kudos kept coming his way. The *Kutztown Patriot* had recently dubbed him "the prince of institute instructors." An 1898 article in the *Pittsburgh Press* declared: "There are not many men in the educational field whose breadth and general information along all educational lines is equal to that of Dr. Brumbaugh. He seems to be able to speak upon any subject and at any moment's notice, whether it be kindergarten work or that for a college senior." The highest plaudit appeared in the *New York Teachers' Quarterly*. That journal had lately described him as "one of Pennsylvania's greatest educators and the most popular lecturer in the United States."

7

Caribbean Call

NONE of Martin Brumbaugh's extant letters, written to family and friends before and during 1898, takes any notice of the Spanish-American War, or the crises that led up to it. So we have no idea how he personally felt about Cuba's revolt against colonial rule, the second in twenty years, that erupted in 1895 and developed into a bloody standoff. The American people, however, generally condemned Spain and sided with Cuba's rebels and their guerrilla tactics. Relations between Madrid and Washington steadily worsened, so that by April 1898 most Americans favored intervening in Cuba despite the risk of war with Spain. Public opinion, goaded by the warmongering of the "yellow press," no longer endorsed a Caribbean foreign policy that did not demand Cuban independence. "Cuba Libre!" became a popular cry in the United States.

On Friday, 1 April, Martin's younger brother Frank forlornly wrote to him (they had patched up their spat by now) that "The war talk takes up all spare time. I lost hope for peace at noon to-day. I hope I am wrong but I 'feel it in my bones' now." What prompted such a pessimistic outlook on Frank's part—why he suddenly "lost hope for peace"—is puzzling. There had been no overnight turn of events, no incident, like the recent *Maine* explosion or the undiplomatic DeLôme letter (both in February), to incite jingo bluster for an immediate declaration of war.

True, the world was anxiously waiting to hear how the Spanish government would respond to President William McKinley's recent three-point ultimatum: (1) put an end to concentration camps; (2) declare an armistice until 1 October; (3) grant independence to Cuba if the United States deemed it necessary. But on Thursday, 31 March, the day before Frank sat down to write his brother, both Huntingdon weekly newspapers (there was no daily) carried reassuring news: the Navy's long-awaited report on the sinking of the *Maine* was finally in, and it contained no peace-threatening findings. The naval board of inquiry concluded (wrongly, as we now know) that an external underwater mine had caused the battleship's forward magazines to explode; however, the court, its report stated, was "unable to obtain evidence fixing responsibility . . . upon any person or persons." Spain was off the hook—at least so far as the *Maine* had become a cause célèbre.

Perhaps, then, Frank's April Fool's Day foreboding, intuitively right as it was, sprang from a day-late reading of Thursday's editorial in the *Huntingdon Monitor*. The editor's musings, accurately reflecting the bellicose hysteria of Congress and the American people, was captioned:

THE CUBAN QUESTION

A crisis is Approaching, and Public Feeling
is at High Pitch—It May Result in War

In another three weeks, the "Cuban Question" did indeed foment armed conflict between Spain and the United States, but not before Congress, in the famous Teller Amendment, had disclaimed any territorial designs upon the West Indian island. The fighting, lasting less than four months, would be mercifully brief; it was brought to a halt in mid-August.

When the smoke of the Spanish-American War lifted, the United States suddenly found itself a world power, with a collection of insular colonies. Not all its overseas colonies—e.g., Hawaii, Wake, and other pinpoint Pacific islands—had been acquired through the war or from Spain. But the Treaty of Paris (10 December 1898) added Puerto Rico in the Caribbean and Guam and the Philippines in the Pacific to American territory. The United States paid twenty million dollars for the Philippines; however, Puerto Rico (including some small adjacent islands) and Guam were ceded as indemnity. Cuba, of course, gained independence, although the Platt Amendment of 1900, for all practical purposes, gave the United States a quasi-protectorate over the island, discrediting the earlier Teller Amendment.

By the nineteenth century's close a large minority in public life had come to espouse America's destiny to control the Caribbean. The Spanish-American War had emphasized the need for an isthmian canal if the United States was to make the most effectual use of a two-ocean navy to meet military emergencies. Puerto Rico, strategically situated at one of the main approaches to the Caribbean, thus became a vital territorial acquisition in carrying out American aggressive political and economic policies in the Western Hemisphere. For better than a year after the Treaty of Paris, the island was occupied by the U.S. Army, until Congress got around to enacting civil government there. The Foraker Act did that on 12 April 1900.

Early that month, in the closing days of Senate debate on the measure, the city of Philadelphia hosted a visit by Admiral George Dewey, the sixty-two-year-old "hero of Manila." The admiral and his bride of a few months came to Philadelphia on Friday, 6 April, to attend the Soldiers' and Sailors' Concert at the Academy of Music. Secretary of War Elihu Root and his wife had planned to accompany the Deweys to the afternoon musical matinee but arrived from Washington too late. In the evening the Deweys and the Roots attended a dinner party in the admiral's honor at the mansion home, on Rittenhouse Square, of Alexander J. Johnston, president of the Pennsylvania Railroad.

Among a select group of guests was Provost Charles Harrison, representing the University of Pennsylvania. During the social affair, he and Secretary Root took to chatting about the pending Foraker Bill and the educational problems a civil government would face in Puerto Rico. Just recently, the *New York Times* had carried an article that charged: "School work has made less advance in Puerto Rico than has any other movement for the betterment of the general condition." In the course of their conversation, according to the *Juniata Echo*, Root casually asked Harrison if he could recommend a proven educator who had a "strong personality" and was an "efficient organizer," someone he could send to that island to put in place an American system of public schools. The provost replied that the person who immediately came to mind was Penn's professor of pedagogy. With that, the two dignitaries went on to talk about other things. A week later the Foraker Bill became law.

On 17 April Brumbaugh received the following typewritten note from Provost Harrison:

> Dear Professor Brumbaugh,—
> I would like to see you as soon as conveniently may be, [*sic*] upon the question of the "Commissioner of Education" to Puerto Rico.
> Please consider this note, for the time being, as personal.
> Very truly yours,
> s/ C. C. Harrison

The message was ambiguous, and Brumbaugh must have thought so, too. He seems to have responded promptly, but apparently wanted some things clarified before he went to see the provost. For example, was he supposed to come ready with a nomination? Or was he, the one who got the note, to give thought to the post of commissioner for himself? If so, would the commissioner be a member of the Executive Council and hence as much politician as educator? Would the appointment be a permanent one? Would accepting the job mean he would have to resign his Penn professorship? These are questions that can be inferred from a second communiqué out of the provost's office that came by mail two days later. It read:

> Dear Dr. Brumbaugh,—
> No, I had been thinking about you and Puerto Rico. The question is a serious one: Whether, if the appointment shall not already have been made, and it would come to you, it would not be your duty to be the Commissioner of Education for Puerto Rico and a member of the Executive Council.
> I do not say permanently, but perhaps for two years,—so that public education throughout Puerto Rico may be thoroughly well organized.
> Very truly yours,
> s/ Chas. C. Harrison

We do not know if Brumbaugh and the provost discussed the Puerto Rico matter any further after the confidential note of the 19th. All the circumstantial evidence, however, suggests he showed absolutely no interest in going to the Caribbean island, even for a short spell.

Nevertheless, Provost Harrison proceeded to put Brumbaugh's name before Root once again, this time in writing. On 25 April, Penn's chief academic officer received the following letter from the war secretary:

> My dear Doctor:
> I am in receipt of your letter of the 24th relative to Professor Brumbaugh. The matter will now necessarily rest until Governor Allen has had an opportunity to look about in Porto Rico and express an opinion to the President. I would be very glad of the fullest information possible regarding Prof. Brumbaugh's past work to send to Governor Allen.
> Very truly yours,
> s/ Elihu Root
> Secretary of War.

Then, on 22 May, Secretary Root wired Harrison saying: "Unless something has occurred since your last letter to change Professor Brumbaugh's willingness to act, or your opinion, the president will send in his nomination as commissioner of education for Porto Rico."* Apparently, by this time Brumbaugh was less adamant about not going to the Caribbean. On the day of the Root-Harrison telegram, he accepted an invitation to talk with the secretary of war and the president the next afternoon in Washington.

Immediately, he wired his cousin Gaius, a District of Columbia physician and son of Dr. A. B., to meet him in Union Station. The two men, only a few days apart in age, had been very close as boys. Years later, Gaius remembered that his Quaker City relative got off the train hot and perspiring. He was in obvious mental agony. "What should I do?" he burst out upon greeting his cousin. Gaius advised him to do as he thought wise after talking with the president. Martin went first to Root's office, in what is today the Old Executive Building, while Gaius waited in Lafayette Square, across from the White House.

Brumbaugh and the secretary of war conversed at some length that afternoon. But Root could not coax the professor into uttering an on-the-spot outright yes. According to the *Huntingdon Globe*, Brumbaugh resisted on grounds of health, Puerto Rico's climate, and academic and writing commitments. Finally, Root said, "Let's go over and see the President." They made the half-block or so walk to the White House and were promptly received in the chief executive's office.†

McKinley put the question to Brumbaugh, "Would you enlist to help your country if it was necessary?" "Of course," the educator replied. "Then this is just

---

*"Porto Rico" was the official spelling then used by the American government, as it was by Martin Brumbaugh.

†Teddy Roosevelt, who dubbed the presidential mansion "The White House," added the west wing in 1902. William Taft created the Oval Office in 1909.

as much a public duty," said the president. "I [am not asking] you to carry a gun to Porto Rico, but I am asking you to carry a school book to the children of Porto Rico." Then the president went on to stress two things, Brumbaugh later recalled. He wanted "to put the conscience of the American people into the islands of the sea"; and he did not intend to send any one to Puerto Rico who wanted to go. It was an appeal—a kind of missionary call—that made the Dunker educator waver in his opposition to the appointment.

He left the White House, however, having begged off giving a final answer. Outside, he walked across Pennsylvania Avenue and joined Gaius in the park, where they sat on a bench and talked for a long time about what was best—and right—for him to do. Forty-eight hours later, at 2:00 P.M., on Friday, 25 May, Brumbaugh's wired acceptance was in President McKinley's hands.

But now he needed to be cleared, at McKinley's instruction, by Mark Hanna, national Republican party boss, senator from Ohio, and the president's most intimate adviser. So the nominee went to Thomasville, Georgia, where Hanna had a vacation home, and passed the final screening test. His nomination as Puerto Rico's first commissioner of education was sent to a Republican-controlled Senate on Monday, 4 June. Congress by then had adjourned for the summer, so confirmation was delayed until Wednesday, 5 December, months after he had gone to the island.

In a letter to Abraham Cassel about library concerns, written in July when his imminent departure for Puerto Rico was much on his mind, Brumbaugh interjected the comment: "I did decline twice to go to Puerto Rico. I finally was led to say yes from a sense of duty. I seemed to be the man the government wanted." But in an October article in the *Juniata Echo,* he wrote much more introspectively about why he acquiesced in accepting the Caribbean assignment. He explained, intimating that McKinley acted as an agent of God, that

> It was a call from a patriotic President to do a patriotic service, the only service I could not conscientiously decline. Some men enlist in the service of their country to wage war against a national enemy. I was engaged to carry American Educational Ideals to the people living in the tropics, in an island I had never dreamed of seeing, and in a climate that my study all too clearly warned me to avoid. But Shakespeare says, "There's a divinity that shapes our ends." It seemed to me such was the case now. God, not man, had put this work upon me, and leaving home, church, friends, professional prospects that were promising, and the work of education in the church I love, I was carried steadily and surely southward.

At another time, he told his *Echo* followers that when "God sends the message it is the duty to go . . . [to] provide human freedom, proper education, religious freedom, and equal rights to all [his] subjects."

Upon Brumbaugh's appointment the University of Pennsylvania gave him a two-year, unpaid leave of absence, effective 1 September. His salary as a federal official in Puerto Rico was set at three thousand dollars, a considerable sacrifice of income. While he was gone, his classes in pedagogy were taught by his friend Nathan Schaeffer, the state superintendent of instruction.

By the time Brumbaugh telegraphed his affirmative answer to the president, the transition from military to civil control in Puerto Rico had already taken place on 1 May, so there was some pressure on him to leave for the island as soon as possible. The next month was a hectic one for him. For one thing, speaking engagements had to be canceled. A big disappointment for him was the need to give up his place on the general committee to represent the International Association for the Advancement of Science, Arts, and Education at the Paris Exposition of 1900. Then, too, the J. B. Lippincott Company of Philadelphia had recently engaged him to edit a new multivolume pedagogical series (it would eventually include nine works over the next several years). Two manuscripts had just come in, and he was sedulously trying to get them ready to go to press.

And there was his family to think of. He and Anna talked it over and decided that she and the children would not go with him at first. They would join him later, in October, when the weather in Puerto Rico was not so steamy hot. That settled only some of the family worries. A decision also had to be made about Flora Belle Parks, who, now twenty-five, had been a part of the Brumbaugh household for six years. Her services would not really be needed in Puerto Rico because Anna, as the wife of a high-ranking government official, would have no trouble hiring an islander as housemaid.

One of Flora Belle's Philadelphia girlfriends was Juniata alumna Fannie Shellenberger. From 1896 until her marriage in 1902 Fannie was the private tutor to the daughter of Thomas Hunter, the founder and president of the Acme Tea Company (later Acme Super Markets). Fannie frequently visited the Brumbaugh home at this time when everybody was mulling over—and openly talking about—Flora Belle's familial fate. It was finally decided, Fannie later recalled, that Flora Belle was more than a household servant; she should be designated "Mrs. Brumbaugh's companion" and accompany the family to Puerto Rico.

Fannie Shellenberger, a great admirer of Martin Brumbaugh, used to tell an interesting story about something that happened to him a couple of years before his Puerto Rico assignment. She was an active member of Philadelphia's First Church of the Brethren—which her paragon also attended—during her years as a tutor. So it very much annoyed her when "some little squirt" had Brumbaugh "counciled" by the congregation for belonging to the Masonic Lodge. The Brethren, in those days, were forbidden to join secret societies, although that did not stop a lot of young Dunkers from doing so. Brumbaugh was one of them, and while county superintendent of schools joined the Mount Moriah Lodge, No. 300, at Huntingdon. But a lodge dimit shows he resigned on 11 July 1892. Why, then, the issue came up several years later is something of a mystery. According to Fannie, Brumbaugh's defense at the congregational hearing was that he had not attended any Masonic meetings for a long time and had no intentions of renewing activities. So the charge was dropped.*

Now, in the summer of 1900, the ex-Mason's mind was on Puerto Rico, not on church discipline. With Anna, Flora Belle, and the children left behind for the time being, he sailed for Puerto Rico on 28 July. He took passage on the U.S. Army transport *Sedgwick* out of New York Harbor, his commission tucked away in his trunk. Early on the morning of 4 August, after a voyage of 1380 miles, he heard a sailor on the bridge suddenly cry, "Land on the bow!" From the ship's deck the curious passenger could make out mountain crests against the distant horizon, then soon the outlines of an island, and finally the gleaming white wall of San Juan.

As the *Sedgwick* navigated into the protected harbor, he saw—off to his left at the end of a sloping, rocky promontory—gray-green El Morro, a formidable-looking fortress towering 140 feet above the sea. Its walls, eighteen feet thick, bore the scars of Admiral William T. Sampson's passing bombardment two years before. On its ramparts stood a lighthouse, damaged by the American gunnery fire. Minutes later the transport dropped anchor, and Martin's gaze now focused on Casa Blanca (the "White House"), built by Ponce de León in the early 1500s as palace and castle. It stood atop an ancient wall a hundred feet above the bay. Then, looking toward the west, he could see an unbroken row of tall coconut palms, shooting up like plumes on the rock-ribbed sea wall, lining the shore. At noon he was ferried to the wharf.

Such was the thirty-eight-year-old professor's first glimpse of the "Pearl of the Antilles," Puerto Rico's fin de siècle nickname (today it is "Island of Enchantment"). The island, easternmost and smallest of the Greater Antilles (Cuba, Jamaica, Haiti, Dominican Republic, Puerto Rico), was discovered by Columbus in 1493. Well within the tropics, it remained under Spanish control for four centuries. Two months after Sampson shelled San Juan's fortifications, General Nelson A. Miles landed in the Bay of Guanica, on the southern coast, with twelve thousand American troops and met with minimal resistance. Peace put an end to his nineteen-day campaign, which occasioned only five or six small but sharp engagements.

---

*It is rather odd that Brumbaugh should be councilled by the Philadelphia Brethren. Although he attended First Church at this time, he did not transfer his certificate of baptism from Huntingdon until 5 May 1912. Counciling was ordinarily carried out by a member's home congregation.

Brumbaugh may have been an inactive Mason, but he always had good things to say about Masonry. In 1912 he addressed Franklin Lodge, No. 134, on its centennial celebration. He spoke of Masonry's "true teachings" that enable the "Brethren" of Franklin Lodge to serve both "society" and "God." On that occasion, he was introduced by the "Worshipful Master," who made an interesting comment: "Franklin Lodge is fortunate today in that it witnesses what I trust will be the resumption of Masonic activities by a man who, in or out of the Lodge, is first and last a Mason, Brother MARTIN G. BRUMBAUGH."

In shape, Puerto Rico is roughly a parallelogram, with a gently rounded-off southeastern corner. In size (35 by 100 miles), it is half as large as New Jersey. It has a coastline of about 350 miles that, unlike Cuba, is almost totally free of fringing reefs. But Puerto Rico, which ironically means "rich port," lacks good harbors. San Juan, landlocked and perfectly sheltered, is by all odds the best, Ponce and Guanica, both on the southern coast, being the only others with adequate depth. San Juan Bay has one serious disadvantage, however: its narrow channel.

A lover of nature, Brumbaugh found the diverse topography of Puerto Rico fascinating; the island was varied in scenery and luxuriant in vegetation. He saw vast primeval rain forests, of which only a few thousand acres remain today. Mountains cover about 70 percent of the island, which is bisected lengthwise by a rugged midland range. Called the Cordillera Central, it climbs at its highest peak, El Yunque (the "Anvil"), to an altitude of 4,389 feet. The mountainous terrain rolls seaward to the north and to the south in heavy undulations, which gradually straighten out to level coastal plains with rich alluvial soil. The southern descent, sharply cloven, is steeper than the gentler slopes to the north. From the central watershed flow hundreds of streams, which become torrents after heavy rains. There are twelve hundred rivers, the principal ones on the northern side of the divide, but none navigable for any great distance.

In 1900 agriculture was practically the only occupation of the people of Puerto Rico, but a mere two percent of the population owned more than two-thirds of the farmland. Hat-making and lace work, however, were significant hand industries. There was also some manufacturing incident to marketing the staple crops: distilling rum, milling sugar cane, and cigar rolling. The three leading exports when the new education commissioner came to the island were coffee, sugar, and tobacco. Coffee-growing, which was concentrated on the shaded mountainsides, usurped nearly half the cultivated acreage. Sugar planters had located their farms along the fertile coastal fringe, particularly in the eastern and southeastern regions of the island. The well-watered inland valleys produced tobacco, a plant indigenous to Puerto Rico. In Brumbaugh's day the plant was called "the poor man's crop." Islanders also planted cotton, but not for exportation, although it had once been an important agricultural export. Tropical fruits—oranges, limes, bananas, figs, coconuts—grew wild and in profusion, but these, too, were a neglected resource.

Puerto Rico, like most Caribbean islands, is subject to periodic hurricanes. On 8 August 1899, one year before Brumbaugh arrived, the island had suffered a frightful toll of life and property as the result of a world-famous storm: Hurricane San Ciriaco. Three thousand people died and a fourth of the island's inhabitants were left homeless and without food. The destruction of vital sugar and coffee crops and the enormous loss of cattle threatened economic disaster. The island, deeper than ever in poverty, was still reeling from San Ciriaco's damage when the Foraker Act ended military control.

It was Puerto Rico's tropical climate, not worry about hurricanes, that prompted frequent meteorological comment from Brumbaugh. He once said, bemoaning the "excessive" humidity: "The Spanish word for tomorrow is *mañana,* and *mañana* is the first word an Anglo-Saxon learns to speak. It tells in a word the [climate's] effect upon conduct." But the temperature, he admitted, was moderate enough—at San Juan ranging between seventy-eight degrees and eighty-two degrees the year round. The coolest months he found to be December, January, and February.

Brumbaugh complained that "rain falls almost every day." In some parts of the island this is true, especially the northeast corner—which averages one hundred inches of annual precipitation. Here the most extensive forest area is located. In San Juan, the yearly rainfall averages sixty inches, about a third more than Brumbaugh's home area in Pennsylvania gets. The island's southern slopes, however, are deficient in moisture and in some areas irrigation is necessary to grow crops. The rainiest months are from April to November, when heavy downpours occur between noon and evening. A glorious sunset and a clear, cool night almost always follow.

In Puerto Rico, even more so than in Louisiana, Brumbaugh had the chance to observe a society of intermingled races. When the fortune-hunting Spaniards descended on Puerto Rico, they were greeted by Taíno (also called Arawak) Indians, whose name for their island was Borínquen. These aborigines were soon all but wiped out; practically all of the males were either murdered, worked to death, or sent to their graves by European diseases. Women, however, were spared to be concubines, from which sprang a large class of mestizos (over 300,000 by 1900).

Beginning in the 1500s, slaves were imported from Africa to work the growing sugar and tobacco plantations. Not as many Africans ended up in Puerto Rico, because of its topography, as on other Caribbean islands. Also, very few black females were ever part of the Puerto Rican slave trade, which is why Spanish settlers took Indian women to populate the country. By the time of the Spanish-American War, Spain had abolished human bondage in all of its Caribbean colonies. The census of 1899, compiled by the U.S. Army, listed 75,000 "negroes" and 250,000 mulattoes on the island. As Brumbaugh learned, although Puerto Rico had no detectable racial problems, mestizos stood higher on the social scale than did blacks.

Whites, rich and poor, represented 61 percent of Puerto Rico's population (about 950,000) in 1900. This was a larger percentage of white people, nearly all of whom were of Spanish origin, than on any other island in the West Indies. From the 1820s on, many Spaniards, because of revolutions in Santo Domingo and other Latin American colonies, emigrated to Puerto Rico. They brought with them capital, some industry, and expertise in sugar and coffee agriculture. The rich landlords, merchants, and professional men dominated the island's political life and economy. Many among this aristocratic clique had a good education, but it was they who opposed the American government after the war.

There was virtually no middle class. The great majority of noncolored people were living in utter poverty when they became United States subjects. Called peons in that part of the world, they did the bulk of the labor on the coffee, sugar, and tobacco estates. Brumbaugh said, "The man with the hoe and machete [was] supreme." When the peon worked—unemployment was as high as 50 percent—he was paid thirty cents a day. Peons lived in crude, thatch-roofed shacks, built of poles and palm fronds. No nails were used in building them; the poles were tied together with vegetable fiber.

Historically, the Roman Catholic Church had been a primary cultural agent in molding Puerto Rico's ethnic mix into a Spanish civilization. In the four centuries prior to 1898, Catholicism, as the established religion, shared with the crown the revenue of the insular treasury. To pre-Treaty of Paris Puerto Ricans, the scepter and the crosier were accepted as dual symbols of sovereignty. State aid to religion ended, of course, after Yankee troops invaded the island. When Martin Brumbaugh landed in Puerto Rico there were fewer than four thousand native Protestants, who were ministered to by missionaries from eight different denominations.

Catholic-nurtured islanders were far better off in the care of their souls than they were in the state of their physical well-being. Indifference to public health problems and the harmful environment shocked the island's conquerors. They saw misery and suffering and sickness and disease on every hand in the towns and countryside alike. They discovered that tuberculosis, dysentery, smallpox, malaria, and venereal disease prevailed throughout the island. (Yellow fever, an import to Puerto Rico, proved no health hazard the way it did in Cuba. Not a single case was reported in the years 1899 and 1900.) Of Puerto Rico's sixty-six towns, only nineteen had a hospital, the capacity of beds totaling about five hundred for the whole island. Only three of the hospitals—at San Juan, Ponce, and Arecibo—measured up to American standards.

San Juan itself was not exempt from all sorts of afflictions, Brumbaugh wrote from the capital. He told how its narrow, cobblestone streets swarmed with infirm, crippled humanity. Reduced to beggary, they would come up to him and ask, with outstretched hand, for "uno centavo American"—one cent. He came upon thousands of men and women with feet swollen to grotesque size, the victims of elephantiasis, a common affliction of poor peons. Large colonies of lepers congregated outside the city wall, ghetto-dwellers under constant vigil. Children, naked and filthy and anemic (because of hookworm), roamed the streets, a sight that touched deeply the Pennsylvania schoolman. Much less of a cultural jolt to him was the island's universal lack of modern conveniences. Hardly a stranger to the lack of modern facilities in rural life, he found out that everywhere—city, town, village, farm—people stoically put up with primitive conditions: no waterworks, no garbage collection, no sewerage.

Dr. Azel Ames, an army surgeon during the occupation who would later become a frequent Brumbaugh correspondent, swore that Puerto Rico was the filthiest place he knew of. More than three-fourths of the dwellings in Puerto Rico had no means of disposing of human excrement, not even outhouses; rural inhabitants, as in Spain, resorted to fields to answer the call of nature. For potable water, towns-people, including San Juaneros, depended on cisterns, wells, and aqueducts, while country folk drank from polluted streams and rivers. Such a way of life took its toll—the life expectancy in Puerto Rico was 33½ years, compared to 50 in the United States.

In all, Brumbaugh wrote seven articles on Puerto Rico for the *Juniata Echo*, keeping the campus posted on what he was doing and what he was seeing. He often described the hardships of the people, but never, except for the rain and the heat, complained about the unwholesome environment. In fact, he thought San Juan, where he lived and worked, a charming place. He liked to say, historical buff that he was, how, since the war, it had become the oldest city under the American flag. With a population of some twenty-five thousand, it was also Puerto Rico's largest city (and still is, but having grown by nearly twenty times). For Brumbaugh San Juan had the pace and intimacy of a small town.

He spoke of the island's capital as a typical-looking Spanish-American city. Most residences, he wrote, were two-storied, their flat roofs covered with rich red tile. According to him, "negroes" as a rule lived on the lower level. The wood, stone, and stucco houses and public buildings were tinted bright colors—blue, yellow, green, pink, and other shades common to hot countries. Overhanging iron balconies, with wrought-iron railings and broad columned porches everywhere graced the bright-hued dwellings. Brumbaugh would have seen no chimneys or glazed windows; all openings were shuttered or jalousied.

Of all public buildings of historical interest, perhaps he marveled most at fabulous San Juan Cathedral, a rare sixteenth-century New World example of me-dieval architecture. The beauty of the beige-and-white church, bathed in afternoon sunlight, must have daily been an inspiring sight from his nearby office.

San Juaneros—at least a few of them—did enjoy the modern convenience of electricity. The capital also had telephone and telegraph service. Two ice plants operated year-round, making it possible to refrigerate food. The cobblestone streets were daily swept by inmates from La Princea Prison (now defunct), attired in white duck uniforms and guarded like an American chain gang.

San Juan is an islet, built as a military stronghold when Puerto Rico quickly became Spain's most important military outpost in the Caribbean. For his first several months, Brumbaugh took lodging in what is now Old San Juan, the forti-fied end of the islet. Today this is a residential and commercial district of seven square blocks. His address was 2 Allen Street, adjacent to chalk-white La Fortaleza, the governor's historic mansion. (It serves to this day as the governor's residence, the oldest in the Western Hemisphere.) Later, after his family joined him, he moved to Santurce, a neighborhood on the main island a short distance away. At that time this area was on the verge of becoming a fashionable suburb, but today it is consid-ered the heart of modern San Juan. From Santurce Brumbaugh had a fifteen-minute ride to work on a rickety, narrow-gauge train from Latimer Station, just across a flower-studded lawn from his one-story brick home. (Latimer Station also served as his address.) But before he left the island a trolley line had supplanted the steam-engine rails.

On May Day 1900, a Tuesday, the residents of Puerto Rico's picturesque capital, a mix of splendor and squalor, witnessed a colorful event: the transition from military to civil control. The ceremony began at nine o'clock on a beautiful, cloudless morning. The military commander, Brigadier General George W. Davis, reviewed from the balcony of the city hall a grand parade of soldiers and sailors marching and countermarching around the capital's principal plaza.* An hour later the inaugural formalities for the civil governor, Charles H. Allen, a Massachusetts banker and assistant secretary of the Navy at the time of his appointment, took place on the flag-bedecked temporary platform in front of the governor's mansion. A crowd of about five thousand persons witnessed the ceremonies and heard the inaugural address. The *New York Times* expressed disappointment that the turnout had not been larger—the reporter thought it should have been more like thirty thousand—since the occasion had been made an islandwide holiday. Martin Brumbaugh, of course, was not in San Juan that day; he was still in Philadelphia, convinced he did not want to go to Puerto Rico.

He also missed the first session of the Executive Council on 28 June—which was dragged out because half of the councilmen did not understand English, and so everything said had to be interpreted. By terms of the Foraker Act, the council—made up of eleven members (six Americans and five Puerto Ricans)—served as the upper house of the legislature. All of them were appointed by the president of the United States with senatorial consent. A lower house of thirty-five legislators, the act further provided, was to be elected by popular vote. The judicial branch rested in sixty-seven justices of the peace, five district courts (three judges for each court), and a supreme court (five judges). The governor appointed the five lower-court benches, the president those of the highest bench.

The six Americans on the Executive Council also constituted the governor's cabinet. Each cabinet member—the secretary of state, treasurer, auditor, attorney general, commissioner of the interior, and commissioner of education—headed up an executive department. Section 25 of the Foraker Act stipulated that the education commissioner

> shall superintend public instruction throughout Porto Rico, and all disbursements on account thereof must be approved by him; and he shall perform such duties as may be prescribed by law, and make reports through the governor as may be required by the Commissioner of Education of the United States, which shall annually be transmitted to Congress.

---

*General Davis became military governor in May 1899, the third to be given that command.

Brumbaugh knew this charge laid no easy mission upon him. As Governor Allen had forewarned, he had taken on a "herculean labor." Later, in praise of the educator's work, Allen said that other members of the Executive Council had duties more varied and wider-ranging, but none had a "more difficult task" than he.

Spain had largely ignored popular schooling in its New World colonies. When the U.S. Army occupied Puerto Rico there were about five hundred schools in existence, but not a single structure had been built as a school per se. In many cases, pupils met in the homes of teachers or the teachers held classes outdoors under the palm trees. On any given day they might, or might not, conduct their individual schools. Military officials found that no more than 8 percent of school-age children on the island had ever spent time inside a classroom of any kind. Teachers had little or no formal training, and most were political appointees, grossly unfit for their positions. The vast majority of them were men, unmarried and very poor; their salaries were often years in default. Teachers could charge tuition and did, thus denying children of poor parents a chance to be educated. But what education they would have gotten was hardly worthy of the name; it consisted mostly of memorizing. It also included a heavy dose of religion and church doctrine. The island had no public secondary schools or colleges. Its four private post-elementary schools, all fourth-rate, were closed at war's end.

Thus the United States had taken over an island whose school system was a mere pretense at teaching and learning. In a population of nearly one million, the military census of 1899 classed 88 percent of the people as illiterates. Only 5,045 persons admitted to more than an elementary education. Some of them, however, were well-educated men who had studied abroad, a practice of those who could afford it during the centuries of Spanish dominion.

American troops had hardly taken over the island when the army set to work modernizing public schooling there. Among other reforms, the military created a binational insular board of education, decreed free education for all children between the ages of six and eighteen (compulsory attendance, although on the books, was never enforced), promulgated a codified school law, built a "model and training school" in San Juan, and located a site for a normal school at Fajardo, on the east coast.

By 1900 the army had mustered a motley teaching force of about eight hundred, a tenth of them Americans and the rest islanders. Military law required each town or city having a graded school to employ a teacher whose mother tongue was English. The first crop of English teachers, mostly young men, included "ex-soldiers, ex-teamsters, ex-packers" and other such poorly schooled riffraff, Brumbaugh once grumbled in disgust at army standards. "None of them knew Spanish," he said, "and some of them knew little English." He ridiculed their limited vocabulary as a hash of "slang and vulgarity." According to him, the quality of language and teaching dramatically improved when women started coming in greater numbers.

Imposing so abruptly an American educational system upon a people of Puerto Rico's cultural past naturally gave rise to frustrating problems. One of the very earliest was the language barrier. Teachers from the two countries had a hard time communicating with one another; it was even worse between Americans and their islander pupils. Moreover, the handful of bilingual Americans had learned Castilian Spanish in school, but many Puerto Ricans, especially in rural areas, spoke a patois. The discord over making Castilian Spanish the official classroom usage was never happily resolved—certainly not when Martin Brumbaugh was in charge—and resentments lingered long. Also, the military mandated English in the curriculum, yet at first had no teaching materials in translation. This predicament, of course, eventually passed; however, hastily translated textbooks often fell far short of the linguistic or pedagogical needs of an alien people.

The biggest problem for the military regime—as it would be for Martin Brumbaugh—came down to the bottom line: a thin public purse. The United States fully expected Puerto Rico to pay its own bills with no help from Washington. But the extreme poverty of the island drastically limited all expenditures for its own societal welfare. During the last year of military control the education budget barely added up to $299,000. The money for schools came from general revenues, although just before Brumbaugh came to the island a special school tax had been levied on certain professional groups.

Occupation forces, therefore, had made serious efforts to Americanize public education by the time a civil regime made its advent. Martin Brumbaugh appreciated much that the army had done, but he believed its board of education had made some flawed administrative and pedagogical decisions. The *Philadelphia Ledger* and the *Pennsylvania School Journal*, however, declared him the one man admirably qualified to set things right. The *Ledger* professed that "the choice of the President is approved everywhere in Pennsylvania." It editorialized, "After our sad experience in Cuba, it is encouraging to know that Porto Rico will have such men as . . . Brumbaugh in public service." The July 1900 issue of the *Pennsylvania School Journal* excerpted the *Ledger* column and endorsed it, noting that "Dr. Brumbaugh's work in pedagogy at the University has attracted widespread interest from the leading universities of the country."

Brumbaugh thought, at first, it would take four years to do what needed to be done, even on a foundational basis, to modernize public schooling in the nation's new Caribbean territory.* Amazingly, he would do the job in much less than two years' time. Even today, a hundred years later, Puerto Rican educators speak beholdingly of what he did for their people in so brief a tenure. In 1972, at a ceremony in which oil paintings of all Puerto Rico's past commissioners and secretaries of education were unveiled, Brumbaugh's work was described as a "feat," "a surprising labor whose influence transcended [his] administration."

---

*His commission from the government was technically for four years, although, as noted earlier, he had only a two-year leave from Penn.

Brumbaugh may have gone reluctantly to perform his island "feat," but he did so with a clear conscience. He refused to look upon his country's colonialism—whether in the Caribbean or the Pacific—as an imperialistic venture. A Dunker pacifist, he could easily have taken up with the Anti-Imperialist League, as many of his fellow academicians and intellectuals did. But he refused to espouse the league's diatribes against American expansionism. He sincerely thought the president was unassailably high-minded in seeking to bestow an Anglo-Saxon civilization—republican institutions and the English language—upon the Latin races inhabiting America's insular colonies. McKinley had told him that day in May he and Secretary Root had gone to the White House: "I desire to make appointments to Porto Rico I can sleep on"—that is, the kind of men, all college-bred, who could honorably build the American way into the life and laws of that Caribbean island. That sentiment, in Brumbaugh's eyes, was the measure of McKinley as a person.

Nothing he experienced once he got to the island changed his mind about the rightness of his country's governing presence there, or about the president behind it. In 1902, not long after resigning as commissioner, he told the graduating class at the Carlisle Indian Industrial School:

> This country has set the pace for the whole civilized world. It has become in a most peculiar sense a vigorous and promising world power. Porto Rico is but a type of our ability as a nation to do great service. Two years ago seven men were sent to Porto Rico and within that short time they have organized one of the most successful governments in history. . . .

That is why, he added, "Its people speak of the . . . President as the founder of human liberty in the Island." The *Carlisle Daily Herald* quoted him as saying, "Our watchword has been 'We will never make a promise to the people of Porto Rico that we cannot or shall not fulfill.'"

The United States had been so honorable in its colonial policies, according to the Martin Brumbaugh scenario, that Puerto Rico's grateful masses had accepted subject status with nothing but genuine trust and high hope ever since the day the Stars and Stripes became their flag. "The people of the island not only did not oppose, but they joyously welcomed American occupation" was the categorical way he put it for the *Pennsylvania School Journal* not long after the Carlisle speech. Even the few elite, he said, were "swept off [their] feet by the celerity of our action." Another time, in his editor's preface to a 1903 book on Puerto Rico, he declared: "Under wise and conservative guidance by the American executive officers, the people of Puerto Rico have turned to this Republic with a patriotism, a zeal, an enthusiasm that is, perhaps, without a parallel."

Such patronizing rhetoric had the ring of a chauvinist, which, in a certain sense, Brumbaugh arguably was; no one in the early civil government did more flag waving or extolling of American virtues than he did. But as a pacifist, he never—at that time, at least—subscribed in any jingoistic way to a "my country, right or wrong" brand of overpatriotism. What his public comments clearly betrayed was his ardent espousal of a popular colonial doctrine of that day: the White Man's Burden. This, as geopolitics of the times evinced, was only a euphemism for imperialism, albeit an altruistic imperialism driven by a deep Anglo-Saxon sense of "duty to God."

Brumbaugh's rosy picture of the Puerto Rican scene the first few years after peace was only partially accurate. An important fact to keep in mind is that the island was well on its way toward self-government by 1898. A strong home-rule movement had developed there decades before the Spanish-American War. Liberals, although splintered into several political camps, generally agreed on some form of autonomy or semiautonomy under union with Madrid. Finally, in 1897, Spain, war-weary from the Cuban imbroglio, declared Puerto Rico an autonomous state. A popularly elected bicameral government (except for the governor) assumed power on 20 July 1898. Ironically, only days later the island's home-rule experiment died aborning at the hands of the U.S. Army.

The liberals and their newspapers registered no protests about the timeliness of the socioeconomic reforms the new rulers promptly introduced. But they did chafe at the paternalistic, exaggerated missionary mentality behind the changes. It also made them exceedingly unhappy that their *Yanqui* conquerors brusquely dismissed the idea of immediate home rule. The Foraker Act, as they saw it, derogated many of the political gains the people had won under Spanish dominion. Highly unpopular, the act gave rise to anti-American politicians who soon held a majority among elected solons. So it was not true that the Puerto Ricans submitted to the presence of Uncle Sam with quite the degree of cheerful goodwill Martin Brumbaugh said they did.

As for the kind of reception specifically given *educational* reform, however, his glowing appraisal of public opinion did not distort the facts. The American flag had been raised in the island only twelve days before the leading citizens of San Juan met and passed a series of resolutions apropos Puerto Rico's antiquated school system. Few scholars would disagree with what historian Vincenzo Petrullo wrote in his book, *Puerto Rican Paradox*. He said, balancing the good and bad sides of American turn-of-the-century colonialism, that the United States "brought to the island, at last, a broader opportunity for education in every way, something which the Puerto Rican leaders had wanted but had not been able to attain in the four hundred years the island had been a colony of Spain." Then he went on to say, in lofty Brumbaugh-like wording: "The people accepted public schooling enthusiastically . . . and threw themselves into the task with a will and a devotion which will always remain as a bright chapter in Puerto Rican history." The opening pages of that "bright chapter," it cannot denied, were brilliantly written by the first commissioner of education.

8

Commissioner of
Education

WHEN Martin Brumbaugh got off the boat at San Juan that Saturday noon in early August of 1900, he had no idea how vengeful the man he came to replace would turn out to be. That man was Dr. George G. Groff, the interim appointee, who himself had been an applicant for the post of education commissioner. The two men met briefly in Groff's office and introduced themselves the Saturday of Brumbaugh's arrival. Then on Monday, 6 August, Groff submitted a letter, in person, offering to stay on as assistant commissioner. But the proposal was declined on the spot. Embittered, the rejected fellow Pennsylvanian sailed for New York that very evening. The incoming commissioner had humiliated him, he later said, by not accepting his expert services. For a long time Groff would brood over the way his successor treated him. He became an obsessed man, driven to get revenge.

So the new commissioner began his work without even an informal briefing. On top of that, the irate Groff had left no record of his work since 1 May, the date of his interim appointment. He did leave a memorandum, however, that identified some things he thought should be done without "an unnecessary moment" of delay. But these were administrative tips and had little to do with the state of the island's public-school system. What is more, a fire on 1 July had destroyed the building in which the education bureau had its offices and stored its files and records.

Brumbaugh did not have much to go on, then, to get a quick picture of what must be done to make ready for the upcoming school year. He relied upon three sources: the War Department's 1899 census; a voluminous report detailing the military's public-school initiatives (prepared in mid-February 1900 by Victor S. Clark, then president of the insular board of education); and whatever information he was able to pick up from his employees, both in the office and out in the field. Thus in one sense the new commissioner was handicapped, but in another was left free to institute whatever course seemed best.

His daily posted office hours were 8:30 A.M. until noon and 2:00-5:00 P.M.— giving him the traditional two-hour midday break. But he likely ignored the siesta ritual and labored right on through the day. He said the early weeks were stressful for him, much more than his busy but self-paced life as a university professor. He felt frustrated, with neither the time to plan nor the resources to make needed changes.

Perhaps, in weary moments that autumn, he sometimes wished George Groff had not been passed over for commissioner. The good doctor could certainly boast the right credentials for the post, which he obviously very much coveted. A physician and scientist, he had enjoyed a distinguished academic career at Bucknell University in Lewisburg, Pennsylvania, prior to the Spanish-American War. He had begun teaching at that Baptist-related institution in 1879 as professor of organic sciences. There he soon became known as "the father of many . . . worthwhile things in the college," most notably of the biology department and of coeducation. The trustees named him acting president for the school year 1888–89. Groff's influence came to be widely known in Pennsylvania's medical community through his writings—mostly pamphlets, brochures, and health tracts. He served as head of the state board of health, and at the time of the calamitous Johnstown flood in 1889 supervised the sanitation work at that stricken city.

When America went to war with Spain, he enlisted as a major in the Medical Corps, eventually being ordered to Puerto Rico as a sanitation officer. Because of his academic experience, Dr. Groff was made a member of the army-created board of education for the island, later becoming its chairman. Then, in anticipation of the shift to civilian control, General Davis named him acting commissioner of education. As the incumbent, Groff had hoped this would give him the edge among other applicants for the position. President McKinley had told Brumbaugh he would refuse to send men to Puerto Rico who wanted to go there, and maybe that hurt Groff's candidacy. But the final say about insular cabinet members belonged to Governor Allen, who, in light of his choice, must have had some doubts of his own about the army officer.

Back in the states, scuttlebutt had it that things had not gone well under Groff's interim leadership. At least that was the word from Nathan Schaeffer. He wrote in July, while Brumbaugh, aboard the transport *Sedgwick,* steamed toward Puerto Rico:

> I hope to hear of your safe arrival at San Juan and that you will find Dr. Groff's work less bad than it is represented to be. Dr. Harris [United States commissioner of education] intimated at Charleston that Groff's work will all have to be undone. At least this is my inference from a remark he made.

Brumbaugh soon found the rumors to have some basis. According to a front-page article in a December 1900 issue of the *San Juan News,* he not only publicly criticized some of Groff's decisions and policies but also blamed him for squandering twenty thousand dollars of scanty school funds during his short interim appointment.

As far as Groff was concerned, however, his successor had walked into an ideal situation. "Military authorities passed over to the Civil Government [a ship] in complete sailing order," he said in a speech soon after he went back to Bucknell and college teaching. Moreover, he felt he had introduced some timely changes of his own in moving Puerto Rico toward wholesale educational reform. For one thing, he had planned a series of sixteen teachers' institutes for the whole island during the summer of 1900, before Brumbaugh's arrival. These institutes, given in Spanish, presented American methods and theory. About half the island's teachers were reached in this way and, in Groff's opinion, did much to reduce prejudice against Americanizing the public schools.

Not so ideal, however, were the commissioner's makeshift headquarters; as a result of the July fire, they were just three small rooms in an upper floor of the governor's mansion. But in September he was given more space (seven rooms) for his departmental complex—in the Intendencia Building on Plaza Alfonso XII, fronting San Juan's Military Square in the central part of Old San Juan. (The offices of the commissioner of interior, the treasurer, and the auditor were also located in this building.) The new location housed his staff of eighteen, a library, a museum, and the shipping department. Here were received all the books, charts, maps, slates, furniture, and other supplies for schools, and from here all shipments went out, by boat, train, and ox team, to all parts of the island.

Brumbaugh had two months in which to get organized for the upcoming school year. Sparing no efforts, he recruited teachers and rented, repaired, and equipped buildings. The military had, for 1899–1900, operated 616 schools; the new commissioner set a personal goal of eight hundred for the first year of the new century. Although he missed the mark in the number of school starts, everything else fell into place. *Echo* readers were told that on 1 October the school year began "with no jar, no discord, no confusion." He also wrote, "The greatest needs are money, new laws, better teachers, school-houses, and efficient local supervision." That sentence, as time would show, nicely defined his agenda as commissioner of education.

Finding "better teachers" stood at the top of the Brumbaugh list of reforms (along with "new laws," about which nothing could be done until the insular legislature convened in December). As he stressed in a truistic comment soon after taking office: "The power of any school is its teacher. The power of the system is the combined skill and efficiency of its corps of teachers."

Unfortunately, there was not much "power" generated by the ranks of native teachers, either individually or corporately. The commissioner complained in his early reports that they knew absolutely nothing about American ideals or modern pedagogy and that the mass of them lacked "the spirit of professionalism." Thus little could be done, at one jump, to upgrade their classroom fitness. Until Puerto Rico had its own normal school, he was forced to mark time, weeding out the superannuated and useless teachers as soon as possible through testing and periodic evaluations. In the interim, his department also provided systematic supervision and conducted Brumbaugh-type teachers' institutes at strategic locations on the island.

The commissioner faced less of a dilemma with another staffing problem that first fall: finding, in a hurry, English teachers for the additional graded schools he had slated to open. Like the army before him, he looked homeward and recruited twenty-six young people, all university, college, or normal-school graduates. Some of them knew Spanish. For most of them, it would be the first time in the classroom. Secretary of War Root obligingly gave the amateur teachers free passage on army transports. The first shipload of them waved "Miss Liberty" a good-bye and headed for blue water on 29 September. Eventually, about one hundred statesiders would brave mal de mer and put in a year or two as Brumbaugh minions. Thus Puerto Rico, like Louisiana a dozen years earlier, also experienced a "Brumbaugh Infusion." When the commissioner gave up island work, his office had nearly five hundred applications on file, postmarked from all states in the Union.

Among the first group to come were a couple of Juniatians: Irvin C. VanDyke and Horace O. Wells, both with fresh diplomas. VanDyke, then a bachelor, spent his entire island stint teaching at San Juan's high school. Wells, who came back to marry his sweetheart from eastern Pennsylvania (a non-Juniatian) in the summer of 1901, moved around a bit more. He started out as a field supervisor stationed at Aguadilla—a harbor town on the west coast—and in charge of sixty schools. The *Echo* reported that only twenty-six of his schools were in towns; the rest were rural, scattered over 250 square miles and reachable solely by bridle paths. His second year, Wells became principal of the high school at Ponce, where one of the teachers was his wife. VanDyke and Wells were the only two Juniata alumni Brumbaugh thought it prudent to hire. It was wrong to show undue favoritism to Juniatians, the *Echo* explained on his behalf, because "it places the Doctor in the wrong light in his administrative policy."

A former Juniata faculty member, Samuel Brumbaugh Heckman, also followed M. G. to Puerto Rico. The thirty-year-old Heckman, a distant relative from the Miami Valley of Ohio and then unmarried, went there as the commissioner's man Friday. Holding bachelor degrees from Earlham and Harvard, he had taught at Juniata from 1895 to 1897, resigning to begin graduate studies at Penn. But he made little progress after 1898 when he began teaching at nearby Cheltenham Military Academy—which is what he was doing when he teamed up with Brumbaugh. After his Puerto Rican duty, Heckman returned to Penn and taught at Temple University (1904–6) while completing an M.A. (1905) and a Ph.D. (1906).*

---

*Heckman's doctoral dissertation was entitled "The Religious Poetry of Alexander Mack, Jr." Mack's father is honored as the founder of the Church of the Brethren. Brumbaugh did not direct the dissertation, but he made his private library, which contained manuscripts of Mack's poetry, available to Heckman. He also made suggestions about how to title the study. It was published in 1912 by the Brethren Press.

In 1908 he began a thirty-one year academic career in psychology and education at the College of the City of New York.

The commissioner fully expected all the individuals who signed on with the "Infusion" to do their island tour out of a deep sense of mission, like his. Too often this did not happen, despite a screening process that involved both Heckman and himself. Still, he could report to United States Secretary of the Interior Ethan A. Hitchcock that

> A few admirable teachers . . . have come as a solemn and sacred sacrifice for the Americanizing of the people of Porto Rico. These are true patriots and are worthy the highest commendation. The teacher who braves a strange climate and a new environment for the good of those to be served is as much a patriot as he who in time of war carries the starry banner to victory.

Historians, American and Puerto Rican alike, have tended to hold the Brumbaugh people in good repute. For example, one scholar, Knowlton Mixer, describes them as having been exceptionally dedicated to their work. In his college-textbook history of Puerto Rico, he claims that they exemplified "a high ideal of service"— more so than Yankee white-collar toilers in other sectors of the civil government. The reason, according to Mixer: "the ability and high character of [education's] first Commissioner."

There was no deus ex machina like the "Brumbaugh Infusion," however, to intervene and dramatically solve the most desperate situation education's first commissioner faced: an island full of untrained native teachers and no college or normal school to prepare a new generation of replacements. But no ditherer, he had within weeks put into effect two projects, both calculated to produce results in a couple of years. One was a plan to send young Puerto Ricans to study in the United States. The other engaged him in scouting out a desirable site for a bona fide insular normal school and drumming up popular support for such an institution.

The study-in-the-States program actually had a twofold purpose: to train teachers but also, in his words, to open a way for "ambitious young men and women, poor but worthy, who yearn to taste of the higher life of culture and power." A career in teaching, therefore, was not necessarily a condition for final selection, a process Brumbaugh personally handled. He sent off letters to academic acquaintances at "leading schools, colleges, and universities" all over the East and Midwest. His list also included three of the most famous industrial schools in the country with a teacher-training curriculum: Booker T. Washington's Tuskegee Institute in Alabama; Virginia's Hampton Institute, founded by the recently deceased Civil War general, Samuel C. Armstrong; and the Carlisle Indian School in Pennsylvania, headed by Lieutenant-Colonel Richard H. Pratt. The various institutions were asked to admit on probation some of the island's brightest minds, all of whom would need grants-in-aid. The response was prompt and openhanded, bringing over thirty positive replies. All offered free tuition, some also threw in room and board.

By mid-October, the first in what would finally be a group of 174 were en route to the mainland. "Every vessel going north," reported the commissioner, "is now carrying some of these pupils." They traveled gratis, on army transports—a War Department service scheduled to end in mid-December, both for incoming American teachers and outgoing Puerto Rican students. Before long, a flood of applications—at least five hundred—deluged the Intendencia Building. Where exactly the lucky ones ended up enrolling for study on the mainland is hard to find out from available public sources. But Brumbaugh's successor reported in June 1902: "They are scattered throughout the smaller colleges and the best preparatory schools in the States." Circumstantial evidence suggests the industrial schools got most of them. In the early rush of applicants, for example, Lieutenant-Colonel Pratt's Carlisle School, cajoled by Brumbaugh, accepted forty-five students (many of them orphan girls), the limit of its dormitories. This generous act, said the commissioner, made Pratt's name "precious" in many Puerto Rican homes.

The commissioner had felt, all the while, that Puerto Rico ought to accept some responsibility of its own for footing the study-abroad costs. He was able to push his fellow legislators into doing this when they convened for their first, historic session in December. The legislature enacted a pair of scholarship programs. The first one doled out four hundred dollars a year to each of twenty-five young males, chosen by competitive examination, to go to the United States to prepare for college or professional school. The second law pertained to a different set of students: those with mechanical or other types of manual-arts talent. It awarded twenty selectees—divided evenly between the sexes—an annual scholarship of $250. But they had to attend one of the better-known industrial schools in the United States. The main body of artisan-minded scholarship winners, it was later reported, enrolled at Tuskegee. The industrial-school students were expected to return and, stated the law, "assist in the improvements of the conditions in Porto Rico." Altogether that first year, through one program or another, the education department sent 219 teenagers north—a "labor of love," Brumbaugh called it.

The commissioner, of course, made sure Juniata College was counted among the very first institutions to open their doors to Puerto Rican students. Two appeared on campus in early October, both enrolling in the three-year normal program. (Tragically, one of them would die of pneumonia in the middle of winter; his body was shipped back to Puerto Rico for burial. Eventually, a second Puerto Rican student died and was buried in Huntingdon.) Some of the others that followed took the business course or attended the academy. In all, Juniata hosted ten islanders—all males—before they stopped coming in 1911.* The most enrolled in any one year was eight in 1902, when the Caribbean octet banded into The Puerto Rico Club. Fellow Juniatians remembered them as quite the Beau Brummels, never without coed admirers.

---

*In the pre-World War I years and into the 1920s, Juniata enrolled a number of non-Puerto Rican Latins from Cuba and several Central American countries.

Brumbaugh's favorite story about one of these early Beau Brummels told of the student's first experience with snow. He found it fascinating and wanted his family to share his pleasure. So he packed a box full of this lovely whiteness, addressed it to his mother, and took it to the post office. By the time he had paid the postage to San Juan, a serious drip had developed. The Huntingdon postmaster, curious about the soggy parcel, asked what was inside it. Informed, he of course rejected it and, quietly amused, returned the postage money. The commissioner recounted this incident so often in his post-Puerto Rico years that it must not have been of apocryphal origin.

Making it possible for scores of young Puerto Ricans to benefit from free schooling in the United States proved enormously successful and popular, as did Brumbaugh's second emergency project: an insular normal school. In September 1899 the army's board of education had acquired the site for a proposed normal school at Fajardo, located on the tip of a miniature peninsula on Puerto Rico's northeast corner. At that time, Fajardo was a fishing village of thirty-five hundred residents (today it is a major sailing and boating center). The site had been donated by the local people, but nothing more was done except to fence the grounds and dig a well.

The commissioner visited the place about five weeks after he came to the island. With the miserable, nearly impassable roads, he found it all but impossible to travel overland. He knew at once it was not a "happy location." Anxious to get started, he nevertheless went ahead and opened a school on 1 October, in a rented house at Fajardo, with five instructors and less than twenty students. But he could see it had no future there, in such a remote area. Over the succeeding months he got the village fathers to agree with him, and they "patriotically" accepted the school's demise when the school year ended. Fajardo, Brumbaugh said, was a "blunder" that cost his project a whole year's lost time.

Meanwhile, he had found what he called an "ideal" new site on a hill seven miles from Old San Juan. It was located in Rio Piedras, a community of twenty-five hundred on the outskirts of Santurce, where he now lived.* A coastal rail line passed through Rio Piedras on its way to San Juan (the same line he rode to work on), and a couple of trans-island roads converged there. The commissioner felt strongly that the normal school should not be situated far from the Intendencia Building—so that he could keep close watch over its progress and its faculty. He ran into some snags buying the desired land—the owner lived in Spain—but he was able to make a deal for fifty acres. This was the only time while he was commissioner that his office had to pay for a school site; all the others were donated by the local people. He pitched in to help Charles G. Post, his school inspector turned part-time architect, and a Puerto Rican draftsman, Angel A. Bugella, plan and design a building scheduled to be ready by the end of 1901 or early 1902.

That summer what Brumbaugh called an "apology for a normal school" at

---

*Both Santurce and Rio Piedras have long since been annexed by San Juan.

Fajardo was replaced by a ten-week session in San Juan while construction work went on at Rio Piedras. The summer institute opened with 16 teachers and 836 normal pupils, a turnout that astonished the commissioner. Nearly 200 of those in attendance won teacher certification under stiff Brumbaugh standards. Then, in October, because the builders had just begun, the inchoate normal school moved to temporary quarters in Rio Piedras: the governor's summer place. Classes were held there until the next spring, when they were moved to a three-story, brick-and-stone T-shaped structure on the campus proper. About a hundred qualified students were admitted the first year.

Puerto Rico was now ready to begin the long, serious task of training its own teachers; for the time being, teachers-to-be would enroll in a two-year program, a third year to be added in the future. The new building, costing forty thousand dollars, was dedicated on 30 May 1902, a ceremony the now-departed commissioner regretfully missed. As he once said, getting the Insular Normal School was "weary waiting," and "at times [he] almost lost the courage of [his] convictions." In another year, under his successor, the normal school became the nucleus of the University of Puerto Rico. One of the busiest streets in Rio Piedras today, which begins at the university and runs through town, is named Calle Brumbaugh. (Near the docks in Old San Juan, there is another street, but much shorter, called "Brombaugh.")

Good schoolhouses, well built and well equipped, were as vital to Brumbaugh's reforms as competent teachers, although for a time he had to improvise. The army had never gotten around to building schoolhouses, relying instead on rented buildings or rooms. Some of these places were quite suitable, but most of them Brumbaugh wrote off as "miserable" locations for schoolhouses. For example, he early visited a graded school where he found one room, twelve feet by sixteen feet, crowded with fifty-four pupils. The children had to stand, because the room was too packed for any of them to sit on the floor. He discovered that it was not uncommon for rural schools to corral forty to sixty youngsters into shed-like structures invariably plagued by leaky roofs. When it rained, everybody got wet. So did books, which were soon ruined (the law called for them to be kept in boxes on the floor, but often the boxes were unlidded). In cities, schools were sometimes held in the lofts of old coffee warehouses, which were dark and unbearably hot. Most schools, rural or town, had no blackboard. Without new, American-type schoolhouses it would be impossible to accommodate the expected explosion in the schoolable population once all the public-school reforms were in place.

The money to put up new schools was simply not there; out of insular revenues only four hundred thousand dollars was now budgeted for education. And local school districts were all but bankrupt. So Brumbaugh fixed upon a bold move: he would go directly to the man who had talked him into coming to Puerto Rico—the president of the United States. Having, by mid-October, filed an updated report to the governor and having seen the 1900–1901 school year off to a reasonably good start, the commissioner sailed for home. He first spent several days in Philadelphia with his family, overseeing last-minute preparations for them to accompany him on a 10 November embarkation for Puerto Rico. Then it was on to Huntingdon for a short visit—to see his parents, attend to personal business, and look after some matters on the Juniata campus.

Early on Friday, 26 October, Brumbaugh took the train to Canton, Ohio. He had indeed succeeded in setting up a private huddle with McKinley, who was waiting out the last days of the 1900 presidential campaign at his pre-White House home. McKinley, renominated by the Republicans, and Democrat William Jennings Bryan, who lost to him in 1896, were at it again. Last time, the president had electioneered from his front porch, receiving selected delegations and making only prepared statements. Conventional wisdom in those times did not think it seemly for presidential contestants to take to the stump, although that did not keep Bryan from piling up thousands of miles on the campaign trail, both in 1896 and in 1900.

But McKinley, as before, again chose to sit sedately on his front porch. He would let the 6 November election turn on his first-term record: he had won a war, added vast oceanic possessions in the Pacific and Caribbean, and had pulled the nation out of the depths of depression to the heights of prosperity. The Republicans chanted their prize slogan, "McKinley and the Full Dinner Pail," in championing the administration's success; the Democrats still harped on "Free Silver," their 1896 battle cry, but declared imperialism the paramount political issue in this election.

McKinley had won in 1896 with just under 52 percent of the popular vote, far from a landslide margin. Political pollsters were unheard of before the 1940s, so the president had no statistical clues about the mood of the American people when Martin Brumbaugh knocked on his door. But nothing the caller ever said suggested McKinley seemed particularly preoccupied with his reelection odds while they chatted. The president had the reputation of being a patient listener, and apparently he was not out of character that day.

Brumbaugh put before him Puerto Rico's desperate need for schoolhouses, most urgently in remote, rural areas. He was quoted by the *New York Sun* as reporting after his return to Philadelphia: "The President is deeply interested in the progress of education in the island and never seemed to tire of hearing about the children, their characteristics, and capacity for learning." He asked many questions about the competence of native teachers and was "greatly pleased" to hear that English was taking hold in the classrooms. According to the *Juniata Echo*, the Canton host "agreed so fully" with what he heard that he promised, if returned to office, to find two hundred thousand dollars somewhere for school construction. No doubt Brumbaugh was sent away with one of McKinley's typically warm handshakes. But whether or not he departed with a red carnation sprouting from his buttonhole—the president's wonted treat for a male guest—history has never recorded.

McKinley, a few days after the two men conferred, once again defeated Bryan (but by a lesser margin of victory than in 1896), extending his White House tenancy.

Not many weeks later, after returning to Washington, the president kept his word on Puerto Rico.

Meanwhile, Puerto Rican voters themselves had gone to the polls in November of 1900 to elect the members of their first legislature under the American flag. Representatives to the new government convened on Monday, 3 December, in San Juan for opening ceremonies. At two o'clock in the afternoon the legislators, in solemn and dignified manner, marched in procession down the Calle de la Fortaleza to the executive mansion. They paid their respects to Governor Allen and then proceeded, led by the Executive Council, to the Disputación Building (the statehouse), four blocks away. The two legislative branches met in a preliminary joint session while the House of Delegates elected a speaker and organized into a law-making body. Then the council retired to its own chamber and did the same thing. The secretary of Puerto Rico, former Montana Supreme Court judge William H. Hunt, took over as president of the Council. Brumbaugh once described the forty-three-year-old Hunt, soon to be elevated to governor, to be "an able, brilliant, patriotic, kindly man."

Once the Council had assembled and committee assignments made, the commissioner of education stood up, was recognized, and said:

> Mr. President, the people of Porto Rico today take upon themselves one of the priceless possessions of the human spirit. They assume, for the first time, the right to legislate for themselves. They receive the blessings of human freedom. This is to them not the gift of a royal decree. It is the gift of a sovereign people to those whom they have solemnly covenanted to protect and to assist. The people of the United States give this inestimable blessing because they themselves possess it and are glad to accord it to the people of Puerto Rico.

He then went on to remind his fellow councilors how the United States had won its own liberty through "a noble struggle against a sovereign but mis-guided state." All during the long Revolutionary strife, he said, the "one commanding, overmastering, matchless soul" was George Washington. "May his name be as sacred here as it is at home!" Brumbaugh exhorted. "It was he, Sir," expounded the commissioner, "who never doubted the issue, and who in the darkest days, at Valley Forge, with God to guide, led the way to this auspicious hour."

Following these prefatory patriotics, Brumbaugh approached Secretary Hunt and presented him with a gavel made from the wood of the old house at Valley Forge used by General Washington as headquarters. The mallet, he said, came from a window sill, the handle from the floor "over which in pain and hunger and distress he stepped to the highest hours accorded a sovereign spirit." Upon handing the symbolic mallet to Hunt, Brumbaugh stated:

> I present this gavel to you, Mr. President, with the firm assurance that in your hand it will always typify American institutions and with the wish and prayer that it may never fall to suppress human rights, but rather, that it may always fall to confirm the

sovereign will of a righteous senate, legislating for the highest welfare of a people whose stars I hope soon to see sparkling in the blue of the flag we love—the grandest flag that flutters beneath an all-protecting eye.

Later, commenting on the reaction of his upper chamber colleagues, Brumbaugh, ever the historian, reported in the *Echo*, "The applause that followed this address was the first that ever rang through legislative halls in this island." Hunt accepted the gavel, made a fitting response, and Puerto Rico's first day of democratic government passed into history.

Brumbaugh held his Executive Council associates in the highest regard, especially those making up the cabinet. (All of the cabinet members, except one, were older than he was.) Once, in 1904, reflecting upon the quality of the men who organized Puerto Rico's civil government, he told a lecture audience:

> They were animated by the true missionary spirit—the spirit of helpfulness. To them as to you, the great concern was not the commercial advantage that might accrue to the United States, but the social education, and industrial uplift of a long-neglected people. And in this conception of their duty they were steadfastly sustained by the wise and sympathetic support of [a] great president. . . . His solicitude for the welfare of the people of the island was such that when appointments to vacancies in the Executive Council were necessary his one question was, "Do you know these candidates to be good men?"

The Executive Council operated through twelve standing committees. Members of that body served on more than one committee; most did duty on four. Brumbaugh's four were education; enrolled and engrossed bills; franchises, privileges and concessions; and public institutions and property. He presided over the first two of these committees, being only one of three councilors with a dual chairmanship. He often fussed about how much of his time was diverted from educational matters by his multiple-committee functions. Things got no better when he was elected president of the council in July 1901, after putting in a month on an interim basis. He took the place of William Hunt, who began to assume more and more responsibilities for the often-absentee Governor Allen. (Hunt became governor that fall when Allen resigned.*

As a lawmaker, the commissioner had one supreme goal in mind: guiding through the legislature a school code custom-made for Puerto Rico. The one he inherited was modeled on that of Massachusetts and "not fitted to . . . conditions" on the island, he reported to Governor Allen in October 1900. His advice: it should be "wholly abrogated" and replaced by a new law when the legislature began working in December. Already he and Heckman had started drafting a more realistic statute.

---

*Brumbaugh's initial salary of three thousand dollars was a thousand less than that of other cabinet members. This discrepancy seems to have troubled him. So in late December and early 1901, he wrote the president, Senator Foraker, Secretary of the Interior Hitchcock,

The code in place when he got to Puerto Rico was not a legislated law but a military directive. It was the product of Dr. John Eaton and his assistant, Victor S. Clark—both career educators—in the early months of 1899. The sixty-nine-year-old Eaton, a former Civil War general, had served as United States commissioner of education in the 1870s under President Ulysses Grant and was more recently a small-college president. He came to Puerto Rico in January 1899 at the request of Major General Guy V. Henry, the military governor, to take charge of the whole educational system. Ill health, however, forced him to leave in late May.

Victor Clark, a confirmed bachelor finishing up a Ph.D. at Columbia who had joined Eaton in February 1900, moved up to top educator. In July the twenty-seven-year-old Clark did away with the one-man-show approach. He created the Insular Board of Education, a more democratic decision-making body, to be the central power in the system of public instruction. He was named the board's president, and it was his 15 February 1900, report to the military governor that Brumbaugh found so helpful when he first took office.

Clark resigned in March 1900 and was replaced by Dr. George G. Groff, Brumbaugh's rival for the post of education commissioner. Groff was supposed to have said that the ailing, elderly Eaton based his school code on but a single fact-gathering trip outside San Juan. But one government document indicates that the old gentleman made two tours of the island, getting to all the large towns, while Clark made it to one-fourth of the smaller towns.

Brumbaugh never much faulted the Eaton-Clark duo for making so few personal inspection treks, although he did think they should have been more observant on ones they took. His biggest quarrel with them had to do with where their code of laws placed the locus of power. Ironically, for someone who time and again professed how proud he was to be a participant in an "experiment in [democratic] government without parallel," he said the army's code left the school system too decentralized. Too much power had been handed to the local school boards and too little accorded to what had since become a new office—that of commissioner of education. "The Little Island of the Sea," he maintained, was not yet ready to run, let alone reform, what had been, and still was, a bankrupt and corrupt system.

As he saw it, the problems were severalfold. First, the authority to employ teachers rested solely with the local boards. Second, the law required no examination if an applicant already held a Spanish or Puerto Rican certificate. Third, licenses, good for five years, had been issued in far greater numbers than there were schools, creating a glut of incompetent teachers. Fourth, the law did not permit school boards to assess or collect money; they were at the financial mercy of mayors and town councils. Since most towns were heavily in debt, they made no school appropriations.

---

and United States Commissioner of Education Harris, making a complaint. He also got some of his well-placed friends in public education, like Oliver Corson, to speak up for him. Among all the administration's bureaucrats, from the president on down, support was unanimous. Congress authorized a thousand-dollar raise, effective 1 April 1901.

Thus the law compelled the boards to make contracts—for teachers' salaries, rent for school buildings, and classroom materials—they were helpless to honor.

Such a situation, complained Brumbaugh, "is fatal to the advancement of the schools." He told the governor he thought it "impossible" to do his duty, as it was defined in the Foraker Act, unless he had more control over teachers and unless school boards could count on the public purse. He said, with a touch of Dunker humility, that he did not personally "covet power," but would be willing to "assume" it in order to make as much progress as possible toward Americanizing Puerto Rico's schools.

The commissioner, therefore, anxiously awaited the beginning of the legislative session in December, when he could submit a reform school bill of his own devising. Very little lawmaking, however, was accomplished that inaugural month, much to the commissioner's dismay. The problem lay in the House of Delegates, whose members had no experience in deliberative ways. The whole month of December was lost as a result.

Since the organic act of April 1900 limited the Legislative Assembly to a sixty-day session, the solons had to put in long hours daily in January in order to finish their business. When they adjourned, late at night on the 31st, they had enacted thirty-six laws. The very first one passed guaranteed a basic American right: trial by jury. Of the three-dozen laws placed in the statute book, twenty-two of them originated in the Executive Council. This is explainable, in large part, because of the advantage of having an American majority familiar with parliamentary workings. Brumbaugh's position got written into a number of measures, including the three for which he had the greatest personal interest: the two study-in-the-States scholarship acts and a totally rewritten public-school code.

The new school law was signed by Governor Allen on 31 January, to take effect on 25 March. It gave the commissioner everything he wanted. First of all, he now had discretionary control over the hiring and licensing of all teachers. The Brumbaugh law required each school board to nominate teachers and send the list of names to the commissioner, who would approve or disapprove each candidate and return the list. Only the approved nominees could be hired. (American teachers alone were appointed by the commissioner.) In addition, all teachers, as in the States, would have to pass annual tests until permanently certified under new, stricter standards.

As for tax-supported public education, the new law stipulated that not less than 10 percent and not more than 20 percent of the revenue of every town be set aside as a separate fund for schools. Each town council had the power to fix the exact percentage. But future school directors would have to stand their watch in the certain knowledge of an annual audit by the commissioner's office.

The Brumbaugh code, as its author readily admitted, was a bureaucratic compromise between the tight central control of education that had obtained under Spain and the decentralized, democratic American system. The Eaton-Clark laws had erred, Brumbaugh said, by moving too fast toward liberal school governance. Despite his public claims that the Puerto Ricans had "turned eagerly to the school as the door to [American] citizenship," too many of them did not. In private, weaker moments he gloomily confessed to encountering widespread indifference, even opposition.

Opposition took the form of passive resistance, apathy, or neglect among the wealthier circles, as it had under the Spanish and the U.S. Army. Aside from obvious reasons of socioeconomic snobbery, the elite proved obstructionist primarily because they knew the tax burden would fall heaviest on them. Many of the more affluent school directors during military occupation had thwarted reform by a do-little—or, more often, do-nothing—policy. Just as problematic was the inertia reflected by many illiterate peons. Living in abject poverty, they saw no purpose in schooling for themselves. Brumbaugh had confronted an impasse like this once before; Puerto Rico was not unlike the situation a decade earlier in Louisiana. He decided he needed to do for the Pearl of the Antilles what he had done for the Pelican State: carry the gospel of public schools directly to the people. But first, he had to begin making use of McKinley's largess.

The president's promised two-hundred thousand dollars (money refunded from the island's tariff revenue) became available about the time the legislature adjourned. Building new schoolhouses gave the commissioner's spirits a big boost, since the results were highly visible and also quantifiable. He happily informed *Echo* readers, "Some of [you] will recall that I had a hand in making plans for several buildings in or near the campus . . . [so] I resolved to make the plans for the school houses of Porto Rico. . . . The work goes merrily along." It did so to the tune of thirty-six schools over the next several months.

Twenty-two of the schools went up in rural areas, at around an average construction cost of $1,765. They were all frame and one-room replicas of those Brumbaugh attended, taught in, and superintended during his Huntingdon County youth. Even so, the low-cost building program was something of a budgetary tour de force. The price tag on materials, much of which had to be shipped from the United States, was high, and with skilled mechanics at a premium, there was the enormous expense of transporting workmen and materials to the trackless interior districts.

All the while, the noise of busy builders also sounded in fourteen towns. The town schools ran the gamut from two rooms to ten rooms. Fajardo and Mayagüez, ports at opposite ends of the island, boasted the ten-room structures. The commissioner pronounced the one at Fajardo, built of cut stone and brick, "the most beautiful" of the fourteen. He also judged the majority of new schools to be the "largest and finest buildings in their respective towns." Only two of the lot, however, had indoor flush toilets.

Neither San Juan nor Ponce, the two most populous towns, joined the construction rush. Both places took advantage of commodious public buildings to house their schools. For one of its schools San Juan handed over to Brumbaugh the

Beneficiencia Building, on the west end near El Morro Castle, which, oddly, also sheltered the insane asylum. He thought this school not only "well-housed" but the island's "best-equipped." He did, however, have a sixty thousand-dollar structure on the drawing board for the capital before quitting his post.

In every case the land for town and rural schools was donated, although the new code of laws did hold over the school boards the threat of eminent domain. As much as he could, the commissioner reported, he used native laborers and home-island materials at every construction site. Nor did he hesitate to point out how he, by personal involvement, saved his department costly architect fees.

Once the school-construction boom was underway, Brumbaugh could at last do something about promoting "an increased healthy sentiment in favor of education" among the people. He decided upon a public relations tour—he called it a "propaganda" tour—beginning in San Juan and stopping off at the more populous centers on the western half of the island. The itinerary included Camuy, Aguadilla, Mayagüez, San Germán, Yauco, and Ponce. A railroad ran part-way along the northern coast, but most of the travel would be by horse-drawn carriers over wretched roads. A reporter for the *Puerto Rico Herald* journeyed over much the same route as the Brumbaugh retinue would several months later. He wrote:

> I recently rode (with the Government mail) from Camuy to Aguadilla—on the main route from San Juan to Mayagüez—and our coach was bogged five times. From

Major public-school towns in Puerto Rico visited by the commissioner. Also shown is Mount El Yunque.

Mayagüez to Yauco, over the only road, few coachmen will venture at double rates, and over three-quarters of the distance horses are unable to drag the carriage, and ox-teams are employed.

Both the newsman and the commissioner were exasperated by the incompetency of American engineers. Under military rule they had put down roadbeds that inconveniently washed out whenever it rained. According to Brumbaugh, who fifteen years later would take pride in his reputation as a road-building governor, schools—and churches—were unthinkable in the interior regions of Puerto Rico unless they could be reached by something more passable than footpaths and narrow byways. In fact, as commissioner of education he saw to it that children in rural areas could walk safely to school, no longer fearful of venomous snakes that infested vine-covered jungle paths. He had the trails widened and cleared out overhead. "Let in the sunlight where children pass to school" became a vigilant slogan of his.

Puerto Rico had only one good—Brumbaugh called it "magnificent"—stretch of road in the early twentieth century. It linked the eighty-four miles between San Juan and Ponce. Known as the "military road," the Spanish had built it as a ready means to transport troops and artillery from one port town to the other. Well-graded, macadamized, and winding over high mountains and through deep ravines, it rewarded travelers, wrote the commissioner, with "the most sublime views in the world, rivaling the scenery of Switzerland." The San Juan–Ponce trip could be made in fourteen hours.

Brumbaugh thought it a good idea to ask one or two well-known American educators to accompany him on the week-long campaign, despite the rugged roads. So he turned to two old friends: Oliver T. Corson, now editor and publisher of the *Ohio Educational Monthly*; and Henry Houck, Pennsylvania's deputy superintendent of instruction. He claimed that the two of them, with few exceptions, had spoken to more teachers than any other educators in America. Both men graciously volunteered their unpaid time and arrived at San Juan on Friday morning, 8 March. They were impressed into service almost as soon as their ship docked. On the 8th and 9th, the teachers of San Juan and Rio Piedras districts attended five sessions in the capital city's theater, on the Plaza de Colon.

Then it was on with the expedition. They went to four other towns: Mayagüez, San Germán, Yauco, and Ponce. Rural schools were visited along the way. It was a grueling week for the three Americans and their interpreter, Dr. Charles W. Drees, a Methodist missionary. They were up before daylight, but most days they covered only twenty miles by nine o'clock, often through a rainstorm. Delays from breakdowns or tardy servants were everyday annoyances. Long rides in a jolting, cramped, stifling vehicle over roads Brumbaugh described as "a disgrace and a danger" were fatiguing. Yet the touring trio was expected to summon up a full measure of energy and enthusiasm for the three or four speeches they usually made at every stopover. Still, what they saw and the way they were everywhere received kept them exhilarated the whole trip.

His American comrades, wrote Brumbaugh in a subtle self-congratulatory vein, expressed astonishment at the scope of the work he had initiated throughout the island. Henry Houck was especially moved by one experience that the commissioner called a "glorious revelation to [his] friends." The wayfarers were traveling through the northwestern coastal area, on the route between Camuy, world-famous for its network of caves, and Aguadilla, where some say Columbus first landed in Puerto Rico. They suddenly rounded a bend in the road and ahead of them stood a small frame shack with an American flag fluttering in the tropical breeze. It was the flag that caught Houck's eye, and he exclaimed, "What's that?" The entourage stopped, alighted, and entered the hut—to find a school in session and forty-two children. The unexpected sight prompted Brumbaugh's Pennsylvania Dutch friend to ask if he could say a few words. Houck had the reputation of being an irrepressible wag, but for the moment he was said to be a very sober-minded man. Misty-eyed, he gave his young audience a little pep talk that, the commissioner wrote, "will long remain a sacred memory."

Brumbaugh's account of the rest of the trip made it sound like a victory march taken by conquering heroes. At Mayagüez, Puerto Rico's third-largest city, children "fairly overwhelmed our party with rare tropical flowers," he wrote. At Yauco a large group of people came out to the main road to greet the travelers in a steady pour of rain. The Yaucoans, with much shouting and singing, then escorted their guests back into town, providing a kind of Palm Sunday triumphal-entry tableau. Everywhere, the schoolmen spoke to huge, enthusiastic crowds, which sometimes overflowed from a public theater into the town plaza. At Ponce the police had to be called out to restore order when the crowd turned into a mob, fighting to get inside the lecture hall.

The traveling trio made every effort to link public schools with ultimate American citizenship. As the commissioner put it when he spoke in the thronged theater at San Germán:

> [T]he free public schools [will be] infinitely more potent in lifting the island than all political discussion; . . . the product of the school, as it is known in the States, will most of all contribute to the speedy placing of a new star in the azure field of the glorious flag of freedom—the star of Porto Rico.

At the hint of statehood, said Brumbaugh, the crowd broke into an uproar. Men cheered "buenos," women sobbed convulsively, children waved The Stars and Stripes. Most probably, it was scenes like this that convinced Brumbaugh, even in moments of darkest doubt, that the Puerto Rican people were basically both pro-American and pro-education. Such demonstrations also led him to think the ten-day, 250-mile circuit was worth all the trouble. By his estimates, about three hundred teachers and at least ten times as many from the general public—town leaders, school directors, ordinary citizens—took in what were, he said, "really the first great educational mass meetings ever held on the island."

Brumbaugh said that during his first year on the island he was on the road as much as his office work and other official duties permitted, making a "detailed study of the entire [educational] problem." He reported in the fall of 1901 having been in "every important town and over every important road." But he let everyone know it was a burdensome, health-threatening chore. He wrote:

> Travel is not agreeable recreation here; it is a sacrifice. To drive as much as 92 miles in one day over poor roads, through deep rivers, and heavy rains, arriving at one's destination at midnight is not pleasant. It is a drain upon one's energies, and I have repeatedly returned quite ill.

Apparently, the more Brumbaugh got out among the people and the scattered school districts, the more he was overwhelmed by the reality of a populace almost totally illiterate. Perhaps that is why he often resorted to strong, pugnacious rhetoric to communicate how embattled he felt. "This is my foe," he told Juniatians through the *Echo,* alluding to illiteracy. It was in this context of militant language that Edwin Stephens, editor of the *Louisiana School Review*, told of one speech Brumbaugh made and the attention-getting gambit he used. As a speaker, the commissioner was always intrigued, said Stephens, by the delayed reaction of Puerto Rican crowds, which had to wait for the interpreter to repeat in Spanish the few sentences he had just uttered. The interval allowed him to study his audience and play upon its mood. So, according to Stephens, he once began:

> "I have only one enemy in Porto Rico!" This caused a murmur—that he should speak of enemies, and Brumbaugh noted it; then he said: "And that enemy I am determined to destroy!" People began to look around at each other, as if to find in what quarter of the audience this enemy might be. Then he said: "And that enemy is *Ignorance!"* When the interpreter repeated this sentence, that mercurial populace tossed their hats in air with bravos.

A good deal of the commissioner's travels had to do with dedicating new schoolhouses. Often he took the governor with him or some other cabinet member. He thought it an important propagandist stratagem to make the day of every dedicatory ceremony—involving much patriotic fanfare—a kind of holiday for the town or barrio. By the summer of 1901, Brumbaugh said, he was dedicating one school a week. Some of these buildings he named after great Spanish explorers, like Columbus and Ponce de Leon. But most of them honored famous Americans: Washington, Franklin, Jefferson, Jackson, Adams, Lincoln, Grant, McKinley, Longfellow, Prescott, Webster, Hamilton, Garfield, Mann, Peabody. Many Puerto Rican schools today still bear the names of these historic figures. Among them also is that of Martin Brumbaugh—on two schools, one in San Juan and the other in Santa Isabel, a town on the southern coast.

The school as a citadel of patriotism was a prominent theme in Brumbaugh's reports, speeches, and writings in these years. As a teacher and textbook author, he had of course always made this a central theme in behavioral outcomes. So, mimicking their mainland counterparts, Puerto Rican children began the school day saluting the flag, after which they sang "America," "Hail Columbia," "The Star Spangled Banner," and other patriotic songs—in English. Brumbaugh wrote, "The first English many of [the pupils] know is the English of our national songs. The influence of this is far-reaching."

For Washington's birthday in February 1901, he proposed that every school conduct special exercises. The response was a pleasant surprise to him; he said at least thirty thousand pupils (out of forty thousand enrolled) took part in "honoring the first American," as did perhaps five thousand adults. The *Pennsylvania School Journal* noted with approval that "Everyone connected with the educational department, from Commissioner Brumbaugh and the district superintendents to the teachers of rural schools, had been at work for weeks in preparing for the day." Exulted Brumbaugh:

> These exercises have done much to Americanize the island, much more than any other single agency. No such demonstration was ever witnessed in Porto Rico. The young minds are being molded to follow the example of Washington. It is one of the most gratifying results so far achieved in our work.

The commissioner also arranged to stage similar school celebrations on Flag Day, in June. His department declared it a half-holiday, engaging close to forty thousand children and upwards of sixty thousand adults in the public observances. In San Juan, twenty thousand cheering children, many costumed in red, white, and blue, marched through the main streets in step with "happy teachers," each carrying a small flag furnished by the commissioner's department. This scene was duplicated everywhere on the island. That Flag Day, said Brumbaugh, "was more generally observed than I have ever known it to be in the States, and more enthusiastically." The governor was so impressed by the success of the two public spectacles that he put the education commissioner in charge of the Fourth of July celebration.

Brumbaugh found the enthusiasm of Puerto Rican schoolchildren, especially those from peon families, to be a "patriotic and soul stirring" marvel. Their eagerness to learn, despite having to attend school barefoot and in tatters, provided him with a stock of heart-tugging anecdotes. The setting for one of his favorites was a little school at Juncos, a village in the island's eastern forested area. On a day spent observing classes there, the commissioner noticed that one of the boys would never turn his face away from him. Puzzled, he asked the teacher why, only to learn the lad's shirt had no back. That day's special visitor, according to later reports, saw to it that the ragamuffin soon had better togs. Another story told of a schoolboy in a mountainous region whose homemade, ill-fitting shirt (made for his father) bore across its back the legend "Pillsbury XXX." Such examples, said Brumbaugh, typified how children of the poor preferred going to school, no matter how clothed, to growing up in ignorance.

But in some places, the commissioner soon found out, this readiness to escape illiteracy and ignorance was modulated by resistance to coeducation. Puerto Rico's Spanish heritage had for centuries forbade the mixed schooling of the sexes. Brumbaugh, determined to change this prejudice, decided it was wisest not to make a public issue of the matter but quietly to increase the number of coeducational schools on an incremental basis. By 1902 this policy had gone a long way toward phasing out separate schools, without friction or protest. Statistics that spring, however, still showed seventy-three boys' schools and sixty-four for girls.

On the other hand, the color question, although racism existed among the aristocracy, created no obstacles to the immediate integration of schools. Among the masses social democracy was "very pronounced," wrote Brumbaugh. In his day about 9 percent of the teachers and 28 percent of the pupils were "colored" (not mulattoes). Many of the colored teachers came from adjoining islands and spoke English. Others came of old slave stock. All the evidence, Brumbaugh reported, indicated that black children did about as well as other pupils. The supervisor of the San Juan District wrote in 1902:

> The negro and the white child have thus far done equally good work in the schools. . . . The negroes are ambitious and like to go to school. They have been prominent in all public exercises, whether in the theater as speakers or on the street drilling. In every case the negro boy has been the best officer.

Mulatto children, by contrast, he described as being "the most indolent" students in the San Juan schools.

Along with coeducation and integrated schools, Brumbaugh, as commissioner, was avidly committed to agricultural training for Puerto Rico's rising generation. He also believed the future wealth of the island and its promise lay in the soil, for centuries the main source of livelihood for the common people. He criticized Groff, Eaton, and Clark for ignoring, in their school laws and curriculums, Puerto Rico's traditional agrarian economy. Schools modeled on America's best, he said, had no place as yet in rural areas. Thus his department turned "heroically" to the mission of teaching agriculture.

Agricultural education, he hoped, would be the prescription for helping the landless poor become landowning farmers. Practically all of the nineteen rural schools built with McKinley money took on this educational function. They were all sited on an acre of land, each enrolling fifty pupils. These schools differed from other rural schools in curriculum and daily routine. Mornings were given to little more than the "three R's," the afternoons to working in the soil under the tutelage of an experienced farmer—or, it was Brumbaugh's ultimate aim, a scientific agriculturist. The students grew such crops as garden vegetables, fruits, corn, and tobacco.

Unfortunately, the schools languished and did not prove the success hoped for. It was hard to find competent teachers, and the commissioner's own department, it was later said, neglected equipping the schools adequately with hand tools. But most important, the people themselves really never caught the vision of small-scale, independent farmers constituting the core of the island's citizenry. Ten years later Brumbaugh was still grieving over the failure of his pet project, convinced the Puerto Rican government—and his successors—could have done more to sustain "those little experiment stations."

Of the 876 schools in operation at the end of Brumbaugh's tenure, 490—or nearly 56 percent—were rurally based. They were taught almost exclusively by Puerto Ricans and were ungraded; the lessons were done in Spanish (except for learning patriotic American songs in English). Graded schools, introduced by the first commissioner of education, were located only in villages, towns, and cities, The curriculum, although taught in Spanish, included study of the English language. Thus every graded school had the services of a teacher whose native tongue was English, usually one for three or four schools. Only the graded school had a principal.

By 1902 about twice as many males as females (605 to 329) staffed the island's classrooms. In every kind of school and supervisory rank, men and women got equal pay. Compensation, however, was below the mainland's average salary scale. Rural teachers in Puerto Rico, for example, made only forty dollars a month, and those in graded schools, fifty dollars. Principals did a little better, taking home seventy-five dollars each month. Low pay troubled Brumbaugh, who wanted to attract talented people, but budgetary constraints kept him frugal-minded on the matter of wages.

The Brumbaugh-designed school system concentrated on elementary education almost to the neglect of secondary education; only San Juan and Ponce had a high school by 1902. As the commissioner said in his first annual report, he would be guided by Bentham's dictum: "the greatest good for the greatest number." He wrote,

> With three-fourths of the population over ten years of age unable to read a newspaper, the elementary branches should for some time occupy and engage the energies of the teachers now working. It is better that 300,000 children should be taught to read and write and cipher than that 40,000 should learn botany, chemistry, grammar, rhetoric, and astronomy.

To meet the need of reducing mass illiteracy in the shortest possible time, he devised a four-four plan: the first four grades were designated "Primary," the second four "Intermediate." The curriculum across all eight grades, besides the "three R's," placed emphasis upon language, nature study, history, and elementary science.*

The Brumbaugh plan not only minimized the value of a system of secondary

---

*Elementary science dealt, not with scientific subjects, but with practical lessons about health and personal care: hygiene, proper diet, cleanliness, sanitation. Brumbaugh was delighted by the immediate communal impact of this part of the curriculum—such as the sudden appearance of whitewashed shacks and flower gardens.

schools for the time being but also saw no defensible need for kindergartens, not an easy decision for a progressive educator of his ardent persuasion. He wrote in his 1900 report:

> Pedagogically the kindergarten is the last refinement of a highly organized system of education that proposes the entire education of the child for the most complex social, industrial, and civic activities. It is distinctly a socializing institution.

As such, he argued, a preindustrial, illiterate society like Puerto Rico, with "thousands of children half-clothed, half-fed, half-housed, half-homed," was not now the place to introduce the specialized methods of the kindergarten. Consequently, when he made his departure kindergartens existed only in the two port cities of San Juan and Ponce.

In addition to rural, agricultural, and graded schools, Brumbaugh instituted—or set the stage for—a number of special schools. Early in his administration he opened night schools throughout the island for those who, for various reasons, could not attend public school in the daytime. In February 1902 night schools were enrolling close to 750 students. But by then the class rosters included many adults, eager to learn English and study United States history. Brumbaugh also guided through the 1901–2 legislature a law establishing three schools to train nurses. One of them he had already started up—in San Juan—before resigning. That same legislative session passed another measure, granting the commissioner of education power to open three industrial and trade schools—one each in San Juan, Mayagüez, and Ponce—as soon as funds permitted. But the task of implementing industrial training was left to Brumbaugh's replacements.

Such programs and Martin Brumbaugh's overall quick-order achievements as commissioner demonstrated he possessed a rare combination of administrative skills: he was both a bold planner and a superb manager. Puerto Rico in his day was divided into sixty-six territorial units called municipalities—political bailiwicks similar to counties in the United States. The commissioner grouped these municipalities into sixteen school districts, to one of which the neighboring islands of Vieques and Culebra were added. (Actually, the military had originally organized the island into these sixteen districts, a number Brumbaugh thought administratively warrantable.)

Each district was headed by a "field supervisor," who reported to the central office in San Juan. Before Brumbaugh's time, supervisors received no expense funds and were obliged to own two or three horses while perambulating over treacherous jungle trails. Their pay was a pittance: seventy-five dollars monthly. Hence many of them had slighted their work and falsified reports. Brumbaugh and his law changed all that. Under his leadership districts had to provide housing and office rent for supervisors. He increased their salaries to twelve hundred dollars a year, gave them assistants, and by law required them to be ex-officio school board members in their respective districts. Brumbaugh also hired a "field deputy"—a bilingual Venezuelan—to be his go-between with the supervisors.

From the beginning of Brumbaugh's public-school command, Puerto Rico also saw the debut of a host of private schools, most operated by religious societies. The Roman Catholic Church and Protestant missions devoted much time and money to this work. Some independent private schools were conducted by teachers who had failed to be certificated. But in Puerto Rico's roadless interior there was not a single private school. Brumbaugh once observed that no matter how much private schooling flourished, as long as it forsook the hinterlands it could never educate the great mass of the population. But he was very grateful for what help private schools were able to provide in lessening the appalling burden of illiteracy. At all times, he said, parochial schools—Catholic and Protestant alike—worked in harmony with his department. Almost universally they adopted the books, supplies, and courses of study used by public schools.

As a pedagogist, the island's first education commissioner won widespread curricular support for one very good reason: his stated commitment to a plan of schooling that would not only produce future generations of informed American citizens but also preserve Puerto Rico's cultural heritage. He envisioned the public schools transforming the Caribbean possession into a bilingual society, a people of dual patriotism—to their Spanish yesterday and their American tomorrow. As Brumbaugh wrote at this time, "It would be a great injustice to the Spanish-American civilization to undertake to remove the language of their native country, so rich in literature, so glorious in history." Philosophically, he was guided by a favorite aphorism of his friend Nathan Schaeffer, one he often quoted as commissioner: "A man is as many times a man as he has languages in which to think." As a result, the public school curriculum at all grade levels duly gave attention to Puerto Rico's Spanish legacy—historical and literary as well as linguistic. Deliberately, to best serve these pedagogical ends, he limited the number of Americans to only about 12.5 percent of the total teaching force, a policy he was always quick to point out for the island's public record.

Notwithstanding all that Martin Brumbaugh did to advance universal education in Puerto Rico, he left the island in 1902 in the knowledge that some three hundred thousand children of schoolable age went untaught for lack of schools. Every district had a long waiting list of pupils. It gave him some comfort, however, to be able to boast that the attendance record of those enrolled averaged 75 percent, a percentage point better than Pennsylvania's average.

Regrettably, though we know much about Martin Brumbaugh the commissioner of education, very little is known about his private life while he was in Puerto Rico. Only seven of his letters from that period have survived—all to his parents. They are brief, hastily scrawled, and give us only a glimpse inside the Brumbaugh household. Mostly they are a son's pleading for parental pity. He complained about his work load and the miseries caused by the rainy season. He mentioned being "sadly rundown and worked out." One time, he wrote, presumably in jest, "Well, if I live to see you, you will see an older son than you ever had," emphasizing he was under "great strain." What he needed, one letter said, was "perfect rest," but "that will come only when I get away from this place." A couple of times he entreated his father, who had just sold out his share of the Brumbaugh Company Store to Martin's brother, Irvin, to visit him (this never happened). He wanted the elder Brumbaugh to see for himself what a heavy work load he carried as commissioner—"I live more in a day than you do in a year." But his mother never got invited, because "the trip would be too much for you." Nobody back home, including his parents, wrote often enough to suit him.

Never once did he mention where the family, regular churchgoers in Philadelphia, worshipped on Sunday mornings.

Nor did his correspondence to the home folks say much about Anna and the children or their daily activities. Once, he said tersely, "Family is well." Another time, he fretted—ironically—that Mabel and Edwin should be in better schools. In one letter, written in the hurricane season, he told his mother not to worry, because his family lived in a solid brick house and were in no danger should a storm sweep the island.

Aside from these letters, we know little about the family's twelve-month island experience. Edwin, when an old man, once reminisced about happy hours spent, as an eleven-year-old, flying gaily colored kites there, still a favorite pastime of Puerto Rican boys. The air currents over the headlands of San Juan harbor were—and still are—particularly frolicsome. As Edwin told it, this was the scene of the unique Puerto Rican game "fighting kites." A boy would attach a sharp, stiff blade to his kite cord several feet below the kite. Then he tried to maneuver his kite, once it was airborne, in such a way as to cut the line of a competitor, causing his kite to be blown away. Said Edwin, "This was not merely exhibition, but serious boyhood competition."

Another source of information is a newspaper interview by a *Philadelphia Times* reporter in November 1901. The whole Brumbaugh family had just returned to the States, supposedly for a month's vacation. The reporter described them as "full of enthusiasm for all things Puerto Rican." He quoted the commissioner as saying that Anna and Flora Belle "enjoy the distinction of having seen more of our beautiful colonial possession than any other American women or foreign women of any country." Brumbaugh elaborated: "They accompanied me in my travels about the island. We sailed all around the coast and traveled the roads of the interior, and practically explored every nook and corner of the island."

We learn a bit more about the Brumbaughs' leisure hours from a March 1901 *Juniata Echo* article. It was written by the commissioner and titled, "New Year's Day in Porto Rico." In it he told of a family outing on that first holiday of the new century. After a breakfast of coconut "nectar," oatmeal, boiled milk, oranges, bananas, bread, beef, and coffee, the Brumbaughs headed for the San Juan quay, where some time was spent bargaining with a boatman. Then they were off sailing southward across the bay, to Cataño, at that time a low marsh-encircled village.

There the Brumbaughs came upon a familiar scene: cock-fighting—a favorite sport in Puerto Rico even today. (In fact, Brumbaugh noted parenthetically, "Near our house every Sunday afternoon a crowd gathers, a score of fights are held, and much money is lost or won.") From Cataño the family took an electric car—the first on the island—out to a coconut grove along the bay. There they spent the rest of the day picnicking on roast pig in company with friends and wading in the surf. For the commissioner, the "unique day" was a "glad memory."

Martin Brumbaugh's *unhappiest* memory of Puerto Rico, he probably would have said, was the news of William McKinley's death in the fall of 1901. The fifty-eight-year-old president, shot by an anarchist on Friday, 6 September, while attending the Pan-American Exposition in Buffalo, New York, died eight days later. Along with the nation, Puerto Rico too mourned the assassinated chief of state, the third White House victim of a gunman since the end of the Civil War. One San Juan paper, the *Boletin Mercantil*, reported that a memorial service on Thursday the 19th "packed [the capital city's theater] from cellar to dome" (about five thousand people).

The cast of twelve speakers that afternoon included the island's commissioner of education, whose address was one of three delivered only in English. He spoke from a platform on which a large picture of the president, draped in black cloth, stood on a pedestal covered with flowers. To the rear of the stage, a portrait of *Columbia* kept vigilance over the scene, while red, white, and blue banners streamed from the ceiling. As might be expected, Brumbaugh's eulogy was studded with superlative verbiage in tribute to his fallen political avatar. His peroration declaimed:

> In expanding American institutions and extending American dominion [the president] was actuated by no selfish motives. To him people were not the objects of conquest and plunder, but fellow citizens whose anguished cries thrilled his soul and compelled him to extend the same blessings which Almighty God had bestowed upon him and his. With altruistic fervor he labored to give as he had received and he is justly entitled to be characterized as the Defender of Human Liberty, the Deliverer of the Oppressed, the Uncrowned King of Mankind.

With the perspective of time, latter-day American historians have not generally accorded McKinley's presidency such an exalted status. Every poll of college and university history professors, since the first one conducted in the late 1940s, places his presidential performance in the "high average" category. It is a ranking that would mystify, if not irk, Martin Brumbaugh were he alive today.

He had been on the island little more than a year when McKinley was martyred. But by that time his work was getting a measure of favorable public notice, both in Puerto Rico and back in the United States. The *Puerto Rico Herald* ran a story in November commending "El Señor Martino," as some took to addressing him, because, it said,

He reconstructed the department of education out of the ruins which he found, through the failures of Eaton and Clark. . . . He has made himself popular throughout the island. All the Puerto Ricans, without distinction of party like him, because he has nobly raised himself by his actions above political factions . . . and the people . . . love and admire him. Few have won so completely the sympathies of the people.

That same November, the *San Juan News* editorialized: "Some years hence the people of the island will be contributing to a fund to erect a memorial to Martin G. Brumbaugh, the founder of our educational system, the mettle of our progressive isle."

Meanwhile, in October an editorial in Connecticut's *Hartford Daily Times* had lauded the commissioner's department as one "we can justly point to with pride as upholding our national principles and traditions." It said of Brumbaugh: "He is one of the few men holding government positions in the island who are admired and respected by the Porto Ricans." This was quite a turnaround in public opinion from his early days on the island when, according to the commissioner, some people were captiously calling him a "czar."

Published plaudits are certainly useful in gauging Brumbaugh's reputation as the civil government's first commissioner of education, but perhaps a more telling bit of *practical* evidence is to be found elsewhere: in the spending record of the legislature and local school boards from mid-1900 to early 1902. In that brief time span, combined expenditures for the public-school system increased from around $400,000 to over $670,000. Brumbaugh, by the time he resigned, had induced Puerto Ricans, an impoverished people in need of many social services, to commit more than one-quarter of the island's total expenditures to education. That was as good or better than any school district or state on the mainland.

No chronicle of Martin Brumbaugh's record as education commissioner would be complete that failed to mention something else that added luster to his name: his role in founding Puerto Rico's first public library. It all happened quite by accident. When he began converting San Juan's Beneficiencia Building into a high school soon after his arrival on the island, he came across some five thousand volumes of Spanish and American works. Uncataloged, they had been haphazardly stored in several rooms and all but forgotten. It occurred to him, he later wrote, that it would be "a public service to utilize these volumes as a public library." So he had them hauled to the center-city post office, took over three upper-level rooms (which he had redecorated), and shelved and cataloged the books.

He got the first legislature, with hardly any debate, to provide modest funding. Governor Hunt promptly appointed a five-member board, naming Brumbaugh its president. The board president wasted no time communicating with steel-king Andrew Carnegie, then in his mid-sixties and dedicated to giving away his enormous fortune for philanthropic deeds, especially endowing libraries. A number of letters were exchanged before the Scottish-born Good Samaritan came through with one hundred thousand dollars in early November 1901. The San Juan library was one of only seven to be built by Carnegie in the Western Hemisphere south of the continental United States before 1919. Ponce and Mayagüez, inspired by what San Juan had done, also established public libraries—but not with Carnegie money.

Months before locking in the Carnegie gift, Brumbaugh had already begun thinking about returning to the University of Pennsylvania. He was in touch with Provost Charles Harrison about the matter as early as April. At that time—and again in October—the provost assured him, as originally promised, that he could have his professorship back whenever he wanted it. He was still pondering what to do when the Brumbaughs took passage on the steamer *Ponce* for New York. They arrived home the third week of November. Everybody assumed the family had returned on a vacation, but their prolonged stay fueled public speculation. During the Christmas-New Year's week, the Philadelphia and Pittsburgh papers ran stories announcing the commissioner had resigned.

Whether or not he himself leaked this news to reporters is not known. But he had in fact made that decision before the holiday season. His letter of resignation—addressed to Teddy Roosevelt—was dated 23 December and was to take effect upon the appointment of his successor. For the next several weeks he sent out no published announcement of his own.

He did, however, let the governor of Puerto Rico know what he had done that Christmastime. For Hunt, it was not at all glad tidings. His very personal response, penned on New Year's Eve, must have deeply moved its recipient. The letter read, midway through: "I am so sorry to have you go, and never will esteem another friend made in middle life as I do you, and never will rely upon another with such unreserved confidence and devotion. . . . [I want] to tell you how affectionately fond of you I became: how I *loved* you and your big heart." The governor was also distraught over missing the Executive Council president's leadership during the current legislative session, already half over.

Not until 30 January—through a formal, printed flyer—did the commissioner inform his Puerto Rican and American cohorts on the island that he would not be coming back. By then, of course, the word was out, bringing about a flood of letters beseeching him to reconsider. His assistant, Samuel Heckman, remained behind and ran the San Juan office until Roosevelt found a new commissioner. Heckman also sold off the Brumbaughs' household effects for them.

9

Back to Academe

IT is hard to say why Martin Brumbaugh, popular as he seemed to be, chose to leave Puerto Rico after only a fifteen-month stint as the island's education chief. His own stated reason for doing so is a perfect study in circumlocution: "Only the greatest demands of imperative duty prompt me to relinquish such a thoroughly noble work." That is what he told his staff and every school-board member, principal, and teacher on the island in his 30 January circular to them.

But other people in subsequent years spoke with greater particularity about what motivated him. In 1914, at the time he was running for governor, the press—though never directly quoting him—gave a twofold explanation for his departure: he disliked administrative work and he thought Teddy Roosevelt ought to appoint his own man. More recently (1972), a document prepared by Puerto Rico's department of education attributed his exodus to a nagging "health problem." This comes as a surprising piece of information. True, the island's education commissioner often mentioned being utterly exhausted, but never once did he so much as hint at a chronic malady. Poor health, if it was a problem, quite likely was not Brumbaugh's but his wife's complaint. Daughter Mabel, many years later, indicated this was the case. When a septuagenarian, she recalled that it was concern for her mother's well-being that forced the family to return to the States. Anna, she said, was subject to malarial attacks.

All of these reasons could very well have had some bearing on why the commissioner decided to resign. But they are not the whole story. Perhaps an October 1901 missive from Charles Sower gets closer to the underlying cause. The publisher wrote: "Your welcome letter of 9th was duly rec'd, and I regret exceedingly that your long sojourn in San Juan has not *all* been one of pleasure and satisfaction." Not only to Sower but to a few others close to him, Brumbaugh had confided that his job seemed to be a "thankless task." But none of his preserved letters or other papers ever divulged why he felt that way.

Psychologically, things took a turn for the worse for him a couple of weeks after he heard from Sower—and therein perhaps lay the precipitating cause for his resignation. He was in the middle of packing up for the family's long-awaited home visit when Governor Hunt passed on to him some unsettling news: a cablegram

169

from Secretary of the Interior Hitchcock had just arrived (7 November) at the Executive Mansion, raising some questions about the commissioner's prudence as a public official. The cablegram read in part:

> Report on Commissioner Education for Porto Rico received. Contains reflections on past conduct of war department. Also upon that of private individuals. All based on hearsay. . . .

Hitchcock further stated that Brumbaugh's report for the year 1900–1901 would not be accepted unless he "eliminate objectional pages."

This referred to his having quoted from the memorandum that George Groff left for his guidance. Groff's notations, intended to be confidential, were critical of the allegedly slipshod way General Eaton and Victor Clark had gone about gathering data preparatory to drafting an army-backed school code. The jottings also belittled Clark's managerial style during military occupation.

Before anything could be done about satisfying Hitchcock's telegraphed terms, the Brumbaughs left for the mainland. Soon after they arrived back home, the United States commissioner of education, wanting to play the role of mediator, brought himself into the dispute. William Harris prevailed upon his subordinate to come to Washington on Tuesday, 3 December, to talk over the predicament. The nation's top education officer held Brumbaugh in the highest regard, so as tactfully as he could he explained what troubled Secretary Hitchcock. Martin's report, Harris pointed out, not only amounted to a breach of bureaucratic etiquette but, so far as the elderly General Eaton was concerned, could be construed "in the nature of persecution." Brumbaugh responded that, although his report cited Groff, he had observed for himself the mistakes and mismanagement of Eaton and Clark. Therefore, he argued, this took the disputed passages out of the realm of hearsay and gave them legitimacy. Nonetheless, he was compelled to back down and acquiesce in Hitchcock's ultimatum; the offensive sentences were deleted.

It was embarrassing to be called on the carpet, even by a well-meaning acquaintance. Harris, a gentle man, understood his friend's chagrin, and told Hitchcock, "Doctor Brumbaugh naturally feels some sensitiveness with the implied censure of his report." What he did not know was that the "Doctor" had finally run out of patience with the habits of bureaucrats; within days his handwritten letter of resignation was on its way to Teddy Roosevelt.

Brumbaugh's San Juan staff was stunned by his decision. Many of them were gripped with angst, anxiously wondering who the next commissioner would be. As one of the male office workers worriedly put it: "Imagine a repetition of Groff, Clark or Eaton!" But such a prospect was a very real possibility; already Clark and Groff were actively politicking to take Brumbaugh's place.

President Roosevelt contacted him on 13 January, seeking his advice about Clark's "fitness for the position." "Unfit" was Brumbaugh's unequivocal reply. A week later, he learned about Groff from John R. Garrison, Puerto Rico's auditor and a fellow cabinet member. Garrison wrote, "It is important that your successor shall be a man well qualified to take up and carry out the magnificent work you inaugurated here with such marked success." Then came the troubling bit of gossip:

> I have heard in a way I cannot well discredit that Dr. Groff is making efforts to become your successor!! It is wholly unnecessary for me to comment on this. Both of us know what the Department of Education was under Groff as Acting Commissioner. We can surmise what it *would be*. *Verbum Sat.* [*sic*].

Soon after this revelation, Provost Charles Harrison dropped a note to Brumbaugh, now back teaching at Penn, saying he saw by the Philadelphia papers that Groff was being "urged as Commissioner of Education." He went on to query, "If Mr. Groff is unfit for the position, as I understand you to believe, do you not think you should so intimate to the President, or to the Secretary of War?" Thus prodded, Brumbaugh wired an anti-Groff caveat to the White House.

The provost and the professor immediately got their heads together and began scheming to put forward a nominee from among the Penn faculty. They settled upon Dr. Samuel Lindsay, a thirty-two-year-old sociologist. Lindsay had been one of Brumbaugh's two Penn companions on his European trip in 1895. President Roosevelt, they were pleased to learn, readily went along with their nomination of the sociology instructor. Appointed on 23 January, Lindsay officially took over his duties on 8 February.

The ex-commissioner had been holding forth in his old classroom in College Hall since early January. Now he lived closer to the university. Since getting back to the States, the family had sold their home on Fortieth Street and bought a larger one at 3324 Walnut Street, a shorter walk from the Penn campus.

Now approaching his fortieth birthday, the once-lanky, well-muscled son of the countryside was beginning to display a middle-age paunch. The six-footer jotted down in one of his early 1900s date books that he now weighed 219 pounds. Bull-necked, he listed his collar size as a seventeen. He wore a size forty-four shirt, and had a forty-two-inch waist. But he carried his bulk on surprisingly small feet—his shoe size was only nine and a half. With his leonine head, the tall, portly professor recalled to mind one of the male characters in Wagner's operas. His beetling brows in a few years would delight newspaper caricaturists. One newsman said of Brumbaugh's eyebrows: "They arch out over his eyes like the beaks of an eagle."

Once back in the academic arena, Martin, now forever addicted to cigars, quickly reverted to his past professorial routine: teaching, writing, and keeping a full lecture card. The second edition of his *Fifth Reader* came out early in the spring of 1902. But the death of its publisher, Charles Sower, in March dampened any rejoicing by the textbook's author over prospering sales. For another Quaker City publishing house, J. B. Lippincott, he was back at work soliciting writers for the educational series he had started to edit before going to Puerto Rico.

He was, upon returning from that island, in great demand as a lecturer on the educational progress made there under the aegis of Uncle Sam. Most requests he declined, but in April he did go to the nation's capital to read a paper on his Puerto Rican experiences before a convention of the American Social Science Association. While in Washington, he and Samuel Heckman, now a Penn graduate student, stopped by 1600 Pennsylvania Avenue. They did so at the president's behest. Roosevelt, his fight with Colombia over an isthmian canal route through Panama still a year off, was worried about other, more immediate problems in the Caribbean. He wanted their firsthand assessment of political conditions in Puerto Rico, where anti-American feeling was on the rise.

The proverbial month of spring showers also brought some now familiar but not altogether welcomed words from his uncle, the doctor: "You were elected to your position as President of Juniata College for the coming year, unanimously." This time, however, he accepted the trustee notification with quiet submission.

With the month of May, his newest textbook, a collaborative effort, was on public-school desks. *The Hall and Brumbaugh Standard Primer*, published by the Sower press, was coauthored with Anne Heygate-Hall, the woman who early in Brumbaugh's Penn career had ranked him with John Ruskin as a major intellectual influence in her life. She now headed the department of practice teaching at the Philadelphia Normal School. This latest primer took an innovative pedagogical approach to teaching reading. Exercises in the first half of the dainty little book appeared in script, in the second half in print. "All good teaching," said the preface, "now follows this order." It was the method advocated at the Philadelphia Normal School.

Maria L. Kirk, who had been the artist for the five-volume series of Brumbaugh *Readers*, did the illustrations, some of them in multicolor, another novel feature of the textbook. The *New York School Journal*, which declared that the *Primer* "marks a decided high point in the literature offered to a young child," gave special praise to Kirk's artwork. The reviewer maintained that her pictures took the small volume "out of the school text-book category and made it suitable to lie on the library table." The *Annals of the Deaf*, put out by Gallaudet College in Washington, D.C., was another periodical, among many others, that saluted the *Primer*. Its pedagogy and its drawings, the *Annals* emphasized, transformed it into "a book of unusual attractiveness and educative value for little deaf children." The *Primer* sold well enough to go into a second printing in 1908.

One of Brumbaugh's first lecture engagements that post-Puerto Rico May was somewhat of a minor historic event. Home-city Girard College scheduled him for a Founder's Day address. The then-famous institution, which opened its doors in 1848, was a free home, secondary school, and what would now be called a junior college for destitute orphan white boys. (Today it is an independent boarding school, grades 1 through 12, with an 81 percent minority enrollment.)

Brumbaugh might well have been the first preacher ever to appear before the

student body up to that time. The school had been founded through the philanthropy of French-born financier Stephen Girard, whose will specified that "no eccle-
siastic, missionary, or minister, of any sect whatsoever, shall ever hold or exercise
any station or duty whatsoever in the said college; nor shall any such person be
admitted for any purpose, or as a visitor, within the premise." The mid-nineteenth
century was a time of intense religious rivalry in America, and Girard wanted to
shield the school's wards from the tensions of sectarian strife. In Brumbaugh's
case, the trustees got around the anticlerical ban by ruling he was only a lay minister and not a practicing man of the cloth. This would not be the last time Girard
College made an exception for its Founder's Day dignitary, as he would discover a
few years later.

June, traditionally commencement month in those days, took him to several
college and high-school graduation ceremonies. One of them was at Ohio State
University, no doubt at the instigation of Oliver Corson, a trustee. While in Columbus he did double duty, addressing also the city's high-school seniors. It was the
largest high-school graduating class in the history of the Buckeye State's capital to
that date, and the ceremony was attended by parents, relatives, and friends of the
graduates "in the thousands," estimated the *Columbus Evening Dispatch*.
Brumbaugh, who had been going up and down the state for the past fifteen or
eighteen years talking to teachers, was a great favorite among Ohio educators. The
reporter covering the high-school exercises for the *Evening Dispatch* probably
defined as graphically as anybody ever did Brumbaugh the platform mesmerist.
He wrote: "[The speaker] was keen, incisive, humorous, pathetic, learned, elegant.
He made his auditors laugh and he brought tears to their eyes."

Commencement-time 1902 produced his first honorary degree, but it was one
that gave him considerable pause. The trustees of Mount Morris College in Illinois, a denominational sister school of his alma mater, notified him in early June
that they planned to give him a doctor of laws degree. Perturbed, the prospective
honoree hurried off a letter to Juniata's Henry Brumbaugh, pleading, "What shall
I do? I do not feel like taking an Honorary Degree from any Institution of Learning. I have always opposed, as you know, such a procedure." He said he preferred
to earn his degrees, adding, "I do not care a rap for them anyhow."

But Henry's younger cousin was not being entirely honest about his feelings.
Betraying a calculating concern, he went on to say that a Mount Morris degree
might prevent him from being honored by "some other and more widely known
Institution."* Commiserating with his relative's "unfortunate" dilemma, Henry
answered that the Mount Morris board would probably understand if he turned
down their award. For some reason he decided not to do that—but did choose to
have the LL.D. conferred in absentia. The story was entirely different come June
1903, when Franklin and Marshall College, a much more prestigious home-state

---

*Mount Morris, which struggled from its start in 1879, merged with Indiana's Manches-
ter College in 1932.

institution, gave him another LL.D. One of several commencement speakers, he gladly made the short train ride to nearby Lancaster to accept the degree in person. (The 1903 commencement exercises marked the college's golden jubilee.) Of the seven honorary degrees he would collect over the years, that of Mount Morris was the only one with a Brethren stamp.

Brumbaugh's first year back from Puerto Rico ended with a business deal that, while in the making, must have stirred nostalgic memories of a near-legendary period of his youth. The calendar for 1902 was only weeks old when Dr. Joseph T. Rothrock, a Penn professor and the state's first forestry commissioner, got in touch with him. He wrote to say he had heard that the Forge lands could be bought and wondered if that were true. Brumbaugh answered that it was, immediately relaying word of this exchange to his parents. They were now in their late sixties and probably in need of greater financial security. (Family oral tradition holds that the son had promised his mother and father to share with them all proceeds from the sale of any property or land of theirs redeeded to him by his uncle Henry, the farmer, in 1883.)

Talking George, recently retired as a farmhand and doing very little preaching of late, tramped over the for-sale territory with Rothrock several times and now and then helped out with the surveying. After months of dilatory but good-faith bargaining, the Brumbaughs sold off five of the original six Forge tracts in mid-December. At three dollars an acre, they pocketed $5,090.40 for the onetime lumbering and iron-furnace site. For a small sum, the son turned over the remaining twenty-seven acres to the state in 1918, after both of his parents were dead. By the time the Great Depression had set in, 541 acres of the Forge area had become Trough Creek State Park (1933), the rest a part of Rothrock State Forest land.

A few months into the next year, Brumbaugh learned from Samuel Lindsay that Puerto Rico's legislature had passed on 12 March a law establishing an insular university. It was to be located at Rio Piedras on the site of the Normal School he had founded. He took this as an indirect tribute to his work as commissioner. But, more than that, he had since returning to the States become a vocal champion of a pan-American university. He called for it to be situated in Puerto Rico, one of the Caribbean's more centrally placed major islands. Perhaps, he now hoped, his proposed new university would eventually become a reality. This dream of a hemispheric institution of higher learning on the island, however, would not be realized until a half-century later, although the campus of present-day Inter-American University is not located at Rio Piedras.

That spring of 1903 also brought irritating news out of the "Pearl of the Antilles." Dr. George Groff was at it again, trying to create a fracas over alleged misdeeds by Brumbaugh while commissioner of education there. Now back teaching at Bucknell, the biology professor was still a very bitter man. He had never gotten over losing out to Brumbaugh for the commissioner's post and then being cast aside as his assistant. He resented even more knowing that Brumbaugh, after resigning, had influenced Teddy Roosevelt against giving him a second chance at the head job. Also—and this came out in a letter to Samuel Lindsay as late as 1908—he was unforgiving that "Dr. B" had so few good things to say about the public-school program of the military government. He wrote, "I think he never once spoke with any regard for the truth in reference to the work of his predecessors"—meaning the writer in particular.

Ever since August 1900, Groff had harassed Brumbaugh in any carping way he could, such as demanding that the Puerto Rican postal authorities condemn him for mail fraud. (The inspector-in-charge said Groff was "loco.") This exasperating behavior once led Governor Hunt to shake his head in wonderment and say to Brumbaugh, "Groff must be a strange character. I am at a loss to comprehend his persistence and what he expects to attain by his continued attacks upon you."

Now, in March 1903, Groff thought he had found ammunition for firing new anti-Brumbaugh salvos. He had read an editorial in the *San Juan News* that month charging the former commissioner with malversation. The "ringing editorial," as Groff termed it, made two specific allegations: As a "public servant," Brumbaugh had illegally purchased one hundred thousand copies of his own *Standard Readers* for distribution to the island's schools; and he "dealt in school desks contrary to the law." Seizing upon these gravamens, Groff communicated with Secretary Hitchcock and Governor Hunt in early April, pressing for a full-scale probe. He told them, "I am sure you will find more than one violation of the law." He also contacted the *Philadelphia Public Ledger*—to bring the charges out in the open and humiliate his enemy on home turf.

Brumbaugh, of course, was forced to defend himself in the eyes of all concerned: Hitchcock, Hunt—and through a *Public Ledger* reporter—Philadelphians. He forthrightly admitted procuring his own *Readers*, saying, "I concluded that mine was as good as any other." (One letter to the editor from a former American English teacher in Puerto Rico testified to the "infinite superiority" of her ex-boss's *Readers* over the others, declaring "this was the almost unanimous opinion of all the English teachers on the island.") But the figure of one hundred thousand was grossly exaggerated, he said; it was more like eight or ten thousand. All disbursements, both for textbooks and desks, he argued, had been perfectly legal and duly audited. (Interestingly, Groff, while acting commissioner, had tried to do what he now attacked Brumbaugh for having done: he had ordered ten thousand copies of a new book he himself had authored, *Hygiene in the Tropics*, for circulation throughout the school system. But Brumbaugh, upon his arrival, promptly canceled the order, which infuriated the physician.)

To a *Public Ledger* newsman, the maligned ex-commissioner dismissed the *San Juan News* editorial as the fulmination of an "Anti-American [and] Anti-Administration organ." About Groff's tactics, he caustically opined: "It appears to me that the malice in his accusation emanated from one who wanted to be Commissioner and failed to get the position." In the end, Brumbaugh emerged from this latest attack on his character fully vindicated, and no official investigation ever took place.

It was around the time of the Groff hubbub that the chivied Penn professor began his long public identification with Sunday-school work. Not that he was unknown as a religious educator in prior years. Several of his Juniata Bible lectures had been published in book form and were quite popular outside the Dunker fold. (The wife of Jacob Riis, the noted New York City urban-reform journalist, bought a copy of his most recent series—on the Gospel of John.) At the 1899 Annual Meeting of his denomination, which in the early 1880s had suffered a major schism, in part, over the issue of Sunday schools, Brumbaugh had spoken about the importance of Christian education in the life of the church. In fact, his 1899 *History of the German Baptist Brethren* averred that the Sunday school was actually an innovation of the Dunkers. According to him, in 1738, thirty years before Englishman Robert Raikes founded *his* first Sunday school, the Germantown Brethren had begun holding young people's Sunday-afternoon meetings. "That this pioneer activity should have been abandoned," he wrote, "is as inexplicable as the resistance with which a few still oppose Sunday schools on the ground that they are an innovation."

And, no hypocrite on the matter, he had not shirked Sunday-school duty himself at Philadelphia's First Church of the Brethren, his place of worship, on the corner of Carlisle and Dauphin Streets. Also, from time to time before his Puerto Rican stint, he had taught a Sabbath-day class for the employees of former postmaster general John Wanamaker, the Quaker City's pioneering department-store titan.

Brumbaugh had also been active in Christian education at the graduate-school level. For several months a year between 1898 and 1900, he had made weekly treks (every Thursday) to the Biblical Seminary of New York City, where he taught divinity students. Then in January and February of 1903 he and a Penn colleague had conducted a ten-week Sunday-morning course of Bible study in the university's Howard House Hall. As publicized, it was "Specially Intended for Members of the Faculty, Graduate Students, and Other Critical Thinkers Inside and Outside of the University." Brumbaugh's five lectures dealt with the method of Jesus' teaching.

But his first national exposure as a Sunday-school enthusiast dated to the summer of 1902, when he gave a major address at the International Sunday-School Association's tenth annual convention in Denver. Wanamaker, an officer of the organization—it was active in the United States and Canada—probably had something to do with putting Brumbaugh on the convention's program. If so, he can be credited with introducing American Protestants to a new voice in the reform of religious education.

As a boy, Brumbaugh had found the Sunday school a bore, its pedagogy a disaster. The approach was evangelistic and dogmatic, telling the child what to believe and how to act. Bible-centered, it failed to use the Scriptures as a guide and source of enrichment for the developmental religious experiences of children or to relate biblical materials to current social problems. Any kind of extrabiblical material was scorned, even biographical studies of yesteryear's Christian heroes. Moreover, the "uniform lesson plan," commonly adopted by Protestant churches shortly after the Civil War, required everyone, young and old, to study the same curriculum. By the 1900s, however, church-school reconstructionists were calling for "graded" lessons, geared more to the intellectual level and immaturity of childhood. Also, since the rise of the Sunday-school movement a century earlier, there had been the perennial problem of well-meaning but untrained lay teachers.

At the center of agitation for Sunday-school reform were many American educators identified with the progressive-education movement, then in its heyday. Their secular pedagogical innovations were inspired by cognitive and child-psychology theories propounded by early nineteenth-century European thinkers like Friedrich Froebel, Johann Pestalozzi, and Johann Herbart, and more contemporary American educational philosophers like Francis Parker and John Dewey. All had something to say about the religious and moral feelings of children and the appropriate pedagogy for exposing juveniles to spiritual and social values.

Some progressive educators, while agitated by problems of the Sunday school—its narrow, ungraded curriculum, its lack of trained teachers, its biased, catechetical approach—were also not altogether satisfied with the nature and quality of moral education in the nation's secular-oriented public schools. They had no quarrel with teaching children right and wrong, as the schools did by helping them to evaluate the consequences of their conduct in a social situation. But they questioned whether moral education could be best taught in the absence of a religious perspective. Still, in their opinion, the public-school approach to forming moral character was preferable to that of confessional and doctrinaire church pedagogy.

At century's turn, therefore, two theories of moral education existed side by side: that of the Sunday school and that of the public school. Some progressive educators and laypeople saw a benefit from integrating both modi operandi into the structure of each institution. So in early 1903 a mixed group of them—Catholic, Jew, and Protestant—met in Chicago for the purpose of discussing how this could be done. Out of this ad hoc gathering sprang the Religious Education Association (REA). Its stated objective was "To inspire the educational forces of our country with the religious ideal, to inspire the religious forces of our country with the educational ideal, and to keep before the public mind the ideal of religious education, and the sense of its needed value."

The REA at once undertook the task of propagating its philosophy in churches, synagogues, and public schools. Among its founding officers were such illustrious scholars as university presidents William Rainey Harper (Chicago) and Nicholas Murray Butler (Columbia). The University of Chicago, which already was the nerve center of the Social Gospel movement, became the REA's headquarters. The association published a bimonthly magazine, *Religious Education*, soon recognized as a powerful medium in molding public opinion. At the University of Chicago, where John Dewey still taught, the REA set up an experimental "model Sunday school." Here it tried out new curricula and pedagogical methods, in addition to promoting alternative strategies for reshaping the educational mission of the church. The REA also inspired the creation of programs of religious education in colleges and seminaries.

The REA's progressive pattern for religious education, while not neglecting biblical materials, looked to liberal theology for its exegetical base. Guided by Dewey's doctrines of experimentalism and pragmatism, REA partisans contended that people (especially children) could be educated in the Christian faith with no need for religious conversion. They never feared being known as radicals or heretics. By their method, no longer would the child be told what to believe. Religious instruction, still using the Bible as a moral guide, would instead encourage children to develop their own individual religious experiences. Sunday-school lessons, the reformers proposed, should confront children with problems of personal or societal interrelationships, the solutions of which involved religious values. By the end of World War I the religious-education movement would bring major changes, not only to the curriculum of Sunday schools of all faiths but also to that of public schools.

Martin Brumbaugh's identification with the Religious Education Association had begun in April of 1903. He was appointed to its Department of Teacher Training, which had a ten-man staff. (The next year he also did a turn as a vice-president of the organization.) In the peak years of his university career, REA-style religious education, especially teacher training, became a corollary professional interest of his that would, as time would tell, give his name international as well as national currency. Few men anywhere on the globe, a contemporary of his once said, were more "potent" in the training of Sunday-school teachers before the First World War than the Dunker professor-preacher. He soon came to be known for his "firm faith in and ardent enthusiasm for the Association," as one of its officers wrote him in appreciation. The REA's first assignment for him was to help plan and to be the on-field director of its second annual convention, with Philadelphia the venue.

By the time of its sixth convention, in 1908, the REA's membership exceeded two thousand. That year's annual assembly met in Washington, D.C., in February. Teddy Roosevelt entertained the delegates at a reception in the White House. He spoke to them on the theme of spiritual training and lauded the REA's work. Uncle Sam's children, he said, "must be trained in the elementary branches of righteousness . . . so that it shall come naturally to them to abhor that which is evil, or we shall never see our democracy take the place it must and shall take among the nations of the world."

Brumbaugh was an ideal recruit for the REA. His reputation as an educator reached across America, and in Pennsylvania he was widely known as an active churchman. Also, his natal commonwealth provided fertile ground for reform—it had more Sunday schools than any other state in the Union. Its 1,723,749 "scholars" of all ages in 1903 exceeded the number of those in neighboring New York by nearly half a million. On an international scale, this enrollment totaled about one-third that of England and Wales combined.

As a pedagogical expert for REA, Brumbaugh immediately became a darling of the Pennsylvania State Sabbath School Association (PSSSA), serving as an officer of its Philadelphia County affiliate. It was he, in 1903, who first introduced teacher training into the Sunday schools of Pennsylvania, teaching a night class of fifty people. This cadre of trainees then went out to the churches to conduct similar classes. Brumbaugh's ongoing work with the PSSSA earned him the firm friendship of not only John Wanamaker but also another wealthy Sunday-school activist, Pittsburgh's Howard J. Heinz, of the "57 Varieties" canned-food industry. Perhaps Brumbaugh's stature within the PSSSA, which was interdenominational in its work, was best epitomized by a public tribute once paid him when he was Philadelphia's chief of schools. A speaker told PSSSA conventioneers: "One of the greatest men I ever knew lives in Philadelphia and he is head of the public school system. I wish it would cloud up and rain men like Martin G. Brumbaugh for forty days and forty nights."

This accolade was prompted, in part, by the role Brumbaugh played in promoting the PSSSA's fiftieth anniversary celebration, held in the Quaker City. The four-day event was highlighted by a massive nighttime parade lasting nearly three hours. Twenty-seven thousand cheering men from all over the state and fifty bands formed a column five miles long. Thousands of marchers carried flags, banners, and placards, many depicting an open Bible. Brumbaugh said, "The parade was the sublimest scene that ever swept the streets of this great city." He watched it from the reviewing stand on Broad Street. This observation spot was an honor accorded him because, on his own initiative, he had organized over a dozen miniparades that day by the city's public-school children.

By the time of the PSSSA's golden jubilee, the Brumbaugh name had been for a number of years also closely linked to The Sunday School Times Company, in Philadelphia. It published the influential *Sunday School Times*, a conservative— some would say fundamentalist—weekly Protestant periodical. (The PSSSA had its own organ, *Pennsylvania Herald*.) Brumbaugh's was thus a name revered both by REA liberals and hyperorthodox evangelicals in the movement to restructure America's Sunday schools.

This was possible because, like a true Dunker, he was no theological dogmatist. His paramount interest was in teacher training, not theology. His own approach to Bible study tended to be expository and historical. He found the Holy Writ a rich lode of inspirational anecdotes, a practical life-centered guide for societal and personal values, and not a sourcebook for theological speculation. A perusal of his Juniata Bible lectures, chapel talks, sermons, and other homilies reveals absolutely no scientific analysis of the Protestant biblical canon, nor any appreciation for such scholarly endeavors. On the other hand, neither do his writings contain objections to the scientific investigation of the Bible.

In 1904 Charles G. Trumball, editor of the *Sunday School Times*, enlisted Brumbaugh to prepare a correspondence course in teacher training. The lessons ran serially in his magazine from November 1904 through the spring of 1905. Later, revised and expanded, they were published in book form and titled, *The Making of a Teacher* (1905). Brumbaugh subtitled it, "A Contribution to Some Phases of the Problem of Religious Education." For decades *The Making of a Teacher* stood as the preeminent work in the field, praised by religious and secular educators alike. Republished twice—1932 and 1947 (once by Harper Brothers)—it ran through eleven editions. The *Juniata Echo* reported in May 1912 that the World Sunday School Association had talked Brumbaugh into making a Chinese translation of the book, but nothing seems to have come of the idea.

The immense popularity of *The Making of a Teacher* is a bit surprising. Although reviewers pointed out that the book is stripped of technical language and easily understood by the average Sunday-school teacher, it is certainly no elementary, quick-read, how-to-do-it manual. Its 351 pages present a deep look at the laws and theories of teaching. Three-fourths of the book discusses the psychology and pedagogy of the Greeks and Romans, the nineteenth-century gurus of the latter-day progressive educators, and other classical writers and thinkers, before getting to the Jesus model. (For Brumbaugh, of course, Jesus was *the* one perfect teacher.)

A few of the author's "sincere friends," he says in a prefatory comment, feared that his "formal" discussions, though couched in simple language, would be over the heads of the "great masses" of teachers or would bore them. He, too, had prepublication misgivings. But a run of eleven editions over four decades proved their worries unfounded. In fact, for many years *The Making of a Teacher* was extensively used by teachers' institutes as a reading course, both in Pennsylvania and in other states. As the Boston-based *Journal of Education* said in appreciation of it, "Although it is primarily for Sunday School teachers and other workers, it is at the same time, one of the best books yet published for any teacher."

Brumbaugh helped author another book put out by The Sunday School Times Company in 1908. He and three other writers of national reputation produced *Training the Teacher*. This four-part volume, hyped by the *Times* as the "Teacher-Training Book of a Generation," was adopted by the International Sunday-School Association as a diploma-granting course.

Brumbaugh's campaign for governor and his four years in office brought an end to his heavy commitment to public Sunday-school work, but not before he went to Zurich, Switzerland—accompanied by Anna and Flora Belle—in mid-July 1913 as one of Pennsylvania's delegates to the seventh annual convention of the World Sunday School Association. A top-billed speaker, his topic was, "The Sunday-School as an Education Force."

Brumbaugh, as a Religious Education Association partner, not only sought to make the Sunday school relevant to the twentieth century, but also shared the Association's concern about the current trend to secularize public education. John Dewey, the REA's saint, had written in 1902:

> There are many who regard the transfer of [the] educational function from the church to the state as more than a matter of regret; they conceive it as a move which, if persisted in, will result disastrously to the best and permanent interests of mankind.

Brumbaugh echoed this sentiment when he once declared:

> The only considerable nation on earth to-day that does not seek systematically to provide its boys and girls with moral and religious training [in the public schools] is the United States of America.

He already had the reputation, since the beginning of his teachers' institute fame, of spiritualizing public education as "service for God and for country," in that order. He preached that educators, above all else, must exemplify Christian ideals. And as Philadelphia's superintendent of schools a couple of years later, he became a prophetic voice for moral training in the public schools.

Among those who admired him for his REA activism was the Reverend William W. Newton of the American Church Sunday-School Institute. Philadelphia-based, the institute was a creation of the Protestant Episcopal Church. It published the *American Church Sunday-School Magazine,* a monthly, which Newton coedited. In the magazine's February 1907 issue, the religious journalist published a six-stanza hymn he wrote in honor of Abraham Lincoln and dedicated to Martin Brumbaugh. The choral refrain, Newton seemed to be implying, was meant to describe the school administrator as well as the Great Liberator:

> Hero! Hero! Sent from God!
> Leader of his people.

Besides wide fame as a religious educator, the immediate post-Puerto Rico years brought the shaggy-browed Penn professor other kinds of academic, civic, and professional recognition. He took a leading role, as a concerned citizen, in initiating major reforms in the Philadelphia school system. In 1903 he had been named to the Council of the International Educational Conference, a body made up of prominent educators from twenty-eight states and four provinces of Canada. That same year, the governor appointed him to a five-year term on the Valley Forge Commission, whose responsibility it was to preserve, maintain, and improve the site of George Washington's famous Revolutionary War military camp.

In early December of 1903 *The Brumbaugh-Hall Primer* attracted singular attention at the opening of the Children's World International Exposition, held in the Tauride Palace in St. Petersburg, Russia. Brumbaugh had sent a copy of the

book to Elizabeth Mavriklevna, the dowager empress, who had called for and sponsored the two-month-long event. He wanted to show foreign educators an example
of an American primary-school textbook. The dowager empress presented the
Primer to the exposition as part of the stately inaugural ceremonies. The silver tray
on which it lay was bordered by small Russian and American flags intertwined
with an arrangement of the empress's favorite flowers.

June 1904 saw him inducted as an honorary member of Penn's Phi Beta Kappa
Society, whose medal he always proudly wore on a vest chain.

There were also speaking appearances before the Pennsylvania State Education Association and the National Education Association (he would address the
NEA a dozen times during his academic career). The year 1904 also marked the
first of several annual delegate treks to New York's Quaker-sponsored Lake Mohonk
Conference of International Arbitration. It was during those years that Brumbaugh's
Penn colleagues elected him to the Academic Council, the faculty's highest au-
thoritative committee.

On more of a human-interest note, Brumbaugh's on-the-street heroics one day
in January 1905 earned him a column in the Philadelphia papers. It was a Monday,
the day after New Year's. He had just left his home on Walnut Street on the way to
his campus office when he caught sight of a runaway horse. The horse, pulling a
small wagon, was galloping at breakneck speed on the sidewalk along Woodland
Avenue, near its intersection with Walnut Street. Directly in its path was a group of
little children, at play, unaware of their danger. Brumbaugh rushed to get in front
of the horse, waving his arms and shouting at it. This caused the frightened animal
to swerve toward the street, barely missing the frolicking tykes. At the curb, the
wagon struck a sapling, breaking it off. The collision overturned the cart, spilling
its load of strawberries, onions, clams, and fish in every direction. The horse broke
away from the shafts and charged on its way another couple of blocks before it was
stopped.

Viewed by Juniata College people as no less heroic later that year was their
nominal president's success in getting Andrew Carnegie to help capitalize the erection of a new campus library. The college, with a total enrollment of 363, had over
the past decade gradually expanded its facilities and curriculums. Major construction included a classroom building (Students Hall, in 1895); a women's dormitory
(Ladies Hall, in 1890); a dining room (Oneida Hall, in 1898); and a gymnasium, in
1901. The campus had also been enlarged to twenty-three acres, part of which was
converted into the athletic field, used for various outdoor games; there were as yet no
varsity sports. On the academic front, the number of four-year liberal-arts students
had grown to twenty-eight. The Academy, opened in 1899 as a residential surrogate for country teenagers deprived of high school, now enrolled seventy-seven.
The Normal School, the Bible School, the School of Music, and the Business School
accounted for the rest of enrolled students. The faculty, none with an earned doctorate, numbered twenty-five. To speak of an endowment was an exercise in fantasy.

By all counts, Juniata, almost three decades old in 1905, was still very much a humble, needy, bucolic college. To appeal to the "Napoleon of the Smokestacks" for philanthropic assistance in building a library must have struck most trustees— maybe even M. G.—as sheer folly. Who first came up with the idea is not on record. But it was probably obvious to board members that M. G., who only three years before had won a Carnegie-built library for Puerto Ricans, should be the contact man for the college. So in late summer 1904 Brumbaugh made his first move. He asked Governor Samuel Pennypacker, a dear friend of his and another history buff devoted to promoting the cause of the Pennsylvania Germans, to route the dwarfish humanitarian, on an upcoming visit to Pennsylvania, through Huntingdon for a possible stopover at the college. But the governor, although sympathetic, was unable to pull off the stratagem.

For the next several months, on into 1905, Brumbaugh doggedly pursued the Scotsman by mail. At last, on 12 March, a Philadelphia mailman delivered the eagerly awaited affirmative reply. The good news came to the Huntingdon trustees via an M. G. letter ten days later. They were told that Carnegie agreed to a grant of fifteen thousand dollars for a library—on a matching-fund basis, of course, a policy he originated in the history of American philanthropy. The college-raised money was to be used for maintaining the proposed structure.

The trustees acted posthaste. Within weeks they commissioned Edward Tilton of New York City to be the architect. Tilton, the designer of most Carnegie-financed libraries, had made a minor splash on the world scene in the restoration of the Heraeum at Argos, in Greece. A fund drive enjoyed instant success; by early winter $20,500 had been raised in cash and pledges.

But a belated needs study indicated the necessity of a bigger facility than originally planned. So Brumbaugh wrote Carnegie at Skibo Castle, Scotland—his retirement manor—and explained the situation, asking for a larger gift. Carnegie, impressed by the progress of the college's financial campaign, wasted no time replying. On 13 October Brumbaugh received a cablegram from the ex-steel baron's secretary that read in part: "Mr. Carnegie . . . wants me to say he will be glad to increase the allowance for Library Building . . . from Fifteen Thousand to Twenty-eight thousand. . . ."

Ever since Brumbaugh's college days, the library had been the academic apple of his eye. The erstwhile student librarian donated thousands of volumes, including the wonderful Cassel collection. In 1904 the college hired its first trained librarian when he offered to pick up the tab over the summer months on condition the trustees continue the position. He also saw to the introduction of card cataloging and a system of classification.

The site of the new structure, the trustees agreed, should not be on the already crowded campus. They wanted a proper setting, one that would allow the edifice to face toward town, like Founders Hall. After much thought they chose the northwest corner of Moore and Seventeenth Streets. This was directly across Seventeenth

Street from the house Brumbaugh still owned. The trustees further decided to purchase several other houses and lots along that Moore block up to Eighteenth Street. The cost of these properties, owned by two faculty members, added up to $6,500.

Once again, as in 1878, the college turned to townspeople for help. This time, however, there was no appeal for outright charity. The trustees proposed a seven thousand-dollar loan, interest free. As an incentive, Brumbaugh spread word that if the town came through he would give an equal sum toward campus expansion. In the spirit of '78, Huntingdonians accepted the challenge and, thanks to them and M. G., Juniata was fourteen thousand dollars richer. (Over the years the extent of Martin's openhandedness would give rise to rumors he faithfully tithed the biblical one-tenth of his income to his alma mater. In all, he was said to have given Juniata more than fifty thousand dollars.)

Work on the Carnegie Library—architecturally a combination of Doric and Ionic styles—began in March 1906. Dedication ceremonies took place on 17 April (Founders Day) the next year. M. G., of course, saw to it that a bevy of dignitaries, political and collegiate, were in attendance (Carnegie declined his invitation). Still Juniata's official headman, he, not his cousin Harvey, presided at both afternoon and evening programs. But he no longer bore the workaday tag of a university professor; since June 1906 Philadelphia had given him a new title: superintendent of public schools.

A peon cabin.

Governor's Palace in Old San Juan, overlooking the harbor and sea wall, with "The Stars and Stripes" stretched out by the breeze.

The commissioner, at his San Juan desk. He had begun to part his hair in the middle, probably to hide a noticeable widow's peak.

The governor of Puerto Rico and cabinet in executive session at San Juan. M. G. is on the far right. Governor Charles H. Allen sits at the head of the table, with Secretary William H. Hunt on his right. Both Allen and Hunt kept in touch with M. G. through letters for many years afterward.

A typical Brumbaugh-built school.

Insular Normal School, Rio Piedras, soon after construction in 1902.

The summerhouse on Back Street in Wayne, Maine—as redesigned and enlarged by architect-son Edwin.

Brumbaugh in seldom-worn clerical garb. The photograph was probably taken for his denomination's 1908 bicentennial.

The history-making 1911 School Code Commission. Seated, *left to right:* M. G.; George Phillips, West Chester Normal School superintendent; Nathan Schaeffer, state superintendent; William Lander, Bedford County merchant. Standing, *left to right*: James Coughlin, Wilkes-Barre superintendent; John Rilling, Erie lawyer; David Oliver, president of the Pittsburgh school board.

Executive Mansion in Brumbaugh's day. The main entrance was on the left.

The governor in his "democratic" bowler. Here he seems to be setting the headgear style for his escorts.

The governor and his new wife Flora Belle. He would often say to her, "Aren't you glad we married us?"

The governor makes the newsreel on "Good Roads Day."

The "good roads" governor and his official car, with chauffeur and footman.

10

Farewell to Penn

BACK at Christmastime 1901, when Brumbaugh chose not to return to Puerto Rico, "welcome home" greetings from Philadelphia friends and acquaintances stuffed his mailbox for days. One welcoming note came from William J. Moran, a ward school director. After stating a few pleasantries, he signed off with the words: "Very glad you are back again once more with us and *hope that I may some day see you as the Superintendent of Philadelphia.*"

There is no reason to suspect Moran's offhanded compliment set the educator immediately to hankering after the municipal post. For the moment, it seemed, Puerto Rico had soured him on administrative work. But, designedly or not, he soon began to attract attention as a spokesman for reformist solutions to Philadelphia's badly deficient public-school system. As a result, in 1903 he was elected vice president of the Public Education Association (PEA). This was at the very time he had been enlisted by another reform cause—that of the Religious Education Association.

The PEA was an influential volunteer citizens' group founded in 1881. It was one of thirty similar large-city reform organizations in several eastern states. The aim of the PEA, its constitution stated, was to "Promote the efficiency and to perfect the system of public education in Philadelphia." For two decades the Association had been the agent provocateur in a whole series of reforms and innovations. But there had not been uniform progress, and much still remained to be done in the way of modernizing the school system. Fortuitously, at the time Brumbaugh allied himself with the PEA leadership the nation was being convulsed by a frenzy of reform. Historians refer to the years roughly between 1900 and 1910 as the Progressive Era. Americans had seen nothing like it since the great Age of Reform, the 1830s and 1840s. It is important to understand how this new-century phenomenon of history ultimately worked to the benefit of the Public Education Association and Philadelphia's soon-to-be superintendent of schools.

The Progressive Era coincided with a period in United States history when the nation was in the throes of turbulent transition from an agrarian society to one of urban life and an industrial economy. This created complex political, social, and economic problems: monopolies, political corruption, societal injustices, crowded cities, rampant poverty, increased organized crime. The transformation of American society began after the Civil War. By the late 1890s the United States stood as the industrial giant among world powers. European immigrants by the millions supplied the unskilled labor pool for this prodigious expansion of manufacturing.

The nation's population more than doubled in the three and a half decades following the Civil War to well over one hundred million citizens. The growth of American cities, the favorite haven of most immigrants, was just as spectacular. Urban population *tripled* between 1860 and 1900; four out of ten Americans were now city dwellers. Multitudes of farm and country folks, like newly arrived foreigners, were also lured to the cities in search of jobs. But pell-mell urban growth would trip off a whole catalog of socioeconomic and political woes, especially in metropolitan centers. The hordes of overseas newcomers and former homeland rustics and small-towners sadly watched their big-city paradises steadily slide into Dantean hells. Among the most disillusioned of urbanites emerged a crusading army of reformers who called themselves "progressives."

These progressives, who were mainly middle-class men and women, never coalesced into a single political party. Active in all parts of the country at all levels of government, they chose to work as Democrats and Republicans toward common goals. As one historian described their impact on the American scene, "The truth is that progressivism was less a minority movement and more a majority mood." That mood decried what seemed to be an outworn political philosophy for dealing with the complexities of the new century: the Jeffersonian ideal of minimal government intervention. Progressives argued the country now needed strong, not feeble, organs of government at all tiers: federal, state, and municipal. Government must become an agency of human welfare.

To a remarkable degree, the wide-ranging gains the progressives eventually scored rested upon journalistic muckraking. The practitioners of the new reportorial style were a group of reformer-writers. Beginning about 1902, these bright, young, aggressive reporters revolutionized journalism. They pioneered in factual, investigative reportage. By dogged research, they exposed the corruption caused by modern industrialization, urbanization, and immigration. Political bosses, urban boodle, collusion between supposedly upstanding politicians and corporate leaders, strangling monopolies—all came under their scrutiny. They relentlessly attacked social evils such as slums, juvenile delinquency, and prostitution.

All of them passionately sought to arouse the public conscience against America's iniquitous ways. Teddy Roosevelt, offended by their zeal, branded them as muckrakers. He compared them to the character in Bunyan's *Pilgrim's Progress*, who, because he was so intent upon raking filth, could not see the angel overhead offering to trade a celestial crown for his muckrake.

But few Americans shared the president's dim view of this "New Journalism." Instead, they swarmed to buy up the latest scandalous revelations about their society. As a result, a bevy of popular monthly ten-cent and fifteen-cent magazines like

McClure's, Cosmopolitan, Collier's, the *American,* and *Everybody's*—all with a nationwide circulation—flourished. They found it hugely profitable to carry a corps of muckrakers on their payrolls. Some of the most shocking but socially edifying serialized articles written by these well-paid troops were later collected and published as best-selling books. One of the most famous of these muckraking volumes was New Yorker Lincoln Steffens's *Shame of the Cities* (1904). It was a reprint of his celebrated series in *McClure's* on urban corruption and the crookedness of boss-rule and machine politics. His major thesis was that the political rot of the nation's great metropolises—and the ills of democracy generally—must ultimately be blamed on the moral apathy of ordinary citizens.

Steffens built his case around spot exposures of what he considered the six most egregiously misgoverned cities in the United States: St. Louis, Minneapolis, Pittsburgh, Philadelphia, Chicago, and New York. His exposé of Philadelphia, written in 1903, was titled "Corrupt and Contented." He began by saying urbanologists blamed immigration for most municipal ills, but that hardly explained conditions in the City of Brotherly Love. True, he said, the unprecedented influx of European immigrants after the Civil War helped swell its population to 1,293,697; only New York and Chicago were more populous. Great numbers of foreigners—mostly Irish, Italian, and Polish—opted to settle in this major Atlantic-coast port, then the republic's chief textile center. Yet, as Steffens was quick to point out, nearly half of its populace was "native-born of native-born parents." This made Philadelphia "the most American of our greater cities," he noted. He also said it was "the city of homes" (one house for every five persons), unblighted, like Gotham, by immigrant-crammed tenements.

Why, then, did Steffens indict this quintessential American city as the worst governed in the country? Because, he argued, it, unlike any other tainted city, was totally—almost "hopelessly"—befouled by machine politics.

The Democratic Party had long ruled New York through infamous Tammany Hall, but for years Philadelphia had been ruled by the Republican machine. The bosses there got their orders from United States Senator Matthew S. Quay, the party's state czar. Quay's chief power broker in Philadelphia in the early 1900s was Israel ("Is") Durham, Pennsylvania's insurance commissioner. Durham spent most of his time at an office in Philadelphia rather than the one in Harrisburg. He and his underling bosses were so powerful that the party controlled, by a miscellany of fraudulent expedients, every stage of the voting process. At least New Yorkers, wrote Steffens, could vote for Tammany Hall, but honest Philadelphians had no vote at all. As he put it, they "have no more rights at the polls than the negroes down South." "Nor," he said, "do they fight very hard for this basic privilege." His stinging conclusion: The City of Brotherly Love seemed quite "satisfied to be a scandal to the nation and a disgrace to democracy."

In fact, not only the city was deprived of self-government, so was the local machine. Its ringleaders answered directly to Matthew Quay, imputed by Steffens to be the latter-day "proprietor of Pennsylvania and the real ruler of Philadelphia, just as William Penn, the Great Proprietor, was." The boss's grip on the city could not easily be broken. It was reinforced by the political circumstances of the time: the Republican Party's tyranny over both Pennsylvania and the federal government. Steffens wrote:

> The people of Philadelphia are Republicans in a Republican city in a Republican State in a Republican nation, and they are bound ring on ring on ring. The President of the United States and his patronage; the national Cabinet and their patronage; the Congress and the patronage of the Senators and the Congressmen from Pennsylvania; the Governor of the State and the State Legislature with their powers and patronage; and all that the mayor and city councils have of power and patronage—all these bear down upon Philadelphia to keep it in control of Quay's boss and his little ring.

Philadelphia's City Councils was a double-chambered diet, with 146 unpaid members, that ruled the treasury. No municipal government in the world approximated its numerical tumescence. Its massive size and gratuitous service made the Councils especially vulnerable to jobbery. Political as well as social reform would therefore entail a daunting struggle in Philadelphia, warned Steffens—perhaps "Nothing but a revolution."

Gustavus Myers, a muckraking comrade-in-arms, agreed that radical, if not revolutionary, actions had to be taken if the birthplace of the Declaration of Independence and the Constitution were to be rid of its systemic corruption. In 1910 Myers would earn his own rightful niche in "the literature of exposure" with a revelatory book entitled *The History of the Great American Fortunes*. But in 1904, the same year *The Shame of the Cities* appeared in book form, he published a scathing article on Philadelphia in the *Living Age*, a weekly literary magazine. He titled his piece "The Most Corrupt City in the World." Even Steffens had not gone so far in defaming the community where Martin Brumbaugh made his home.

Both Steffens and Myers deplored the apathy of prominent Philadelphians who would not join reform movements. Clergymen, Sunday-school leaders, lawyers, realtors, shopkeepers, heads of charities—all knew what was going on but went along for a variety of reasons. Even Charles C. Harrison, the provost of the University of Pennsylvania, refused to join a revolt. The man for whom Brumbaugh had great respect as an academician demurred because, he said, "it might impair his usefulness" to Penn. The people, Steffens caustically observed, "seem to prefer to be ruled by a known thief than an ambitious reformer."

Not that boss-rule went unchallenged. Public-spirited groups like the Municipal League, the Allied Reform League, and the Law and Order Society fought the machine's politico-financial control over various city franchises. But their collective list of members numbered far too few to be effective.

Among the free-spoken, individual reformers, one man stood out as most combative: John Wanamaker, the piously inclined Philadelphia giant of retailing.

Wanamaker, who would become a confidant of Martin Brumbaugh, epitomized the Henry Clay-coined phrase, *self-made man*—rising from bookstore errand-boy to founder, in 1869, of one of the country's first large department stores. (He would later, in 1896, establish another one in New York City. Both stores catered to the carriage trade.) As a self-made man, he built his merchandising fortune with prayer as well as business genius. He was a model family man, world-renowned as a leader of the Sunday-school movement and the Young Men's Christian Association. But he was just as prominent in the political life of his country as he was in its business and religious life.

Wanamaker got his introduction to national politics when he served the Republican party (now coming to be called the GOP—"Grand Old Party") as chief money-raiser during the presidential race of 1888. The Republican banner-bearer was Benjamin Harrison, an ex-senator from Indiana and a Civil War veteran. For the Democrats, it was Grover Cleveland, running for reelection. Thanks to Wanamaker's enterprise, the GOP raised more than three million dollars, the biggest campaign chest to date. The Democrats' campaign funds in the 1888 race for the White House never came close. Even so, Harrison barely won (in the Electoral College, not by popular vote). The new president rewarded Wanamaker for his key role in the narrow victory with a cabinet appointment: postmaster general. Unfortunately for Republicans—and the postmaster general—Harrison turned out to be a one-term White House tenant.

As a cabinet politico, however, Philadelphia's merchant prince discovered he liked holding high public office. In 1896 Pennsylvania's senior United States senator, J. Donald Cameron, retired. Wanamaker conducted an all-out campaign to get his party's nomination for the vacant post. He was backed by the reform wing of the party, but Matthew Quay, the holdover senator and state chairman, fought against it. The Quay faction supported Boies Penrose, the future Republican boss of Pennsylvania, and the man Martin Brumbaugh would have to deal with in his quest for governor a dozen years hence. Penrose won the nomination handily, later also winning the statewide election.

Wanamaker's defeat angered him and led to a ceaseless war against the reign of Quayism. He made the *Philadelphia North American*, a newspaper owned by his son Thomas, a militant anti-Quay organ. He did succeed temporarily, just before Brumbaugh left for the Caribbean, in damaging Quay's reputation and throwing his well-oiled machine out of gear. But the big boss and his forces soon regrouped, and Brumbaugh returned to find the political picture in Pennsylvania *status quo ante* Puerto Rico. Nevertheless, he saw much to admire in Wanamaker, who, perhaps as much as anyone else in the state, embodied the civic ideals of a progressive and the fury of a muckraker.

Brumbaugh and his PEA cohorts especially valued the help of Wanamaker's *North American* in exposing the Quay-Durham team as a plague on education. It was one of the papers that had uncovered a recent machine attempt to corrupt schoolchildren into gambling through illicit "policy" games (buying "numbers"). Ring-linked gamesters plied their nefarious trade, at a few cents a chance, in the vicinity of schools. The exposé put an end to the racket, but paid-off police officers got off unpunished.

About the time of the policy-selling scandal, further evidence of the machine's brazen attempt to corrupt education came to light. In this case the public-school system itself was threatened. It was no secret that teachers and principals owed their positions to political pull (ward bosses), like any other city employee. It infuriated PEAers and Municipal Leaguers, however, to learn the latest trick of the Republican City Committee in the spring of 1903. Just before the municipal election the committee sent a letter to every male teacher asking for "voluntary contributions." But blue-penciled, in one corner of the notice, appeared "2 per cent" (of the recipient's salary). Professor Martin Brumbaugh was outraged by such hubris. He publicly denounced the "rake-off" ploy: "I desire to raise my voice to curse [this] method."

A court trial that April revealed to what extent political pull, at least in one ward, amounted to outright extortion. Steffens wrote about this case, and so did Clinton R. Woodruff. (The trial itself was covered by all the city's newspapers.) Woodruff was a progressive par excellence. He was a member or officer of numerous reformist groups, both national and local, including the Philadelphia Education Association and the Municipal League. (He and Martin Brumbaugh, it is of incidental interest to note, were well-acquainted; joiners both, they belong to many of the same clubs, historical and genealogical societies, outdoor organizations, and professional associations.)

In December 1903, Woodruff, a frequent contributor to leading American journals, wrote a muckraking article for the *Educational Review*. He titled it "A Corrupt School System." He set the context for the April trial by assailing the conditions that allowed the Republican machine to subject the Philadelphia schools to politics. The "first stepping stone in the path of political preferment," he wrote, was to become a school director. And, he charged, ward bosses, themselves vassals of the city boss, had the final say on who got to be one. Thus school directors were "political henchmen" controlled by ward bosses. Therefore, the bosses, not educators, Woodruff deplored, managed Philadelphia schools at the local level. At the same time, the public did not elect the city's central board of education. Its members were appointed by a panel of judges from the Court of Common Pleas.

What brought this sordid fact home to the people of Philadelphia was the trial of three school directors from the twenty-eighth ward. The defendants included the ward's school-board president and the secretary. They ended up convicted of extorting money—sums ranging from thirty dollars to one thousand dollars—from teacher-applicants. One witness testified that her payoff came to $120—which she did not have. She said, according to the court records:

They told me they didn't want the money for themselves, but that it was necessary to buy the other faction. Finally I agreed to the proposition, and they told me that I must be careful not to mention it to anybody or it would injure my reputation. I went with my brother to pay the money to Mr. Johnson. He held out a hat, and when my brother handed the money to him he took it behind the hat.

Hoping to excuse himself of bribery, the board president said, with sound logic, that the real culprit was the boss of the twenty-eighth ward (a Mr. Sterr). "He is the whole school board . . . and he is the one who should be indicted," the man reasoned. The accused candidly admitted: "The directors themselves are mere figureheads, and Sterr manages the schools." The Superior Court of Pennsylvania, in late 1903, upheld the lower court's verdict.

To be sure, not all sectional school directors were dishonorable or hacks of the machine. Take Dora Keen, for example, secretary of the Philadelphia Education Association from 1900 to 1906. The daughter of a world-famous surgeon, she had been a director of the ninth ward for six years when she ran afoul of bossism. In March 1903 Boss John K. Myers refused to renominate her as a board member because, as a PEAer, she had fought for a policy he opposed. She wanted to hire and promote teachers on the basis of merit; he wanted to do it by political pull—in other words, through payola.

The problem of school governance had been for the PEA a matter of study and agitation since the mid-1890s. Every annual report called for overhauling educational administration. The association brought to Philadelphia eminent educators and university presidents to speak at public meetings about the need to restructure metropolitan school systems. Then came the rash of incidents in 1903: the "rakeoff" letter, the bribery trial, the Keen-Myers showdown. Roweled by these scandals, the PEA's executive committee, which now included Martin Brumbaugh, began to study public-school management in eight major cities. This investigation prompted a spread in the newspapers a few days before Christmas 1904: "Appeal to the Citizens of Philadelphia." The ad assailed the city's public-school bureaucracy as "archaic, cumbersome, and utterly inadequate to deal with the problems that confront it today." It detailed some of the system's most serious defects and the terrible results. The finger was never directly pointed at boss rule for the bad conditions, but the implication was there.

The purpose of the "Appeal," however, was not merely to recapitulate ten years of PEA grievances against an outdated educational structure. Its object was to issue a call for the creation of an "Educational Commission," composed of known men of expert knowledge, ability, and integrity. The commission was to be charged with drafting legislation "making any changes deemed wise and desirable for the first school district of Pennsylvania." The organic school law, stated the "Appeal," had failed to keep pace with the city's tremendous growth in wealth and school population since the Civil War.

The PEA, then with a membership of seven hundred, sensed that the times were ripe for deeds on this important issue; progressivism and muckraking had seen to that. Also, it so happened, bossism was in a state of some disarray in Philadelphia—and Pennsylvania—in 1904. "Is" Durham was a very sick man, and the seventy-year-old Quay had died in May. His groomed successor, Boies Penrose, did not yet have control of things. At any rate, after the holidays the board of education took the initiative and appointed a five-man task force. Professor Martin Brumbaugh was named to it as the educational "expert."

In 1904 Philadelphia had one of the most byzantine, chaotic, underfunded public-school systems among the nation's largest cities. It was the outgrowth of village conditions a half-century before. The PEA stigmatized the resultant bloated bureaucracy as "triple-headed." There was the city board of education, made up of one representative from each of the forty-two wards. But each ward had a separate twelve-member board. These sectional boards, male-dominated and boss-ruled, alone elected the teachers and janitors for their own schools, the central board and the superintendent having no say whatsoever.

Nor did the board of education have complete control of school appropriations. It could not levy a separate tax for running the schools. It depended for its financial resources solely upon allocations from other departments of City Councils—the third head. For example, the Councils' Department of Buildings, not the board, had oversight of all school property, including the lighting, heating, and sanitation. School maintenance, therefore, was funded in competition with other claims upon that bureau's purse. The board never knew, from one year to the next, how much it would be able to spend. And as might be expected, overlapping powers and functions in the bureaucracy led to chronic warfare within the three-tiered system over limits of jurisdiction.

The funding chaos explained in part why Philadelphia's school expenditures lagged so far behind that of other major cities: 3 million dollars compared to New York's 33 million; Chicago's 23 million; and Boston's more than 10 million. Among all big cities, Philadelphia ranked a lowly thirty-fourth in per capita spending.

The superintendency, in place only since 1883, carried little more than advisory powers and involved mostly clerical work and petty routine details. For all practical purposes, it was a paper-shuffling position, without a fixed term, and not greatly respected. The superintendent did have some supervisory authority over the elementary grades, but the board totally controlled the secondary schools.

Brumbaugh, a firm proponent of change, accepted appointment to the Educational Commission without demur. The bill it prepared ended up a compromise. But one commission member later said that what they did get owed a lot to Brumbaugh, who "had large influence in the deliberations and conclusions" because of his "excellent knowledge of education" and "his excellent judgment." The bill finally got Governor Samuel W. Pennypacker's signature on 22 April 1905. It was to take effect the first day of 1906.

Although the new law fell far short of PEA expectations, its leaders identified three important steps toward centralized management. First, the board of education was reduced in number by half, to twenty-one. Second, although sectional boards remained, they only had visitorial, not elective, rights. Election, promotion, and dismissal of teachers now fell under the authority of the central board. Third, the school system was guaranteed—at least in theory—an adequate, automatically increasing income. Though Councils still made the annual appropriation for specific public-school expenses, the new law required the system to get a sum not less than five mills on each dollar of the real estate tax. The position of superintendent, however, was not strengthened by the legislation.

When the board of education met to organize in January of 1906, its reduced membership of twenty-one included eight fresh faces. Within three months the recomposed board faced the task of finding a new chief of schools. Dr. Edward Brooks gave notice in April that he would step aside at the end of the school year. At age seventy-five he was incapacitated by impaired health and unable to discharge his duties. The septuagenarian had been superintendent for fifteen years; he came to Philadelphia from his principalship at Millersville Normal School.

In the ensuing weeks the board narrowed the list of candidates to two names: Dr. Cheesman A. Herrick, chair of the commercial department at the Boys' Central High School and a highly respected teacher, and Martin Brumbaugh. Batches of letters supporting Brumbaugh came to the search committee from all parts of the country east of the Mississippi. His endorsers represented a variety of professions and walks of life. Most, as would be expected, offered glowing testimonials. The school superintendent of Louisville, Kentucky, for example, called Brumbaugh one of the "strongest" educators in the United States, rivaled by few as "an authority on educational topics." Chicago's superintendent said that, among the nation's educators, "He is recognized as one of the foremost leaders." The top schoolman of the state where a young Brumbaugh had spent five summers in teachers' institute toil declared categorically, "[He] is regarded in Louisiana as the greatest educational leader in the country."

But the Penn professor was no shoo-in as a nominee. The board found itself split into two factions, and its president, Henry R. Edmunds, and the powerful Simon Gratz openly favored Herrick. The way the press analyzed this division, it fundamentally revolved around the future of Boys' (Central) High School. The faculty there—long of reputed excellence—wanted to see the secondary school converted into a college, to be called the College of Philadelphia. Central's high-powered alumni association also favored the procollege scheme. This would mean adding two more years to the curriculum. So when Brooks resigned, the alumni and Herrick's colleagues immediately nominated him, knowing he sided with them in plans to transform Boys' into a college.

The Brumbaugh camp, on the other hand, was said to represent the interests of the University of Pennsylvania. Penn officials, so the story circulated, discouraged talk of another Philadelphia college (Temple, La Salle, and St. Joseph's also conferred liberal arts degrees). Newspapers, therefore, reported that an intense behind-the-scenes political contest marked the search for a new superintendent.

The board decided to caucus on Friday evening, 25 May, to take a straw vote. The agreement was that the winner would be declared unanimously elected at its next regular monthly meeting—on Tuesday, 12 July. This one, of course, would be open to the public. One version of the 25 May conclave, reported by newspapers but denied by the board, had Herrick winning by a single vote on the first ballot. But one man who voted for Herrick asked permission to reverse himself, it was said, thus giving *Brumbaugh* the bare majority.

What must the victor have thought, after getting news of the result! The election in City Hall was a perfect replay of the one in the Huntingdon County Court House twenty-two years before. But Brumbaugh's date book entry for that day simply reads: "8 P.M. Board of Ed. agreed on me for Supt. Schools."

The breakdown of the balloting surprised newsmen, as bits of inside information were passed to them. Some board members had taken unexpected sides, like William H. Shoemaker, who had headed the search committee. He got up out of a sick bed to vote for Brumbaugh, which was not what the board expected him to do. Of greater interest to journalists, however, was how the sides lined up. Brumbaugh garnered every vote, except one, cast by new members of the board—eight in all. The press interpreted his victory, so far as board politics went, as both a triumph for new members, presumably more progressive, and the University of Pennsylvania.

Rumors abounded that the Herrick faction would renege on the 25 May accord, and intense lobbying by both factions to change votes did go on over the next two weeks. But nobody defected. So on the afternoon of 12 July Brumbaugh's election was pro forma. ("I was unanimously elected," his date book for the 12th reports.) The main item on the agenda had to do with remuneration. The new superintendent would start out with a salary of $7,500 a year (up from the $5,000 Brooks got). Some board members wanted it to be $10,000, comparable to salaries of superintendents in other large cities.

No one was more pleased by Brumbaugh's election than Edward Brooks, who penciled a congratulatory note the day after the board meeting. He said he was happy that "one of my own pupils and friends has been chosen to succeed me, which I feel to be an honor to me." In a later letter to Dora Keen he took great pride in reciting the ways he had been a determining influence at pivotal points in Brumbaugh's career:

> I have watched his career with much interest since he left my old school at Millersville, and have been proud of his educational work and the well merited honors that have come to him. It was on my recommendation that he was elected professor of pedagogy in the University of Pennsylvania. I was consulted in respect to his appointment as a member of the Educational Commission, and it was on my assurance of his

attitude on questions connected with the revision of our school law that he received the appointment. When there was doubt about his selection as my successor by the Board of Education, I wrote a strong letter of indorsement to several members of the Board which I was informed, influenced a number of members to give him the slight majority by which he was elected.

But there was something Brooks did not know when he went on record with the board as a Brumbaugh-man. Ever since January, three months before he resigned, the trustees of The Pennsylvania State College (it became a university in 1953) had Brumbaugh's name under consideration for president of their institution. The incumbent, George W. Atherton, was quite ill and anxious to be replaced. In fact, at this very time he was in Los Angeles, where he had gone hoping to recuperate. Former Governor James A. Beaver, a Civil War hero and now a judge on the Superior Court of Pennsylvania, was trustee chairman. He arranged for Brumbaugh to visit the campus in February, on Lincoln's birthday.

But apparently the visitor showed little interest in the little land-grant college nestled in the rich farmland of Nittany Valley. Beaver was disappointed but did not give up. To the trustees he advised "making haste slowly" in wooing the reluctant Penn professor. The two men corresponded over the succeeding weeks. They met again, on Monday, 19 March, for dinner at the Union League, when Beaver was en route to Atlantic City.

Next month the ailing Brooks decided to retire, and Brumbaugh was immediately touted as a possible heir to the superintendency. This complicated Penn State's search for a president, because Brumbaugh allowed his name to remain in contention for the Philadelphia post. Beaver now began to press the matter. He wrote Brumbaugh that Atherton's poor health (he had returned from California more ill than when he went) necessitated finding his replacement "at the earliest possible moment." The judge arranged for Atherton to talk to Brumbaugh personally, thus enabling the Philadelphian to see for himself the president's alarming condition.

The two men got together, presumably on Monday evening, 7 May, at the Continental Hotel, where Atherton was staying. By authorization of the trustees' Executive Committee, Atherton invited Brumbaugh to give the commencement address on 13 June. At that time he could meet all of the board members, who, he had already been told by Beaver, "are unanimously of the opinion that you would fill the [presidency] better than any man of whom we have knowledge."

But Atherton's visit was in vain. On 10 May Brumbaugh wrote to Beaver and turned down both the presidency of Penn State and the commencement invitation. The judge acknowledged the letter, saying he fully understood. But he added: "I think that in the long run you could have rendered better and more lasting services to the state if you had come to the hub than if you remain on the edge." Brumbaugh never put down on paper why he decided against going to Penn State. Certainly in early May he had no assurance he would be elected to succeed Brooks. Perhaps he found the town of State College too bucolic; many a time he proclaimed his "love" for Philadelphia, its cultural enhancement and its exhilarating social life. Then, too, Huntingdon was only thirty miles away, southward over Tussey Mountain. It could be he was afraid that being so close to the Juniata campus would only get him more involved with internal operations there—something he was unwilling to encourage.

At any rate, elected superintendent in June, he moved into his office (Room 696) in City Hall on the 13th. Officially, his duties began on 1 July. He found his desk adorned with a mass of American Beauty roses, supplied by well-wishers. There was no public induction ceremony, although the board of education did hold an informal reception in his honor that afternoon in his office. He told the press that he would spend the summer getting to know his job. When asked if he contemplated any immediate reforms, he said there would be "no radical, rash, or precipitate changes. . . . We will move slowly and surely." To do otherwise, he added, would be "foolish and probably dangerous." The next evening he left on the 8:59 train for a New England vacation.

Orienting himself to his duties that summer, however, kept Brumbaugh tied neither to desk nor Philadelphia. Since getting back from Puerto Rico, he had been scouting about for a summer retreat in the north country, somewhere the fishing was good. Before he went to the Caribbean, the devoted disciple of Izaak Walton had rented a house at Valley Forge two or three summers for his family. In an old straw hat, wearing galluses, he spent the days bass fishing on the Schuylkill. After returning from Puerto Rico, the Brumbaughs vacationed three summers on a small island in the St. Lawrence between Alexandria Bay, New York, and Kingston, Ontario. It was a Waltonian paradise.

Then he was told by its state superintendent of schools that Maine was an "ideal" summertime sanctuary for rod-and-reel hobbyists. Brumbaugh at first thought Rangeley met all his conditions, but before going there he got contrary advice from a good friend of his in Atlantic City, also a native-born down-easter. The man wrote, in March of 1903: "Rangeley is a good place but the fishing is not all of the time as good as at some other places. Wayne for one place." At Wayne, Brumbaugh was informed, he could catch "white perch, black bass, pickerel, yellow perch, etc., etc.—all you want at any time of the year." The village, located about twenty-five miles west of Augusta, lies at the head of Androscoggin Lake. It took only one summer's stay to convince Brumbaugh that Wayne should be the perennial site of his vacation pied-à-terre.

The family first rented the home of a widow, Mrs. Jane Johnson, the social arbiter of the village. Soon after the First World War, they bought a small farm atop Morrison Heights, Wayne's little mountain. It overlooked Lake Androscoggin and had a view of Mt. Washington and other Presidential peaks far away in New Hampshire. But it took too much time and trouble to get from the view to the fish. So they sold the farm in the mid-Twenties and bought a typical village house in Wayne on about three acres, with water on three sides. From then to the end of his life,

Brumbaugh, the ultimate piscator, could step from his back door into his boat. Edwin Brumbaugh eventually worked architectural wonders with his father's cottage, transforming it into the most imposing residence in Wayne—then and now.

Late in life, Brumbaugh composed a little tribute to the Pine Tree State for the *Portland Evening News*. He titled it, "Why We Summer in Maine." The seasonal immigrant wrote, "We count the days in the storms and sleets of winter until comes rosy June. Then we hie to Maine." Here, he said, the family found "rest, repose, quiet and good fishing." He described how the climate, the scenery, the isolation "all combine to build new ideals and finer fitness for the duties of life." Thus, proclaimed the article's final words, "Maine for us. It is God's glory-crowned country." Obviously, Brumbaugh could rhapsodize as effusively over New England's youngest state as he could over his beloved Pennsylvania.

At Wayne, then, the superintendent-elect spent several weeks the summer of 1906, preparing for his new duties. Not, it is certain, to the total neglect of baiting the hook. There were also times, no doubt, when he fell into moments of wistful reflection. He must have suffered spells of unease at taking over a school system as notorious for political corruption as the city government itself. What would this do to him, a man of honor? Moreover, his midlife change of career would now deprive him of all academic joys. He had dearly loved the stimulating intellectual life of a professor and scholar, the excitement of being a bannered speaker at teachers' institutes. Now, at age forty-four, he had opted to give it all up. So far as we know, he never confided in anyone what made him do this.

The Brumbaughs returned to Philadelphia in mid-August, a month before the school year began.

11

City Superintendent

THE lead editorial for the October 1906 *Juniata Echo* began by advising its readers:

> Keep your eye upon a very Hercules of the Educational World in his voluntary struggle with the combined forces of political graft in the city of Philadelphia. It is our own Dr. M. G. Brumbaugh in the role of Superintendent of Schools . . . , trying to secure the modernization of the public schools and public school system of his city. . . .

Juniatians were told: "The people and the press seem to be on the Doctor's side." That was indeed the case; expectations were high in progressive circles. Brumbaugh's election, declared the *Philadelphia Inquirer*, "is a guarantee that the reforms demanded by the people and sanctioned by the Legislature are to be carried out." The paper went on to predict: "There is made certain a series of changes and innovations which will revolutionize the public school system of Philadelphia and sound the death knoll of the present curriculum and system of school government." But, given the city's core corruption and its school system's distressed conditions, the *Inquirer* warned, "it is certain that time will be required to produce the best results." The *Echo*, for that reason, worried that "Dr. M. G. may lose."

That summer, meanwhile, Governor Samuel Pennypacker appointed Brumbaugh to the Pennsylvania College and University Council, a twelve-member governing board for higher education. (He would be appointed to a second four-year term on the council in 1910.)

The 1906 school year opened in September with 172,000 pupils (K–12) trooping into the classrooms of more than 250 Quaker City schools. This represented an enrollment increase of almost five thousand over 1905's first day count. As in past years, such numbers could not be adequately accommodated. More than ten thousand grade-schoolers were forced to enroll for only half-days. Close to two hundred others attended "double-sessions schools"—where two classes crowded into one room, each taught by a different teacher. Several hundred more were debarred entirely for lack of space; they were put on "waiting lists." Thousands of children attended makeshift classrooms in rented buildings, condemned by the new superintendent as "wholly unfit." Other, city-owned school buildings were so antiquated and in such disrepair as to be a hazard to the health and safety of youngsters.

For years the school system had been absorbing about five thousand newcomers annually. Brumbaugh projected no abatement in this trend for some time to come. His extrapolation would prove to be close to the mark; in 1914, when he resigned, the public-school population had grown by more than thirty thousand. Yet the board of education had spent, for 1905–6, only a million dollars on repairs, renovations, and new construction—mostly of elementary schools—out of its operating budget. It would take millions more than the $6,070,000 budget Brumbaugh inherited to modernize the school plant. Quite apart from overcrowded, decrepit schools, it greatly distressed Brumbaugh to see the inconveniences imposed upon pupils by the lack of such basic furniture as desks. "It is a fact," he wrote in his 1906 annual report,

> that the children are sitting on broken benches, that they are sitting on boards in aisles between benches, that they are sitting on boxes, that they are sitting on window sills, and that in some cases they are actually sitting on the floor. . . .

Students from diverse linguistic, cultural, and ethnic backgrounds presented another serious problem. A survey of major U.S. cities in 1909 found that at least half the school-age immigrants did not speak English. They spoke German, Russian, Polish, Italian, or Greek. These children had to be taught without the technology and sophisticated methodology at the disposal of public schools today.

Of equal concern to the new superintendent was the urgent need for more high schools. In 1906 Philadelphia had but four secondary schools, none coeducational and all located in center city: Central (or Boys') High School; Girls' High School; Girls' Commercial High School; and Girls' Normal School. Brumbaugh had stated forthrightly, his first day in office: "I am heartily in favor of district high schools. I shall do all I can toward their establishment." The number of high schools was abysmally low compared to that of other municipalities. Among the country's twenty-four largest cities, Philadelphia ranked twenty-third in the number of high school students out of its total public-school enrollment.

It troubled Brumbaugh to know that New York City, for 1906, was spending upwards of nine million dollars on secondary schools while Philadelphia had committed a paltry few thousand dollars toward new construction. He could very well have said of the Quaker City what, in 1891, he had thundered about the Keystone State to a gathering of school directors at Harrisburg: "It is a stigma upon us that Pennsylvania is not now making preparation to bring the high school in sight of every child in the Commonwealth. We can have it if we will—if we *want it.*"

But before new schools, even before curriculum review, the newly inducted chief told the press in June of 1906, he would first and foremost give attention to "the teaching body." "I believe that the life of the school is the life of the teacher," he said to reporters, "and I help schools most when I help teachers." This, of course, was a familiar credo of his; the "teaching body" in Huntingdon County and in Puerto Rico had heard similar rhetoric. For Brumbaugh, as one scholar has noted, the teacher was, "in the end, the curriculum." He reported to school-board members that he had spent much of the 1906–7 school year "meeting personally practically all the teachers of our city" and every principal, counseling and encouraging them. His rapport with teachers would be remembered as one of his most notable traits as superintendent.

As an incorrigible teacher-advocate, he made his office readily accessible to classroom minions in need of a "father confessor." It was said of a visit to his office: "His disarming smile caused trouble and worry to vanish." To try to call him up at home in the evening for a few words of wisdom, however, was an impossibility. In order to protect his domestic privacy, he had long ago refused ever to install a telephone in his house.

In Brumbaugh's eight-year superintendency, Philadelphia's "teaching body" grew from just over four thousand to some fifty-three hundred—which, in 1914, was almost double the number of teachers in the state's second largest school system, Pittsburgh's. The gender breakdown that year showed 651 males and 4,704 females handling the daily teaching chores.

Philadelphia, then as today, had one of the highest urban black populations in the North—more than 50,000. Although there was no de jure segregation, a number of all-black schools did exist. But Brumbaugh inherited only 49 African-American teachers in 1906. He actively worked to improve this racial imbalance, and by the end of his superintendency had doubled their numbers to 97.

More than they have been given credit for—although Brumbaugh himself never stinted praise of them in public—the administrative staff during the years 1906 to 1915 made a major contribution to the transformation of Philadelphia's school system. The Brumbaugh Establishment included four associate superintendents, ten assistant district superintendents, eight directors of special services (like kindergarten, music, drawing), plus—by 1915—about two hundred principals. Women held nearly half the principalships, all at the elementary level. Two of the special-services directors were female. Racially, of course, all administrators were lily-white in 1906. (There would be three black supervising principals by 1914, however.) On the sixth floor of city hall, the public-schools' central-office people liked to speak of the superintendent as "The Chief."

The first year went well enough for the new superintendent. A May 1907 *Ledger* editorial applauded him for "daily proving his efficiency as an executive." By that time citizens could see some visible progress toward alleviating the problem of overcrowded classrooms. A dozen new or remodeled elementary schools were opened in rented buildings, and construction was begun on seven others. Additionally, the board of education appointed a committee to look into the matter of district high schools.

A noteworthy event took place in October 1906: the erection of the Philadelphia Trades School, the first of its kind in the United States. Brumbaugh did not originate the idea—a board member did—but, a strong advocate of manual training, he implemented it. Also, he established two evening trades schools, which provided classes in various crafts for boys above the age of fifteen who worked during the day. Local contractors and businessmen welcomed these innovations.

Like Carlyle, Brumbaugh believed "all work is sacred." Like Dewey, he was of the opinion that the public schools should prepare its wards to take a productive place in the life of a democratic society. He was saying this as early, if not earlier, than the philosopher. He told board members, restating a doctrine of Bentham, that the urban school system must be "many-sided in order to accomplish the greatest good to the greatest number." (Puerto Ricans had heard him quote the same benthamic precept to define his strategy there.) In the years ahead, he would make the Philadelphia schools pioneering laboratories of vocational education.

Brumbaugh's break-in year as superintendent saw him make another futile attempt to give up his presidency of Juniata College. The trustees there had kept him busily involved with two major projects over the last couple of years. One of them had been the Carnegie Library; the other one had to do with revising the college's charter. Carnegie's legal advisers, before Brumbaugh finally wooed twenty-eight thousand dollars from the latter-day Maecenas, questioned whether Juniata qualified for a charitable gift. First of all, it had been founded as a joint-stock corporation (its stock, in 1907, had a value of about $15,000). But as Brumbaugh explained to Carnegie's people, the college never intended to, and never did, pay dividends. Still, to allay the generous Scotsman's doubts, the trustees decided to recharter Juniata expressly as a nonprofit institution.

Carnegie's agents also raised questions about the college charter itself; they interpreted it as defining Juniata's mission to be sectarian. It dictated that all trustees must be of the Brethren faith and stated the college's educational purpose to be that of advancing Brethrenism. To revise the charter, the trustees faced the huge task of tracking down every shareholder's certificate—close to two hundred of them. Each one, it was hoped, would be ceded at no cost to the college. Martin volunteered to handle the exceptional cases: balky or deceased shareholders and lost certificates. As it turned out, he had to do more wheedling and detective work than he had bargained for.

He also took on the responsibility of drafting the appropriate amendments to the charter. His legal counsel was George Henderson, a Quaker City attorney and officer of the Philadelphia Education Association. The two Philadelphians set out to cleanse the charter of any hint of sectarianism. Some trustees, and especially Acting President Harvey, did not take kindly to such radical changes. The final document had two important consequences for the college. One amendment expunged the test of Brethrenism for membership on the board of trustees. The other one rephrased Juniata's mission statement. In place of "preserving the doctrines of the Bible as believed and practiced by the Brethren," the new, M. G.-worded state-ment read: "The purpose or design is to establish a college or institution of learn-ing which will provide the young with educational advantages as will fit them for the responsibilities and duties of life." This was precisely what he was telling Phila-delphians their public schools should be doing.

These college-related matters took more time from his superintendency than he liked. Another time-consuming presidential chore also increasingly irritated him: answering the repeatedly bad-humored letters from disgruntled Juniata fac-ulty members. Mostly they groused about their salaries. In December 1906, caught up in the burdens of his new job, he wrote a testy letter of his own to Harvey, his on-campus surrogate. He accused the Juniata professoriate of not being self-deny-ing enough for the sake of the college. He said, "Let them remember that I made the sacrifice for ten years, and that ever since I have been away I have sent back to the treasury of the College more money than I could possibly have earned had I remained in the faculty."

Professors had taken to backbiting, he learned. Although hurt, he felt he could not really blame them. His was in reality a fictional presidency, complicat-ing the administrative process and damaging Harvey's image as a leader in his own right. So, in the spring of 1907—with the new library built and charter revision well along—he felt he could now press the matter of his resignation. First, though, he dutifully presided at the dedication of the Carnegie Library in April and then gave the commencement address on 20 June. But on that day he handed his Uncle Andrew a sealed envelope. In it was a typewritten letter, dated the 17th. It read:

> Gentlemen:
>
> In view of the fact that I hear from time to time that my relations to Juniata College, as its nominal president, and as a member of its Board of Trustees interfere with its normal development and its more effective usefulness, and inasmuch as I have a larger desire to see the College become all that it should be, than to promote any personal interests either of mine or of anybody else, I hereby tender my resigna-tion as president of the institution to take effect immediately, and my resignation as a trustee to take effect at the next annual meeting called for the purpose of electing trustees, and I insist that both these resignations shall be acted upon in the way indi-cated, in order that the trustees may be absolutely free to carry out whatever in their judgment is best for the interests of the College, and in order that all responsibility may be definitely fixed exactly where it belongs.

Brumbaugh also penned a covering letter addressed to his uncle. He said in part:

> I can assure you and all the Trustees that this step is taken wholly in the interests of the College, that I have no personal motive in this act, and that my interest in the College will not be lessened by this cessation of official relations. That it may make for the success of the College is my prayer.

At their regularly scheduled meeting the last week of June, the trustees deferred action on his dual resignation. His uncle wrote him, begging him to reconsider. But the nephew, all set to leave for a Maine vacation, dictated a terse, adamant reply on 10 July. He left it for his secretary to type and to sign for him. Meanwhile, he had apparently changed his mind about leaving the board, because his second note makes no reference to pulling out as a trustee:

> When I sent my resignation as President of Juniata College I meant it, and your notice of the action of the Board, under date of June 25, does not change my opinion.
> I write again to say that I must insist that that letter be received for exactly what it says and that I be at once relieved from this position. There can be no change in this decision.

True to form, the trustees soft-pedaled M. G.'s strongly worded demand, and for several years more the catalog listed him as "President." As M. G. saw it, however, he had relinquished that title the day he moved into city hall. Later, as governor-elect, he was asked to furnish data for a biographical sketch in *Who's Who in America*. For the years of his Juniata presidency, he gave 1894-1906. As for his trusteeship, he continued to allow himself to be reelected every three years.

The resignation issue erupted at a time when, as superintendent, Brumbaugh had begun some crucial initiatives. One of them concerned the state of the school plant. The previous fall he and his contingent of associate and district superintendents had spent three months evaluating the condition of buildings and equipment. The deplorable evidence of physical neglect shocked the superintendent. He figured it would take a loan of at least five million dollars just to meet current needs, not to mention those of the future as a result of the city's normal growth. A sympathetic board of education petitioned City Councils to authorize a loan of that amount. Philadelphia's two most activist proschool groups, the Public Education Association and the Teachers' Association, publicly supported the board. But Councils would delay any action on the loan petition for more than a year.

Meanwhile, the eight commonwealth senators from the Philadelphia area had read the superintendent's 1906 damning report on the wretched condition of the city's schools. They called for an official hearing. The Senate appointed an in-body committee of three, headed by Senator Ernest L. Tustin, one of the Philadelphia eight. For several days in mid-March 1907, the senatorial trio summoned a host of witnesses—from the mayor to members of the board of education and Councils to ordinary citizens—to testify before them. Strange as it may seem, neither the superintendent nor any teacher was subpoenaed.

The reception of the investigators by the educational community and certain newspapers was not at all cordial. The Wanamaker-owned *North American*, for example, ran an editorial captioned, "HANDS OFF THE PUBLIC SCHOOLS," on the day the committee began its work. The piece raised the fear of political intrigue: "Just what the investigators of this inquiry are after is not clear. . . . The movement, however, is suspicious. It looks like the first step in an attempt to bring the schools back again into politics." Readers were reminded: "There were fine pickings for insiders in former times, when schoolhouse sites were sold to the city for ten times their value, and when ward heelers were made the janitors in school-houses." And Senator Tustin and his team were advised that restoring "Republican Gang" control would not be tolerated: "Public opinion now counts for something in Philadelphia." Ultimately, the editorial charged, blame for the "shameful decay" of schools must "rest directly" upon the niggardly Councils.

The senatorial visitation also frightened the Philadelphia Teachers' Association (PTA). They met in mass protest against the investigation and passed a series of resolutions. In substance, these resolutions denounced unsolicited legislative interference and expressed complete confidence in the Brumbaugh regime and its plans to solve the local problems. The PTA's president told newsmen that in only a few months time far more had been accomplished than had been in the all of the previous five or six years.

The three lawmakers finished their hearings in general agreement with the superintendent's grim assessment of things. They returned to Harrisburg convinced that reform was right and necessary. It was most imperative, they urged in their report, that Councils act at once on a five million-dollar loan in order, as they bluntly worded it, "to put the school plant upon an American and civilized basis."

During 1907 the debate about floating a large loan dominated Philadelphia's public-school agenda. The most vocal opponent was State Senator James "Sunny Jim" McNichol, a Philadelphian and a powerful figure in the Republican machine. It was at this time that Brumbaugh coined his crusading slogan: "A Decent School and a Decent Desk for Every Child in Philadelphia." The sectional boards now became a direct voice of the people; most of the forty-one women directors joined the Public Education Association, the Philadelphia teachers, the board, and the superintendent in putting pressure on Councils.

But in the very midst of the fray, Brumbaugh found himself concurrently engaged in a broader cause: drafting a new state school code. It had become increasingly evident to many Pennsylvania educators that the commonwealth's school laws amounted to a jumble of conflicting legislation. Everywhere, calls were being heard to bring order out of this legal chaos. Moreover, within recent years every state bordering on Pennsylvania had created its school system anew.

Accordingly, the General Assembly of 1907 passed a resolution authorizing the governor to appoint a seven-man Code Commission. Its task was to revise, collate, and digest all the acts and statutes relating to or touching the laws of the public schools of the commonwealth. That September Governor Edwin S. Stuart, a former popular Philadelphia mayor and a friend of education, followed through on the resolution. Brumbaugh was named one of the commissioners; four were administrators and the other three were a school director, a merchant, and a lawyer.

They were charged with producing a comprehensive measure by the time of the legislature's next biennial session.

The Code Commission, chaired by State Superintendent Nathan Schaeffer, faced a stupendous assignment. Beginning in January 1908 it met seven times over the next twelve months, as recorded in Brumbaugh's date book. Meetings were held in Philadelphia, Wilkes-Barre, Harrisburg, and Pittsburgh, usually for two or three days each get-together. In between, each man worked on individual projects. Their efforts resulted in a bill that had a rather stormy passage through the legislature of 1909. The solons dealt with little else, subjecting the proposed code to a battery of changes. When it reached Governor Stuart, he vetoed it. He did so on the ground that the legislature, by a mosaic of "contradictory" amendments, had destroyed the harmony of the original bill.

Public sentiment, however, demanded that the fight for a unitary code go on. From many parts of the state came requests that the commissioners stay by their work—unofficially—during the legislative interim and come back with a second draft for the assembly of 1911. All seven readily agreed, and for another year they continued to meet periodically at their own expense.

As with the school code, Brumbaugh had suffered a dose of disappointment when Councils finally got around, on 3 October 1907, to doing something about a major school-construction loan. Under Mayor John Weaver's stern gaze, the councilmen had only enough courage to authorize half the needed amount. The dejected superintendent recorded in his date book for that Thursday: "Beginning of the struggle. What is the end?" Kindly old Edward Brooks, sick as he was, immediately penciled a commiserating letter to his successor. He wrote:

> You are defeated in your fight, as I presumed you would be, but it is a defeat with honor. While the enemies of the public schools have won the actual victory, you have won the greater victory by the place you have secured in the hearts of the people of the city. You have the cordial approval of the teachers and friends of public education in the city, and you will live in their hearts as the friend of the public schools, when the oligarchy that rules the city today will be forgotten or only remembered in the archives of infamy.

Brooks went on ("in rather stormy language but my feelings are even stronger than any words") to castigate the "dastardly conduct of the Mayor in robbing the public schools of their due." He said it was a backhanded tribute to Brumbaugh that the mayor never publicly criticized him for pushing for the unprecedented five million-dollar school loan. "But," said Brooks, "I could see the cloud of hatred upon his brow as he listened to the hearty cheers that greeted you in your eloquent appeal for the public schools at the dedication of the new Manual Training School." The old educator advised against fighting the mayor and Councils for a larger loan. The best thing to do, he thought, was to take the $2,500,000, and together with such moneys as could be siphoned off annual appropriations, spend it "where and in such a way that the city will reap the greatest benefit."

Even so, Brumbaugh was warned, the mayor and "his gang" would keep a watchful eye on how the loan was spent. They would look for "faults" in an effort to discredit the superintendent in the eyes of the public, Brooks cautioned at the end of his letter. It was wise counsel, and Brumbaugh shied away from another public confrontation with city hall for the time being. His legions of supporters, however, would not be silenced.

Although dealt a partial defeat as superintendent in 1907, Brumbaugh did enjoy two notable—and interrelated—successes that year. One was the formation of the Home and School League of Philadelphia. The idea for a parent-teacher group in Philadelphia came from Mrs. Edwin C. Grice, a prominent socialite who was active in the National Congress of Mothers. (The Congress, founded in 1897, changed its name to National Congress of Parents and Teachers in 1924.) Mrs. Grice had tried for several years to generate parental concern about the local schools. But she made little headway until Brumbaugh became superintendent. He blessed her work at once and put the weight of his office and popularity behind it.

The Philadelphia League came to canonize him as much as Mrs. Grice for its inception. Declared its annual report for 1914:

> The honor of the work should be laid at the feet of him [Brumbaugh] who with courage faced the untried way in the beginning, and with faith and great patience wove out of the crude material of community interest and enthusiasm the present system of social activity that is spreading through our schools to-day. . . . He has succeeded in drawing out the latent forces of the various groups of social workers forming the League and has guided and directed it toward civic betterment.

The League lay "close to his heart," Brumbaugh once said, because "The parent and the teacher are the dominant forces that build manhood and womanhood for the Republic. The touch of each should be consistently the touch of the other. For that reason I believe in the holy union of home and school."

Early in the 1906–7 school year, the superintendent—in conjunction with the local chapter of the Mothers' Congress—initiated parent-teacher meetings at various neighborhood schools. Close to two hundred of them were held over the following months, attended by more than thirty thousand parents. Sometimes during this early stage the superintendent spoke as many as five times an evening to various parents' groups. Aroused public interest led to the formation of the Home and School League in October 1907. The superintendent, with the board's approval, furnished a room at 1522 Cherry Street as its headquarters. By 1914 as many as two hundred thousand mothers and fathers were setting foot in schools at least once a year for one purpose or another.

The league's work soon attracted international attention. The superintendent's report for 1914 noted that inquiries about the organization had come from numerous countries: Argentina, Japan, Italy, England, South Africa, Australia, Mexico, Cuba, Russia. No doubt other American cities, especially those that had formed Leagues before Philadelphia did, were similarly canvassed by foreign educators. But certainly nowhere in urban America could there have been a closer working relationship between a local league and its superintendent than in the Quaker City.

Brumbaugh also acted as foster father of a second civic program, this one more schoolchild-oriented: playgrounds. The nation's urban centers had begun to provide outdoor play areas in the mid-1890s for health and safety reasons and to combat juvenile delinquency. Philadelphia's first public playground was opened in the summer of 1894.

The following year, thanks to philanthropic citizens, the yards of four elementary schools acquired some play apparatus and were placed under trained supervisors. Over the next decade the playgrounds movement grew slowly. In 1903 the Public Education Association conducted a study of ways to increase the play space around each school. Some schools had yards so small that all the pupils, standing shoulder-to-shoulder, could not crowd within their confines. Further attention to play needs of children came from the incipient parent-teachers coalition; early on, its leaders gave outdoor play a high priority on its agenda.

Like other progressive educators of his day, Brumbaugh appreciated the educational, social, and moral value of playtime. He told the board of education in 1907: "Play is the birthright of every child." Another time he remarked, "No child can do his best in thought or in conduct who does not play freely in God's out of doors." The day he took office, the *North American*, in the context of a comment he had made to the press along these lines, wrote of him: "Martin G. Brumbaugh . . . is not a stern pedagogue who believes in books, and books alone, as a means of education." Therefore, the paper went on, under his supervision "the public schools are more likely to be filled with happy, healthy children than with stooping pedants. . . . He would like to see a playground connected with every school, if possible." A year later, he passionately raised that very issue with his board: "I plead for large playgrounds around each school and ample space in the basement for rainy-day exercises."

Play was important in the pedagogy of progressives for many reasons, health and physical fitness being only two of them. Its greatest value for child development, in their thinking, was to foster socialization. That was a basic concept of the progressives' sage, John Dewey. It was a concept that Brumbaugh expounded every bit as early as the great philosopher. In 1907 he told the board of education: "The boy or girl who plays freely in the open air on the school playground is learning most of the fundamental needs of life in an ordered community. It is the great socializer of our complex life."

Thus play, through object lessons, builds character, his argument went. Children learn the need for self-restraint, the significance of cooperation and team work, and that cheaters are ostracized by playmates. Brumbaugh even asserted that fun and games can nourish patriotic and spiritual attitudes: "They make [the child] a worker for his country . . . [and] a reverent believer in his God." Unfortunately, he never explained how this happened.

The key component of Brumbaugh's philosophy of play was *supervision*. Time and again he declared in his talks and reports that Philadelphia's sons and daughters did not know *how* to play. Their unsupervised games reflected cat-and-dog strife, anarchy, violence. Therefore, he argued, children must be taught how to play as well as how to work.

This theory of play—that juvenile sport begets character and a respect for others—had practical schoolroom application, or so assumed the educational avant-garde of the early 1900s. To paraphrase Brumbaugh, the playground unmasks the inner dynamics of individual children—their attitudes, their problems, their potentialities. Thus the observant teacher, while on recess duty, can best learn how to teach and handle each pupil.

Brumbaugh also linked play and physical fitness in his pedagogy. "All children need muscular as well as brain exercise. It should be part of their education to be taught to keep their body fit," he said the summer of 1906. That fall he wasted no time creating a department of physical education, with a director and ten assistants. Thus did "gym classes"—the gymnasium being the school yard—gain entrée to the curriculum of Philadelphia's elementary schools.

It took him another year, however, to get a public playgrounds program in place. He had as a model the Playgrounds Association of America, organized in 1906. Also, by 1907 seventy-seven cities were operating summer programs. In mid-February that year, he wrote to a number of civic-minded men and women of the Philadelphia area and invited them to meet in his office. He wanted them to "discuss the great movement sweeping the entire country." Out of this dialogue developed the Playgrounds Association of Philadelphia (PAP), formed on 22 May. Brumbaugh was named its first president.

Within a year's time there were 116 dues-paying members. But PAP needed a broader financial base in order to extend its work citywide. So one day in the spring of 1908 the president called one of its members, Otto Mallery—who, incidentally, was on the board of education—into his office. He proceeded to talk Mallery into becoming "field manager," whose job it was to find other sources of funds. Mallery resorted to a stratagem made famous by today's baseball Little Leaguers in shopping malls and on street corners the country over: Tag Day. The first one was held that May. Tag Day became a spring rite in Philadelphia for the next several years. The money raised this way was used to buy vacant lots, adjacent to schools where possible, as playground sites and to equip them.

Brumbaugh envisioned, however, moving support away from private philanthropy toward municipal control as soon as possible. He knew that in 1904 Los Angeles had created a Playground Commission, the first such department in any city. Other cities soon followed suit. At his urging, Mayor John E. Reyburn, by act of Councils, appointed a Public Playgrounds Commission on 27 May 1909. The purpose of the commission was to survey the play needs of Philadelphia and to study what other cities were doing to sponsor outdoor recreation. The report was submitted in 1910, and the following year Councils created the Board of Recreation. The mayor named Brumbaugh the president. In 1913 all playgrounds, except one or two, would be taken over by the city.

Brumbaugh now presided over two playgrounds organizations. The original one, the Playgrounds Association of Philadelphia, would still serve a vital purpose: "to continue our propaganda for supported play until every citizen is a friend of the inalienable right of the child to supervised play in the open air." By the time he became governor, the association listed close to thirty-five hundred members. And Philadelphia by then had thirty-eight playgrounds, all in use year-around. The progress the city had made in seven short years was far from negligible. A proud president told PAP members in 1914: "It is now true that our . . . play facilities are unequalled." Later, in the early 1920s, he would come to enjoy repute as one of the nation's most eloquent spokesmen for physical fitness, urban playgrounds, and outdoor recreation.

Of the early years of his superintendency, that of 1908 turned out to be an especially sad one for him, bracketed as it was by the death of his favorite uncle and his mother. Dr. Andrew B. Brumbaugh died at an early-morning hour on 27 January in Philadelphia, where he had been rushed from Huntingdon by train for an emergency appendectomy. At age seventy-one, he withstood the operation fairly well but succumbed to peritonitis. "His death is an awful shock to me," Martin wrote his father. He and cousin Gaius had sat at bedside to the end.

Four years earlier, while vacationing at Gananoque, along the St. Lawrence River in Ontario, Canada, he had addressed an affectionate birthday message to "My dear Uncle (A.B.B.)". He wrote: "I congratulate you upon your 68 years— years full of effort and unselfish service to others." He said, "You have been an inspiration to many—to me often." The nephew attended the funeral in Huntingdon, one of the largest ever seen in the town; it had to be held in the Presbyterian Church to accommodate the throng of mourners.

The evening of his uncle's death, Martin sat down and penned to his parents what was probably the tenderest letter he ever wrote to them. As usual with letters to his folks, however, it tended to be preachy. He admonished his father, two years older than his suddenly deceased brother:

> Now, for goodness sake, you ought to take care. . . . Surely this is a lesson to you and I pray God to help you to quit worrying, take your rest, let others work. Do this for our sake, who love you and who want you to keep well many years.

Then, becoming more inclusive in his filial solicitude, he ended the letter saying,

> I fear mother can't come to funeral [*sic*]. The weather is too cold. But both of you must now take care. You only pass this way once—both of you—and I do want you to

have a peaceful, restful old age. Get help in the house and at the farm and both of you take it easy. The money I can supply. But I can't buy my parents. Won't you do your part? Please.

In early July invalided Martha Brumbaugh became bedfast. She died seventeen weeks later at age seventy-six—on 15 November, just before dawn. She was buried in the little hilltop cemetery on the Brumbaugh homestead farm at James Creek, next to the graves of her daughter and infant son. A couple of years later, Martin would begin sending his widower-father south every winter, to escape the seasonal cold under sunny Floridian skies.

Within days of his mother's death, Huntingdon and Philadelphia newspapers reported a boom to make him the chancellor of the University of Nebraska. Upon the resignation of the incumbent, Dr. Benjamin Andrews, William Jennings Bryan was soon touted as the front-runner for the job. But some of Brumbaugh's friends out West began talking him up as a rival to Bryan. Bryan had just lost, two weeks before, to Republican William Howard Taft for the White House prize. Three times he had failed his party since 1896, an unprecedented record in United States political history. But out in Nebraska many people idolized him as the "Great Commoner" and were bewitched by his populist oratory. Rural Protestant America had no voice more eloquent than his in a time of rising cities, corporate power, and ethnic and religious diversity.

Brumbaugh had no interest in the chancellorship and on Thanksgiving Day wrote to say so to his western claque. As he told the press later, "Pennsylvania is good enough for the Dutch. . . . I love my dear old Pennsylvania too much to go West and wish to continue my career in this good old Commonwealth." He went on to say that Bryan was "eminently suited" to head a university because of "his political experience, facility in public speaking, and scholarly attainments." But as everyone knows, the Nebraskan himself chose to be a noncandidate, preferring politics over academics.

Brumbaugh's own "scholarly attainments" while superintendent were perforce minimal. He did turn out an occasional article for professional journals. And in 1908 he even found the time to put together a volume entitled *The Life and Works of Christopher Dock*. Published by Lippincott, it was a compilation of Dock's works both in the original German and in English translation. Brumbaugh hailed the pious Mennonite schoolman on the Skippack River as America's pioneer writer on education. His fifty-two-page *Schul-Ordnung*, written in illuminated text, was the first treatise on pedagogy and school management printed in the New World, Brumbaugh argued.

Ex-governor Samuel Pennypacker wrote the introduction to the Dock volume, while the editor provided a brief biographical sketch. Pennypacker, then president of the Pennsylvania Historical Society, pointed out to fellow-member Brumbaugh in a postpublication letter that the book offered an important corrective to Keystone State—and educational—history. It revealed, he said, that "the dawn of our science of pedagogy originated with colonial Mennonites, contrary to the historical romance that the 'Plain People' had always disregarded learning." For Brumbaugh and Pennypacker, Dock's *Schul-Ordnung* represented another star in the historical firmament of the Pennsylvania Germans.

That summer of 1908 Brumbaugh also did a good turn for his own religious order, which shared the "Plain People" label with Mennonites. It was he, the previous year, who had suggested that, in 1908, the Brethren hold a bicentennial celebration of their beginnings. He proposed that it be done the week of Annual Conference, in June. This would give the Des Moines, Iowa, yearly meeting a chance to look to the past as well as to the future, he pointed out. It so happened that a major piece of business on the agenda for that year was the issue of a denominational name-change: from German Baptist Brethren to Church of the Brethren.

When scheduled for a principal address, Brumbaugh balked; he begged off, citing the demands of his superintendency. But Daniel L. Miller, editor-in-chief of the *Gospel Messenger* (the brotherhood's weekly periodical), wrote him in amiable defiance:

> No! There would be general disappointment all over the Brotherhood if you failed to be with us at Des Moines to give your address. You are really responsible for this Bicentennial. You persistently kept at it until it came. Now for you to drop out would be like Hamlet with Hamlet left out. No! It cannot be thought of for a moment.

Brumbaugh not only spoke but also made available for an exhibition his invaluable collection of Sauer-printed Bibles and other colonial Brethren works. Miller later wrote him, rating his address on eighteenth-century Brethrenism as "easily the best and most interesting of all that were heard."

Following that eventful week, Miller was asked to edit the bicentennial proceedings into a book. He borrowed the title for it from a suggestion made by Brumbaugh: *Two Centuries of the Church of the Brethren*. Those were the words he had jotted down in Miller's notebook while the two of them sat side-by-side on the conference platform. He had done this the day before delegates got to a vote on the controversial question of a new denominational label. The name-change passed, which led Miller later to write Brumbaugh, "It seems you had the spirit of prophecy." He also told the Philadelphian, because of all he had done to make the bicentennial a success, "it is most fitting that you should write the introduction [to the book]." Which request he dutifully honored.

While 1908 left the Brethren historian sad memories of departed loved ones, it also gave him a couple of personal honors, incidental though they were, that he always remembered with considered pride. One was being appointed by Mayor Reyburn to a committee charged with solving a problem of local history. To the ten committeemen—all librarians except two—fell the task of determining the date Philadelphia formed a municipal government. Their report settled on the year 1683, perhaps as early as 23 January, based on a careful search of original documents in various libraries and archives. The report was drafted by Brumbaugh. Its closing paragraph made "bold" to call for a "suitable recognition" of the city's 225th anniversary. The idea likely came from the report's author, who had also initiated a commemorative event for the Brethren that year and who was ever ready to beat the drum for the Keystone State's glorious role in history. A celebration of some kind, he urged, would enable "historians and the people at large . . . to appreciate more than they have in the past the commanding influence . . . the Province of Pennsylvania and the City of Philadelphia [had] upon the history of the development of the United States of America." The mayor hailed the suggestion and proclaimed 5–12 October as "Founders Week."

The other honor to befall Brumbaugh that year was his election, in April, to the ranks of the prestigious American Philosophical Society (APS). The APS had been founded by Philadelphians—Benjamin Franklin among them—in 1743. It was America's first scientific association, modeled after the century-older Royal Society of London.

Two days before Thanksgiving that year, less than a week after his mother's funeral, the longtime Philadelphian decided to sell his Huntingdon home. He sold it to Tobias T. Myers, his one-time Quaker City pastor and now Juniata's professor of New Testament Studies. The price: forty-five hundred dollars. For the time being, however, the house's seller held on to his other Huntingdon property, the downtown store building.

Over the next two years while Philadelphia's chief of schools was caught up in a number of causes—playgrounds, school construction and loans, a revised state school code, parent-teacher coalitions, and, of course, Sunday schools and religious education—two more academic institutions made serious bids to name him their president. One was Franklin and Marshall College, oldest liberal arts school founded by the Reformed Church in the United States (today the United Church of Christ), which had awarded him an honorary degree a half-dozen years earlier. In early April 1909, at the time a clique of state assemblymen were filibustering the school code, he received a letter from Nathan Schaeffer, the Code Commission's chairman. Schaeffer wrote:

> Dear Friend,
>   In case the School Code is defeated, how would you like to be made President of Franklin and Marshall College? If you wish to cut loose from Phila. give us a hint, and Hon. W.N. Hensel will do the "legging." I know his thinking of you.

An ordained German Reformed minister who once taught at Franklin and Marshall, alumnus Schaeffer was a member of the search committee. (William Hensel, a former state attorney general, was trustee chairman.) President John S. Stahr's resignation was to take effect in July, after commencement. Nothing among Brumbaugh's papers or correspondence confirms that he got a bona fide offer from college officials. But among his memorabilia is a once-sealed envelope, meant to be opened posthumously. Inside was a handwritten note, dated "2-28-1910," identifying three college presidencies tendered him within the preceding four years. Franklin and Marshall was named as one of them. He explained that he did not go there out of "loyalty to Juniata and in justice to my family. My present work, though more arduous, is more remunerative. I can give more to Juniata."

The second presidential overture—the third having been Penn State, in 1906—came from Girard College. Its longtime president, Adam H. Fetterolf, resigned in January 1910. Interestingly, Fetterolf had been Philadelphia's superintendent of schools himself before going to Girard. The Board of City Trusts soon put the current superintendent at the head of its list. He met with some City Trusts officials on Thursday afternoon, the 27th, in their board room on the estate. The parley confirmed the interviewers in their high estimates of the schoolman.

As once before in his case, they finessed the anticlerical ban in Stephen Girard's will, this time offering him the presidency. He declined, he wrote in his sealed-envelope note, because "The 'pent-up' character of the place depressed me." He had reference to the "solid wall," specified in Girard's will, that enclosed the campus. It was a high wall, fourteen inches thick, and capped by marble and iron posts. Most prisons did not have a fence so formidable, Brumbaugh often said. Philadelphians liked to joke, he said, about whether the wall was there to keep people out or to keep the orphan boys in. Ironically, the Girard presidency finally went to Dr. Cheesman Herrick, Brumbaugh's rival for the superintendency four years earlier.

Having spurned two top college posts in 1910, Brumbaugh did not hesitate to accept academic kudos from a third institution that year. Lutheran-related Gettysburg College awarded him a Doctor of Laws in October, during inauguration ceremonies for President William A. Granville.

In 1909 the Philadelphia schoolman had gotten a letter containing a noncollege proposal that intrigued him more than a little. Quaker City residents learned about the contents of that letter from a *Public Ledger* article that blazoned: "CALL BRUMBAUGH TO A NEW FIELD—Millionaire Wants Superintendent to Head a 'Character Development League'." It was from the superintendent himself that newsmen got word of this "call." He said it came from a New York philanthropist named James T. White.

White, reported Brumbaugh, was a recent retiree from the publishing business, and had written to say he wanted to devote the rest of his life to promoting moral instruction in the nation's public schools. "I realize how little I alone can do," he confessed, "and desire to associate with myself, one who is recognized as a world-wide authority in all matters pertaining to the education of youth." The New Yorker declared he would back the work to the extent of a million dollars.

The league presidency, Brumbaugh publicly admitted, looked very tempting to him. "While he is not seeking to connect himself with another organization," the *Ledger* article quoted him as saying, "he wishes to do all in his power to further this movement." As the superintendent explained it to reporters, the league would develop materials for different grade levels to be used as part of the classroom curriculum. These materials would illustrate by means of stories about famous Americans the values and virtues they embodied.

Brumbaugh, as his career clearly demonstrated, had always looked upon the school, along with the home and the church, as a major force in character education. In his educational philosophy, the teachings of the heart—the moral sense— deserved to be taken as seriously as the lessons of the mind. He, in company with many progressive educators, bewailed how the nation's secular-based public schools neglected teaching religious and moral values. That was why, in 1903, he joined the leadership of the Religious Education Association. He once said, speaking as an REAer, "Religious instruction is a vital part of all right instruction." But, he admitted, the Constitution "wisely" forbids the state to engage in it. Therefore, only the Sunday school and family can—and must—do it, he preached.

Brumbaugh firmly believed, however, that the public schools had an obligation to reinforce the religious instruction of home and church through systematic nontheological moral training. Thus would all three institutions be bound together in a vital unity of purpose. In this pedagogical view, he was a disciple of arguably one of the greatest men in all of educational history, Johann H. Herbart (1776– 1841), the German philosopher-educator. Herbart became the master spirit of the age for most turn-of-the-century American progressive schoolmen. The supreme end of education, the philosopher had contended, was to develop personal character and social morality. He stressed that the best moral ideas can be found in the study of history, literature, and science. (This is a popular theme once again in the mid-1990s.)

Herbartians in the United States organized a club during the 1892 meeting of the National Education Association at Saratoga Springs, New York. In 1895 the club was reorganized into the National Herbartian Society for the Scientific Study of Education. The name Herbartian was dropped in 1901, because the society no longer felt limited to the thinker's ideas. Most of the major educational journals, up to the 1930s, were staffed or edited by Herbartians. Brumbaugh himself joined their society, probably sometime after his return from Puerto Rico, and would later put in a term as its president.

Well-doer James White had good reasons to go after the Philadelphian as the man to lead his Character Development League on grounds other than the educator's Herbartian convictions. He had an established record as a writer and speaker on the topic of moral training for the young. Churches and synagogues often served as a pulpit for him. Also, in April 1906, a month and a half before his election as Philadelphia's superintendent of schools, the local New Century Club had named him chairman of a committee to formulate "a working plan" for moral education in the city's public schools. Later, as superintendent, he made a lengthy case in his 1907 report to the board of education for teaching basic values to public-school children. He wrote that everything about the school should be "redolent of moral purpose."

By moral purpose he meant—to quote from the "working plan"—"an earnest and reverent seeking for truth, a deep feeling of wonder and awe, a responsive spirit of love, and a spirit of humility combined with a passion for human service." "It is vastly more important that the growing citizen should be well mannered," he told the board in 1907, "than be well informed." For this reason he would do very little tinkering with the curriculum of the elementary schools; the basic subjects, he once said, "are today overtaught . . . and [not likely] to be undervalued."

Brumbaugh's commitment to making the Philadelphia schools a model system for moral training attracted the notice of the National Education Association. In 1907 he served on one of its committees to draft a paper on teaching morals in the public schools. There were those, however, who questioned the wisdom of making the formal study of moral principles a curricular concern. But the committee reported back in 1908, its recommendations winning universal acceptance.

Brumbaugh returned from the NEA's Cleveland convention in June all enthused, observed Philadelphia's fourth estate. Armed with his NEA committee's outline, he was ready to implement "moral as well as mental instruction" into the hometown schools. His blueprint passed the scrutiny of a committee of twenty teachers and the board of education. According to the press, "The list of virtues that are to be inculcated is formidable, but it is not proposed that this instruction be rammed down the throats of the young people. Instead, it is to be given in ways that will appeal to youthful minds."

As a pacesetter among early twentieth-century urban superintendents, Brumbaugh took the position that moral training could be given in various ways, not merely by classroom tutelage. He agreed with John Dewey that big-city schools, in the work of Americanizing the masses, should transcend their traditional role and become "neighborhood centers." They should be kept "open day and night for every legitimate use that the community as a whole can vision," he once avouched before an audience at a convention of the National Education Association.

He began preaching this idea of the school-as-social-center to the Philadelphia Board of Education from year one of his superintendency. They heard him say: "Nothing will more quickly break up more bad habits and tendencies to lawlessness than social centers, where the children, under wise guidance, are given such a moral uplift as to make them hunger for the cleaner and the sweeter, and the better things of life." He stood convinced that just as the playground served the after-school, daytime welfare of the young, so, too, did decent and entertaining afternoon and evening activities. They countered the alluring temptations of the streets and "cheap amusement halls," he said.

In the fall of 1906 the superintendent had already decided to act upon his convictions. With the cooperation of the Public Education Association and the Civic Club, he took it upon himself to designate the Agnew School as a social center, Philadelphia's first. The following year he had other schools post afternoon and evening hours, but now with the board's sanction. The newly begotten Home and School League readily volunteered time and personnel. Its report for 1911–12 listed eleven social centers, which, as a rule, were located in the poorer and more densely crowded sections of the city. In 1913 the league passed to the municipal board of recreation the supervision of these sites. Thereafter they were called "recreation centers," but were reduced in number to six. The most popular activities were entertainment (chiefly home talent), lectures, singing, dancing, gymnastics, basketball, skating, cooking, manual training, and sewing.

Such was the philosophy and reputation of the man James White hoped would lead his cause. But, curiously, after White's letter made headline news nothing more was ever heard of the Character Development League, Brumbaugh's "presidency" of it, or the million-dollar bonanza. Sometime later, however, in a Pennsylvania Education Association speech, Brumbaugh did obliquely mention the outcome. He said:

> A friend of mine wanted me to enter on a moral propaganda [campaign] in the schools of America. To him the idea was good, to me only partly so. No people on earth have more material lying around in literature [in history and biography] than we.

Early in 1910, a few months after White's Character Development League made its newspaper splash, the Philadelphia superintendent took a nasty fall outside his home. One wintry day he fell descending the front steps. He slipped on an icy spot, striking his back against the edge of a step as he tumbled down. The pain was excruciating and did not go away. He self-diagnosed his backache as lumbago, not imagining it would become nearly incapacitating by the year's end. The nagging pain, on top of tensions due to his superintendency, plunged him into deep depression. His date book for this period carries inscriptions such as "Never felt more heartsick and discouraged" or "Day ended in gloom to me."

It was in this state of mind that he wrote to his cousin Harvey from Wayne, Maine, in June. (He had sold his downtown Huntingdon store building in May for $25,000.) He proposed that the two of them collaborate in forcing the trustees to face reality about Juniata's presidency. So both of them in July submitted letters of resignation.

The trustees were taken aback by Harvey's complicity in the episode, having been able in the past to ignore M. G.'s periodic resignation attempts. They tried to head off the crisis by a resort to semantics. In August they voted Martin the title of chancellor and Harvey that of president. But both men would have nothing to do with this ploy; they knew it meant no real empowerment for Harvey, the de facto president. Their bluff did not work; the trustees dallied over a decision for months. It was Harvey who finally forced their hand.

Harvey Brumbaugh had put up with a lot in his eleven years running the college in his cousin's shadow. But he was not egoless. In October he issued an ultimatum of his own. And so the spring of 1911, on 6 March, Trustee Chairman

Henry B. Brumbaugh's forty-one-year-old son was elected Juniata's fourth president. At long last, M. G. had been excused as titular head. Not a hint of this leaked out until it was announced at the first chapel service in September. In fact, the trustees' acceptance of M. G.'s resignation had been kept an absolute secret for a whole year. Hence, the chapel announcement caught everybody off guard. Said the *Juniata Echo* in a belated explanation: President M. G. resigned because of a "great multiplication of duties and actual and threatened sickness."

The "sickness" referred to his back problem, which, over a year later, still at times drove him to his knees in agony. During the fall of 1910 it had got so bad that going to his office in city hall amounted to "an exercise in sheer will power," the press reported. He was finally advised to go to the seashore (Atlantic City) for bed rest and medical treatment by two specialists. He left the day after Christmas, placing the office in charge of a deputy superintendent. An X-ray examination fueled rumors of a possible operation, but that proved unnecessary.

He did not return to Philadelphia until 7 February, still unable to go to city hall for regular work. He spent several days in mid-March seeking hydrotherapy at Warm Springs, Virginia, which was followed by a week-long stay at Magnolia Springs, Florida. All the while, his condition forced him to spend half his time in bed. Until mid-May 1911 he made periodic trips to Atlantic City for continuing treatment.

That May he got some nonmedical news that helped perk him up: the revised state school code had become law. On 28 February the Code Commission had placed its redrafted document before a joint session of the House and Senate committees on education. In the legislature itself, the document encountered stiff but not broad opposition. Some lawmakers contended that the measure had been forced upon Harrisburg by the Philadelphia "Ring" to spare the city the burden of increased taxes. Passed by an overwhelming majority, the code was signed on 18 May by Governor John L. Tener. As a body of law, it covered 152 pages.

The School Code of 1911, as it was called, received almost universal approval by the press and state educators. The *Pennsylvania School Journal* hailed it as "among the best in the country." It was described by the Philadelphia Education Association, which had a major input into the code, as "the most extensive and radical instance of educational legislation that has ever been accomplished in this country." It "marks the beginning of a new era," the periodical prophesied. Others called it the "Magna Carta of the Pennsylvania Public Schools."

Two men on the Code Commission, it was generally said, performed brilliantly and exhibited "indomitable courage": Martin Brumbaugh and Dr. George M. Phillips, principal of West Chester Normal School and the commission's secretary. For one thing, they were the most vocal among their colleagues in favor of a state board of education. It was defined as basically an advisory body, but having general oversight of the schools. Some commissioners, including Chairman Nathan Schaeffer, questioned the need for such a board, fearing it would centralize too much authority at Harrisburg. The law specified that this new body be composed of six members, plus the state superintendent of instruction, and be appointed by the governor for terms of six years. All were to serve without pay. Appropriately enough, Governor Tener placed on the first board the very men who had devised the school code.

The School Code of 1911 affected Philadelphia in many ways. One way it did so was by restricting the school boards of first-class districts—Pittsburgh was the only other one—to fifteen members. They were still to be court-appointed, much to the disappointment of many progressives who had hoped they would be elected at large. The Quaker City's new downsized board met for the first time on Monday, 13 November. But before the directors and their superintendent could take advantage of certain new powers granted by the code, there arose a temporary distraction involving the superintendent himself.

At the other end of the state, Pittsburgh's reorganized board was desperately looking for a superintendent. Brumbaugh's name had early been bandied about. He learned this from a letter he received from a principal in the Three Rivers area: "A strong Brumbaugh sentiment was launched last Saturday [October 28] at the rooms of the Teachers' Association." The letter went on: "All we are praying for just now is a good, broad man who can play the part of Moses." A few days later he heard from David B. Oliver, the new board's president. Oliver, a wealthy industrialist, ex-United States senator, veteran school director (thirty-five years), and member of the Code Commission, belonged to a family influential in the Republican politics of western Pennsylvania. Ironically, in another five years Oliver, his brother George (who succeeded him in Washington), and fellow senator Boies Penrose would team up against Brumbaugh in an attempt to destroy him politically. The Pittsburgh school director arranged to meet with the across-state superintendent in Harrisburg on 8 November, when the state board of education next convened.

Philadelphia papers got wind of what was going on and began fretting that the "Smokey City" might "annex one of our most useful citizens." Brumbaugh was called "a pedagogical expert [known] all over the United States and abroad." Articles referred to him as "a man of prophetic vision and an inspiring personality." They said he had "made himself indispensable to this city," and was an "efficient administrator" whose services were "imperatively needed." Brash reporters were sure the board of education would eagerly concede anything he might ask for.

A week before Thanksgiving Day, Brumbaugh got a letter from an old Bostonian friend, Dr. Arthur E. Winship, editor of the *Journal of Education*. Winship, who would be hailed as dean of educational journalists before he died in 1933, wrote:

> I was in Pittsburgh last Saturday and met several members of the Board of Education and with other persons of influence.
>   Of course I do not need to tell you that you can have the superintendency at

$10,000 if you want it, but I do not believe that you do. . . . I can no more think of you out of Philadelphia than I could think of myself out of Boston.

On Saturday, 9 December, Brumbaugh took the train to Pittsburgh for a "confidential talk." He and the school board there conferred over dinner that evening at the Duquesne Club. A month later a letter came from David Oliver formally bidding him to accept the Pittsburgh superintendency. But Brumbaugh replied with a graciously worded refusal, explaining that, on New Year's Day, he had been unanimously reelected by his own board. He said he had accepted his reelection "in good faith." "My Board," he continued, "has been most kind to me and I do not think it at all well for me to resign this place—where, with a united Board and an outlook full of promise, I think I can render my best services."

If Philadelphia's superintendent honestly thought he had a harmonious board behind him, then he was badly deluded. He full well knew that he had vexed several members by engineering two provisions in particular into the School Code of 1911: reduction of board size and greater powers for the superintendent in first-class cities (those with a population of five hundred thousand or more). Thus when the scaled-down board met to amend its bylaws and rules to conform with the new law, it split into two factions over the superintendency.

One division—called "the progressives" by the press—argued for giving the superintendent unlimited sway. The other set wanted to continue to retain board supervision of the high schools. The weeks-long gridlock resulted in a compromise: Section 16 of the amended bylaws amplified the authority of the superintendent to include a say in the hiring of high-school teachers and in curricular and administrative matters. He was also given the privilege of voice and vote on all board subcommittees. Disappointed progressives described these concessions as only "a very short step" toward placing major power in the hands of an "expert." This factional tension would fester until it burst into the news twenty-four months later.

The directors enjoyed greater agreement, however, on another provision of the code: the independent taxing and borrowing powers of school boards. No board member welcomed this change of law more heartily than veteran director Simon Gratz, first appointed in 1869. He had voted against Brumbaugh's election in 1906 and would be the agent of a future showdown with the superintendent. In 1911, however, the seventy-one-year-old Penn alumnus became the storm center of protests from businessmen and property owners when he proposed that the board adopt a six-mill tax rate. He said this would generate at least a million and a half dollars of increased revenue. The added revenue would obviate, Gratz argued, the necessity of floating another permanent loan for public-school purposes. The board of education courageously supported him, thus enabling the Brumbaugh superintendency to give the city thirty-six modern buildings over the next three years. The superintendent's rallying cry of "A Decent Seat in a Decent School for Every Child in Philadelphia" came close to being realized by the time of World War I.

Empowered by state code and board bylaws, Brumbaugh at once seized the initiative to reorder the city's cumbrous high-school system and its muddled administration. In 1912 there were three different types of high schools: academic (Boys' and Girls'); manual training (three); and William Penn (for girls), built in 1909 and providing academic, commercial, and vocational curriculums. Several of these schools had "annexes," some in outlying districts. Each school and its annex was a disparate unit as managed by the board. There was little, if any, coordination of curriculums. Brumbaugh's staff, therefore, set to work to phase out this bureaucratic nightmare. They abolished the three manual-training schools and converted them into what were called "composite" or "comprehensive" high schools. Thus all the city's high schools would eventually offer a standard four-year, three-program curriculum—academic, commercial, manual arts—modeled to some extent upon that of William Penn's. All students had to take core subjects in what Brumbaugh called "Humanistic studies."

Much to the unhappiness of Boys' Central alumni and faculty, who voiced loud opposition, this restructuring plan deprived the institution of its special status as a quasi-junior college. The Brumbaugh-refabricated system of upper-level schooling anticipated by a half-dozen years similar recommendations promulgated by the National Education Association, through its Commission on the Reorganization of Secondary Education.

By 1914 Brumbaugh's superintendency had increased the number of high schools to seven, four of them located in outlying districts. (Several more were projected for the near future.) Their enrollment at that time came close to realizing a stated Brumbaugh goal: 7 percent of the total student population. (It had been four percent in 1906.) But against these accomplishments stood some humbling comparative statistics: New York and Chicago each had twenty-one high schools; Boston, fifteen; Cleveland, twelve. None of the Quaker City's seven was yet coeducational. Nor were all annexes abolished.

In giving Philadelphia modern high schools, Brumbaugh did not intend to degrade vocational education. He was well aware, in a society that still condoned child labor, that the vast majority of urban youth would not go to—or if they did, finish—high school. Progressive educators, therefore, argued that the industrial arts should be an integral part of public schooling. They stressed two reasons: as an expedient to deter potential school dropouts and to provide some training for those who do. Not until 1900 did Americans begin to accept the idea of teaching the trades at public expense. As for vocational education, it dates to 1906, when the National Society for the Promotion of Industrial Education was organized.

In Philadelphia the Public Education Association had long agitated for industrial training. Between 1906 and 1912 the PEA conducted a series of studies of industrial education and vocational guidance in various cities throughout the country. So Brumbaugh and his board had in the PEA a strong, informed ally. Vocational education, as the superintendent defined it, meant "a type of training that fits [the pupil] for the competition of the industrial world." But several years before John Dewey got around more famously to argue it, he told the board in 1907 that industrial education must be an "apprenticeship in democracy." This kind of training, he explained, "is strongest when it makes flexible and facile minds for the public." The desired democratic and academic experience for future industrial workers of America could best come from the comprehensive high school, he contended. By requiring prescribed subjects for all students, it provided a

> common point of contact for the entire student body of the school. This is not only necessary but highly desirable as enabling the school to perform . . . a most important social and ethical function. The commingling of the students in class-room work will prevent as nothing else could the formation of cliques and of class distinctions arising between groups entering upon different lines of work. The students learn to respect one another and one another's work when they meet upon a common basis of cultural data in the curriculum.

Brumbaugh also encouraged "all forms of industrial and manual education" in primary and grammar schools. This was in response, he said, to the community's demand for a "new content in the curriculum" for teenagers who did not go on to high schools. By 1912 70 percent of grammar-school pupils were getting some type of formal vocational discipline, while *all* those in the primary grades were.

That year the Public Education Association submitted to the superintendent a plan to establish a "vocational bureau" as part of the public-school administration. The following year the association urged the appointment of a "skilled Director of Industrial Training" to head the bureau. Acting on these suggestions, the superintendent, in the spring of 1914, created the Department of Vocational Education and Guidance, a forerunner in municipal-school management.

Meanwhile, in March of 1912, Brumbaugh had become a homeowner in Germantown, one of the historic sections of Philadelphia. He bought a property at 254 West Walnut Lane for $26,425 (it was assessed at $32,000). For an avid disciple of Clio like him, the mansion-size house was perfect; it evoked memories of the Revolutionary War and the early national period. With more than a dozen huge rooms, the three-story stone structure had served as a British field hospital at the time of the Battle of Germantown, 4 October 1777. And here was entertained Lafayette on 20 July 1825, during his second visit to the United States. Moreover, only a few blocks away stood the Germantown Church of the Brethren, mother congregation of the denomination, founded on Christmas Day 1723. Its early life and leaders had been the subjects of much of his research and writings on Brethren colonial origins.

As a Germantown resident, he took to catching a ride to his office with John Wanamaker, driving in to the store from his Jenkintown home. The bond between the two Sunday-school buddies grew closer as a result of carpooling, but their mutual admiration went beyond a common devotion to religious education.

Wanamaker applauded his passenger's fight to purge the school system of politics. And Brumbaugh genuinely respected what his chauffeur was trying to do in the way of continuing education through the Wanamaker Commercial Institute, a school for his employees. The superintendent had once called the institute a "great educational experiment." Only recently the press had quoted him as saying Philadelphia's public schools ought to be run like the Wanamaker stores—that is, with utmost efficiency. With the fall of 1913, Wanamaker would make his appearance on the board of education.

Brumbaugh had grand plans for the coming summer. He was going to the international Sunday-school convention in Zurich, Switzerland, as a delegate and star speaker. He was also scheduled to preside over a meeting of the executive committee of the International Congress on Home Education, to be held in Ghent, Belgium. He was serving as its world president. Furthermore, the board of education had given him a leave of absence to spend time in Europe visiting public schools.

He, Anna, and Flora left New York on 7 June, passengers on the *Oceania*. But two weeks into the trip Philadelphia newspapers began to run stories about persistent rumors that the superintendent planned to resign to become president of Drexel Institute of Arts, Science, and Industry (today's Drexel University). Brumbaugh's date book and letters indicate he was indeed the prime candidate in the institute's search. Further talk of his resignation was scotched, however, when newspapers published his denial on 28 June. He had written to some friends categorically disclaiming any intention of abandoning his superintendency.

The educational purpose of his many-sided European trip was to look, in a general way, into the school systems of several foreign countries: France, Belgium, Switzerland, Germany, Holland, and England. But his predominant interest was to see at first hand the kind of industrial training provided in the schools of Germany. He hoped to bring back ideas suited to the needs of Philadelphia's vocational programs. He returned, however, convinced, he told his board of education, that "we have more to teach others than we have to learn from them." He crowed: "Our public school system in Philadelphia is more definitely serving the needs of this community in a way that a school system in a democracy can work, than are the schools of any of the countries I visited."

As it turned out, the superintendent's homecoming—his workplace was now in the Stock Exchange Building, on Seventh Street—was soon marred by a rancorous aftermath. The board became embroiled in a fractious debate over an alleged breach of its bylaws. Progressives were angered that the "stand-patters," as the press called them, had ignored the superintendent in an important high-school administrative decision. In banner-captioned stories, the local papers followed the course of the month-long fray with graphic reportage.

The working relationship between the board and the superintendent in the past had at times been tense but not necessarily antagonistic. The remarkable accomplishments over the last five years attested to that. Brumbaugh had been reelected each year without a dissenting vote. In fact, in January his salary had been raised to nine thousand dollars, although that was not high enough to suit the progressives. But they were defeated in an attempt to put it on a par with that of superintendents in New York City, Chicago, and Boston: ten thousand dollars.

The factional war began on Friday evening, 19 September, when the board's two committees on high schools and elementary schools met in joint session. The business at hand was to select a new principal for Girls' High School, subject to the approval of the full board at its next regular meeting, on Tuesday, 14 October. Only one name came up, that of Frederick Gowing, handpicked by Simon Gratz. Gowing, a textbook salesman with a Ph.D., had never taught in the Philadelphia schools. Progressives, led by John Wanamaker, tried to postpone a decision but lost by a vote of six to five.

Of all the city's newspapers, the *Public Ledger* gave the Friday night conclave the most sensational headline: "BRUMBAUGH SHORN OF FULL CONTROL: Superintendent May Quit." Coverage by the press indicated John Wanamaker was the most outspoken in rebuking the Gratz faction—and board president Henry R. Edmunds—for not consulting with the superintendent about the Gowing nomination. Said the board newcomer, "Under the existing circumstances if I were the Superintendent of Schools I don't think that I would stay around here very long." "You would for nine thousand dollars a year, wouldn't you," Edmunds dryly snapped back. This insulting rejoinder piqued Brumbaugh, whose face reportedly turned red, his eyes "sparkling." He and Edmunds then fell into a sharp exchange of their own. The meeting ended when Wanamaker's motion to defer action until Brumbaugh officially registered his opinion narrowly failed.

Two days later, on Sunday, parents and teachers hastily assembled to discuss the committee's action. Reported the *North American*: "The slurring remarks aimed at Doctor Brumbaugh by Henry R. Edmunds, president of the board of education, aroused indignation among Doctor Brumbaugh's friends." The sympathetic paper further noted: "Members of the Public Education Association of Philadelphia, representing the highest type of citizenship interested in clean administration of the schools, are planning to go into court." The intention was to file a taxpayers' suit against Gratz and what the *North American* dubbed "his pullback colleagues."

The adjective "pullback" was meant to describe the reactionary effort to defy both the board's bylaws and the School Code of 1911. The code, insisted the PEA, expressly stipulated that superintendents in first-class cities were in charge of "all" schools. And the board's bylaws contained a similar proviso, it was argued. Gratz and his partisans rebutted the Brumbaughites by noting, quite correctly, that the PEA was wrong about the board's own rules: they stated that the superintendent could only "inform" the board on the qualifications of high-school teachers; he could not make recommendations. As for principals, the Gratz camp pointed out, that whole matter had been decided two years ago when the bylaws were last revised.

At that time the majority of the board members believed the duties of the position were purely executive and should come under the exclusive supervision of that body, they said.

All during the imbroglio, Brumbaugh made clear, his unhappiness with the board was strictly a matter of "principle," not of "personal grievance." He explained, according to the *Philadelphia Press*: "The question is, Should the superintendent of schools, no matter who he might be, be consulted on subjects for which he is paid to consider?" The dispute had not prejudiced him against Gowing or any other non-Philadelphian candidate, he said. But, "all things being equal," he made it clear, "a Philadelphian would be [his] choice above all others." The city's teachers strongly endorsed his philosophy of a merit system of advancement, especially since more district high schools were in the offing.

Contrary to the scare headlines of the *Public Ledger*, the superintendent never seriously considered resigning. The reason he did not, scuttlebutt had it, was because his resignation might dash chances to be the Republican nominee for governor in the upcoming 1914 elections. Newspapers reported the subject had already been broached to him by party leaders, who "found him in receptive mood." It was even being insinuated that Brumbaugh had refused the presidency of Drexel Institute because he thought it would put an end to his political ambitions.

The Gowing episode ended on 14 October in a three-hour session described by newspapers as "one of the stormiest in the history of the board." A spirit of hostility permeated the board room: personalities were not spared; frank opinions were expressed about power-hungry members; charges and countercharges filled the air; speakers were shouted down. Epithets such as "a damnable lie" and "a deliberate untruth" lent color to the ruckus. At one point John Wanamaker interceded to plead for peace and order. Brumbaugh got in his own lick at the Gratz cabal: "You don't debate issues to reach a proper conclusion, and I must tell you that your methods of procedure are conducive to inefficiency."

The acidulous evening adjourned following a surprising vote: by a seven to six margin—with Edmunds changing front and siding with the progressives—Gowing's election was annulled. The position of Girls' High School principal was reopened, with the superintendent to approve the qualifications of all candidates. After the meeting, the stand-patters left the room singly while the progressives hung around to discuss their victory. The press quoted Wanamaker as saying that "the vote showed an awakening to the necessity of more up-to-date and progressive methods on the part of the board."

"PULLBACKS LOSE IN SCHOOL BOARD WAR" was the *North American's* caption for its story on the stormy session in its next-day edition. The paper exulted over the defeat of "autocrat" Simon Gratz and "his reactionary followers" in "their arrogant plan" to push Gowing on the board of education. "PROGRESSIVES IN CONTROL" proclaimed the headlines of a *Public Ledger* article on the meaning of the Tuesday-night vote. Its lead sentence sanguinely predicted: "A new era has dawned upon the public school system of the city."

Two months later the superintendent got the principal of his choice, although not without further squabbling among board members. Yet the Gratz set held no spite after their defeat. When Brumbaugh submitted his resignation the following spring, upon his nomination for governor, the board refused to accept it. Gratzites respected Brumbaugh because he always scrupled at exploiting the ideological division on the boards. Never once did he court the vote of any man in the face of a divisive issue.

By the time he finally gained ascendancy on high-school matters, Brumbaugh had won three salary raises for elementary-school teachers. Equitable compensation for women, a long-standing professional concern of his, had been one of his stated goals as superintendent. In 1906 men of Philadelphia's classrooms, most of them high-school teachers, averaged $177.56 in monthly pay. By comparison women, the almost exclusive mainstays of the kindergartens and presecondary grades, earned $78. Statewide, the averages were $51.81 and $39.14, respectively—which placed Pennsylvania twenty-eighth in a list of forty-five states. An ordinary industrial laborer in the commonwealth just before World War I was paid about fifteen cents an hour—thirty-six dollars a month.

When Brumbaugh left for Harrisburg, he had nearly tripled the monthly income of female teachers—to $94. Quaker City menfolk, on the other hand, had seen their monthly paychecks decrease to an average of $166.40, primarily because of younger teachers staffing the new high schools. Three raises did not eliminate the salary gap between the sexes, but it did bring Brumbaugh's women teachers to a parity with the pay of their counterparts in Pittsburgh. Male teachers, however, took home $15.75 less each month than those in the Steel City.

Philadelphia teachers came to revere their superintendent not only for materialistic reasons. They also knew him to be a humane administrator who genuinely cared about his classroom troops. He always sought "the personal touch" in his working relationships, a fellow educator said of him. The *Public Ledger* once published the following anecdote of his tenderhearted treatment of a discharged female teacher who desperately entreated him to return her to duty:

> Because of the infirmity of age and mental derangement, [she] had to be dropped from service. She visited the office of Doctor Brumbaugh, almost haunted it, seeking reinstatement. This he could not grant her, but he listened patiently to her appeals and recital of her troubles. One day he crept from his office, tears in his eyes, leaving the poor unfortunate behind. He emptied his pocketbook, borrowed all that an associate had, and sent his secretary to the woman with a big gift.

Commented the *Ledger*: "Such things he did in one form or another almost daily."

The persistent rumors in late 1913 that the superintendent might well stand down and run for political office dismayed the educational community. Many felt that his work was not yet finished. Perhaps some of them wished they could thwart losing him in the same forceful way Mayor Blankenburg had recently done when it appeared the superintendent was ready to give up another civic post. On the eve of sailing for Europe that summer, Brumbaugh had written the mayor, proposing to resign from the board of recreation. Blankenburg addressed an overseas response immediately. He wrote in part:

> I do not know how we could keep house without you on the Board of Recreation, not only owing to your deep interest in the welfare of the children, but also to your splendid executive ability. So 'good-bye' to that impossible, unwarranted, unspeakable thought.

For all practical purposes, the year 1913 marked the close of the Brumbaugh superintendency. The early months of 1914 were spent seeking the nomination for governor on the Republican state ticket at the May primaries. In June the board of education, by a unanimous vote, granted him an unpaid leave for the months of September and October for full-time campaigning. But on Tuesday, 14 July, he submitted his resignation, determined to quiet any charge that he was using the superintendency to advance his political interests. The board, upon a John Wanamaker motion, tabled a decision until its September meeting.

Brumbaugh's achievements as Philadelphia's chief schoolman were far more comprehensive than delineated in this chapter. But enough has been narrated to illustrate that, for those transitional, reformatory times, he had indeed distinguished himself as a "statesman in education." Perhaps his friend George Henderson best put his educational diplomacy in historical perspective when he credited the superintendent with being responsible for

> the three greatest strides that have been made in the public schools of Philadelphia since the consolidation of the city in 1854: First, the reorganization of the central and local boards under the act of 1905; second, the adoption of the School Code in 1911; and third, the evolution of the superintendency of public schools.

Brumbaugh's statesmanlike qualities were conspicuously evidenced in his fight to divorce the public-school system from politics. Philadelphians saw in him a man of utmost integrity who went about his business with the rare grace of a diplomat. That is the point Colonel William Lander, a colleague of his on the state board of education, was making to a *Public Ledger* reporter in November 1914 when he said, "He is [always] the frank, fearless advocate of right things. Brumbaugh always works in the open." As a result, said Lander, "In a short time [he will] have the most reluctant opponent on his side as an enthusiastic supporter. . . . Small-minded people become great by the contact of his presence—they partake of his own greatness and gather strength from him."

Brumbaugh made his superintendency's valedictory in his last annual report to the board of education. He wrote:

> To give up my life work, to turn to new duties after thirty-six years of constant service to the schools, is no easy task. My heart will always be with the childhood I love and with the schools in which I have wrought. I reluctantly relinquish a work in which I found abiding inspiration and to which I have given myself unreservedly. I pray you keep the teachers and children near your heart and so legislate as to bring to our beloved city a system of education so splendid, so clean, so efficient, that all may know we count our greatest agency for constructive good the schools of the people.

Perhaps board members, reading these words, called to mind something the *Public Ledger* had printed months earlier—in its 22 March edition. It was a statement supposedly made by an anonymous but creditable educator. To the question, "Who are the three foremost superintendents in America?" this person immediately answered that Brumbaugh's name would be on the list. Then he asseverated: "Men would differ as to the name of the other two, but one place would be his unquestionably."

This perception that Brumbaugh ranked among the country's trinity of most respected school administrators was shared by John A. Garber, then of Washington, D.C. A member of the Church of the Brethren and a government employee, Garber was working on a doctorate at George Washington University at this time. He often repeated a story similar to that of the *Public Ledger*--except he would identify the eulogizer as another brilliant academician-turned-politician: Woodrow Wilson, when he was governor of New Jersey.

12

Gubernatorial Campaign

THAT Martin Brumbaugh was a Republican and proud of it was no secret to many Philadelphians. But as their superintendent of schools, he had won his reputation for public integrity by refusing to mingle in politics. And he remained untouchably independent of political intrigue in his work as a member of the state board of education and the College and University Council. Even so, his name was being mentioned in connection with the 1914 gubernatorial race as early as the previous autumn. That September of 1913, stories circulated that Brumbaugh "smile[d] about rumors" of his interest in the governorship, an ambition he was quick to disavow.

The next month, former Governor Samuel Pennypacker and Brumbaugh were both on the centennial program of Philadelphia's First Church of the Brethren, on Sunday the 18th. Pennypacker was scheduled to speak first, and began by praising his friend as a great public servant and churchman. Then he said, "Now they call him Doctor and me Governor. I would be very pleased and not at all surprised if one of these days our titles should be changed." Pennypacker, of course, knew a lot more about the inside political situation than his remarks indicated. Huntingdon's *Daily New Era*, in November, reported that "for several months" the Brumbaugh candidacy "has been carefully groomed in various sections of the state."

It is certainly something of an anomaly that the schoolmaster, with his conservative moral ideals, allowed himself to be lured into the political life of an old boss-ridden Eastern state. Many reformers, this late in the Progressive Era, still regarded Pennsylvania as politically the most corrupt state in the Union. One pamphlet, printed in 1914 and anonymously signed "A Pennsylvanian," made the following indictment:

> I have lived in Nevada in boom times. I have lived in New York through several administrations. I have lived in the easy virtue of official Washington. Pennsylvania beats them all. Pennsylvania has every kind of political deviltry I ever saw or heard of elsewhere, and a few more she has evolved herself.

Pennsylvania's—and the state Republican Party's—bad reputation derived in large part from the political hegemony of Boies Penrose. Penrose, a native Philadelphian, was born in 1860 into a family of great wealth and social prestige. An honor graduate of Harvard, he briefly practiced law before making politics his career. Beginning in 1881 he served twelve years in the General Assembly (two in the House and ten in the Senate). In 1897 he was elected to the United States Senate through the influence of Matthew S. Quay, whose trusted lieutenant he had become. He remained in the Senate until his death in 1921, having inherited control of the state Republican Party in 1904 when Quay died.

Penrose, burly in stature (6' 4", 200 pounds), was blessed with a brilliant mind and great political talent. A protectionist in trade and thus an apologist for industry, the "Big Grizzly," as his admirers called him, showed no interest in constructive legislation, good government, or attaining the status of statesman. As a party boss, to his credit, he never became a grafter, being independently wealthy. He craved only political power. Jealously, he trained no one to succeed him, and his death marked the passing of the last of the statewide bosses.

By 1914, however, Penrose and the state Republican Party were in deep trouble. The celebrated triangular presidential race in 1912—involving William Taft, Theodore Roosevelt, and Woodrow Wilson—had badly split the Republicans of Pennsylvania. Roosevelt had made a personal tour of the state during the campaign on the third-party Progressive Republican ("Bull Moose") ticket. The Rough Rider's swing through Pennsylvania threw Penrose's party into disarray. A host of reform-minded Republicans and Independents leagued to form the pro-Roosevelt "Washington Party." William Flinn of Pittsburgh took charge as field marshal of the Republican defectors.

In the nation at large, T. R. came in second, with 27 percent of the popular vote. Pennsylvania was one of five states that gave him a plurality over Taft and Wilson.* It was the only time between 1856 (when Pennsylvania's James Buchanan was elected) and 1936 (when Franklin D. Roosevelt won) that the Keystone State's electoral vote had gone to any presidential candidate other than a regular Republican. Moreover, the Flinn-Roosevelt faction had further routed Penrose by usurping pilotage of the Republican State Committee. The regular element of the party had never before been dislodged from control in its half-century history.

By this time two Philadelphia Southside regulars, brothers William S. and Edwin H. Vare, were on the rise in local politics. Edwin was a General Assembly senator and William was then a United States congressman (he would go to Washington as a senator in 1926). They had been loyal Penrose men until 1911, when the senator undercut William's bid to become the Republican nominee for the mayoralty. As William wrote in his autobiography, *My Forty Years in Politics*, this "was the prelude to further differences with Penrose which were to enliven Philadelphia and state politics in the years to come."

---

*Wilson entered the White House with but 41 percent of the popular vote. The minority president became the first Democrat in twenty years (since Grover Cleveland) to be elected the nation's chief executive.

According to John T. Salter's little treatise, *The People's Choice*, a study of William as Philadelphia's Republican czar after World War I, the Quaker City politico had the ability to read "the sign of the times." He divined that the Progressive Era was attracting popular educators into politics. Woodrow Wilson was the classic example. At the state level, Ohio's Simeon D. Fess had gone to Congress from the presidency of Antioch College. The Buckeye State also had sent Ohio Northern University professor Frank B. Willis to the General Assembly for two terms and was now about to elect him governor. Both Fess and Willis were Republicans. In 1912 Michigan, a rock-ribbed Republican state, had already elected a "teacher statesman" to be governor: Democrat Woodbridge N. Ferris. And in Pennsylvania, of course, there was the everywhere-revered longtime former deputy superintendent of education, Henry Houck, now secretary of internal affairs since 1906.

Vare said in *My Forty Years in Politics* that all his public life he had supported public education and school reform, both in Philadelphia and the state. He called himself an "ardent champion" of the School Code of 1911, which Brumbaugh had helped draft and which completely divorced the schools from politics. "It was the splendid success of . . . Martin G. Brumbaugh as the Superintendent of Schools of Philadelphia," he wrote, "which caused me to urge his nomination and election as the Governor of Pennsylvania." He said he had known and admired Brumbaugh for many years, having closely followed his career since he came to Philadelphia in the 1890s. "[I] realized that he had great popularity up-state, and recognized him as a man advanced in progressive ideas and one with a record as a public benefactor."

Both Vare and Brumbaugh were sons born of farm families, and came to be known for their sleepless drive. But in most other respects they were opposites. Bill Vare, shorter by several inches and five years younger, "was in no sense a cultured or highly civilized person," writes Salter. "He never had time to read, and he knew nothing about the liberal arts. . . . He was the politician without informed ideas on the majority of great public questions." Salter observes, "Instead of a high order of intelligence, he possessed a 'happy shrewdness' that enabled him to succeed where more intelligent men had failed."

Unlike Martin Brumbaugh, he lacked a charismatic personality and captivating eloquence and enthusiasm as a public speaker. Also unlike Brumbaugh, he was a man of great wealth, making his money out of a variety of city contracts meted out by the local political machine he rose to control. As a matter of fact, Harvard-educated Boies Penrose had much more in common culturally and intellectually with Brumbaugh than Bill Vare did.

In any case, convinced that the present political trend of the country favored the election of educators, Vare returned to Philadelphia from Washington "one day in the early winter of 1914" with his mind made up for Brumbaugh.

He learned from his brother Edwin, however, that Penrose and his chief aide in Philadelphia, State Senator James McNichol (he who had thwarted Brumbaugh's appeal for a five million-dollar school-construction loan), were prepared to force a gubernatorial candidate of their own on the Republican ticket: former Governor Edwin Stuart. Vare pointed out to his brother how he thought the political climate called for an educator. As he said of their conversation:

> I then asked Ed to name the most prominent school man in Pennsylvania and he immediately replied, "Brumbaugh." "He's the man for us," I said. My brother agreed with me.

He now faced the task of persuading the state Republican organization. But he knew that Penrose, a candidate for reelection in 1914, had reasons to patch up differences with the Vares: there was a Democratic president in the White House; Flinn men held two important offices at Harrisburg (state treasurer and auditor-general); in "Old Dutch Cleanser" Rudolph Blankenburg, Philadelphia had a reform-minded, anti-Penrose mayor; and Pennsylvania's independent voters and progressive Republicans were very restive with Penrose-ism. Moreover, the party boss needed all the support he could get, since the recently ratified Seventeenth Amendment to the Constitution provided for the direct election of senators. It also happened that 1914 would mark the first Pennsylvania primaries for the direct nomination of all state officers.

A few days after the Vare brothers agreed on Martin Brumbaugh, they called at Penrose's office in Philadelphia. McNichol and William E. Crow of Uniontown, state Republican Party chairman, were there but not Penrose. Recalls Vare:

> "Jim," I said to McNichol, "we have another candidate."
> "Who is it?" he asked.
> "Brumbaugh," I stated.
> Penrose entered at this time and McNichol told him what I had said. Penrose looked sour, but made no declaration at the time.

According to the *Philadelphia Ledger*, the senator grumbled afterward, "We have too many schoolmasters now."

Crow held an arranged interview soon after the tête-à-tête in Penrose's office, defying the Vares. He said upstate counties strongly favored Stuart as the Republican gubernatorial candidate. William Vare went to McNichol and protested: "This isn't a square deal. Crow ought to say something nice about Brumbaugh." McNichol passed the word on and Crow acquiesced. In another interview he mentioned the school superintendent as a possible candidate, stressing his popularity in the Pennsylvania German counties.

Vare put more pressure on the Penrose machine when he returned to Washington. He polled a delegation of sixteen state Republican congressmen on their gubernatorial preferences. Fourteen of them, he writes, "declared emphatically for Brumbaugh." Back in Pennsylvania Edwin saw to it that this tally promptly got circulated among the party's state committeemen. Then, according to Vare,

Shortly afterward my brother Ed saw Penrose and had a heart to heart talk with him. He warned Penrose of his own danger of defeat and told him bluntly that Brumbaugh would make the strongest candidate the Republicans could name for Governor as he would attract the thousands of independents who had left the Taft ticket two years before and would put the party back on its feet in the State.

The Vares promised to work for Penrose's reelection if he would give way on Brumbaugh. Robert C. Bowden, in his *Boies Penrose: Symbol of an Era*, explains why the senator eventually relented in his opposition to the Vares' choice:

Penrose had learned to hate the honest school teacher while he was the efficient Superintendent of City Schools of Philadelphia because he fought to keep the schools free from political domination. That was enough to arouse the undying hatred of any self-respecting politician. But now he was ready to do an about-face, and politically embrace the honest school master, for Penrose shrewdly realized that at the moment the scholar in politics was in high favor. Woodrow Wilson was riding the crest of popular favor. Why not capitalize on the popularity of such a partnership, more especially since Brumbaugh had a very strong following in the state. So Penrose very graciously used the upright Brumbaugh as highly attractive window dressing for his own senatorial aspiration, [and] swung into step with the parade.

But also, writes Bowden, the United States senator awaited the election in "fear and trembling" for his own political survival.

The Brumbaugh papers are utterly mute about the behind-the-scenes complicity of the Vare brothers in the Republican Party's gubernatorial nomination process. Later, after he declared his candidacy, Brumbaugh always vigorously scorned charges that he was "slated" for the nomination by the undercover intercession of Bill Vare on that winter's day the congressman met with state party kingpins in Penrose's office. He scoffed at rumors he had knowingly allowed Vare to orchestrate his speaking schedule six months before he went public with his decision to run. Educator friends, not bosses, persuaded him to get into the race, he would indignantly insist.

The persuasive moment came, as he told it, in late February 1914, at a conference of school superintendents in Richmond, Virginia. Many Pennsylvania fellow administrators there urged him to enter the May primaries. But, as the *Public Ledger* once quoted him, "Had there been no open primary I should not have been a candidate. I could offer myself only through a direct appeal to the people upon a platform of my own composition throughout and free from the influence of any political leaders or group."

Thus at the time of the Richmond conference, according to the *Huntingdon Daily New Era*, all that Brumbaugh would say publicly was that he *would not* run unless "there came wide demand from the people of the state." The Republican slate must have "popular approval," he said.

He kept what the *Public Ledger* termed a "sphinx-like silence" about his political plans for another several weeks. One of the paper's reporters told of Brumbaugh's noncommittal behavior at a meeting of the board of education's Committee on Elementary Schools on Wednesday, 4 March. In a relaxed moment, David H. Lane, a board member and "Peerless Leader" of the Republican City Committee, made known that his "favorite son" for governor was the superintendent, just back from Richmond. This elicited the question, "Well, Doctor, what do you have to say about that?" voiced in chorus by several board members. Brumbaugh, the reporter said, only "shrugged his shoulders and twitched his heavy eyebrows but made no answer." Moments later a messenger boy interrupted the meeting with a telegram for the superintendent. He read it in silence, prompting Simon Gratz to speak up and say, "It's only another county that has gone for Brumbaugh." There is no doubt board members greatly respected him, even though some of them, like Gratz, occasionally held to separate agendas from his.

Not until Monday morning, 16 March, did Brumbaugh officially announce his candidacy; the deadline to file was 21 April. He called a press conference in his office in the Stock Exchange Building. By that time, according to the *New Era*, polls of counties all over the state revealed a "decided preference" for him among Republicans. The candidate said he was led to place his name on the primary ballot in response to the "home folks" of his native county and "thousands of other good citizens." He emphasized that he would not be "an office-seeker in a partisan sense." He made it clear that he was entering the race as an Independent Republican, free of "entangling alliances."

The next day the *Public Ledger* reported that Republican Party VIPs in the state had "without exception today expressed unstinted approval" of the schoolman's candidacy. They saw it as a welcomed antidote for the party, alleged the paper, because of all the bad press Penrose was causing.

The *Huntingdon Globe*, with excusable pride in a local son, greeted the news of Brumbaugh's candidacy with a bit of historical analogy that, in light of his oft-confessed admiration for William McKinley, must have greatly pleased the county native:

> In our political experience, covering a period of over thirty years, we have never witnessed a more spontaneous and universal call for the public service of any man than in the case of Doctor Brumbaugh. It is on a par with that great uprising of the people in favor of Major McKinley for President in 1896, when every other candidate, no matter how worthy, was but a drop of water in that stupendous avalanche which swept the "Little Napoleon" from Ohio to Washington.

What reason did Brumbaugh give for abandoning, at age fifty-two, a lifetime in school work to enter active politics? He knew that, if elected, he would be governor only for four years, since he could not serve two successive terms. Then what? Pennsylvania, he told an interviewer, reflecting upon his decision, "is a good old State and I love it. I want to set it straight." He went on:

In 1913 in this State we adopted a Statewide primary law and I saw at once that only a man whose record would bear scrutiny could hope to win the nomination for governor. That was my opportunity. I was not ashamed of my record. I saw that there was a chance for a school man of wide acquaintance and I saw also that no boss could control that nomination. . . . [So] I determined to go into the primaries.

Almost every Juniatian hailed with pleasure their ex-president's candidacy. But not so at first did one popular forty-year-old professor on campus, Charles C. Ellis, a former student under Brumbaugh at Penn, and like him a great attraction at teachers' institutes (including down in Louisiana). Ellis, a match for M. G. in the pulpit and on his way to becoming a denominational leader and president of Juniata, feared that his old professor would be ground under by "gang" politics. Felix Schelling of Penn also worried about the political safety of the man whose Ph.D. dissertation he had directed. He closed a congratulatory note by wishing he "might see [him] in better company." But Brumbaugh, secure in his religious faith, felt no vulnerability. As he wrote to Juniata alumna Flora Shelly, "I have prayerfully gone into this contest." And in an open letter to the student body of his alma mater in April, he said he had concluded that it was his "Christian duty" to run.

Many Brethren felt, however, that if he had really spent much time in prayer he would not have declared his candidacy. In some parts of the brotherhood it was still considered scripturally wrong to become involved in politics. As recently as 1912, Annual Conference had reaffirmed the doctrine that a Christian's citizenship was in heaven and that "the church of Jesus Christ is no part of the world system." On this basis, Brethren were advised: (1) not to allow themselves to "become entangled in politics"; (2) neither to vote nor accept any office of any kind unless they were convinced that by so doing they could "more completely fill their mission in the world"; (3) to accept no office, the duties of which might "require the use of physical force or might compromise, in any way, the nonresistant principles of the Gospel of Christ."

According to Charles Ellis, M. G. rationalized his decision to seek the governor's chair by citing the second proviso in the 1912 Annual Conference ruling. His election, confided M. G. to the skeptical professor, would do two things for his denomination: bring the Brethren into public notice and deal him a golden opportunity to put the principles of the church to work in the political arena. Already, newspapers were playing up his "Dunkard" (the word he chose to use) heritage, portraying him as a "stalwart scion" of the Pennsylvania Germans. As an article in the Sunday edition of the *Public Ledger* the week he announced his candidacy noted: "Unlike the many descendants of the German sectarians in Pennsylvania who have undergone a change of heart in religious matters, Doctor Brumbaugh has closely adhered to the faith of his fathers."

The moment the educator jumped into the primary race, schoolteacher friends of his—from cities, towns, and hamlets—in immense numbers volunteered to help him in the preliminary work. In short order, they collected seventy-two thousand names on his nominating petitions. He prepared a four-page pamphlet that summed up his political creed. A proven wizard at crafting slogans, he declared in the little manifesto: "My life's work must be my platform and my pledge." Brumbaugh assured the electorate of his political independence as a Republican. Among other things, he announced against child labor, and for workman's compensation; good roads; local option (as the "practical solution" to the "vital problem" of the liquor traffic); woman suffrage; public-school vocational training in agriculture; conservation; state civil service; and a high "moral standard in all public service."

The press reported that the school superintendent said he would refrain from any stumping prior to the 19 May primary election. Schoolteachers and other educators did it for him. They addressed copies of his platform pamphlet and sent them to as many registered state Republicans as time allowed.

On the party ticket, Brumbaugh was pitted against three other candidates. But he won over them easily, polling 253,788 votes out of 320,097 cast for all four GOP aspirants. That gave him four-fifths of the party's total tally for the gubernatorial nomination. (About 300,000 registered Republicans failed to cast their ballots in the primaries.)

Brumbaugh carried every county in the state, while Senator Penrose, with a total of 219,871 votes, lost thirteen counties running against only one opponent (J. Benjamin Dimmick, of Scranton). In all, the school superintendent outpolled Penrose in fifty-eight of the sixty-seven counties. As someone on Dimmick's campaign staff, much impressed by the bumper vote for the Philadelphian, commented to newsmen:

> Doctor Brumbaugh never had been before the people for an elective office and practically had no organization behind him. It therefore must be conceded that the vote for him was purely personal and a wonderful tribute to his widespread popularity in every section of the state, and striking evidence in the universal belief in Doctor Brumbaugh's integrity and wonderful ability as an executive.

A few days after the primaries, the Brumbaughs set out by car for Wayne, Maine, to get away from all postelection hullabaloo. On the day they arrived at their summer home—Sunday the 24th—Mrs. Brumbaugh "took sick." That is all Martin's date book notes about her illness. Her medical condition, never publicly identified, continued to worsen following the Brumbaughs' return to Philadelphia. The family physician diagnosed her ailment as terminal. The news was a heavy blow to the husband at what should have been a time of great jubilation. By mid-June it was evident her death was only days, possibly only hours, away. Her husband's date book records for Sunday the 28th: "Mother very low." She died "peacefully" that night a few minutes after two o'clock, the doctor at her bedside.

Anna Konigmacher Brumbaugh passed away three months after her fifty-third birthday. For years she had been a near-invalid. She had been a quiet, unassuming woman of simple tastes, called "Anna K." by her friends. She had cared nothing for the social life that offered itself as her husband rose in public service. The prospect of being a governor's wife had caused her some apprehension, although she never seemed to resent being married to a man much in the limelight. Devotion to the church and charity work, especially for the elderly, had sufficed to satisfy her social interests and needs. Her saintly ways made her a beloved citizen in the eyes of many Philadelphians.

The funeral service was held at home on Wednesday, 1 July, conducted by Juniata professor Tobias T. Myers, her former pastor for many years. Interment, strictly private, followed at the West Laurel Hill Cemetery. Martin, Mabel, and Flora (Edwin had married in February) left a few days later for Wayne, to try to forget politics and to grieve.

On Tuesday, 14 July, Brumbaugh presented, in absentia, his letter of resignation as superintendent of schools, effective the first of September. It designated Dr. William C. Jacobs, senior associate superintendent of schools, to act in his place pending the election of a successor. As noted in chapter 11, on motion of John Wanamaker the communication was tabled by a unanimous vote and would not be acted on until September.

Philadelphia newspapers applauded the board's refusal to act on the superintendent's resignation. So did other dailies elsewhere in the state. The *Harrisburg Telegraph*, for example, said tabling it gave lie to the biblical dictum that "a prophet is not without honor save in his own country." Brumbaugh was so indispensable to the Quaker City school system, the *Telegraph* declared, that the board was wise "to retain his services even if only in an advisory capacity to the last possible minute." "But," the article went on, "the people of Philadelphia must come to an early understanding of the fact that Dr. Brumbaugh will be able to hold his office as superintendent of schools only a short time longer at best. . . . [H]is election is as certain as anything can be."

By this time, Brumbaugh's friends had set up a campaign base on the ground floor of what was then the Betz Building, in which the Vare Street Cleaning and Construction Company offices were located. Soon pledges of support from men of every party from all parts of the state and nearly every county swamped the headquarters. The *Telegraph* published one signally approbatory letter from a physician in Tidioute, Warren County—a dyed-in-the-wool Democrat. The doctor, employing allusions to historical and literary figures, wrote:

I know Doctor Brumbaugh well and have known him for thirty years. I was a pupil of his when a child and again when I was preparing for my professional careers, and I know he possesses the qualities that make the Statesman. *He has the great, kind heart of Lincoln, that seals the appeals of a people for civic righteousness and moral uplift; he has the intellect that, like Webster's, suggests the remedy, and he has the indomitable will power of Jackson to carry out his convictions. His character is an inspiration to the thousands of students who studied under him, and like Goldsmith's "Vicar of Wakefield" "he lures to bright worlds and leads the way."* [Italics added]

Therefore, the country healer assured his readers, Brumbaugh's "patriotism is a passion of love for his native state, and if elected Governor of this great Commonwealth his ambition will be to give the people a government that will earn the respect of the whole nation."

Meanwhile, the Republican State Committee meeting in Harrisburg in mid-June had fixed a late-August date to open its political campaign. Pittsburgh was to be the place. Originally, the rally date had been set for 15 July, but party leaders had run into problems trying to draft a platform that would reconcile some of the diverse views held by Brumbaugh and Penrose. Generally, however, it was projected that Pennsylvania's GOP campaign would focus on the issue of prosperity and the impact of the Democratic tariff—sloganized as "bread and butter." The slogan would serve to remind voters of the GOP's successful national shibboleth in 1900: "The full dinner pail."

A number of minor political parties had fielded candidates for the gubernatorial contest. Brumbaugh expected to face two major challengers: Democrat Vance C. McCormick and the Washington Party's William D. Lewis. McCormick, from a highly respected aristocratic family, was a wealthy Harrisburg newspaper publisher (of the *Patriot* and the *Evening News*). In the historic three-cornered presidential contest of 1912, the former mayor of Pennsylvania's Capital City had been national chairman of the Democratic Party and campaign chairman for Woodrow Wilson.

William Lewis, a former faculty colleague of Brumbaugh's, had resigned as dean of the law school at the University of Pennsylvania to run. The future director of the prestigious American Law Institute had been chairman of the platform committee at the "Bull Moose" Chicago convention in 1912.

It was as fine a set of candidates for governor as any state had ever—or would ever—put before the electorate.

For the senatorial race, Boies Penrose would have to contend with Democrat A. Mitchell Palmer and Gifford Pinchot of the Washington Party. Palmer, a Quaker graduate of Swarthmore College, had been a congressman since 1908. When Wilson proposed to make him secretary of war in 1913, he turned down the cabinet post because of his religious faith. (Later, appointed attorney general in 1919, he would earn the title of "Fighting Quaker"—and notoriety—because of his overzealous crusade during the time of the infamous "Red Scare.")

Gifford Pinchot, a Connecticut native, was a Yale graduate who became the first professionally trained American forester and the chief agent of systematic forest management in the United States. He had great influence upon Theodore Roosevelt, the nation's most famous champion of conservation. During T. R.'s presidency he became, upon creation of the Forest Service in 1905, the government's "chief forester." In a famous dispute over conservation policy, President Taft forced Pinchot to resign in 1911—a development that infuriated Teddy. This ultimately contributed to the break between Roosevelt and Taft and the politically costly split in the Republican Party during the 1912 presidential election. (Pinchot would become a two-term governor of Pennsylvania, elected in 1922 and 1930.)

Both the Democratic and Washington parties, then, had placed men with national political reputations on their ballots for the two top races. Their campaign committees got the jump on platform ballyhoo by mid-June, while that of the Republican had been placed on hold.

As scheduled, the Republican Party went to work on its own platform the last week of August, its leaders ensconced in the Fort Pitt Hotel. Brumbaugh, upon his return from Maine on Tuesday the 25th, departed Philadelphia on the 11:15 P.M. train for the next morning's conclave in Pittsburgh. Senator Ed Vare and other Quaker City party pillars accompanied him on the Pullman coach run. Bill Vare and Jim McNichol had gone on ahead the day before.

A mass meeting was then held the evening of the 26th in the Fort Pitt Theater, officially kicking off the Republican campaign. According to the *Harrisburg Telegraph*, Brumbaugh's first public appearance since the primaries brought the theater crowd to its feet in a "tremendous" demonstration that Wednesday evening. He gave the keynote address, devoting his attention to state issues. (Penrose, who followed, dwelt on the national scene and "the follies" of the Wilson administration.)

The nominee for governor stood by his pledges of the primaries, although his and the state party's platform planks, except on local option, were practically synonymous. He declared, paraphrasing the words of Jesus, that "Having put my hand to the plow, I shall not look back, but forward, plowing as straight a furrow as I know how to plow, as straight as God helps me to plow." He lauded Republicanism: "A party that has in a brief period . . . not forgotten to be generous when just, that has liberated the bondsmen, carried enlightenment and help to the people of the islands of the sea, that has been truly progressive without being rash or reactionary."

Two days after the GOP's Pittsburgh powwow, the "Guns of August" began booming in Europe; a terrible war had come to the world.

Both Penrose and Brumbaugh would stump almost continuously over the next two months, making jaunts by automobile or train to every county. Brumbaugh tarried in Pittsburgh on the 27th, meeting with local "marms and masters" in Schenley Park and then touring the industrial plants about the city: the Pitcairn shops of the Pennsylvania Railroad; the Westinghouse works; and the J. Edgar Thomson steel mill in Braddock. Then he was off to Huntingdon for a "Home Folks Day" on Friday.

M. G. was met at the railroad station by a large delegation, which included his uncle Jacob and cousin Harvey. Escorted by his relatives, he made his way through the crowd to the Leister House, across the street from the station platform. At the hotel door awaited his eighty-one-year-old father, who had not seen him since the May primaries. "Hello, Dad," saluted the son. "Hello, boy," said George. Dewy-eyed, they embraced and kissed. Then, "Hello, Marty," or "Hello, M. G.," greeted him on every side as his admiring friends and onetime neighbors kept him busy hand-pumping for the next several hours.

Despite a slight drizzle that evening, a "monster" parade (so testified the *Huntingdon Globe*) convoyed the town's honored visitor to the "packed-to-the-doors" Grand Theater. At almost every street corner along the procession's route could be seen huge banners that greeted the nominee, riding in an open car accompanied by his father. Old George, his chest heaving with sobs, wept in pride as his son doffed his hat from side to side to the cheering throngs that lined the sidewalks, several ranks deep. At the Grand Theater, Huntingdon's largest auditorium, some five to six hundred people crowded in.

Among them was Juan D. Miranda, a native of San Juan, Puerto Rico. Brumbaugh, while commissioner of education there, had reached down into his own pockets to send Miranda to Juniata College. Then, when the Puerto Rican had received his sheepskin, Brumbaugh, now head of the Philadelphia schools, sent him to the University of Pennsylvania under some kind of arrangement worked out with Dean Lewis. As a Penn graduate, Miranda began practicing law in Philadelphia, deeply indebted to two of the gubernatorial contenders for his career start. He chose, however, to campaign for his original benefactor. Giving up his practice for the duration, he spent his time canvassing Juniata College alumni.

It was Frank Brumbaugh's memory that his brother and Penrose never spoke to each other as campaigners. That is hard to believe, since the two men's itineraries sometimes put them on the same rostrum. From the start, however, Martin Brumbaugh harped on the theme that he was his own man, especially when appearing at a rally in the company of Penrose. Over and over again, he denounced bosses, saying, "I have to live with my conscience whether I hold office or not." Sometimes he could use colorful language in professing his political virginity. One early October day three thousand voters in Philadelphia's Town Hall heard him snarl: "I hate a boss as much as you hate a boss, and if ever a slimy thing throws itself in my path I will scotch it."

His repeated denunciations notwithstanding, he only obliquely alluded to Republican bossism. He never named names. He was quick to defend the principles of the Grand Old Party and the honor of the state it controlled. He even condemned anyone critical of Pennsylvania's government as being guilty of treason. Thus when the *Philadelphia North American* challenged him to repudiate Penrose-ism, he scornfully refused to do so. The paper had promised, upon a public repudiation from him, to support his candidacy, make him head of the Republican Party in the state, and boom him for president. In response, Brumbaugh issued a press release on 14 September, saying, "I have no boss. I never will. Even a newspaper cannot boss me." Bossism, voters heard him imply a few days before the *North American's* publicized dare, had not taken a serious toll morally or economically in the Keystone State. "Pennsylvania should not be judged by the actions of an unworthy few, who play upon her for their own sordid ends. At heart the state is healthy and sincere," he gave assurance.

Throughout the campaign he faithfully endorsed the party's entire ticket—which, understandably, only convinced some people that he was in truth a dupe of Penrose. As a campaigner, however, he chose to paddle his own canoe, although his itinerary occasionally coincided with that set up by the party for its other candidates. He enjoyed immensely those times when he and Henry Houck showed up together some place. Their bantering with each other made crowds roar with laughter.

In mid-September the Washington Party came to a sudden demise. The first death-blow came from Pittsburgher Richard R. Quay. In his office in one of the city's tallest skyscrapers, he told the press he was leaving the party. Son of the late senator and state Republican high chief, his had been one of the strong voices in the Roosevelt movement of 1912. But now, he said, his vote would go to Brumbaugh, who appeared to be the most progressive of the candidates. The very next day, Dean Lewis, after a visit to Oyster Bay, Long Island, to talk to Roosevelt, withdrew from the ticket, recommending that the Washington Party fuse with the Democrats and back McCormick. (He would go back to teaching law at Penn for the next few years.)

Party leaders, meeting in Harrisburg that same Wednesday, made the fusion official. The *Telegraph* gloated that the disintegration of the Washington Party was causing Independents to "flock" to the Brumbaugh camp and not, as Democrats had hoped, to that of McCormick.

In the early heat of campaign battle, Brumbaugh sometimes turned to an old political pro for encouragement: John Wanamaker. The nominee wrote the merchant in September, confessing that "in these days of stress and worry," it was a great comfort to have someone like him—"for the strength of a hand clasp and a word of counsel and cheer." "I am grateful for you every day," Brumbaugh wrote in a later note. This missive came following Wanamaker's offer to provide certain offices, free of rent, in the Lincoln Building as headquarters for the Brumbaugh Citizens Committee. The committee had been working out of a cramped room in the Witherspoon Building. Subsequent letters were just as cordial, none more so than the one sent on 10 October:

> I wish I could send to you through the air what I am now sending to you by mail—my sincere love, my hearty appreciation and my very deep gratitude.
>> God bless you.
>> Sincerely, your Boy.

The Brumbaugh Citizens' Committee had meanwhile accepted Wanamaker's offer of office space and on 18 September moved into the Lincoln Building, at Broad Street and South Penn Square. Candidate Brumbaugh had vowed to accept no funds from his party's campaign chest (except for some promotional literature the State Committee took it on its own to print and distribute). The movement for a support group spread rapidly. Its chairman was a former judge and current school-board member, Dimner Beeber; James S. Hiatt was the secretary, and Louis J. Kolb was the treasurer. The thirty-five-member executive committee was state-wide in scope (fifteen Philadelphians, ten Pittsburghers, and ten from a scattering of counties). Early in October a huge banner, bearing a likeness of Brumbaugh, was unfurled across Broad Street, in front of campaign headquarters. Inscriptions on it assured voters of "An Aggressive Administration: Honest, Capable, Efficient."

In only a month's time, Brumbaugh had developed into a formidable cam-paigner. The schoolmaster had learned to rely on that day's equivalent of the "sound bite"—the short, snappy sentence. He gave up the windy language of the lecture room and county institute. As the *Huntingdon Globe* put it, "He has translated his speech from that of the schoolhouse to that of the 'stump,' and nothing has been lost in the translation." Of course, the campaign pace—rushing from town to town—helped to force him into this new speechmaking mode.

He could also impress crowds with a politician's flair for the dramatic. No newspaper reported that he went around kissing babies, but he made a big hit with the lumbermen of Williamsport. When paying court to the employees of the Penn-sylvania Lumber Company there, reported the *Philadelphia Public Ledger*, he

> threw aside his coat and hat and by riding on the big gangsaw proved to the sawmill men that he was right at home. As further proof he exhibited a scar on one of his fingers received years ago while at work in one of the sawdust makers.

Earlier, the paper had said of his behavior as a campaigner in the Pittsburgh area: "The Philadelphia educator is . . . famous . . . for an unquenchable desire to meet the voters face to face, shake hands and swap reminiscences." "Yesterday," its 16 September edition related, "They dragged him out of a boiler room where he was holding forth with two stokers stripped to their waists."

In a 3 October letter to a Brumbaugh supporter, James Hiatt recorded his own portrayal of the candidate's campaign style: "The Doctor is out amongst the people taking off his coat, sawing wood, rolling logs, shaking the horny hands of prole-tariat, embracing hewers of wood and drawers of water." Hiatt declared, "He is proving himself up to the minute and several jumps ahead of the ordinary expert in the Political Game." Needless to say, he had a rapport with audiences of teachers, Sunday church worshippers, and farmers that the high-born McCormick could never match.

Grangers instantly related to him when he reminded them:

> I was born on a farm, I have worked on a farm. I have had to do with farming nearly all my life. I think I know the farmer's problems and his difficulties.

They cheered when he deplored the relentless rural-to-urban population shift in Pennsylvania and declared, his fist raised in the air: "The state should give all possible aid to the farmers. We are too rich a Commonwealth to deal niggardly with the tiller and his soil." Rural dwellers were also delighted when he spoke about Pennsylvania's need for "good earth roads, well crowned, scientifically graded and thoroughly drained." Everywhere he went he guaranteed a boodle-free road-building administration, one that would also keep roads in good repair.

By early October oddsmakers in Harrisburg were taking two-to-one bets that Brumbaugh would win the gubernatorial election. This advantage followed not only news about the Washington Party's demise, but also stories about major defections in the Democratic Party. Larue Munson of Williamsport, who could have had the Democratic nomination for governor in 1910, shocked his party's faithful when he came out for the GOP front-runner. "Thousands of Democrats were ready to make their adieux to the party," he said, "and will turn in for Dr. Brumbaugh and the entire Republican ticket."

At Bradford that October the "Doctor" had uttered what many Independents and Democrats were pleased to hear from him, who heretofore had been so reluctant to criticize the GOP. He said the Republican Party had been "chastened for its conservatism" in 1912 and must now give Pennsylvanians "every wise and beneficent legislation" that would "protect," "safeguard," and "promote" the welfare of the people. And that meant, he stressed, "a large social program of legislative reform."

It could be said that ultimately the outcome of the gubernatorial election boiled down to a contest of personalities, not issues. The two candidates had few quarrels with each other over what the pressing socioeconomic problems were in their state. Theirs was a relatively canard-free rivalry as a result, although the Harrisburg publisher kept questioning his opponent's "sincerity" about despising bosses. But there was one campaign issue, not involving McCormick, around which controversy exploded, provoking more vituperation, slander, and mendacity than all the others put together: local option.

Historically, local option has meant empowering any discrete political unit in a state, even one as small as a ward, to vote on the prohibition of liquor within its limits. As a policy by Drys, it was viewed as the most expedient way to canvass and mold public opinion on outlawing strong drink. Thus its advocates never intended local option to be a final triumph, but only the first step toward statewide—and ultimately national—prohibition. The nonpartisan Anti-Saloon League (ASL), founded in 1895, broadened its attack on the liquor interests after 1904 to include the enactment of state local option laws. It perfected the practice of lobbying in America, and its organized pressure ploys on lawmakers foreshadowed the power wielded by special-interest groups today.

Local option, then, had become the watchword of the antidrink forces in Pennsylvania by 1914. The previous year, however, the Pennsylvania Anti-Saloon League had dropped the ward, township, and borough features of previous local option bills in favor of a straight county unit plan. For the first time in the state's history,

Democrats incorporated a local-option plank into their gubernatorial platform for the campaign of 1914. So did the Washington Party. An attempt to get the Republican State Committee to follow suit at its Pittsburgh meeting in August was defeated 96 to 5, despite the pleas of Brumbaugh.

On Thursday, 17 September, Drys from all over the state attended a rally in Harrisburg to agitate for the local-option cause. The rally-goers endorsed McCormick, Lewis having pulled out the day before. The next day the executive committee of the Pennsylvania Anti-Saloon League put out a press release from its Philadelphia headquarters that sanctioned the action taken by the temperance forces at Harrisburg. League officers confessed being "almost embarrassed" by its "multiplicity of friends."

McCormick preached the doctrine of local option all during the campaign. He had proclaimed his position—à la Patrick Henry—at a party rally in Lewistown on 15 September:

> I not only stand for local option, but fought before the primary for its adoption in this party's platform and won, and if elected, will fight to the end of my administration for its adoption. If this be treason, then make the most of it.

It became his strategy to attack the Republican Party for dodging the issue, and to chide Brumbaugh for "remaining quietly at home" and permitting Penrose to "slap his face" with a state platform silent on the alcohol crusade. As everyone knew, both Penrose and Frank B. McClain of Lancaster, Brumbaugh's running mate for lieutenant governor, were friends of the liquor lobby.

Brumbaugh, of course, had made local option a central plank in his personal platform at the time of the primaries:

> The problem of the liquor traffic is a vital one facing the people and the Legislature today. In harmony with many thoughtful persons, I submit that local option is a practical solution. Any legislative measure looking to an improvement of the conditions regulating this traffic will receive my support.

Despite reiterating this position everywhere he stumped, the Anti-Saloon League would not budge in opposing him. Its leaders were dubious about his ability to defy the Republican machine on the liquor question. This suspicion was nurtured by his unwillingness to break openly with Penrose. In its 23 October issue of the *Keystone Edition*, the league's official Pennsylvania organ, there appeared a full-page spread in bold type charging that Brumbaugh, Penrose, and McClain were backed by "Brewers and Boodlers," "Philadelphia Contractor Bosses [the Vares] and Allied Liquor Organizations of the State," "Gamblers and Grafters," and the "Personal Liberty League." State Superintendent Edward J. Moore, a Methodist minister turned lawyer, wrote an article in the same number titled "Why McCormick,

Not Brumbaugh." He elaborated on the league's fears that Brumbaugh could not live up to his campaign promise on local option.

Frustrated, the Republican nominee complained to the *North American*:

> I have declared for local option and stand by that declaration. I have assured people in a score of utterances that I shall do all I honorably can to promote legislation favoring local option. What more can an honest man say or do?

He wrote the Reverend Moore a long letter of protest, alleging that the league was misrepresenting his stand on the alcohol subject. He accused Moore, who had returned to his native Pennsylvania from Missouri, of being "a stranger" to the state, "wholly misled by self-seeking, if not wholly unscrupulous politicians, using the Anti-Saloon League as a shield." The organization's blue book, he pointed out, professed a policy of "neutrality" when both candidates for political office were allies of the temperance cause. The letter ended with the bitter query: "What is your secret purpose in misrepresenting me to with the people with whom I have had a lifelong association, and who know that I keep my word?"

Moore's reply of 5 October was equally blunt: "I challenge you to show a single word that the Anti-Saloon League has put forth during these months [since March] that has in any way misrepresented you or that has 'unwittingly dragged' great Christian denominations into this strife against the rum traffic." The Drys' pontiff said that the league had not found Brumbaugh's local-option pledge "satisfactory," although its members had "confidence in Dr. Brumbaugh, the man." How could the ASL do otherwise, he concluded with a question of his own, when the Republican candidate was endorsed "by a State Committee that was 96 to 5 against local option?"

Pro-Brumbaugh testimonials, to Moore personally or published as "letters to the editor" or as press interviews, failed to move the ASL's leadership. Antidrink spokesmen like evangelist Billy Sunday, Russell Conwell, Methodist bishops, and other prominent clergymen and lay Sunday-school workers (Howard J. Heinz and John Wanamaker), were of no avail at the ASL's top level. Juniata's Charles C. Ellis sent off an angry letter to Moore, chastising him for his intractability.

Even *open* letters, like the one composed by C. Tyson Kratz, who had been a "Bull Moose" delegate in 1912, made no difference. Kratz, in similar words to Munson's, warned that, with Lewis out of the picture, most Roosevelt men like himself would switch to Brumbaugh. The Norristown resident, a member of the Brumbaugh Citizens' Committee, fumed in an interview by the local *Times* that Moore had set back the cause of local option in the state for ten years and ought to "return to the wilds of Missouri, where he belongs."

The temperance question turned briefly calumnious the last week of October, seizing newspaper headlines. Evangelist Henry W. Stough, who was holding a series of meetings in DuBois, ignited the episode. The *Clearfield Progress* carried a story on 22 October in which it quoted Dr. Stough as saying he had reliable information that Brumbaugh and certain members of his troupe were "lousy drunk" during his recent circuit through Clearfield County. Brumbaugh, who had gone on to Greensburg, promptly denied the charge. He responded with a statement that read in part:

> I can scarcely believe that a so-called evangelist would write such a slanderous lie. I shall at once consult counsel and give him and the paper a reasonable time to make explanation and apology. It must be made decisively and just as publicly as the libel was issued or I shall see that the full consequences of the law are meted out. . . . I AM NOT AND NEVER HAVE BEEN A DRINKING MAN.
>
> I do not intend to allow anyone, even in the garb of a calling that ought to be heaven high above scandal, slander and lying, to reflect upon my reputation or attack my character.

The threat of a lawsuit spooked an immediate telegram out of the editor of the *Progress*, who apologized for putting the revivalist's accusations in print without checking with Brumbaugh (whose denial he said he believed). He also published a retraction in his own paper, but declared Stough had not been misquoted.

The preacher, in defense, swore he had been. In a letter to Brumbaugh and in a press release, he disclaimed having "intimated" Brumbaugh was under the influence. He stood by his story, though, that certain of the men escorting the candidate were intoxicated. Also, he refused to recant his comment that Brumbaugh did not shun the company of saloon-keeping hotel owners. The closest he came to an apology was to say, "I am not forgetting, Doctor Brumbaugh, that you are an exemplary man in your private character." "That's a dirty letter," the candidate retorted in characterizing Stough's communication for newsmen.

With the so-called "dirty letter," however, the week-long incident passed from the pages of newspapers. This left somewhat ambiguous just what the alcoholic state of the Brumbaugh entourage had been. On the other hand, the episode "resulted in a shower of friendly and sympathetic messages" upon the campaigner, reported the *Philadelphia Public Ledger*. In fact, no other issue in the campaign so swamped the Brumbaugh headquarters with cordial letters and telegrams as did local option.

Besides Moore and Stough, only one other person riled the Republican candidate into use of angry rhetoric: ex-President Theodore Roosevelt. The "Colonel," as newspapers liked to refer to the Spanish-American War hero, made a four-day swing through Pennsylvania the last week of October. Traveling by special train, he purportedly made his excursion to plump for Pinchot. Simultaneously, the Flinn-Roosevelt combine circulated more than a million postcards over the Rough Rider's signature. But Teddy also used the trip to attack Brumbaugh, calling him "the woolly lamb" (an ad hominem reference to his steel-gray, unmanageable hair and pacifism) for not denouncing Penrose straight from the shoulder. A *Philadelphia Inquirer* headline on 31 October blazoned: "BRUMBAUGH HITS BACK BIT-TERLY AT COLONEL ROOSEVELT—Resents 'Slanders and Lies' and Demands a Square Deal."

That was the daily's caption for its article on a speech by Brumbaugh to a West Chester audience. Growled the future biographer of T. R.:

> The man who is attacking me knows better. He is not honest and he knows he is not honest, and I challenge him to point to one single act of mine that has not been as clean and as square as any of his ever was.
>
> It is strange that an outsider should come here to run this great Commonwealth and to try to run me out of Pennsylvania. He cannot run me out of Pennsylvania. He has another guess.

The *Ledger* described Brumbaugh's reply to the Rooseveltian reproach as deliv-ered "with the speed of a piston and sounded like the blows of a sledgehammer." In "staccato words," he urged voters not to be misled by the "slanderer and liar." "Isn't it strange," he thundered, "that this same man should come into this state in the last week and prate about me and try to drive the same man out of Pennsylvania that he tried to keep in Puerto Rico twelve years ago?" He said he resigned and came home for reasons he would not go into until the campaign was over (which he never did). He lamented, "How are the mighty fallen," that someone like a former president, in the bitterness of a campaign, would forget his "manhood, dignity and honor" to resort to "falseness, slander and ugliness."

Brumbaugh, playing tit for tat, went on to accuse the Bull Mooser himself of having been boss tainted: he had relied on the New York "machine" to get elected governor, would sign no laws without its leave, and was under its command in distributing patronage. The indignant schoolman said, "I would rather dig in a trench here in Philadelphia for my living."

In an unbossed Brumbaugh, many Pennsylvanians took to saying in public places, voters would not only be electing a governor but a future president. These prognosticators considered him Woodrow Wilson's peer in every regard—intellec-tually, morally, politically. He even had an advantage; as a onetime farmer and lumberman, he better knew the "needs of honest toil," one admirer put it. The perception of Brumbaugh as presidential timber was best summed up in a *Public Ledger* article that appeared on election-day eve. It ended this way:

> The Democratic President wrote some books, while Doctor Brumbaugh has written many. I cannot find any quality in Woodrow Wilson that Martin Brumbaugh does not more than equal. He has the advantage of being on the right side of the tariff ques-tion. When he uttered these words: 'What the people of Pennsylvania want is less laws and more bread; fewer promises, more meat; less war tax and more tariff,' he placed himself far beyond Woodrow Wilson in the estimation of Pennsylvanians.

We are not only electing him Governor of Pennsylvania [tomorrow], but we are making a President of the United States.*

In these days when would-be governors spend many millions running for office, the Brumbaugh Citizens Committee filed $20,899.61 as the total of its campaign expenses.

As election day approached, the heralded future choice for the White House was himself more immediately looking to the Executive Mansion in Harrisburg, confident of victory. For days he had been predicting, based on what he had seen while stumping, that he would win by no less than a 250,000 majority. Also, he had another reason to be optimistic. As he wrote to Russell Conwell, "I have campaigned in the confident assurance that our banners have upon them the smile and privilege of our . . . Father in Heaven. For I will never walk where I cannot pray."

The day of 3 November dawned with the promise of fair weather throughout the state. This came as "cheering news" to the Republican Party, which hoped for a big voter turnout. Its candidate for governor, suffering with a bad cold, appeared at his polling place in Philadelphia's twenty-second ward at 8:48 A.M. The press said he greeted the judges and other voters with the words: "'Tis a splendid day for victory for Penrose and Brumbaugh and the whole Republican ticket. I am sanguine of victory." He then went behind the half-curtain to mark his ballot, numbered ninety-one.

As he slipped it into the box outside the booth, newspapermen turned the act into a photo-op event. Brumbaugh made a comment to reporters reminiscent of Richard Nixon's attack on the press after the former vice-president was defeated for governor of California in 1962: "This is the last time they are going to pick on me." The smiling Germantown voter, of course, was being playful, unlike the embittered Nixon.

As it turned out, Brumbaugh fell considerably short of his optimistic prediction; he ended up with a majority of 66,158 (over five rivals). But his 588,706 total votes were the most Pennsylvanians had given a candidate for governor before woman suffrage. (Daniel Hastings, however, had won by a greater plurality, in 1894.) In Bill Vare's analysis of the election outcome, the whole Republican slate had been swept into office on Brumbaugh's coattail. Keystone State Republicans not only sent Penrose back to the Senate (with 519,810 votes), but gained ten more seats in Congress, outnumbering Democrats and Progressives thirty-one to five after the election. To the schoolman belonged the credit, Vare would always say, for revivifying the Republican Party in Pennsylvania following the "Bull Moose" debacle.

The day after the election, the *Public Ledger*, which in two years would turn critical of Brumbaugh, ran an all-agog article about him. The column described him as a "man of inflexible will and dauntless courage." It went on:

---

*This article would come out in pamphlet form prior to the national Republican convention of 1916 with the caption: "One Prediction Has Come True. What About the Other?" The original piece had been written by Attorney Harry A. Mackey, then a Vare ward chieftain. He later served as chairman of the Workman's Compensation Board during Brumbaugh's governorship and as mayor of Philadelphia.

He is a progressive, responsive to the new life which has quickened the public conscience, a man of far-reaching vision, keen perception and broad sympathies.

One day, months later, the gubernatorial victor sat for an interview by a writer
from the *Outlook* magazine and reflected upon how he, a professional educator,
had come to be elected to high political office. He suggested three reasons. First of
all, over the years he had gone from "one place to another in school work and
lectured at church and school conventions. . . . Before many years I knew most of
the teachers of the State. What came afterward was the natural result of the past."
That is, he was implying, from the start he had a solid, multipartisan political base.
Second, as head of the nation's third largest school system, he had boldly fought—
and prevailed against—boss control of public education. This won him the reputation of a machine-free servant of the people. And third, during the campaign he
told Pennsylvanians, "[T]he Republican party in the past had been long on prom-
ises but short on execution, but that if I were elected I would do what I promised."
He said he guessed the voters believed him. All these factors combined to making
his victory as "easy as taking candy from a child," was the way he summed up the
election outcome.

How or with whom the governor-elect celebrated the honor bestowed upon
him by the vox populi remains an unanswered question for the biographer; the
page in his date book for 3 November is a blank, except for the word "Election."

But on the Juniata College campus the celebration was "loud and long," the
Echo reported. It began election night. When the telegraphed late-hours count au-
gured certain victory, the tower bell began "to peal forth the good news." Classes
were canceled on Wednesday, which was given over to gala parades, snake dances,
mass meetings, M. G. eulogies, singing "Hail to Juniata," and a huge bonfire in the
evening as the culminating event.

Out in Marklesburg, Frank Brumbaugh made a list of thirteen Democratic
neighbors who voted for Vance McCormick. He kept this list in his desk for years,
and as each one departed this life he scratched off his name with relish. In his own
mind he was certain where they were going in the hereafter.

Many conservative Brethren in eastern Pennsylvania took no pride in the gubernatorial outcome, according to the *York Dispatch*. Just before the election, members of the denomination in that area received a pamphlet warning that "it was
wrong for a true Christian to vote," and saying "all sorts of unpleasant and bad
things" about the Dunker nominee.

The Tuesday after election day, Brumbaugh went to Huntingdon to visit his
father and brothers in Marklesburg. Huntingdon gave him another "rousing old-
fashioned welcome" that evening, as it had in August to set his campaign going.
Paraders carried banners with such inscriptions as "Now for 1916" and "Huntingdon,
Harrisburg, Washington." He was the second—and last—governor the county produced (David R. Porter preceded him, 1839–45) but its only native-born one.

He then left by train the next day for Southern Pines, North Carolina, to rest for three weeks. At nearby Pinehurst Country Club, site of today's World Golf Hall, he played the links for the first time. He was immediately smitten by the sport, which came to rival fishing as his favorite outdoor recreation. He would continue to go to Pinehurst regularly until the end of his life. At Southern Pines he made a friend of A. McNiel Blair, a physician and fellow stogie smoker. Brumbaugh sent Blair a box of Blackstone cigars, his favorite brand, that Christmas, which elicited the following thank-you note: "I [now] realize that you are a connoisseur in the selection of tobacco. When I saw the real black ones that you smoked here, I had my doubts, but these are all that could be desired."

For the month of December he went back on the board of education's payroll as superintendent of schools.

William Vare tendered a big dinner in his honor on Monday evening, 7 December, at the Shoreham Hotel in Washington. There he was introduced to Pennsylvania's congressmen and to Frank P. Woods (chairman of the Republican National Congressional Committee), James R. Mann (Republican leader of the House), and James J. Fitzgerald, Democratic member of the Appropriations Committee, of which Vare was a member. In all, about seventy guests, including Ohio's governor-elect and Brumbaugh's friend Frank Willis, showed up for the banquet. Would-be kingmaker Vare said of Pennsylvania's incoming governor in introducing him:

> In reuniting the Republican party of the State of Pennsylvania, which has always been known as the Keystone State, Dr. Brumbaugh has performed a service to the Republican party throughout the nation. He is the man who caused the stampede back to the party in his own state, which was the stronghold of the Progressives. . . .
>
> [W]hen the time comes the people of Pennsylvania will offer Dr. Brumbaugh to the people of the nation a Protection-and-Prosperity President. And if he should be called to that high office, the American people will have reason to be proud of Pennsylvania's gift to the nation.

Three days later, back in Philadelphia, he was inducted into the Union League Club, a political remnant of the Civil War. Vare-scholar John Salter called this fraternity the "highbrow citadel of Republicanism" in the Quaker City. It was *so* highbrow that Bill Vare, himself coveting the honor, never gained admittance. Brumbaugh was sponsored by the club's president, William T. Tilden, a realtor and member of the board of education whose famous tennis-playing son would one day become the first American to win the men's singles at Wimbledon. Like the doctor at Southern Pines, Tilden also got a box of the inductee's favorite cigars at Christmastime. (Cigars seem to have been a common Yuletide gift from Brumbaugh over the years.)

The governor-elect was an "ideal club man," as a reporter for the *Public Ledger* described him at this time—a perfect quality for someone seeking political office. The newsman wrote: "He likes companionship and the good fellowship of the club-house. He is a born comrade, fond of the society of his fellows and the interchange of wits at the dinner table." In addition to all the professional and historical societies he belonged to—more than twenty of them—he was a member of the University Club, the Franklin Inn Club, and the Five-O'Clock Club (its "best entertainer" and sometime president). Characterized as a "free-from-care man of the world" in the *Public Ledger* piece, Brumbaugh must have been an enigma to his late wife, whose own social life had been the very antithesis of woman-about-town. (The *Huntingdon Globe*, around this time, called the home-county native the "best mixer" since McKinley.)

It was the "clubman's" educator friends, however, who gave him the biggest send-off to Harrisburg. They sponsored a testimonial dinner at the Bellevue-Stratford Hotel for him on Thursday evening, 17 December. More than six hundred filled the banquet room. John Wanamaker was the toastmaster until laryngitis silenced him; Juniata College's barrister friend, George Henderson of the Public Education Association, doubled for him until the program's end. A string of speakers, men and women representing the various civic and educational groups he had worked with, paid tribute to his "brilliant" work and laudable legacy.

John Wanamaker, as long as his voice lasted, chose to speak about Pennsylvania's political future. He began by noting that the citizens of the United States had come, of late, to be "blessed with a new vision" of public duty: honest and unbossed conduct in political office. He quoted James G. Blaine, the GOP's giant of an earlier national era, who often said: "As goes Pennsylvania, so goes all the States." Turning to the guest of honor beside him, the hoarse-voiced toastmaster pressed his point home like a Dutch uncle: "Governor Brumbaugh—take friendly and formal notice. . . . You are now the chosen leader of Pennsylvania, and by its wisdom and example, it is in your power to set the pace of good government for all the States." He denounced "wire pullers" and warned against pandering to them. Sadly, it turned out, the toastmaster was mouthing political ideals he himself could not live up to. This failure on his part would soon sour his relationship with the man he envisioned as being a pacesetting governor.

Their broken friendship still weeks ahead, Wanamaker arranged to present Brumbaugh with a special Christmas gift. This would make all the more ironical the circumstances of their future estrangement. The department-store nabob had read widely on the life of Oliver Cromwell, "The Great Independent" of seventeenth-century English history and the stubborn foe of Stuart royalty. In thinking about a unique present for his friend M. G., now about to play the role of statesman, he hit upon the idea of something symbolic in nature. It was designed to link the lives of two men he admired, and to identify what he hoped would be a Brumbaugh-redeemed Commonwealth of Pennsylvania with Cromwell's righteous Commonwealth of England. On Wednesday the 23rd he had the governor-elect stop by the store for lunch, after which he unveiled his creation and presented it to his unsuspecting guest. On it was attached the gift-giver's calling card, inscribed with the following quatrain:

> To My Friend of Iron Will
> The Governor's duties to fulfill
> This Replica of Oliver Cromwell's Chair
> Offers its lesson with my prayer

The intended lesson of the miniature sterling-silver keepsake? In Shakespeare's words, "the dauntless spirit of resolution."

Brumbaugh got another pleasant surprise that December, this one delivered by holiday mail. It was a Yuletide greeting from his old nemesis on the board of education, Simon Gratz. The note read:

> I want to express the hope and belief that, in the high position you are soon to assume, you will be no less successful and win no less honor than in the superintendency from which you will retire.

It was a gracious, conciliatory gesture that epitomized the goodwill and spirit of the season.

That Christmas, the first without Anna, was much less joyous than past ones for the Brumbaugh household. But there must have been exciting bustle in getting ready for the move to the Executive Mansion, then located along the state capital's North Front Street with a magnificent view of the Susquehanna River. Brumbaugh must surely have known he would be carrying a unique set of credentials to the governor's residence: the first career schoolman; the first college president; the first with a Ph.D.; only the second clergyman. What he did not know was that, in every case, he would be the last one.

As Pennsylvania's twenty-eighth governor, his salary would be a mere thousand dollars more than as superintendent of schools—but with many perquisites.

Governor Brumbaugh Forgot an Early Lesson

AS A PUPIL   AS A SCHOOLMASTER   AND AS GOVERNOR.

A newspaper cartoonist spoofs M. G., trained in literature, about the Oliver check.

Frank Butler, Dave, and Annie Oakley.

Flora Belle and Fritz.

A damaged photograph shows the governor hoeing his victory garden after Fritz baptized the press camera.

Sizing up a difficult "chip shot" at Pinehurst, North Carolina.

Fund-raising via honorary degrees, in April 1926. *Left to right:* Pennsylvania's chief justice Robert von Moschzisker; M. G.; Howard Heinz; Charles M. Schwab; U. S. District Judge of Central Pennsylvania Albert W. Johnson; Juniata College Vice-President Charles C. Ellis.

M. G. and his "partner-pal" Flora strolling Atlantic City's boardwalk in January 1929. *The Boardwalk Illustrated News* referred to the former governor as "One of Pennsylvania's most popular and powerful-minded chief executives."

The Mission House and M. G.'s intended presidential home, 1995.

Brumbaugh's historic home in Germantown, as it looks today.

13

Governor versus Gang: 1915–16

DREARY midwinter weather conditions moderated a bit for the new governor's inauguration on Tuesday, 19 January. A drenching rain had fallen on Harrisburg all the previous day and into the early morning hours. Then, as the forenoon wore on, a rift appeared in the heavy, leaden clouds, and there was sunshine. Even so, it was windy and cold, and not too pleasant.

The gubernatorial party left the Executive Mansion for the inaugural site at half-past eleven in a caravan of automobiles, outgoing Governor John Tener and Brumbaugh riding in the front car. A few minutes later they reached their destination, a stage that had been erected in front of the capitol's west entrance. Before them stretched a vast open-air assembly of perhaps as many as eight to ten thousand persons from all parts of the commonwealth. The crowd extended far out State Street, almost to Front, and up and down Third a block each way. People were hanging from utility poles and cornices of nearby buildings. In a commodious grandstand sat members of the General Assembly, state officials, other dignitaries, and their spouses.

Chairs on the speakers' platform had been reserved for Brumbaugh's family and relatives. Edwin and his wife were there, as was Mabel. Of the clan, several were present: a brother—Frank with his wife and daughter; an uncle—Jacob, from Juniata College; and a cousin—John S. Brumbaugh of Pittsburgh, a member of the campaign committee. Curiously, newspapers made no mention of Flora (who may have stayed behind at the Executive Mansion to supervise preparations for the postinaugural luncheon). The Teners had graciously vacated the governor's home the day before so that the Brumbaugh guests could be put up there. Martin's younger brother, Irvin, was absent because his wife was ill, and "infirmities of age" kept George from attending his son's inauguration.

A staff correspondent for the *Philadelphia Public Ledger* observed that as Brumbaugh walked up the steps and on to the platform

It was evident . . . he felt keenly the tremendous weight of responsibility he was about to assume. It was a new Brumbaugh, in a way, self-contained but serious. He did not smile, except now and then in response to a greeting.

He "seemed to be in something of a reverie," wrote the reporter. Other members of the news corps noted that the governor-elect wore an "ordinary black derby," in contrast to the high silk headgear worn by the retiring governor and numerous state officials. This "demonstrated his democracy," one writer opined.

The inaugural ceremony began promptly at noon, upon the last toll of twelve that sounded from the tower of the Presbyterian Church a half-block away. Elder William J. Swigart, a former professor of Brumbaugh's at Juniata and a college trustee, gave the invocation. The clerk of the Senate then read—reportedly in a faint voice—the legislative certification of election, after which State Chief Justice J. Hay Brown administered the oath of office.

Tears trickled down Brumbaugh's cheeks as he stood facing the begowned chief justice. With his right hand raised, he chose to be sworn into office by affirmation—saying, "I promise to do so"—in keeping with his religious faith. Journalists reported that when he bent over to sign the oath, he took a handkerchief out of his overcoat pocket and brushed it across his teary eyes. The official band broke into strains of *America* as he inked his name.

Straightening up, he turned toward the crowd and began his inaugural address, a typewritten manuscript clutched in his hands. But he rarely glanced at the prepared text. He spoke, said the *Public Ledger*, "with all the fire and vigor of offhand oratory." The *Philadelphia Record* characterized his speech as "a brief and forceful renewal of the pledges" on which he had built his campaign. It struck a "popular chord" because it was "unaffected and businesslike," and had "the ring of sincerity," the paper pointed out.

The governor vowed to secure good, enforceable laws. But, he declared, "We have been overlawed." This unnecessarily burdened the people, he explained, and, by bloating bureaucracy, only worked to the benefit of self-serving politicians. Looking toward the grandstand, he enjoined the legislators, his voice rising almost to a shout, to enact the "few vital" laws put forth in his platform and then go home. The crowd let out a great roar of approval when he said this and here and there was heard a "Hurrah for the next President." As both lawmakers and the crowd soon learned, the governor would stand by this paradoxical idea of progressive reform girded with the clout of a chief executive's veto.

Brumbaugh then went on to cite those "few vital" laws "the people have demanded and we have promised." None of them elicited "the spontaneous and deafening" outburst more than that of county local option, according to newspaper accounts:

Men threw up their hats and cried, "Hurrah!" Women in the grandstand rose from their seats and cheered, and there was a vast rumble of approval in every heart of the audience. It was a full minute before he could proceed.

In striking contrast to this uproar, near silence greeted the governor's call for woman suffrage. Only "a few feeble handclaps, lasting, perhaps, 10 seconds, were heard. . . . That was all," reported the *Public Ledger*. Otherwise, frequent applause greeted each salient point in the rest of the governor's proposed legislative agenda. The *Public Ledger* quoted one unnamed Republican lawmaker as saying, after the ceremony was over: "It was the greatest inaugural address I ever heard, and I have heard many, here and at Washington." (Could the lawmaker have been Bill Vare?)

No other governor in recent memory, if ever, had so unabashedly confessed in an inaugural the need for heavenly help and people's prayers as did Brumbaugh. The very first words of his address acknowledged that "I can do my duty [only] when aided and guided by the Divine. In His name and for His people I enter upon this new field of endeavor." And the very last ones were: "Let us all devotedly pray for this great State and by our words and our deeds humbly help our common God to save, to honor, to exalt this splendid Commonwealth He has given into our care and keeping."

Odd as it may seem to us today, newspapers did not ridicule such pious language as mere religious—or political—cant. In fact, nobody, inside or outside the newsroom, had publicly raised the church-state issue vis-à-vis the election of Brumbaugh. His ministerial status was common knowledge. Likewise, nobody had fretted in print when he, as a candidate, had sometimes on a Sunday morning preached in a Protestant church.

In all, the platform exercises lasted only forty-five minutes. When they ended, huge, ruggedly handsome Irish immigrant John Tener quickly turned toward his successor, towering over the six-footer, shook his hand, and made a dash to the railroad station to catch a train for Chicago. There he would take up duties as president of the National Baseball League. (He had played several seasons in the Windy City for the Cubs.) The new governor himself took a motor tour of the inaugural parade route, along which an additional six thousand or more spectators lined the streets. He then returned to the speakers' stage, which had been converted into a reviewing stand.

From there he watched an elaborate parade, enlivened by thirty-five bands, pass by for over an hour. One of the big hits of the spectacle was provided by the well-represented Philadelphia Republican Club. Its delegation had brought along two elephants and a diminutive donkey. The donkey's right eye was covered by a sling and over its back was draped a blanket inscribed with the words: "Seriously Injured, 1914." To the great amusement of onlookers—and the governor—the two Jumbos performed a proper inaugural act upon reaching the reviewing dais. They stopped, made a shuffling turn toward the elevated row of VIPs, and raised their trunks high in salute.

A trainload of Huntingdon Countians also participated as marchers. Marklesburg somehow rounded up a sixty-piece band. Several Juniata professors, including Charles Ellis, took part in the cavalcade. They let out with "some spectacular [college] yells and songs" along the way, said the *Echo*. Many from the home area carried banners and signs that read "1916, Huntingdon to Harrisburg to WASH-INGTON" or "Solely for the People" or "No Entangling Alliances; No Agree-ments." Fellow countians familiarly called out greetings such as "Howdy, Marty" and "Good Luck, M. G." as they marched by the reviewing stand. Only for the "home folks" did the governor remove his derby hat in salutation.

After the parade the new governor hosted an early afternoon luncheon at the Executive Mansion. The day's celebration ended with a public reception in the caucus room of the capitol. His hostess at both events, quite likely, was Flora Belle Parks.

There is some confusion in the record about who of the two women in the widower-governor's domestic life—Mabel Brumbaugh or Flora Parks—filled the distaff place of honor the first year of his administration. According to the *Phila-delphia Public Ledger*, the governor's ward at once became "his constant compan-ion when officially engaged" and had "full charge" of his household and the Ex-ecutive Mansion. (The Brumbaugh household in Harrisburg would now consist of nine employees, including a black butler.) But LeRoy Greene's *Shelter For His Excellency*, the lively history of the Executive Mansion with profiles of a hundred men who occupied it (up to the 1950s), says it was Mabel who took her deceased mother's place as chatelaine of the Front Street residence. Writes Greene, she pre-sided over the mansion "with modesty and simplicity."

The *Huntingdon Globe*, however, seems to side with the *Public Ledger*. Its Valentine Day's issue noted that "Miss Mabel" was "back in the classroom," to the great relief of her pupils who worried that they were about to lose her. As yet unmarried, the governor's twenty-seven-year-old daughter was a kindergarten teacher at the Philadelphia Quaker school on the corner of Girard Avenue and Seventh Street. According to the *Globe*, she did not know about her future plans and would stay at the school until the end of the term.

The safe bet is that Flora Belle was the one who acted as the "Governor's Lady" at times of pomp and circumstance from the start, and also assumed the duty of mistress of the mansion. After all, she, a onetime home-economics student, had been the family cook and housekeeper for two decades. She had looked after the correspondence of Anna, who had been sickly for years. And it was Flora who made all the funeral arrangements after Anna died, Martin being tied up with his gubernatorial campaign.

The conviviality of state Republicans attending the luncheon belied political reality. Inauguration day, unfortunately for the new administration, marked but a brief time-out in what would develop into a vicious four-year-long contest for party power between the Brumbaugh-Vare faction and its Crow-Penrose opponents. Al-ready, when the 121st General Assembly met during the first week of January, Penrose loyalists had flung down the gauntlet in both legislative chambers.

In the House of Representatives, they opposed the Brumbaugh candidate for

Speaker: Charles A. Ambler, of Abington, Montgomery County. The governor wanted a friendly Speaker, wrote Bill Vare in his *My Forty Years in Politics*, "because he had an unusually pretentious humanitarian program for presentation and he realized well in advance the opposition this would meet from the reactionary forces of the Republican Party." In Pennsylvania the post of Speaker was a very powerful one, which set the standard and fixed the character of a legislative session. By his authority the Speaker held "in his hands virtually the power of life and death over legislation," as the *North American* once put it. The fight on Ambler was finally dropped by the Penrose people after the Vare-led members of the House from Philadelphia met at the city's party headquarters and declared for the governor's man.

The opening session of the Senate, meanwhile, produced what the *Public Ledger* called "The Sandbag Committee." Its official name was Committee on Executive Nominations, a body created by a resolution introduced by Republican Party chief, Senator William Crow. At stake were thousands of appointive positions in the state bureaucracy under the governor's control. Constitutionally, the privilege of confirming or turning down appointments made by the governor belonged to the Senate as a whole, acting in executive session. But Crow's novel piece of legislation empowered a select group, to be named by President pro tempore Charles H. Kline, a Penrose henchman from Pittsburgh, to pass on the qualifications of all gubernatorial appointees. It was a power play that could destroy the integrity of the Brumbaugh administration. Readers of the *Public Ledger* were warned:

> In case the Governor should become too independent, this committee will be used as a club to curb him. The senatorial prerogative will be waived, and this committee will be most powerful and really constitute the Senate, so far as nominations are concerned.

Brumbaugh, however, had been in no hurry to award Capitol Hill jobs prior to taking office. This dilatory approach, the *Philadelphia Record* approvingly noted, drastically departed from the policy of past new governors. They had been only too ready to let political shakers take patronage troubles off their hands, entrusting to them the nuisance of dispensing the spoils of office. Meanwhile, the go-slow line was a great frustration to a legion of "original" Brumbaugh men, each clamoring for an office-holding reward from the cornucopia of cronyism.

The governor held back on early jobholder decisions for several reasons. He felt that his appointees clearly had to reflect his independence from the martinets of political power. Also, he wanted to find the mugwumps within the Republican Party who would facilitate pushing his agenda through the legislature. Then, too, it bothered him terribly that, as custom dictated, he was expected to play the patronage game—even to removing, in many cases, men of proven merit.

A month after taking office, the governor spoke at a Penn alumni dinner in

Philadelphia and referred to this personally troubling predicament. He said he was "amazed" to find that there were fifty-four hundred bureaucrats he could replace at will. Then, speaking from the heart, he went on to say:

> What do you think of that! What are you going to do with them? Are you going to do with them what is being done elsewhere, just get them out of the way? That's wrong, gentlemen. You have got to stand with me, gentlemen, for a State Civil Service that will protect good men in office.

A few days later he again anguished over his control of patronage at a dinner of the Reading Chamber of Commerce. At one point he said, "No man, I care not who he is, should have such unlimited power over his fellowmen." For the benefit of newsmen he commented:

> It was stated a few months ago that if the election went a certain way, there would be trainloads of men leaving Harrisburg. I heard it, did you? Well, they may go more gradually. Mark you, wielders of the pen, I said "may," don't say "shall."

As it turned out, he did go the "shall" route—because, of course, at his mercy were a multitude of Republicans. Even so, his independence must have pleased one old Chester County warrior of newsprint who, editorializing, had openly urged him to do what he thought best and ignore all the "dam phool" kibitzers.

It could well have been at this inceptive stage of his governorship that he and John Wanamaker parted ways. Family tradition says that the merchant took umbrage when someone he recommended for a job lost out to another Brumbaugh appointee. The two men never spoke to each other again. There is the story that soon after their alienation some person asked Wanamaker, "Do you know Governor Brumbaugh?" Wanamaker snapped back, "I once knew a *superintendent* by the name of Brumbaugh, but I don't know a *Governor* Brumbaugh." On his deathbed, the department-store king is supposed to have expressed deep regret that he and his former friend never reconciled.

If the Sandbag Committee did in fact bully the governor on the matter of patronage, neither the *Public Ledger* nor any other newspaper made an issue of it. One of its rivals, the *Record*, however, was quick to point out that Brumbaugh's attorney general, Francis Shunk Brown, had "long been known as a Vare lawyer." Moreover, the paper charged, "It is apparent that [Israel] Durham during his time of greatest political activity depended upon him for legal if not some political advice, and when he died he made him one of the executors of his large estate." Though boss tainted, Brown, admitted the paper, was "personally a man of charming manner" and a "lawyer of ability." The *Huntingdon New Era* also credited the appointment of Brown to Vare influence.

The new attorney general and the new governor were fellow members of Philadelphia's Five O'Clock Club—as were the Vare brothers. As clubmates, they became fast friends. Brumbaugh needed a right-hand man who would loyally take charge of his controversial proposed legislative program; he needed a man both of political skills and legal acumen. In Brown—whose salary would be two thousands dollars more than his own—the governor honestly thought he had that deputy, Vare cohort or not. The attorney general, a graduate of the law school at Penn, was the descendant of two Pennsylvania governors on the Shunk side of the family as well as the son of a state senator who became a United States congressman.

Despite all his plaints about the national and state trend toward passing too many laws, Brumbaugh thought that the people should have a law if they wanted it, "because the people in their cool and matured judgments are always right," the *Cincinnati Enquirer* quoted him as telling a reporter. He saw his own legislative prospectus as being a direct response to the popular will. His philosophy of law-making had something of the populist accent Americans would hear preached by Texas billionaire Ross Perot in his presidential campaign of 1992 —laws should come *from* the people, not *at* the people.

But he was capable of political rhetoric spouted by contemporary pre-World War I progressives, too. "The greatest national needs of the day are to be found in the words, social justice," he told the *Enquirer* journalist. He said the two words were self-defining, but then went on to explain that the term embraced the interests of the silent majority—those bystanders "now excluded from debates, editorials and legislative enactments." He had been elected on a platform, he indicated, that promised to bring social justice to that muted mass in Pennsylvania —the workers, the children, the women, the farmers. His final comment was, "I mean to do many things with the help of the Pennsylvania Legislature. If I cannot do them with [its] help I will go to the people."

One mandate the people had given him, Brumbaugh had no doubt, was to prod the legislature into enacting a county local option law. He gave this political hot potato first billing in his inaugural address. Lawmakers in the grandstand heard him tell them that the people of Pennsylvania had "a perfect right" to decide the alcohol question for themselves. They must be given that legal power without delay, he urged. His final inaugural words on a local option law were a reminder that its enactment would be in keeping with the GOP's forward-looking record in Pennsylvania:

> The party that has given this great State its industrial and educational development has now the sacred opportunity of giving the State a great moral uplift. I trust we shall not fail the people on this issue.

Brumbaugh worked closely with Attorney General Brown in drafting what was perceived to be his pet measure of the 1915 legislative session. It was commonly referred to as "the governor's bill." Indeed, Brumbaugh told newsmen, "I want it known as *my* bill." The Anti-Saloon League, reversing its preelection position, now praised the governor for having the "nerve to seriously discuss the liquor question and make a fight for a definite policy." The league gave the Brumbaugh-Brown county local option bill "unqualified support" and, unlike in the past, declined to introduce one drawn up by its own legal staff. In the ensuing legislative struggle, the governor stood out as the recognized impresario of the local-option drama, not the Anti-Saloon League.

No other political issue claimed so much of his time and energy in 1915 as this one. He worked assiduously for bipartisan support and won the backing of Congressman A. Mitchell Palmer. In response to a telegram from Brumbaugh, Palmer wrote in an early March letter: "I shall be very glad to personally urge every Democratic member of the legislature to redeem our party's pledge and vote for local option. . . . The people of Pennsylvania are for local option by a large majority and their will should prevail." At the same time, however, the Pennsylvania State Brewers' Association (PSBA) repeatedly attacked the governor as "an assumptive political boss." The PSBA ridiculed him for trying to push upon the people an "impractical measure" against the wishes of the Republican Party. And by early March he knew he would get no support from the Vares, whose proliquor position was public knowledge.

At the public hearing before the House Law and Order Committee on Tuesday afternoon, 6 April, Governor Brumbaugh made an unprecedented appearance, although he did not testify. Leaders of the Dry movement were present in full force. Among the testimony they gave was a letter from John Mitchell, president of the United Mine Workers of America. The labor chief called local option "a fundamental principle of American liberty." The grand master of the Pennsylvania State Grange gave witness to the thousands of Grangers who favored a local option bill. Perhaps the most dramatic attestation came from the Reverend Father John J. Curran, president of the Catholic Prohibition League of America. He said emphatically: "I am sick and tired listening to the argument that local option will violate personal rights. There is no right to manufacture and sell liquor. It is a privilege."

The day of the hearing, special trains from Philadelphia, Pittsburgh, and other cities brought thousands of local optionists to the capital for a mass demonstration in the evening. The demonstrators paraded in the streets waving flags and wearing white ribbons and singing prohibition songs. The *Harrisburg Patriot* estimated the number of marchers to be eight thousand. "It was," said the daily, "probably the greatest demonstration for a single piece of legislation Pennsylvania has witnessed in all its history." That night the governor addressed the main rally in the Chestnut Street Auditorium.

Three days later Brumbaugh publicly appealed to Christian churches to make Sunday, 11 April, a day of prayer for a local option law. He also sent out six thousand or so letters to clergymen throughout the state. On that Sabbath the governor himself attended services at the Hummel Street Church of the Brethren in Harrisburg and gave a brief extemporaneous talk. The *Patriot* reported that in Pittsburgh thousands of churchgoers dutifully knelt in prayer on Local Option Sunday. Everywhere ministers preached on the righteousness of the cause. Rural areas, in most cases, were natural dry territory, but cities were wet.

Late into the night of Tuesday, 20 April, the day before the House voted on the bill, Brumbaugh held a number of strategy conferences in his capitol office with cohorts from the legislature. He told them, "The State has not had such an awakening in many a day. . . . There is no other issue so important, so far-reaching, so vital, as this." He went to bed confident the bill would pass.

Hundreds of spectators thronged the House chamber the next afternoon for the bitter four-hour debate. The bill's sponsor, George W. Williams of Tioga County, emphasized its wide public support among all segments of society: professional, business, blue collar, farmer. He warned that local option was "stronger than any political party." And if the legislature turned down such a law, "there will be a nonpartisan uprising in Pennsylvania, not in the name of the Anti-Saloon League, but in the name of the people."

Opponents of the Williams bill made scathing attacks upon Brumbaugh, the real author of the measure. One of his vilifiers was Miles B. Kitts, a Democratic educator and lawyer from Erie County. Sporting on the lapel of his coat a miniature American flag, the badge of the Wets, he made a long speech in which he said:

> I came to Harrisburg to represent the people of my [legislative district], not to represent the Governor of this Commonwealth. . . . Yet this agitation has not been brought on by the people of this great Commonwealth, it has been brought on by the Governor himself.

Echoing similar sentiments, another lawmaker charged:

> We, as members of this House, are now asked to lay aside our independence as members of a co-ordinate branch of the government and pass this bill, not because of any demand in our district, but because the Governor wants it.

Every one of the 207 House legislators was there for the debate and vote. The vote against the bill was surprisingly strong—128 to 87 (one representative abstained). Only 62 Republicans cast a yea, and just 5 of 40 Philadelphians did so. In an interview afterward Brumbaugh expressed keen disappointment in the bill's defeat. But he said,

> I am in this fight to the finish. . . . This campaign has only begun. Great reforms are not wrought in a day. It takes time and effort to secure results worthy of our Commonwealth. . . . The right will win.

Sometime later, he threatened to stump every district whose representative voted against local option. He never did, but he would be ready with another bill in 1917.

Years later, Bill Vare admitted in his autobiography that he, his brother, and their courtiers had made a big mistake in not letting the people decide on the sale of strong drink, as Brumbaugh and the temperance forces were demanding before World War I. It was a strategic political error, he wrote, because had the local optionists in Pennsylvania and other states carried the day, the United States would probably have been spared thirteen years of national prohibition. John Barleycorn, however, did not escape completely unscathed during Brumbaugh's first year in the governor's chair. That June, as commander-in-chief of the militia forces, he issued an executive order banning all intoxicants (including beer) from National Guard camps. It was the first time in Pennsylvania's history that a "white ribbon" directive to the military had emanated from Harrisburg.

Although humiliated by party regulars on local option, the governor got more cooperation from them in 1915 on other legislation he and the party had mutually called for in their separate platforms. Of all the acts passed during his administration, the one he took most pride in was the Child Labor Law, which he called his "crowning achievement." In 1915 Pennsylvania employed more children under sixteen than any other state in the Union—and twice the number of working juveniles in New York. Child labor was a social evil the governor had loudly deplored while superintendent of Philadelphia schools. It grieved him that each year he had to issue an average of twenty-five thousand work certificates. He told the *Outlook* magazine:

> That meant that the school days of all those children were over. The boy might go to a place and work a week, and then the employer, finding him useless, would dismiss him, and the boy would go out on the street. . . . We had licensed loafers learning crime.

The Progressive Era pronounced industrial child labor a national shame. In 1906 John Spargo wrote *The Bitter Cry of the Children*, filled with scandalous sociological findings on the abuses of child labor. The next year Senator Albert Beveridge of Indiana, progressivism's most eloquent voice in Congress, began the fight to ban products made by children from interstate commerce. In 1914 Representative A. Mitchell Palmer and Senator Robert L. Owen of Oklahoma cosponsored a federal child labor bill in Congress that incorporated this interdict. But the United States Supreme Court thwarted any federal legislation on the problem until the late years of the New Deal.

By 1915, however, thirty-three states, including Pennsylvania, required children to attend school to the age of sixteen, unless they were regularly employed and had obtained a work certificate. Only thirteen states prohibited boys and girls under sixteen from working over eight hours a day, or forty-eight a week. Pennsylvania was not among the thirteen, despite the perennial pressure for stricter laws by the state's Child Labor Association, established in 1904. This organization was a spawn of the National Child Labor Committee of the American Bar Association, founded the same year.

The Pennsylvania industries that employed most teenagers were coal mines, textile mills, and glass factories. Although glass factories posed severe health and safety hazards (extreme heat, dust-laden air, work-related tension, alternating night shifts), the worst horrors were experienced by breaker boys in anthracite regions. John Spargo's *Bitter Cry* graphically described their plight as they "crouched over chutes," sat "hour after hour," and picked "out the pieces of slate and other refuse from the coal as it rushe[d] to the washers." Their cramped positions disfigured them, he wrote, making them "bent-backed like old men." He told of "cut, broken, or crushed fingers," "clouds of dust" that caused "asthma and miners' consumption," of boys "mangled and torn in the machinery" or disappearing "in the chute to be picked out later smothered and dead."

Between 1904 and 1915 Pennsylvania progressives and the Child Labor Association confronted stiff opposition. Manufacturers argued that stricter laws would put them at a competitive disadvantage with less-restrictive states, and many parents insisted that the extra income was needed at home. Reformers had managed, however, to raise the minimum age for factory and mine workers to fourteen and lower the working hours of children to ten a day. Boys were limited to fifty-eight hours a week and girls to fifty-four.

As governor, Brumbaugh was determined to "blaze the way" in the reform of child labor. To the businessmen at the Reading Chamber of Commerce dinner mentioned earlier, he declared that if youngsters under sixteen must work, they should not have to put in more than forty-eight hours a week on the job. He said, "Get that straight; spell it out, f-o-r-t-y-e-i-g-h-t." So long as he had his way in Pennsylvania, he vowed to his audience, no child would be "sold cheap to any man, or to any industry, or to any interest, in this Commonwealth."

Child labor reform was a common plank in the platforms of all three major parties during Pennsylvania's 1914 election campaign. The Republicans boasted that the GOP had made an "earnest effort" in the legislative session of 1913 to enact a bill regulating the employment of minors under sixteen years old. It carried almost unanimously in both chambers but lost when the House nonconcurred on Senate amendments (70 to 66). This close vote encouraged Brumbaugh, upon taking office, to act promptly on a reform bill, which was drafted—like the one in the last session—in collaboration with the Pennsylvania Child Labor Association.

It ran into a noisy group of manufacturers—and some legislators—who decried the bill's unfairness. But it passed the General Assembly handily. The *North American* quoted Owen R. Lovejoy, general secretary of the National Child Labor Committee, as saying of it: "Pennsylvania [now] has one of the best child labor laws in the country and one which is winning the support of the manufacturers." The law provided for a fifty-one-hour work week and a work day of not more than nine hours for children under sixteen (not applicable on the farm or in the home).

These were longer hours than Brumbaugh had advocated, but the law contained other restrictions that were more satisfactory: prohibition of night work and the employment of a child under fourteen years old, regulation of street trades (e.g., newsboys and shoeblacks) and messenger service, and tougher controls over work certificates.

The innovative feature of the law—a Brumbaugh touch—required children to continue their education while working. This ameliorated a work week longer than the forty-eight hours the governor wanted because eight of those hours had to be spent in school—at the expense of the employer. In other words, Brumbaugh got what he had once envisioned for the city of Philadelphia when superintendent of schools there: continuation schools. Pennsylvania would start out appropriating a million dollars a year for these vocational schools. They would be staffed by teachers familiar with shop conditions in the workaday world, and thus able to adapt school work to practical educational needs. The overjoyed governor exclaimed to an *Outlook* interviewer:

> How I'd like to teach one of those classes! I think it is providential that a great industrial State like this has had a chance to blaze the way in this reform that will make good citizens out of these boys who have to go to work.

No other state had gone so far in combining work reform and schooling opportunities. Some seventy-five thousand working teenagers would be affected by this landmark legislation.

Coupled with this novel program for industrial education went provisions for strengthening the compulsory attendance law, so poorly enforced in some localities. Now an employer had to mail working papers back to school authorities upon dismissing a boy. This made it possible to keep better track of employed school dropouts and prevent them from playing perpetual hooky when let go from their jobs. The National Association of Manufacturers praised the compulsory attendance law and cited Pennsylvania for having "entered upon one of the greatest educational accomplishments of the generation."

These public-school advances necessitated the creation of a State Bureau of Vocational Education with two divisions: industrial and agricultural. Along with Wisconsin, Pennsylvania could now claim the front rank nationally in preparing the young for the trades and the farm. In 1917 when the Smith-Hughes Act established a Federal Board for Vocational Education and first provided grants-in-aid to individual states, Pennsylvania qualified for the second highest subsidy.

Other education bills—more than forty—amended and strengthened the School Code of 1911, as might have been expected during an administration headed by one of its principal authors. Most of them modified the classification and organization of school districts. Teacher preparation, a lifetime's passion of the governor, also got a boost. The Code of 1911 had given authority to the state board of education (of which Brumbaugh had been a member until becoming governor) and the legislature to purchase the thirteen privately owned state normal schools (all-black Cheyney was not then included). Four hundred thousand dollars had been allocated for this purpose, but expenditure cuts by Governor John Tener delayed the work. By 1914 only four of them had been taken over. During Brumbaugh's term seven more would be acquired—three of them in 1915.

There was not only legislative momentum carried over from 1913 for child-labor and continuing public-school reform, but also for a workman's compensation law. But the governor decided not to take any chances, seeing the roadblock local option had run into at the capital. He would lay the whole matter before the people before lawmakers could undercut it. On Saturday, 27 February, every newspaper in the state published the text of a Brumbaugh-seconded workman's compensation act. The press release also included arguments both for and against the law, in simple, nontechnical language. The governor told diners at the Reading Chamber of Commerce meeting on the 26th:

> This is probably new in legislation. They said to me when I first proposed it, "If you do that, you will get a lot of criticism; people will object to it." Well, hang it, that's what it is for. The sooner you get a chance to kick, the better for you, and I know it is better for us who have to sign the act . . . if we know before the beginning of the process of lawmaking what the will of the people is.

"It is just a schoolmaster's notion," he added self-deprecatingly. But he said he believed in taking the people "honestly and completely" into his confidence and "tell the truth." "I don't care a hang who likes it."

Maryland had been in 1902 the first state to come to the rescue of injured workers. By 1915 twenty-three states had fallen in line. Pennsylvania was not one of them. A bill by the 1913 legislature failed when the two chambers could not concur, a defeat, labor unions wailed, perpetrated by Penrose lackeys. In the 1914 campaign all party platforms declared for employer liability and workman's compensation. So Brumbaugh did get his law, but it still took some battling. Eight other states and the territory of Alaska passed similar legislation in 1915. In Pennsylvania minors were included under provisions for compensation. To head the newly created Workman's Compensation Bureau, the governor appointed Harry Mackey, the Brumbaugh-booster and Vare deputy from Philadelphia.

Other legislation gave greater protection to the distaff side of the labor force by limiting the hours of employment for women.

Pennsylvania's great workforce of farmers also benefited from promised legislation. Among other things, a State Commission of Agriculture was established, of which five of the seven members had to be men of the soil. Another law created a Bureau of Markets. The legislature also took advantage of the Smith-Lever Act, passed by Congress in 1914, which provided county-agent extension work through land-grant colleges.

Nor did the Brumbaugh administration disappoint farmers and Grangers in their cry for good roads, although the 1917 legislature would be more productive. The office of state highway commissioner had been created in 1903. The commissioner divided annual appropriations among the several counties in proportion to their road mileage. Two years later the Automobile Act required a license fee to operate a motor-propelled vehicle; the revenue was to be used for road improvements. But this never happened; the receipt from fees always got shunted into the general treasury. Then in 1911 Pennsylvania began taking over county roads as state highways. By 1915 this added up to over ten thousand miles. Only New York had more mileage of good roads. Supervision of roads, at all bureaucratic levels, had by then developed into a rich political plum under the patronage system.

During the gubernatorial campaign, Brumbaugh had been privately critical of highway officialdom; he accused it of nepotism, waste, and incompetence. It was a foregone conclusion, therefore, that the incumbent highway commissioner would be one of the first non-Brumbaugh bureaucrats to go. Once the new governor had his own man, he liked to go around declaring, "I will make good roads with my Dutch fist, my highway commissioner, Mr. [Robert J.] Cunningham, will make good roads with his Irish fist—and we will have good roads!"

Once in office, Brumbaugh set about taking the Highway Department out of politics and putting it into the hands of expert road engineers. And though a fiscal conservative, he badgered lawmakers to double the annual three million-dollar appropriation for highways. He demanded that, as the law provided, license fees go exclusively for road maintenance.

For the first time in the state's history, the 1915 legislature put before the people a constitutional amendment authorizing a fifty-million-dollar bond issue for highway construction. The Pennsylvania Motor Federation (PMF) pushed hard for its adoption. Its literature indicated that Pennsylvania had eighty thousand automobiles on the highways, or one automobile to every twenty families in the state. Good roads, the PMF proclaimed, would keep young people on the farm, lower the cost of hauling farm products to market, ensure better attendance at rural schools and churches, and increase land values.

Meanwhile, the governor, a pitchman par excellence, proclaimed Wednesday, 26 May, "Good Roads Day in Pennsylvania." Counties, townships, and automobile clubs were urged to get out and repair local roads. More than eight thousand volunteers, the governor among them, turned out with picks and shovels and some eleven thousand teams of horses. Then in late July he announced plans to make a personal inspection of state highways in the fall.

The General Assembly also stood with the governor on another issue of growing current interest everywhere: woman suffrage. By 1915 a dozen states had granted women the right to vote. But the suffragettes' biggest adversaries came from the liquor interests, which feared that giving them the vote would hasten prohibition. This slowed to a near halt the state-by-state pace of extending suffrage. Nevertheless, by a legislative resolution Pennsylvania's men were given leave to render their verdict on enfranchising women in November. They said no, by a margin of 55,000 votes out of 800,000 cast.

The 1915 legislative session officially ended with a quaint century-old ceremony; it took place in the rotunda of the capitol on Monday, 20 June. According to the state constitution, the title of every bill approved by the governor was to be read to the citizenry within the thirty days allotted for action after the legislature adjourned. So James C. Deininger, executive clerk to the governor, followed the custom and read from a sheaf of papers two feet thick. The "citizens" making up the rotunda audience consisted, at one time or another, of several guards and a couple of sightseers. It took more than an hour to get through the whole list. Deininger sighed at the end and said, "Thank Heaven, that is over for another two years."

But late that night, in the corridor outside the governor's office on the second floor of the capitol's south wing, he went through the ritual once more for all the vetoed bills. At that hour he had only one auditor: another executive-department subaltern.

A 22 June editorial in the *Beaver Valley News* gave a grand doff of the hat to Brumbaugh as a first-year governor. The New Brighton daily called him a "fair minded man, a noble leader, and a statesman of the kind that makes for good." It took great delight that he kept his word not to be "a tool of the machine." The ex-schoolman, asserted the paper,

> has met the hopes of the best citizenship of the State for good work, and stands today as the most independent executive, and the best representative of the people of the State, that has occupied the Governor's chair in the last half century.

Other newspapers also hailed what the *Harrisburg Star-Independent* called his "defiance" of gangland special interests. Its own editorial on 22 June declared that the governor had boldly "thrown down the gauntlet to a very considerable portion of the old-line Republican leaders" in Pennsylvania. Many Bull Moosers, Progressives, and other dependents had become admirers of his, said the article. The *Philadelphia Evening Ledger's* assessment of the chief executive's 1915 performance matched the eulogistic prose of any newspaper:

> Doctor Brumbaugh may make mistakes—he has made some—but the great, big, salient fact that stands out is that at last we have a Governor who is a man, fallible, but courageous, honest and independent, who does what he thinks he ought to do and does not care two fiddlesticks whether the leaders or other people like it or not.

He "really believes in democratic government and is not a hypocrite," stated the paper.

The most obvious evidence of his independent attitude, in the eyes of the press, was the liberal way he "meat axed" bills, in the parlance of Capitol Hill: 211

of them during the legislative session of 1915. (But he also signed 792 bills.) The *Philadelphia North American,* on 23 June, ran a pro-Brumbaugh article that said his veto record "not only set a new high-water mark for achievements of this kind, but, taken in its entirety, forms a remarkable human document." (The previous record-holder was Brumbaugh's predecessor, John Tener—with 171 vetoes, in 1913.) The *North American* article went on:

> Dealing with a legislature as abjectly subservient to machine and corporation dictation as any that ever sat in Pennsylvania's legislative halls, Governor Brumbaugh not only succeeded in forcing through his program of social legislation, but by the determined exercise of his veto power struck down a veritable mass of vicious legislation, all of it inspired by special interests of one kind or another and all aimed at an invasion of the rights of the people.

It pointed out that such terms as "preservation of popular rule," "social justice," "protection of the health and safety of the people," and "fair play" punctuated the rationale of his vetoes. On the 25th the *North American* editorialized, under the caption "THE MAN WITH THE AX":

> If Governor Brumbaugh's term were to end now, after a duration of less than six months, his veto record alone would insure for him public approval and for his administration lasting distinction in the records of the state government.
>
> This judgment, we believe, will be generally indorsed. But only those who understand the vicious nature of many of the bills which poured in upon him can appreciate fully the sound, patriotic and consistent course he pursued.

Republican-machine spoilsmongers entered the 1915 session with two objects in mind, apparently thinking they could outwit a political naïf in the governor's office. One was to tighten up election laws to minimize popular revolt against machine outrages. The other part of their program was to create as many additional jobs as possible in the state bureaucracy, various counties, and particularly the native city of Penrose and the Vares: Philadelphia.

To accomplish the first objective, a series of a dozen or so election bills, known as the "McNichol flock," was rammed through the legislature with the help of Vare lawmakers. One of them, for example, restored Boies Penrose to the State Republican Committee. He would have replaced Henry G. Wasson, a Flinnite, on the Republican National Committee, from which he had been booted in 1912. Another one, the "anti-fusion" scheme, would have prevented party mergers after the primaries. The Penrose-McNichol-Vare axis had counted on Brumbaugh's compliance in this ploy because as a campaigner he had been himself handicapped by the Lewis-McCormick deal. But the governor, who had never apologized for his position as a party man, argued in his veto that the GOP was historically too principled to take advantage of its dominance in the legislature over any independent party.

On similar principles, he killed a bill—calling it a "ripper" measure—that displaced the Democratic Party of first place on the presidential ballot, won as a result the election of 1912.

Another batch of laws felled by the ax-wielding governor had provided for the multiplication of jobs and what he deemed reckless salary raises. A number of pork-barrel laws directly affected Philadelphia and many of its municipal employees. But as the budget-heedful chief executive told the *Outlook's* journalist,

> I had to hold a tight hand on the purse strings. . . . I sent for the leaders [in the legislature] one day and told them that we were planning to spend more money than we would have. My hint was not taken . . . and I had to veto bills carrying appropriations of $7,000,000.

To the people, he said he deeply regretted the necessity "to reduce the Commonwealth's bounty to many deserving" charities and institutions—especially higher education, "to which [he] gave so much of [his] life." The slashes resulted in a final budget figure of close to $65,500,000 for the next two years. This was around $750,000 less than the appropriations of the 1913 session, a reduction, said Brumbaugh, appropriate at a time of a national recession.

The Brumbaugh vetoes generally won him editorial back-pats from the state press. But sometimes not, like his "no" vote on the Full-Crew Repealer Law. This not only sparked journalistic criticism but brought down upon him the wrath of railroad companies and lobbyists. Even the *New York Sun* ran a blistering editorial headed "Governor Brumbaugh's Serious Miscalculation." The Tener administration had passed a law in 1911 requiring railroads to employ on all trains an adequate number of crewmen. The 1915 "full-crew repealer," as it was called, would, however, effectively eliminate one man on passenger and freight trains. Some newspapers accused the vetoing governor of playing "demagogic" politics at a cost of a million and a half dollars annually to the railroads. But he argued that the "extra man" on a train "may save life or property or both."

For this stand the *Trades Union News* of Philadelphia hailed him as "the greatest champion of labor among all *public officials of the country.*" Richard V. Farley, a labor-union member and the only Quaker City senator to vote against the "repealer," said of the veto: "The Governor has proved that the pen of an honest executive is superior to the sword of a hired lobbyist." In doing so, he "has gained the respect of union labor in this State and every other State," added the senator.

When the lengthy list of vetoed bills became known, surprised Republican bosses avoided public comment upon the governor's actions. Penrose had just returned to Philadelphia from Atlantic City, where he had spent the last ten days under the weather. No boss, or underling, dared criticize the governor openly, but newspapers reported grumbled epithets of "traitor" and "perfidy" among the inner circles of the machine.

"Nothing like it has even been known in all the history of action on legislation," commented a *Harrisburg Telegraph* editorial, referring to the way Brumbaugh had kept everybody guessing on what he intended to do with many of the important bills. Not until Saturday evening, 19 June, did the list of his vetoes and approvals get in the hands of newspapermen, who were pledged to secrecy not to release them until the next day, after the rotunda ritual. But by that time he had already slipped out of the capital for Philadelphia undetected, his whereabouts to be kept out of the papers. He would not return to Harrisburg until 1 July, the public was told.

Out in the prairie-land West, the Brumbaugh record earned a July editorial in the *Nebraska State Journal*. The piece observed that Penrose and his ilk were just as "grieved," if not more so, than New Jersey bosses had been "over their college president governor" (Wilson) several years before. The writer said he did not know much about this "schoolmaster" turned politician. But one thing he knew for sure: "Life ever since has been a succession of sadnesses for Penrose and his subjects."

The governor, he went on, had "proved himself an ingrate not to be trusted by any political machine." The editorial advised: "The country would do well to get better acquainted with Prof. Brumbaugh" because "His friends have begun reading the stars and saying presidential prayers in his name." Summing up the Pennsylvanian's political prospects with a chicken-coop analogy, the *State Journal* said:

> To judge from his acts as governor he was hatched in the same incubator with Woodrow Wilson, though one by a Plymouth Rock democrat and the other a Leghorn republican.

Back East that July, Pennsylvanians were called upon to lay aside their Laodicean patriotism. For the first time in the state's history, the legislature, with Brumbaugh's blessing, had decreed it the annual duty of the people to "observe the anniversary of our national life," the celebration's venue to be Philadelphia. Speaking at a banquet at the city's Bellevue-Stratford Hotel on the evening of 3 July, the governor declaimed on a familiar theme of his: "We need a newer baptism into the faith of our fathers." But he gave more time to Valley Forge, whose "lessons" we must never forget, than to Independence Hall. That lesson—"heroic sacrifice"—must ever be taught in the home, the schools, and the churches, he urged. Then on Sunday afternoon of the 4th he led religious services at Valley Forge, near the Washington Memorial Monument.

Later in the month, he spent a week at Mount Gretna, where the Pennsylvania National Guard was encamped. The 1915 legislature had enacted the reorganization of the state militia. And now, since the sinking of the Lusitania in May with the loss of 128 American lives, there had been a revulsion of public opinion against Germany. Brumbaugh himself publicly espoused neutrality for the United States, which, of course, sounded orthodox enough for the peace-loving Brethren. He had preached at the denomination's Annual Conference at Hershey in June, fascinating Dunker boys as he arrived in a big black car with license tag number "1."

The governor's use of tobacco and newspaper pictures of him, on horseback, reviewing troops at Mount Gretna displeased a lot of Brethren, but the delegates at Hershey voted a resolution commending him "for the high ground he has taken upon all moral issues." It went on to laud him in his fight for local option as a "stepping stone" to national prohibition. The resolution concluded:

> We pray that God may guide him in his responsible office to the end that he may be an instrument in the hands of the Master in giving to the people of this great state a clean, capable, and righteous administration of its public affairs.

The governor's biggest ceremonial appearance that summer took place in San Francisco at the Panama-Pacific Exposition. He sped through Huntingdon on the train, late afternoon, 24 August, with a wave of his hand from the rear platform of the observation car. A small crowd, informed of his schedule, had gathered at the station in the hope of getting a look at him. On the way, he and the Pennsylvania contingent stopped off in Chicago and Salt Lake City, where he was the guest of United States Senator Reed O. Smoot.

Smoot, the same age as Brumbaugh, was a leader in the Mormon Church. History has branded him a notorious advocate of tariff protection. (In 1930 he would coauthor the Hawley-Smoot Tariff, the highest in the country's peacetime history; it was blamed for drying up international trade and hastening the Great Depression.) At parting, the senator gave the governor a hide rug made from a Utah lynx he had shot. A favorite story of Brumbaugh's about the rug had to do with his pet dog, Fritz, a ruby-eyed Tibetan spaniel. The pelt floor covering—with the wildcat's glaring eyes wide open—was placed in the living room in the Germantown home. But Fritz, who hated the smell of cats, refused to come near it despite its very inviting location in front of the fireplace. Just walking through the room he gave it the widest berth possible.

At the Exposition, "Pennsylvania Day" was Saturday, 4 September. The spirit of '76 reigned in commemoration of the 140th anniversary of the first meeting of the historic Continental Congress in Carpenters' Hall, Philadelphia. The Liberty Bell was there, shipped from its cross-country home. More than five thousand spectators gathered in front of the Pennsylvania pavilion for a program of speech-making, music, and tree-planting. There was also a military parade, which included the second battalion of the Pennsylvania National Guard. Over one hundred prominent men comprised the state's delegation.

Brumbaugh, of course, delivered the main address, in which, as no surprise, he gave due honor to the "great State of Pennsylvania in whose first city this Nation was born." He said the country's cherished ideals of federal union and liberty formulated in Philadelphia have found emblematic expression in a now "silent but eloquent" icon: the Liberty Bell. "We of Pennsylvania guard it for the Nation."

Every visitor that day had been given a souvenir badge from which hung a miniature Liberty Bell. Then the governor, plying a silver spade, planted an oak tree
brought from Valley Forge.

In the twenty-one-day continental crossing to California and back, Brumbaugh
gave twenty-five speeches. No two were alike and all were given extemporane-
ously. Their theme: Pennsylvania—its history, its scenery, its rich cultural birthright.

In early October Brumbaugh, probably with much horn-honking, set off on
his publicized road-inspection motorcade across the state. The governor of no other
state had attempted such an excursion. Brumbaugh had dubbed it the "Seeing Pennsylvania First Tour." Flora rode along with him in the back seat of an open touring
car, the second in line behind the lead car occupied by Highway Commissioner
Cunningham and his wife. "Automobilists" had been invited to join in the six-day
circuit, planned to cover nearly a thousand miles. The itinerary mostly followed
stretches of what became Routes 11, 15, 22, 30, and 220, traveling an elongated
east-west loop through the states' midland. In all, about one hundred auto enthusiasts participated in various legs of the drive. (The good-roads promotional activity
by the governor and the Pennsylvania Motor Federation, however, did not convince enough voters, who rejected a constitutional amendment for a highway loan
on the November ballot.)

On 19 October, Lafayette College conferred on the governor his fourth honorary degree (Litt.D.) at the installation of his friend Dr. John H. McCracken as
president. Francis Shunk Brown received a Doctor of Laws the same day.

The rest of Brumbaugh's first legislative term passed without further major
personal or political event.

The year 1916 would be an off-year for the General Assembly, but for the
chief executive it turned out to be anything but a quiescent, do-nothing twelve
months. For one thing, he remarried, making him the only Pennsylvania governor
to wed while in office. Since Anna's death, gossip had him first romantically linked
to a teacher at the Girls' Normal School in Philadelphia and then to Elizabeth
Kolb, the twenty-year-old daughter of a very close wealthy Philadelphia friend and
member of his staff, the bakery baron Louis J. Kolb. Elizabeth had been seen with
him a few times in public, once at a major-league baseball game.

The Kolbs had accompanied him—on President Wilson's yacht, *The May-
flower*—in mid-March to Newport News, Virginia. There Elizabeth christened *The
Pennsylvania*, then the mightiest battleship in the world, when it was launched. At
that time the governor called her "the sweetest girl in Pennsylvania." Rumors that
the governor was preparing a nest for a bride took off when he arranged to have the
Executive Mansion renovated and refurbished.

But newspapers never matched him with Flora Belle Parks. Maybe this was
because they were relatives, or because there was a Pygmalion aspect to their social stations. Flora had no college degree, although she did take some courses at

Drexel Institute between 1906 and 1909 in American and English literature, poetry, rhetoric, composition, and general history. Everybody, then, seemed to have been caught by surprise when they married on Friday, 29 January. Newspaper headlines sensationalized the fact that the newlyweds were fifth cousins and Flora the governor's ward.

Brumbaugh had always protected the privacy of his home life, and so he planned a secret wedding. He put his private secretary, William H. Ball, in charge of all preparations for the ceremony and honeymoon. No inkling of the matrimonial union became public until the governor appeared in person at Philadelphia's City Hall to obtain the marriage license.

The nuptials took place at the Germantown Church of the Brethren, near his home, not at the Dauphin Street church where he attended. A "regiment of newspaper reporters" descended upon the little stone meetinghouse, said the *Inquirer*, "augmented by a battery of photographers, including two or three 'movie men.'" Fully two hundred spectators had gathered by the time the governor's limousine arrived a couple of minutes before four o'clock.

Secretary Ball tried to shield the governor and his intended from the photographers. As a result, the best shot of the couple caught them crossing the threshold as they entered the church. But it really was not very good. To quote LeRoy Greene, historian of the governor's mansion: "They looked like fleeting ghosts in the newspaper pictures."

The ceremony, which was officiated by the pastors of the two Philadelphia Brethren congregations, took just four minutes. The groom, writes Greene, said he wanted "to get it over with as quickly as possible." There was no best man or bridesmaid, and no ring, in keeping with the Dunker custom. The interior of the church was decorated with palms and pines and white lilies. There were forty guests present, including Mabel, Edwin and his wife, and brother Frank's family. After the ceremony and the traditional nuptial kiss, Mabel stepped forward and bussed her new stepmother several times.

The *Inquirer* described the bride as "tall, rather stout and dark, with an exceedingly pleasant face." The paper quoted the governor as having frequently said of her, "She is a woman of great common sense." According to the *Juniata Echo*, the new Mrs. Brumbaugh was "a woman of quiet tastes and gentle disposition," with a "large circle of friends." The new husband was fifty-seven years old, his wife forty-four. After the wedding, the governor and his wife left for an extended honeymoon at Pinehurst, North Carolina, then a winter resort. On the way they made a stopover in Washington, D.C., at the New Willard Hotel.

At Pinehurst the honeymooners deepened their friendship with the legendary Annie Oakley.* After her sensational career with Buffalo Bill's "Wild West Show," Annie and her husband, Frank Butler, had come to Pinehurst in late 1915. They

---

*Frank and Annie had been invited to their wedding, but it is not known when the Butlers and Brumbaughs first met.

joined the staff of the Carolina Hotel there, and every winter Annie gave exhibitions and shooting lessons and Frank took charge of the skeet range. Of Quaker background, "Little Sure Shot," a nickname bestowed upon the Ohio-born markswoman by "Sitting Bull," gained a Brumbaugh stepfather at age eight. She grew up in a community where Dunkers were among her friends and neighbors.

Annie was two years older than the Pennsylvania governor, and the two distant relatives took to calling each other "cousin" during their Pinehurst friendship. After watching a shooting exhibition by Annie, her honeymooning "cousin" offered to make her a "police captain." Both the governor and Flora would become members of her Pinehurst Gun Club, and she would visit them in Philadelphia in subsequent years. Flora became a good shot, and after only one year under Annie's tutelage she won a fourteen-carat Winchester rifle pin.

Annie had a fondness for dogs, like the governor and his wife. Her setter, Dave, became part of her act. He would perch on a high stool and calmly allow his mistress to shoot apples from his head. Annie liked to think her Dave and Fritz Brumbaugh enjoyed a long-distance palsy-walsy relationship. She and Flora exchanged pictures of their pampered canines, and Annie, in her letters to Flora, sometimes added the postscript: "Love from Dave to Fritz." It was the maternal talk of two childless women.

In March the University of Pittsburgh conferred on the governor, at its Charter Day exercises on the 20th, his fifth honorary degree—that of a doctor of laws. Also honored with a degree was John A. Brashear, the far-famed astronomer and precision lens maker from Pittsburgh, a member of the board of trustees, and popularly known as "first citizen of Pennsylvania."

By that springtime, Brumbaugh had pretty much made up his mind to test just how sturdy he was as possible presidential timber. The Republican Party in 1916 was about to engage in its first favorite-son campaign in twenty-eight years. The last time this happened was in 1888, when the man of that hour, James G. Blaine, took himself out of the race. A free-for-all immediately developed.

The same situation presented itself again in 1916; there appeared to be no figure of presidential size ready and willing to be the man of *this* hour. But in Pennsylvania it had long been bruited that Brumbaugh might make an effort to win a majority of the state's delegation to the national GOP convention in behalf of his own candidacy. The big question was: What would Penrose do to head off such a move? He had given no sign, except to say it was not likely that the presidential candidate would come from Pennsylvania.

Brumbaugh had visions of emerging as the leader of a harmony ticket at the preferential primaries on 16 May. But he did not make public his candidacy until 12 March. This came in response to a letter from Henry G. Wasson, a Republican National Party committeeman from Pennsylvania and ex-Bull Mooser. Wasson had told the governor that he alone could unite Progressives and the Old Guard. The *New York Times* and Philadelphia newspapers rightly predicted an "extremely bitter contest." The press saw his candidacy as a bid to final combat over the leadership of the state GOP between the Penrose and anti-Penrose factions.

The senator meanwhile had been sounding out sentiment among Republicans throughout the state. He was reported as confident that he had a majority of county bigwigs on his side in the event of a factional fight with the governor. In March, newspapers said Penrose planned to support a movement to send the Pennsylvania delegation to the Chicago convention in June uninstructed. Also, it was reported, the senator was ready to "unloose a thunderbolt" against the governor and the Vares before many days elapsed. He remained in seclusion in his office in the Commercial Trust Building in Philadelphia, available only to his staff.

The Penrose thunderbolt struck in the form of political blackmail and with the connivance of the Oliver brothers. Brumbaugh learned of the conspiracy through a member of his cabinet, John S. Rilling, a Democrat from Erie. Senator George Oliver had phoned Rilling one day in mid-March, suggesting he come to Washington on "a matter of importance." Suspecting trouble, the former chairman of the State Democratic Committee (he had also helped draft the School Code of 1911) reported this at once to Brumbaugh, who told him to make the trip.

Rilling returned to Harrisburg on 16 March with the following story. He had met with Oliver behind a locked door in the Senate office building. Thus closeted, he was shown a photocopy of a check for one thousand dollars the senator's brother, David, had sent Brumbaugh the previous autumn, during the gubernatorial campaign. Also exhibited were facsimiles of Brumbaugh's endorsing signature on the back of the check, along with a letter and a follow-up telegram of thanks from him for the financial gift. Senator Oliver claimed that the money was a campaign contribution, which the candidate had pocketed and failed to report in his expense account filed in November. He intimated that unless the governor withdrew from the presidential race, the whole thing would be given publicity.

Brumbaugh was stunned by the perfidy of the Oliver brothers. As recently as January 20 he had written a thank-you note to George Oliver for a favorable editorial in the *Pittsburgh Gazette Times*, owned by the senator, on the Brumbaugh administration "after one year." And January the year before, the governor had offered to make octogenarian David Oliver, whom he called "one of my dearest friends," a colonel and member of his staff. But the old gentleman, pleased at the proffered honor, demurred, citing the "pains and penalties" of age.

Brumbaugh had indeed deposited the thousand dollars in his private checking account. But he did that on the basis of a handwritten covering letter Oliver had sent with his donation. It read:

Dr Brumbaugh
My Dear Sir —
personal
I send you the enclosed as a ^ contribution towards your personal campaign expenses (which must be heavy) and with it my very best wishes for your success.

You are carrying yourself *first-rate*: Keep it up on your present lines, avoid en-
tanglements without giving cause for offense, and you will "get there" without fail.

Yours sincerely,
s/ David B. Oliver

Exactly how he meant the money to be used in a "personal" way is ambiguous. But
on New Year's Day 1916, Brumbaugh and Oliver talked about the matter in
Harrisburg's Commonwealth Hotel after a state board of education meeting. According to the governor, at the time of their chat Oliver said he wanted the gift to be
"a personal and not a political one." He was thankful that his name as a donor had
not been made public—because as a school-board member in Pittsburgh, he did
not want "in any way to be known as having a part in politics." Whatever he had in
mind, he had not concerned himself about the absence of his name from the list of
contributors at the time Brumbaugh's election funds were published several months
before.

Obviously, David Oliver had had a change of heart toward the man whose
gubernatorial candidacy he once said "meets with the enthusiastic approval of all
our people." Several letters of his to the governor in early 1915 clearly indicate
why he changed his colors. He had wanted Brumbaugh to reappoint Robert McAfee,
a former officer of the Oliver family industry, as secretary of the commonwealth.
When his—and George's—wish went ignored, he wrote of being "disappointed,"
even "humiliated," as a result of the fledgling chief executive's disregard of their
friendship.

There was a further passage of emissaries between Washington and Harrisburg after Rilling's initial visit to Senator Oliver's office in March of 1916. It was
finally agreed that some prominent businessman and good Republican—someone
who had kept out of the past factional fights—should prepare a special letter to the
governor. This letter should urge him to withdraw from the presidential race in the
interest of "harmony and prosperity." Alba B. Johnson, president of the Baldwin
Locomotive works in Philadelphia, agreed to write the letter, which was not to be
made public until the governor answered it. Both of them would then be released
to newspapers at the same time. Johnson's statement was a masterpiece of diplomacy; ironically, Brumbaugh helped compose it. But at the same time it made
clear that the business leaders of Pennsylvania wanted two things: the country's
return to Republican rule and the end of factional fighting within the party.

But the Oliver-Penrose cabal overplayed its hand: it pushed too hard and talked
too much to the newspapers. Stories of the Oliver check had circulated among
Pennsylvania's newsmen for weeks, and the *Public Ledger* had even got hold of
the photographic facsimiles of the check. The scheme soon backfired. The very
day the two letters were to be simultaneously made public, as the plan called for,
newspapers began to predict Brumbaugh's withdrawal. The *New York Times*, in a 6
April article, reported that this was a fact "practically conceded tonight" at Harris-

burg. Other papers hinted darkly at a "club" over his head, the nature of which was not mentioned.

The governor's aides, angered that he could not now save face, urged him not to withdraw. They said it was too late—he was already "disgraced" by innuendoes of tricky dealings. Meanwhile, Alba Johnson had given out a copy of his letter to the governor for release by the press. Three weeks had passed since Senator Oliver first talked to John Rilling.

The vehemence of his advisors apparently put new fight into the governor. On Thursday, the day of the *Times* piece, he retired to his study in the Executive Mansion and put his half-finished letter to Johnson aside. Without consulting any of his key aides, he then prepared a statement exposing the whole Oliver affair and announcing he would remain a presidential candidate. This anticipatory move on his part, he hoped, would blunt the thunderbolt his foes threatened to strike at him.

The governor admitted getting a check from David Oliver but said he and his campaign staff had been of the opinion that it was a "personal gift" for private use. A letter accompanying the check and telling him to use the money as he saw fit was lost, the governor claimed. (Perhaps the letter *was* lost at the time, but it can be examined today among the Brumbaugh papers.) And the only man who could find it—James Hiatt, his private secretary and ex-campaign chairman—had recently died.* According to the statement, Hiatt had been the first one to point out to him that the check was not a campaign contribution. The governor, stressing that he was for Republican harmony, charged that his enemies were out to discredit him and prevent him from healing the breach in the party.

Brumbaugh spoke of looking up to David Oliver as "a father and wrote him as I'd write my father." He said he "still loved" the Pittsburgh resident "and cannot bring myself to think of him in any way other than as a gentleman of the highest character."

Unfortunately, the Brumbaugh-Oliver scandal inevitably raised questions about the governor's own high character, even in heretofore friendly newspapers. Up in Clearfield, for example, the *Raftsman Journal* carried an editorial that began: "Pennsylvania has been shaken to its centre by recent political revelations coming out of Harrisburg . . . [that have] humiliated and confused [the governor's] admirers and followers." Like the *Raftsman*, big-city dailies also wondered whether the governor had been guilty of dishonesty—or of indiscretion. Declared an editorial in the *Pittsburgh Sun*: "Let us get to the bottom of this rottenness so that the people may know . . . what sort of a man is our chief executive, and if his conduct merits it, the legislature should impeach him."

For the press, the "missing link" to show who was telling the truth was the Oliver letter. But neither its sender nor its receiver seemed inclined to go public

---

*On 17 January 1916 Brumbaugh hired William H. Ball, chief of Philadelphia's Bureau of City Property, to replace the dying Hiatt. The two men became like brothers, and Ball's admiration for the governor bordered on veneration.

with it. The *Sun* for that reason did not let David Oliver off the hook. It blasted him for "not doing his duty" by coming forward with *his* copy of the letter. Why, the editorial asked, did the Oliver brothers keep quiet for months about the check until the governor "disobeyed the mandates of the senator"?

All this while, there circulated talk of other checks said to have gone into a slush fund for Brumbaugh while a candidate for governor. Reports given out by Penrose henchmen allegedly identified thirty contributions from seven different individuals and totaling around fifteen thousand dollars. Senator Oliver, responding to the new accusations, said he had "no personal knowledge" of other illegal checks. But Penrose people promised that "they will be made public in due time." The governor kept his silence about these latest allegations. Up to this point, Boies Penrose had been an amused spectator, untouched and politically benefited by the scandal. People were pointing the finger of scorn at a reform governor, not at someone of the Old Guard or at the "Big Boss" himself.

At this juncture in the lost-check flap, the governor had to deal with a labor strike in the Oliver brothers' home city. In April, Pittsburgh-area steelworkers joined Westinghouse strikers, demanding pay boosts and an eight-hour day. On 2 May a riot occurred at the United States Steel plant at Braddock. The sheriff, fearing loss of life and property, appealed to the governor. On Saturday evening, the 6th, the governor released a statement on the tense situation, sent units of the National Guard to the Three Rivers industrial city, and went there himself for a personal inspection of conditions.

His press release had a Lyndon Baines Johnson ring, emphasizing "Let us reason together." A hero to labor unions, he made clear that the state had "no favorites." The National Guard, he said, would not be used for police duty but police forces must not be abused. He insisted that both sides must observe the law and resort to mediation, "the first legal step in a peaceful adjustment." Fortunately, no general strike materialized and there was no bloodshed or serious acts of disorder. And steelworkers did end up with better hourly rates.

On 9 May the Penrose faction made good its promise to adduce additional slush-fund evidence against the governor. Isadore Stern, a state representative from Philadelphia, accused Brumbaugh of failing to report a five thousand-dollar campaign contribution from Louis Kolb, now an honorary cabinet member. Stern, a candidate for reelection, pledged that if he won again he would be the Penrose-McNichol floor leader in the House at Harrisburg. He urged the governor to call a special session of the legislature and vindicate himself. Otherwise, he threatened, the Penrose-McNichol wing of the GOP would seek to impeach him in the 1917 session of the General Assembly. Brumbaugh denounced the latest charge as an out-and-out lie (which it was) and "unworthy of attention."

Meanwhile, the beleaguered governor had quietly written a placatory, undated letter to David Oliver. He wrote:

> If I have misconceived your purpose, or if I have misinterpreted your motive, it was done in a wrong impression I had of your professed friendship for me and interest in my future as a professional leader of men to better political, moral, and social questions.

Enclosed with the letter was a check for a thousand dollars, with interest.

This is where the political feud stood at the time of the preferential vote for president in Pennsylvania on 16 May. Brumbaugh's was the only name on the GOP ballot, and he received 233,095 votes. (Woodrow Wilson won on the Democratic ballot, with 142,202 votes.) He was also elected a delegate-at-large to the national convention. The governor had hoped the voters would send delegates pledged to him, the popular choice of the party in the state. But Penrose came out the victor; a majority of the seventy-six delegates were committed to him. This practically guaranteed that he would replace Henry Wasson as a member of the Republican National Committee and elevate him once again to the titular leadership of the Republican Party in the Keystone State.

Nevertheless, Martin Brumbaugh, backed by Congressman Bill Vare, was prepared to wage a vigorous fight for the chairmanship of the Keystone delegation at Chicago. He had, however, renounced his own candidacy for president in favor of Teddy Roosevelt. So, although he would allow himself to be nominated, he did not go to the Windy City really as a native-son candidate. In the battle for delegates, the former Bull Moose splinter group had thrown its support to the governor.

The Republican convention opened the first week of June in the Chicago Coliseum. Brumbaugh's name was put in nomination on 9 June by Deputy Attorney General Emerson Collins of Williamsport. When the roll call got to Pennsylvania on the first ballot, Boies Penrose stood up and requested a poll of its delegates. He, John Wanamaker, and thirty-four others voted for Pennsylvanian and ex-secretary of state Philander C. Knox. Brumbaugh tallied twenty-nine votes. When the roll call of states ended, Supreme Court Justice Charles E. Hughes, former governor of New York, came in with a big lead, but he did not receive a majority of the ballots cast.

When this was announced, wild and prolonged cheering broke out. Amidst this deafening din, Martin Brumbaugh jumped up on his chair, reported the *New York Times*, "and a silence fell over the big hall." He said, in a raised voice:

> I wish to thank my friends for casting their votes for me, but I withdraw my name from the contest. I want to say that if our platform is so fair, why not nominate a candidate to fit it? Why not nominate a man who is loved at home and revered abroad? Why not nominate Theodore Roosevelt?

This little speech set off a short but loud demonstration for the colonel.

Hughes failed to win a majority again on the second ballot, although he made a big gain. Senator Penrose, the *New York Times* reported, "continued in the great waiting act [of seeing] which way the cat would jump." He cast the thirty-six votes he controlled for Knox on both ballots. Finally, Hughes came in a winner on the third go-around. This time the Penrose delegation had voted for the triumphant nominee. Not since 1888 had the Republican convention taken more than one ballot to choose its banner-bearer.

Three weeks later, the Pennsylvania GOP feuding factions and the Bull Moosers got together in Philadelphia in what was essentially a harmony conference. They endorsed the Republican national, state, and legislative tickets and the platform written at Chicago. The governor was delegated a major role to help end the party's incessant catfighting. He put to this use his Committee For a Reunited Republican Party, which he had masterminded in March to promote his presidential bid. Until the November elections, the committee, headquartered at Harrisburg, kept him on the go week after week preaching party accord. Sometimes he carried this message into other states. It was an "important service," he told Republicans of Altoona in one speech, to which he freely gave himself.

As the messenger of party unity, he also stumped for the bewhiskered Hughes. A good Republican protectionist, Brumbaugh excoriated Wilson's low-tariff policy. He said this was "one of the really vital issues" of the presidential campaign. He praised the GOP nominee for supporting a constitutional amendment on woman suffrage and predicted that this stand would help sweep him to victory over the incumbent president, who did not. He decried the Democratic wile of trying to scare the American people into believing a vote for Hughes was a vote for war. Hughes had invited the stigma of warmonger by demanding sterner military preparation. This elicited fear, fueled by Democrats, that he had Colonel Roosevelt in mind as his secretary of war—in which event resort to arms was certain, many believed. Wilson's campaign slogan, "He Kept Us Out of War," by contrast, made him, the idealistic son of a Presbyterian minister, somewhat more attractive to pacifists and other antiwar groups.

But Martin Brumbaugh thought it oxymoronic that the country's president could be both a Calvinist and a principled peace-lover. He had sent United States troops—including the Pennsylvania National Guard—to Mexico in pursuit of Pancho Villa. And he had the nation in a state of active preparedness, with plans for a bigger army and navy. Brumbaugh agreed with Peter Jansen, a Mennonite from Nebraska, who wrote him in late October to say that the historic peace churches ought to be warned of Democratic deceit in blackening Hughes as a jingoist. Hughes was a "devout Baptist," said Jansen, who left the bench to enter the presidential race because it was "a call from Above." He had "fought the matter out with his God" in the privacy of his library, the Mennonite wrote of Hughes.

So the Pennsylvania governor acted on Jansen's exhortation at once; he drafted a statement for his denomination's magazine, the *Gospel Messenger*. In a cover letter to the editor, his old friend Daniel Miller, he said Wilson "could not do otherwise" than keep the country at peace—because, he noted sardonically, "nobody wanted to go to war with us." Thus "there is absolutely no sense in our people being caught up by such cheap claptrap as that." Miller, who had written Brumbaugh several months earlier to say it was "One of my strong hopes that the Lord may spare my life to know that you are elected President of Our Country," proved to be of the same mind. But he regretted that the caveat had arrived too late for a preelection edition. Nevertheless, he ventured, "I do not believe our people will be caught with that sort of claptrap."

Enough non-Brethren Americans, however, were swayed by the "He Kept Us Out of War" slogan to reelect Wilson—but only just enough. He won in the Electoral College with a final vote of 277 to 254. At the polls he also barely edged Hughes, losing to him in Pennsylvania. Failing to win by a majority margin, the White House occupant went down in history as the second and last two-time minority president (Cleveland had been the other one). Fortunately for him, the voters returned a Democratic Congress.

But Pennsylvania's governor, unluckily, could not look ahead to so compatible a statehouse for 1917, despite a Republican command of 39 to 11 in the Senate and 208 to 49 in the House. At the end of the General Assembly's off-year, Martin Brumbaugh found himself a badly wounded chief executive, dealt severe political blows by Penrose operatives. He and Flora escaped to Pinehurst for a golfing vacation the first week of December, bracing themselves for more savaging when the legislature convened in January.

But the governor wanted his political adversaries to know, if they did not already, that he was not the "woolly lamb" Teddy Roosevelt once made him out to be. So, upon his return from Pinehurst, he went directly to the people in a published statement. He reminded them that he was a "consistent Regular Republican" and, what is more, still an unbossed one. As their governor, he had struggled to make the party "white and clean," he said, with "no personal advantage" to himself. During the 1917 legislative session, he went on, he would stand firm in his campaign pledge: to wage "warfare against enemies of the people and in defense of their sacred rights." He ended his manifesto on a defiant note: "The control of the Republican party in Pennsylvania by the special interests of which Senator [Penrose] is the acknowledged political agent must and should be broken if the party is to live."

On Sunday, the day before Christmas, the governor jotted in his date book: "My dear Father passed over at 10:45 A.M. I am heart broken." George Brumbaugh was eighty-two years old; he had lived with his son Frank's family in Marklesburg ever since Martha died. He was in a state of dementia at the time of death. Martin apparently did not attend the funeral at Marklesburg on Wednesday, though that is hard to imagine. But neither local newspapers nor his date book puts him there.

On Thursday evening he and Flora entertained a special overnight guest: William Howard Taft.

14

Outganged Governor
and World War I

WEEKS before the 1917 session of the General Assembly convened in January, the Republican factions based in Philadelphia joined battle again, as in 1915, over the speakership of the House. Penrose put forth as his candidate for this powerful post Richard J. Baldwin of Delaware County, a twenty-year veteran as a Harrisburg lawmaker. The *North American* ran articles disparaging Penrose's pick. The paper described Baldwin as a legislator of "unsavory reputation" and a dupe of the liquor interests who had "never attained any positions of conspicuous honor or importance in the House." One of its December editorials noted that he had been one of only three members of the House to vote against the popular election of United States senators. Yet Penrose praised Baldwin's legislative record as "beyond criticism."

Pitted against Baldwin was Edwin R. Fox of Philadelphia, the very "antithesis" of the Penrose nominee, huzzahed the *North American*. The paper characterized the Vare-Brumbaugh candidate to be "in every respect a decent, upright, able man." He had led the fight for the child labor bill in 1915 and had supported every other humanitarian measure advocated by the Brumbaugh administration. He had also sided with the governor on local option. This was a clear sign that he, like the governor, had the political courage to take an independent stand against Vare policy at times, emphasized the Quaker City daily.

Male voters had not only given the Grand Old Party a totalitarian majority in the General Assembly at the past November elections, but they also strengthened the Penrose soldiery, which proceeded to pull off a resounding victory for Baldwin at the party caucus in January. An editorial in the *New York Times* expressed shock and dismay at this setback to the Pennsylvania governor, who, it said, "never acts for political reasons . . . [but] for moral reasons only." In mawkish prose the *Times* declared that everyone "must love a mind so lofty and a soul so sweet." Therefore, the editorial concluded, "Outlanders cannot understand how even sons of Belial like McNichol and Penrose can continue to combat the angel band of Vare-Brumbaugh-Flinn Republicanism."

The so-called angelic governor, however, was at the time engaged in some devilish political bullying of his own. He had not only made anti-Penrose administrative appointments during the 1916 legislative recess, but since December was cashiering Penrose placements in the state bureaucracy by the dozens. "My heart goes out to him, but he has to go," the *New York Times* quoted him as saying when he bounced a man from office. He cited "moral reasons"—meaning political ideology—as the explanation for his actions.

Penrose generals in the Senate, promising that loyalty would be rewarded, threatened not to confirm the Brumbaugh appointments. To this the governor responded that he would recommission rejected appointees after the Senate adjourned. "Never in the history of Pennsylvania politics," observed the *Huntingdon Monitor*, "has there been such a period of uncertainty among the job-holders on Capitol Hill"—from department heads on down.

To add further drama—and intrigue—to the political scene, Penrose kingpins in the state legislature repaired to Atlantic City the second week of January. Penrose drove up from Washington on the evening of the 10th to preside at the gathering. Over the next couple of days the boss and his minions schemed how to wage what the *Huntingdon Evening Journal* called a "war on the governor." This parley was unique in the annals of organized politics in Pennsylvania, said the paper. Heretofore, the machine men always sneaked off to some secluded spot, attracting as little attention as possible. But this one was "widely advertised," the *Evening Journal* pointed out, "to give the impression the Penrose people were completely in control."

Named by Penrose to the "War Board," as the *Huntingdon Monitor* angrily dubbed it, were nine key politicians—"Gangsters to the limit, everyone of them," fumed the *Monitor*. All were men in high co-opted posts or chaired powerful committees in the General Assembly. From the Senate the "board" included Penrose's chief aide "Sunny Jim" McNichol, chairman of the Elections Committee; William C. Sproul of Chester, chairman of the Finance Committee; Edward E. Beidleman of Harrisburg, president pro tempore; West Chester's T. Larry Eyre, chairman of the Public Roads and Highway Committee; and Charles A. "Pickler" Snyder, from Pottsville. Snyder, elected auditor general in November, would not take office until 1 May. But once installed, he would become an instant bête noire for the governor. For eight years progressive Republicans had held the auditor general's office, but, lamented the *Monitor*, the word "progressive" was not in Snyder's vocabulary.

Three of the nonsenators at Atlantic City were Speaker of the House Baldwin; Representative James F. Woodward of McKeesport, chairman of the House State Republican Committee and slated to be head of the Appropriations Committee; W. Harry Baker, secretary of the State Republican Committee; and William S. Leib of Pottsville, resident clerk of the House.

The plotters left their New Jersey war-council site vowed to four ends during the upcoming 122nd legislative session: discredit and embarrass Brumbaugh and the do-gooder Vare wing; thwart the governor in all his appointments; kill any progressive legislation; and gain absolute control of the party in the Keystone State. They gloated that the governor had already lost some political prestige by his defeat at their hands over the speakership. The first goal, they therefore concluded, could easily be achieved by orchestrating a bill to impeach him. Penrose told the press that the legislature was prepared to bring action against Brumbaugh on three counts: perjury in connection with his 1914 campaign fund; malfeasance in office; and bribery. He said his men had "the goods" on the governor. For weeks he would spend more time in Harrisburg than in Washington, zealously overseeing the impeachment plot.

The gang generals returned to Harrisburg in time to listen dutifully to the Governor's Message on the 12th. Brumbaugh put in an order for passing a few new laws—especially one on local option—and amending several others. He also pleaded for large appropriations for roads and schools.

Three weeks later the War Board turned its guns on the governor: William Sproul introduced a resolution in the Upper House calling for an investigation of the state administration. That Sproul, a two-decade veteran of the Senate, should be the person to do this must have been very hurtful to the governor, for the senator's name had long been identified with constructive legislation in the areas of education, good roads, and general welfare. The very public plans of the Penrose gang to impeach the governor immediately "touched off a newspaper political picnic," writes LeRoy Greene in *Shelter for His Excellency*. To Brumbaugh's shock, the *Philadelphia Public Ledger* proved signally receptive to the gang's bill of indictment.

Articles in the *Ledger* in late January accused the governor of wheedling a thirty thousand-dollar contingency fund out of the legislature for the operation and maintenance of the Executive Mansion. It continued to print other stories of alleged prodigal living by the governor, fed to the press by the gang. House Speaker Baldwin, for example, was quoted as saying the people of Pennsylvania were paying fifteen thousand dollars a year more to keep the present governor happy than they had for any of his predecessors. The gang passed out to newsmen copies of state-paid expense vouchers that, as LeRoy Greene writes, "laid before the people the most personal sort of history of a Chief Executive."

The *Wayne Independent*, published at Honesdale in the northeastern corner of the state, never deserted the governor in the heat of the scandal. But one of its editorials admitted, in retrospect, that "the citizens of Pennsylvania and the whole country stood aghast" when the stories broke about the putative spending habits of the man in the Executive Mansion. It was shocking, explained the piece, because "The charges made were very serious, the forces arrayed against him were most ferocious, and the situation looked ominous for the governor."

What made Brumbaugh angriest, and prompted his public rebuttal to the *Ledger* articles, was the malicious, twisted, and in many instances fabricated Penrosean interpretation placed upon the voucher entries. The gang insisted the vouchers showed that the state had paid virtually every personal expense incurred by the governor except the purchase of clothing: it had paid for his honeymoon; boxes of cigars and cartons of cigarettes; stays at "fashionable" hotels while on vacation; train tickets and gas for the car; entertainment of hundreds of private guests at Juniata College dinners; records for his phonograph; visits to the doctor; laundry; and groceries—to mention only a few specific examples of alleged misuses of tax money.

All the talk about impeachment and the press's frenzied feeding on it naturally humiliated the governor. Hate mail, most of it postmarked from Philadelphia, maligned him mercilessly, just as it had at the time of the Oliver scandal. As before, it was probably instigated by Penrose henchmen in the Quaker City.

But the Democrats turned the gossip of the time into political picnicking too. Party leaders were ready to steal the show from Senator Sproul and move first on impeachment proceedings, but they were quickly put into their minority place. Raymond R. Stayer, a retired dentist and Juniata alumnus, was a teenager in 1917. He remembers a Democrat neighbor who liked to tell people how many taxpayers' dollars the governor had spent on "silk pants for his bride." Some Democrats—as well as some Brethren—took to whispering innuendos about the governor's premarital behavior with Flora. (Such rumors still persist in certain Brethren circles.) The mother of Dr. Stayer, however, would get "annoyed" when she heard gossip about the governor's personal life, and she believed none of it.

In answer to *Public Ledger* articles and Penrosean charges, the governor issued "A Statement of Facts" to the press. In it he cited all the major accusations leveled against him, following up each one with the tag phrase "The truth is"—and a refutation. Some allegations were patently trumped up—like the one accusing the abstinent governor of spending tax money to lard his liquor cabinet. As the mansion host he always made cigars and cigarettes a table provision but never alcoholic drinks. Just as unfounded were wild stories that public funds had paid for the governor's honeymoon trip as well as several vacations in Maine.

The "Statement" began with Brumbaugh's denial of ever having asked the legislature for thirty thousand dollars to be used at his discretion for mansion and travel expenses. Such an alleged request was the basis upon which his enemies built their case smearing him as a spendthrift chief executive. The truth was, he answered, the General Assembly, not he, had initiated action on the contingency fund after he took office.

That happened twice, he pointed out. First, the amount allocated for the fund, to cover the years 1915 to 1917, had already been depleted by his predecessor, John Tener, by December 1914. So the legislature, in a deficiency bill on 15 February 1915, appropriated five thousand dollars for the remainder of the fiscal year. But Brumbaugh cut the sum to four thousand dollars and "lived within this income absolutely." The cost of the mansion's nine employees, placed there by the General Assembly, he continued to bear out of his salary as governor.

Then in mid-May he got a letter from the auditor general, Archibald W. Powell. Powell wrote to say he had heard that the governor was footing some of the bills for the mansion's staff out of his own pockets. Brumbaugh was told he did not have to do that. The Executive Mansion was "the guest house of the Commonwealth," the auditor general explained. So Brumbaugh began applying these costs to the contingency fund, which, the "Statement" noted, was expendable at the governor's discretion. Even so, he felt obliged to file regular accounts with the auditor general's office. Therefore, he argued, the fact that he scrupulously vouchered all his official expenses when he did not have to "ought to be sufficient proof . . . [they] were in every respect proper and honest." But, of course, it did mean a larger appropriation for the fund, especially after Brumbaugh began redecorating the Executive Mansion in late 1915.

As LeRoy Greene observes, "It was altogether impossible for a man, on a Governor's salary alone, to maintain the Mansion and its servants." But, he writes, until the 1940s, post-World War I governors "took careful and costly steps to protect themselves" from the "pain and embarrassment" Brumbaugh suffered by the "disclosure" of his mansion bills. None of them had "the faintest idea where to draw the line on Mansion expenses" and each was thus guided by his conscience, Greene, himself a governor's aide, relates. That all changed after the Second World War, when the law finally and explicitly put the governor, his family, and all mansion employees under full maintenance.

Brumbaugh, as it turned out, billed the State Treasury for $109,433.70 during his four years as governor (compared to John Tener's $65,051.33). A wartime governor, of course, could not avoid running up greater official expenses. Travel in itself became a major cost.

On 6 February William Sproul brought to the Senate the Penrose machine-scripted resolution to investigate the governor. It squeaked through that body by a vote of 29 to 19, only 3 votes more than the constitutional two-thirds. And it ran into a hot debate when it came before the House on the 14th, where it carried by vote of 110 to 80—with just 6 votes to spare. It was signed by the presiding officers of both chambers on the 20th. Now the governor was in a "bad fix," reported the *Huntingdon Monitor* in worriment. Penrose had prepared a "thorny bed" for him, because if he vetoed the joint resolution it would look like an admission of guilt.

But Philadelphia's *North American* headlined an editorial: "VETO IT, GOVERNOR." It attacked the Penrose scheme as "so flagrantly dishonest, its purpose so manifestly political, and its provisions so palpably crooked, that Governor Brumbaugh would be justified in vetoing it and would perform a public service in doing so." For seven weeks lawmakers had been squandering fourteen hundred dollars a day pushing the resolution through the assembly, objected America's oldest daily.

When the resolution came up on second reading in the Senate, Brumbaugh sent the legislature a special message denouncing its proposed investigation as grossly partisan. He offered his full cooperation in carrying out an investigation guaranteed to be "free, frank, impartial, and thorough." But his protest was ignored. So, having already made his defense to the people in his "Statement of Facts," he took the *North American's* advice and killed the resolution. He dismissed the measure as a "power that should not be given to anyone," nor, he said, could it be "legally" exercised by "any legislative committee in a constitutional government." Some post-Watergate Americans, of course, might find fault with that kind of reasoning.

While the resolution made its way through the legislature, the gang circulated pocket-sized cards all over the state that exhorted:

Evidence Now Ready
Why Not Impeach
Gov. Brumbaugh

A la Sulzer

The last line referred to William Sulzer, the Democratic ex-governor of New York. He had been impeached and removed from office in October 1913 as a result of a Tammany Hall onslaught against him for fraud and perjury. The Penrose gang professed to see a comparable situation in the Keystone State. But, unlike Tammanyites, they never had the satisfaction of carrying *their* case all the way to a removal. Brumbaugh's veto, his "Statement," and the gang's lack of solid evidence put an end to the political witch hunt by late spring.

In the eyes of the *Wayne Independent*, the governor came out of the fight "vindicated." In late July it editorialized:

The weary months have passed, the white light of exposure has fallen on those cruelly determined persecutors, their motives have been revealed; the organization to a certain extent has disintegrated; many of the reluctant followers have sneaked ashamed into the background; the legislature stands before the public vindicated. It is for our citizens a source of real satisfaction.

But if the machine failed to destroy the governor's good name, its influence with the legislature all but undid the somewhat progressive reputation he had won as a result of social measures enacted in the 1915 term. Penrose-goaded lawmakers often resorted to obstructionist tactics and kept pressure on the governor by prolonging adjournment until 28 June. The 1917 session ended up the second longest since the 1873 Constitution went into effect.

The *Huntingdon Monitor* disgustedly called it "Penrose's do-nothing legislature." That assessment was shared by the rival *Huntingdon Globe*, a Democratic paper, although its acerbity was directed at the governor: "[The legislature leaves] behind a record of fewer revolutionary laws than any previous state law-making body." And in the state capital the *Patriot* gave even a harsher one-sentence Democratic appraisal of the 1917 legislature: "It never rose above the stature of what might be expected of deliberative bodies in Zululand, and the depths of political servility and asininity it reached are bottomless."

Local option was one "revolutionary" law the legislature did nothing—or very little—about. Defeated in 1915, it was kept before the people during the 1916 off-year by the State Local Option Committee (SLOC), brainchild of the governor. Like the Anti-Saloon League, which cooperated but was now committed to national prohibition, SLOC was nonpartisan and nonsectarian. With the governor's imprimatur, it waged an all-out campaign to win a sympathetic legislature come November.

In his Governor's Message in January, Brumbaugh again, as in 1915, placed it first on his legislative agenda. On the 29th a local option bill was read in place in the House. The liquor lobby immediately demanded a public hearing. This stalled further action until 21 March, when the hearing was held. It was marked by bitter acrimony on both sides; hoots, hisses, and jeers filled the air. The governor sat through it all and at one point rose to speak on behalf of the bill. But to no avail; on the 27th it lost on second reading by a vote of 147 to 72, a worse defeat than in 1915. Unlike then, the gallery was far from overcrowded during the two and a half hours of debate. And the ranks thinned out even more by the time the House got around to balloting. Since November the outcome had never been in serious doubt; the electorate had disappointed the Drys. Until the 1930s local option would be a dead issue in Pennsylvania.

Although stymied at the state level, Brumbaugh and other Pennsylvanians of the no-drink persuasion took hope in national wartime prohibitory laws. By the onset of 1917 nineteen states had gone dry. After America's entry into World War I in April, the Anti-Saloon League lobby registered several significant victories in Congress. A clause tacked onto the Selective Service Act dried up the army and navy. Prohibition laws also did the same for Alaska, Puerto Rico, and the District of Columbia. The Lever Act outlawed the use of grain and other foodstuffs in the manufacture of alcoholic beverages. And, of course, Congress was engaged in rancorous debate about a prohibition amendment.

That April a poll listed Brumbaugh's name along with those of twenty other governors who favored national prohibition now that the country had gone to war. His was the only name on the list not from a dry state. Two months later he sent a telegram to Senator Philander Knox in support of what Drys hoped would become the Eighteenth Amendment. He said he spoke for "all the best thinking people of Pennsylvania."

In Brumbaugh's day Pennsylvania had come to be called the "Gibraltar of the Liquor Traffic." Yet his idealism seems to have blinded him to this socioeconomic reality. He persisted in the expectation of an imminent reversal of his home state's image, despite being defeated twice on temperance reform while governor. This optimism won headlines in the *New York Times*, which ran an article on a Thanksgiving sermon he preached at Pittsburgh's Second Presbyterian Church. The article was captioned: "EXPECTS STATE TO GO DRY: Brumbaugh Predicts Pennsylvania Will Oust 'King Alcohol'." He was quoted as saying:

> I thank God that King Alcohol is on the retreat [in America]. . . . There are now twenty-eight 'White States' . . . and the outlook is better now than it has ever been for Pennsylvania to become one of the White States in the very near future. No lesson of the near past is so definite as this. If we could not make good soldiers in camp and cantonment until we had banished rum from camps and cantonments, surely we cannot make good citizens until we have banished rum from the country. I most earnestly hope that the Assembly will heed the lesson of the hour and put Pennsylvania in the light-bearing states by a prompt and effective ratification.

In this same vein he prepared a statement for the Pennsylvania Anti-Saloon League a few days after Congress, on 19 December, passed on the Eighteenth Amendment to the states for ratification. (The league's national staff had done much to write the amendment.) He reminded enemies of booze that for three years he had "steadfastly" endorsed a local option law. "Now," he said, "this cause is in such a thoroughly entrenched position in the public conscience of this Commonwealth that I believe in the next Legislature it will be very easy to pass a local option law. . . ."

Then he went on to say wartime needs and the proposed Eighteenth Amendment had taken him beyond a stand merely for local option. Now he was in favor of national prohibition "at the earliest possible moment." He concluded by asking that nobody be nominated for governor or the legislature "who is not in sympathy with and whose past record does not justify sincere support for the amendment." And in his swan song to the legislators a month later, he urged, with homiletic passion, its immediate ratification.

Pennsylvanians did elect a pro-Eighteenth Amendment governor—William Sproul, ironically the man who had worked hard to impeach Brumbaugh. But the "Gibraltar of the Liquor Traffic" would only by default become a "White State." Before the General Assembly got around to acting on the amendment, the thirty-sixth state (on 16 January 1919) had ratified it, making it national law.

Brumbaugh, on hearing the news, publicly responded: "It is a disgrace that Pennsylvania, one of the greatest states in the Union, has not ratified the prohibition amendment before this." To his further disgust, Pennsylvania upheld its infamous reputation among Drys by ending up the forty-fifth ratification state—and then only by a close margin. Edwin Vare voiced the attitude of most members of the General Assembly at that time. He said he voted for the Eighteenth Amendment, not because he was opposed to hard drink, but because he thought "a vote against [it] is a vote against what is already law." True to its wet notoriety, Pennsylvania defiantly never did pass enabling legislation to enforce prohibition within its borders.

Brumbaugh, himself, would be a foe of "Demon Rum" to the very last. A couple of weeks before his death in the spring of 1930, he wrote to President Hoover offering to testify against repeal of the Eighteenth Amendment at a judiciary committee hearing. And on 4 March, ten days before he died, he sent a letter to an Altoona man proclaiming, "I'm strongly for keeping this country dry—keeping it for God and not for the demon rum."

Brumbaugh went down in defeat the second time around on another future constitutional amendment he took pride in lending his name to: woman suffrage. Pennsylvania had dashed the hope of its suffragists at the statewide elections in November of 1915. By this time women everywhere had begun to repudiate the state-by-state strategy and turn to Congress as the shortest route to the ballot box. They mobilized by the millions in 1915 and adopted a six-year timetable for obtaining voting reform through a federal amendment to the Constitution. That year the Pennsylvania Woman Suffrage Association moved its headquarters to Harrisburg and began publishing a publicity organ, *Pennsylvania Suffrage News.*

America's entry into World War I hastened the victory of women. Large numbers of them volunteered to sell war bonds, work for the Red Cross, and take jobs in factories and on the farm. Soon after America declared war, Brumbaugh appealed to a dubious president to speak out for a suffrage amendment. He could see, months before Wilson was able to, that "War ha[d] made the vote for women necessary."

When the 1917 General Assembly convened, Governor Brumbaugh hoped that the intensified feminist movement had, over the past two years, changed the political climate on equal rights in the Keystone State. His team of loyalists in the House submitted a voting rights bill along the lines of the one in 1915—in the form of an amendment to the state constitution. It came up for debate and vote on 17 April.

Suffragettes showed up in full force that Tuesday and filled the galleries, armed with a twelve hundred-foot-long petition inscribed with 56,444 names. The bill failed after a two-hour debate—101 to 94, four votes shy of a majority. Some sponsoring legislators, because of their near victory, wanted to resubmit the bill. And on 28 May the governor sent a message to the General Assembly urging that this be done. His appeal was ignored. At the time, he and Auditor General Snyder, a member of Penrose's anti-Brumbaugh "War Board," were in the middle of a fierce patronage battle. Snyder had just made the shift from his Senate seat to the auditor general's chair on the 1st.

As with prohibition, Pennsylvania thus became a spectator state in the climactic years of a major national reform movement during the Brumbaugh administration. In November, New York State adopted a constitutional amendment giving the ballot to women. Victory there gave impetus to movements in other states; it was clear that President Wilson and Congress could not hold out much longer. In September 1918 Wilson, in words reminiscent of Brumbaugh's, told the Senate that woman suffrage was a "vitally necessary war measure." But not until June 1919 did the Senate pass the Nineteenth Amendment and submit it to the states for ratification. That same month Pennsylvania became the seventh state to ratify it, with Brumbaugh, its ardent champion, now on the political sidelines. With intensive lobbying, the amendment became national law in time for women to vote in the November 1920 presidential election. The majority of them who did preferred the Republican candidate, Warren G. Harding.

It was also a "source of regret" to Brumbaugh that a bill to abolish capital punishment failed to pass the General Assembly. Forty-one states had the death penalty on the statute books in 1917. Pennsylvania's law—since 1794—limited the sentence of death to murder in the first degree. Like other Brethren, Brumbaugh was guided by his own conscience on capital punishment, since the denomination at that time had never explicitly stated its position on the right of the state to take human life.

In late February a mass meeting against capital punishment was held in Philadelphia's Academy of Music. William Draper Lewis, Brumbaugh's opponent for governor in 1914 on the Washington ticket, was now head of the Prison Reform League of Pennsylvania. He had written his old friend asking to use his name as vice-chairman of the rally. Brumbaugh readily gave his consent. In April he wrote Charles P. Sweeney, a reporter for the *Philadelphia Ledger*, in appreciation of the "commendable and courageous fight" the daily put up in support of the defeated bill. He expressed hope that Pennsylvania would "sometime" outlaw execution as a punishment for crime.

The assembly was more amenable to the governor's agenda, however, in the matter of public-school legislation, just as it had been in 1915. Four more state normal schools were purchased, leaving only Indiana, Mansfield, and Cheyney for the next administration. But their supply of male trainees was by now in great jeopardy. Since 1915, when the United States set out on military and economic war-preparedness programs, the lure of higher wages in factories and businesses had eroded Pennsylvania's potential teaching force. (In 1914 Henry Ford, for example, had begun paying his assembly-line workers five dollars for an eight-hour day.) This suddenly became more critical after the country went to war. Greater numbers of competent young men left the classrooms either for military service or jobs in war industries, where wages would nearly double between 1914 and 1918. Their places were taken by untrained teachers; professional qualifications became inconsequential in many school districts.

The session of 1917 passed four laws in an effort to check the desertion of trained or experienced talent from the classroom. One was a minimum salary law for elementary teachers. (The last such law had been passed in 1907.) It raised basic monthly pay by five dollars at each certificate level: provisional ($45); professional ($55); and state ($60). Unfortunately, this failed to keep pace with wartime inflation, and in 1919 the next administration legislated further increases.

Another 1917 law boosted minimum salaries for county superintendents to twenty-five hundred dollars, paid monthly instead of quarterly. A third created the position of assistant county superintendent.

The fourth law was one the governor and the National Education Association had trumpeted for a long time. It established a general pension system for public school teachers. By 1917 twenty states had adopted some form of a teacher pension plan. Most of them provided for shared contributions, as did Pennsylvania's law. It created a retirement board of seven members, three of them elected from among the teachers. Contributions to the pension fund were to come from employees (one half), the state (one fourth), and the school district (one fourth). The voluntary retirement age was fixed at sixty-two, the compulsory age at seventy. Pensioned teachers would receive annuities amounting to one-eightieth of their average salaries over the previous ten years multiplied by the number of years in the classroom. The law was to take effect in 1919.

Lawmakers of 1917 also increased appropriations for school districts by two million dollars—to eighteen million, a figure Brumbaugh thought could be much higher by tapping certain untaxed sources.

The good-roads movement, as in 1915, also got support from the predominantly anti-Brumbaugh legislature. Senator Sproul, whose name for a dozen years had been identified with state aid for a modern highway system, saw to that. A big incentive was the country's first federal aid highway act passed by Congress in 1916. On a matching-grant basis, it made funds available to states for road-building programs. The legislature again turned to the people for a fifty million-dollar bond issue, to be voted on in 1918, and this time it carried. Lawmakers also put an end to the practice of shunting license fees away from the Highway Motor Fund, where an earlier law said they belonged, and into the general treasury.

Unfortunately, the war curtailed any ambitious response to the 1916 federal overture; only forty-two miles of new roads were built the last year of the Brumbaugh administration. But some three thousand miles of highways were either resurfaced or oiled between 1915 and 1918. The last two years of his administration, Brumbaugh had a new highway commissioner in Frank B. Black of Meyersdale, having lost his first one, Robert Cunningham, by death.

Nevertheless, the governor's "Good Roads Day" and his state jaunts by car in 1915, 1916, and 1917 were a tour de force in propaganda. They helped overcome the public's perception of highways as a speedway for the rich. On "Good Roads Day" farmers and city dwellers alike were persuaded to take off their coats and pitch in to smooth out hummocky and rutted roadbeds. Some places, women provided free luncheons for the volunteers, and many businesses gave men time off to join in the work.

Practically all roads were still packed clay. The *Harrisburg Evening News*, in a flashback article in 1930, described what the governor's entourage looked like within a half-hour of a new day's journey on the tour of 1916:

[I]ts several faces were brown with dust from the swirling cloud rising above the treetops. None who participated will forget the odd appearance of Governor Brumbaugh's monstrous, shaggy eyebrows when they accumulated their coating of grime. Mrs. Brumbaugh and other women wore veils, which afforded little protection. The entire party was accoutred in ankle-length linen dusters, and foresighted members provided themselves with beetle-eyed goggles.

In May 1917, however, "Good Roads Day" gave way to "Farm and Garden Day." Explained the governor, the food crisis, now that the country was at war, was paramount to highway work. And in the fall he renamed his annual highway inspection odyssey an "Agricultural Tour."

The annual tours also represented a protest against existing toll roads and toll bridges. There was general hostility to these vestiges of the state's famous turnpike past, and Brumbaugh was determined to open highways to free travel. He boasted in his 1919 Governor's Message that 278 miles had been unpiked during his four years in office. That year the Lincoln Highway (later Route 30) ran toll-free from the Ohio to the Delaware. And the William Penn Highway (later Route 22) was likewise completely open, except at one point. The governor predicted that the last turnstile in the state would come down by 1921.

One of the seven hundred or so bills to reach the governor's desk in 1917 was somewhat of a landmark in Pennsylvania tax legislation: a 2 percent direct inheritance levy. Brumbaugh reluctantly signed it, giving as his reason the drop in potential state revenue because of the current national recession. In 1919 he denounced the law as an inhumane law and hoped it would be "so modified as to make it an Act worthy this Commonwealth." At the time, Pennsylvania was one of the lowest-tax states in the country.

He affixed his signature, however, to 198 vetoes, totaling 409 for his administration. His valedictory message in 1919 complained that the General Assembly always appropriated money greatly in excess of revenues, and he said he had tried to put an end to "this wholly reprehensible procedure," but to no avail. Hence, he lamented, "The Governor is given the thankless task of reducing these appropriations by vetoing in whole or in part many items that possess merit and some that are purely meritless." He went on, "The Governor should not be obliged to bear the criticism that properly belongs elsewhere." He chose not to veto, however, a pay raise for legislators from $1500 to $2500 a session.

Just as the 1917 session began with a patronage fight, so it ended with one. Two Penrose allies, elected department heads by popular vote the past November, assumed their posts in May. Senator Charles Snyder became auditor general and Harmon K. Kephart of Connellsville took over as state treasurer. Immediately, they made moves to appoint Penrose brothers-in-arms to posts in their respective departments. The governor and his crowd then put out word that for every Brumbaugh man dropped by either the auditor general or the treasurer at least five Penrose men would get the pink slip in other executive offices. The governor's threat worked, and a list of two hundred new appointees, shrewdly sent to the Senate at midnight before the day of adjournment, won last-minute confirmation. In late June the *Huntingdon Monitor* cheered that "Penrose forces have been out-generalled at every turn" by the county's son in the Executive Mansion.

Soon after the session ended, Brumbaugh appointed seven more men in four different departments. Auditor General Snyder refused to pay their salaries, claiming they lacked Senate approval, but Attorney General Brown took the governor's case to the courts and won. Thereafter, for the last eighteen months of his governorship, Brumbaugh, caught up in wartime duties, remained aloof from political infighting. But the Vare-Penrose vendetta waged on in Philadelphia. In November a policeman was shot dead during an election-day row.

Needless to say, all the political brawling with the Penrose gang gave the governor many low moments. But he always managed to bounce back to renew battle. As he wrote in a February letter to Francis Shunk Brown:

> Sometimes I wonder whether it is all worth while and then in such occasions I know it is and I shall both in and out of office keep steadily to the task of making Pennsylvania too decent politically for Penrose and his sycophants to combine to violate all the tenets of decency and fair play.

In the final analysis, it was not vicious political infighting, nor a progressive agenda of legislation, but the Great War that defined the Brumbaugh administration. As Colonel Henry W. Shoemaker,* a confidant of the governor and later overseas diplomat, state archivist, and publisher of the *Altoona Tribune,* once wrote:

> Though born and brought up and ordained in a peace-loving sect, Martin Brumbaugh left a priceless heritage as War Governor of Pennsylvania in the first World war to afflict the United States. It was probably his outstanding service to state and nation, the flawless manner in which he conducted Pennsylvania's participation.

It is oddly ironic that a man who came from a religious faith that extolled nonviolence should be remembered as an adept wartime administrator. Both as a Brethren pacifist and an educator he hated war. In his view, it not only violated the teachings of Christ but also, as he often said, vitiated the humanizing values and ennobling ideals inherent in the search for truth. His Thanksgiving Proclamation of 1915 expressed sadness at the sufferings of war-ravaged Europe and professed that "the law of love is the only abiding law of progress." According to Colonel Shoemaker, "It was his dream, like Woodrow Wilson's, that World War I was a war to end all wars."

But after war came to this country, Brumbaugh, the God-fearing patriot, could

---

*It was then the practice for the governor to retain a staff of honorary colonels as civilian overseers of the state's National Guard. This custom was abolished under Brumbaugh's successor.

not imagine a defeated America. For him, the world's armed combat had now been transformed into a holy war. As he preached from a Pittsburgh Presbyterian pulpit in November 1917: "I firmly believe we are fighting the battle of Christ Jesus when fighting America's fight in this war. We are carrying the cross side by side with the Stars and Stripes and we are marching to a worthy victory." In the October 1918 issue of the National Education Association's *Journal,* he justified America's entry into the war with similar theological reasoning:

> We shall win, because we are right. God never wars on the side of the wrong. We shall come from this baptism of blood a revivified and regnant race, leading the world in all that makes for righteousness, decency, and justice.

It was Brumbaugh's sense of eternal right and justice, then, that triumphed over his Brethren pacifist ethic after America declared war. Even before that, as diplomatic relations with Germany grew gravely tense, he urged Wilson to stand fast for an "honorable peace." This was the essence of a telegraphic message he sent the White House in February, shortly after the president's famous "peace without victory" speech to the Senate.

For over a decade, of course, Pennsylvania's pacifist governor had showed a paradoxical enthusiasm for honoring America's military past as a perpetual member of the Valley Forge Park Commission. He also participated in planning the nation's observance of the fiftieth anniversary of the Battle of Gettysburg in 1913, and was greatly insulted that he did not get proper recognition for his part. But for him the hallowed site of Valley Forge marked the most famous encampment in the world's history. He once called it "the mecca of Americans."

Despite its martial significance, he regarded the ragged, half-starving, ill-clad Continentals and their indomitable leader who endured the harsh winter of 1777-78 there as immortal patriots—brave, self-sacrificing heroes in the cause of liberty and democracy. He thought it a benediction of history that he should be governor when the national government presented his state, in June 1917, with the Washington Memorial Arch, erected at the park's entrance.

The unveiling ceremony took place on Tuesday afternoon, the 19th, with Speaker of the House Champ Clark making the formal transfer of the stone monument. Scores of senators and congressmen attended the ceremony, witnessed by an estimated crowd of twenty-five thousand spectators. (President Wilson, because of the war, decided not to come.) The date 19 June was the anniversary of when the troops of George Washington broke camp and began the march to Philadelphia in pursuit of the redcoats. In accepting the victory arch for his state, Brumbaugh said the spirit of the Revolutionary War scene was increasingly becoming "the spirit of the human race" in its search for an "ideal government." It was "with the Allies in the western line," he declaimed, and justified America's present "Washingtonian sacrifice to defend our national honor and keep our spotless record unsullied."

It had been exactly a year before that the Dunker governor first assumed the improbable role of a military figure. That happened when Woodrow Wilson decided to chastise Pancho Villa for his repeated raids across the Mexican border into Texas and New Mexico and the murdering of a number of Americans. Abandoning his policy of "watchful waiting" toward Mexico, President Wilson called out 150,000 militiamen, including Pennsylvania Guardsmen. Governor Brumbaugh, their commander-in-chief, mobilized all state units on 19 June. He ordered them to assemble at Mount Gretna (south of Lebanon), long the training ground of the Guard, by the 24th. The governor was there to greet the arriving civilian soldiers, saluting and being saluted.

A few days later, he saw them off to Camp Stewart, near El Paso, Texas. This force of 818 officers and 14,178 men, however, did not join General John Pershing's Expeditionary Force in pursuit of the wily Villa, who fled into Mexico's heartland. Instead, they spent the long hot summer drilling. As a result of this basic training, say state military historians, Pennsylvania Guardsmen went into World War I as well trained as any of Uncle Sam's troops that fought in Europe. Part of the Camp Stewart units came home late in the year, the rest doing so early in 1917. But life in mufti was soon ended for all.

On 6 April of that year, the United States declared war against Germany. By that time the state National Guard had again been mustered into federal service. Eventually all the units would be sent to newly established Camp Hancock, Georgia, outside the city of Augusta. Here they would spend the next nine months in a routine of marches, reviews, sham battles, bayonet practice, trench digging, target shooting, and gas-mask drills. Thus was born the famed Twenty-Eighth Division, wearers of the "Red Keystone" insignia patch at the French front.

There were unbudgeted costs connected with the Guard in the periods it was not federalized. As commander-in-chief, Governor Brumbaugh requested additional appropriations to cover the emergency expenses. He assumed, by virtue of this office, that he should be the man to allocate the funds. But in April the Penrose faction, playing politics to the hilt, demanded that a legislature-controlled board, not the governor, be invested with that power. Brumbaugh's tormentors insisted that he could not be trusted to handle the funds without supervision. Their impeachment case would prove that, they said. In the end, the would-be impeachers were forced to back down on the idea of a board.

As governor of a state in which one-third of the population was of German origin (it was about twelve percent for the nation at large), Brumbaugh had his share of troubles gaining undivided support for the war effort. The German-American Alliance had been active in Pennsylvania since 1914, stirring up sentiment for neutrality and opposing help to the Allies. In fact, on 28 January 1915, the governor himself presided at a noisy anti-British rally in Philadelphia's Academy of Music, sponsored by German-American members of the American Neutrality League. But he backed off from such public appearances once America and the Allies won the propaganda war by depicting the Kaiser's soldiery as fiendish "Huns."

Socialists and Industrial Workers of the World also proved troublesome. They denounced the draft and distributed literature against it, which led to police raids and arrests in Philadelphia.

Hate hysteria soon swept the state and the nation against Germans and things Germanic. Sauerkraut became "liberty cabbage," and hamburger was renamed "liberty steak." German-composed music was banned, and teaching the German language was forbidden in many schools and colleges. In Harrisburg, State Police stood guard at the capitol the clock around. Rumor-mongers spread tales that German agents were attacking America through its food, causing gastrointestinal epidemics and worse sicknesses. In the hamlet of Nokesville, Virginia, everybody believed peanut butter was being mysteriously filled with ground glass.

The Brumbaughs enjoyed telling how Attorney General Francis Brown got carried away with this hysteria. He was having lunch at the Executive Mansion with the governor and his staff. It was a brilliant spring day, and Flora decided to serve sassafras tea—without announcing it in any way, or considering that city people might not know what it was. Mr. Brown was talking and eating enthusiastically. He reached for his teacup and took a deep swallow. Immediately, he blanched and in shocked self-pity exclaimed: "My God, I'm poisoned!"

By the time Congress passed the Selective Service Act in May, the Pennsylvania legislature had already gone on record endorsing such a law. It also had pledged all the state's resources, and immediately made all roads available for military purposes. On 25 April the governor and the attorney general took the oath of wartime allegiance. The next day the governor ordered all employees of the executive branch to do the same thing or face dismissal.

In early May he prevailed upon another avid golfer, ex-President Taft, to address the General Assembly on "war aims." After being introduced by Brumbaugh, Taft remarked: "I am a busy man. I had many conflicting invitations, but Martin Brumbaugh is a friend and I could not refuse him. I always try to accommodate a friend."

The future chief justice of the United States, at the time a professor of law at Yale, was so busy, it seems, that he rushed off from New Haven with his tuxedo and shirt but no collar. (Shirt and collar were separate in those days.) The sartorial crisis threatened to keep the illustrious guest from a state dinner in his honor at the Executive Mansion. Flora drafted all the aides she could find and dispatched them to all the men's shops in Harrisburg to see if they could find a seventeen-inch collar for the Brumbaugh's corpulent (350 pounds) guest. Closing time was rapidly approaching, but someone managed to come up with a collar or two and save the day.

The mobilization of manpower and of industrial and agricultural resources were beyond anything demanded of the Keystone State in earlier wars. To cope with the myriad problems, Brumbaugh resorted to a plan put to use during the American Revolution: a Committee of Public Safety. This war emergency body was the outgrowth of a conference of five governors (those of Pennsylvania, New

York, New Jersey, Maryland, and Delaware) hosted by Brumbaugh at the Union League in Philadelphia on 18 March.

Three weeks later, after America declared war, Brumbaugh invited over two hundred prominent citizens from every part of the state to a meeting in Harrisburg. A Committee of Public Safety was formed, with Philadelphian and later United States senator George Wharton Pepper as chairman. Its stated purpose: to support the national government "in every patriotic way." This was to be done by mobilizing and conserving all resources essential to the federal war program. The name of the committee was later changed to the Pennsylvania Council of National Defense.

The council was divided into fifteen departments, each headed by a director. Eventually its roster grew to include fifteen thousand influential citizens—the largest public organization ever created in the state up to that time. Its headquarters were in Philadelphia's Finance Building. Brumbaugh's Sunday-school comrade, Howard Heinz, served as the council's food administrator for Pennsylvania.

The governor, lieutenant governor, auditor general, adjutant general, and state treasurer collectively controlled the disbursement of appropriations for the council's multitudinous war-work programs. There were seventy subdivisions of the council in the sixty-seven counties, usually with a man as chair and a woman as vice-chair. These county organizations carried on all the council's war-defense activities, including Red Cross work, the Liberty Loans, promoting the draft, and relief aid. The momentous impact the council and its subordinate county units had statewide is summed up in *Philadelphia in the World War: 1914–1919:*

> Splendid as were its physical accomplishments, perhaps the greatest service rendered by the Council was its fusing of the patriotic endeavor of all creeds and classes into a singleness and unanimity of purpose—that purpose a fixed and unselfish resolve to spare no effort and to shirk no duty that would help to win the war.

Brumbaugh initiated another war-emergency measure early in 1917. Anticipating that the Pennsylvania National Guard might soon be called into federal service, the governor saw the imperative need for stand-in militiamen in the event of disorder or riot. The State Police, scarcely two hundred in number, was far too weak numerically to handle such situations. (Brumbaugh himself would appoint half of this force's manpower by his term's end.)

So after consulting with Adjutant General Thomas J. Stewart and his deputy, Colonel Frank D. Beary, he directed the two officers (along with retired General Charles M. Clement) to prepare a bill for the legislature creating a utility force. Since this was intended to be a temporary military organization, the bill did not give it the status of the National Guard under the National Defense Act of 1916. It was to be a state military unit, consisting of three infantry regiments (around four thousand men), under the federal militia laws and called "The Pennsylvania Reserve Militia." The plan easily won legislative sanction in late June.

By that time Susquehanna University had awarded the governor his sixth honorary doctorate, an L.H.D.

With summer, the regular Guardsmen left the state for Georgia. Thus in October the planned militia became a reality. But it was impossible to obtain arms, clothing, ordnance, and other matériel from the Federal Government for homefront use. So the governor and Colonel Beary, who had now become adjutant general, had to scrounge for supplies and equipment. The Reserve Militia adopted the color of forest green for its uniforms, and was organized, armed, and quartered in the existing state armories.

Fortunately, there was no mob violence or sabotage in Pennsylvania during the war. Over a thousand officers and men from the green-clad corps would volunteer duty during the flu epidemic of 1918-19. Three decades later Beary, as an octogenarian, wrote of his commander-in-chief: "[He] initiated many activities for the betterment of our Keystone State, but none exceeded in value his insistence on an organization of a body of volunteer citizen soldiers, devoted to the maintenance of peace and order in our state during a war period." In scope it was "vaster by far" than Governor Andrew Curtin's part in the Civil War, said the adjutant general, and "of equal genius for organization."

On the national scene, meanwhile, Pennsylvania's industrial might was pivotal during the war. The Keystone State abounded in raw materials and natural resources. Its coal, petroleum, and timber were strategic resources in war production. It had the largest machine shops, mills, factories, shipyards. Government contracts went to 2,733 industrial plants in Pennsylvania. They turned out cannon, explosive chemicals, rifles, helmets, trucks, ships, locomotives, piping, tin cans, and other miscellaneous supplies. Nearly two-fifths of America's wartime production came from Pennsylvania's industry.

The industrial contributions of the Philadelphia area made it a veritable arsenal of weaponry and military gear. Forty-seven percent of the rifles carried by United States troops were supplied by the Remington Arms plant at Eddystone. The Budd Manufacturing Company produced more than a million steel helmets (over one-half the total), affectionately called the "Doughboy's Iron Lid," an innovative piece of accoutrement for American troops. Philadelphia's Ford Motor Plant painted every single helmet worn by the Yanks. The Baldwin Locomotive Works built 5,551 "Iron Horses" of all sizes, shapes, and gauges for the European Allies and the United States.

Pennsylvania's six shipyards launched 170 vessels, from freighters to destroyers, on the Delaware River. Nearly 20 percent of the total tonnage of America's shipbuilding activity was turned out by Pennsylvania. Hog Island, often then referred to as the "eighth wonder of the world," arose Aladdin-like from a tract of swamp land south of Philadelphia in the winter of 1917–18 to become what was then the largest shipyard in the world.

Indeed, the Quaker City housed the "brains" of the whole unprecedented program of constructing and operating a merchant marine for Uncle Sam during the last six months of the war. President Wilson had appointed Martin Brumbaugh's boyhood chum, steelmaker Charles Schwab, as director-general of the Emergency Fleet Corporation in the summer of 1917, and Schwab manipulated things so that the vast shipbuilding activity ended up headquartered in Philadelphia. Out of the work of the corporation came the postwar U.S. Merchant Marine and the nation's status as a maritime power.

Western Pennsylvania's steel mills and coal fields, meanwhile, rivaled the output of Germany's great industrial region of the Ruhr Valley. Pittsburgh steel was everywhere evident along the Western Front long before the Yanks got there in person. And 80 percent of Uncle Sam's own munition steel was produced in the greater Pittsburgh district. Seventy-five percent of the bituminous coal used by munition makers came from the mines of surrounding counties.

Besides its heavy industry, western Pennsylvania was also known as a center of other kinds of war goods. New Kensington Aluminum Company of America turned out nearly two-fifths of the meat cans used for army mess equipment. Pittsburgh Plate Glass furnished the several branches of the military with a variety of optical instruments: binoculars, telescopes, periscopes, cameras, gun sights. Westinghouse Electric produced munitions, forgings, railroad cars, and other equipment.

Pennsylvania, with a population of 8,600,000, also made an enormous contribution in money. Its citizens subscribed to nearly three billion dollars worth of Liberty and Victory bonds and paid taxes to the Federal Government of over one billion dollars in 1917–19. War Savings Stamps accounted for additional millions of dollars. Four of the five national Liberty Loan drives occurred during the Brumbaugh administration. Only more populous New York State exceeded Pennsylvania's total subscription on each drive.

During the Third Loan campaign, Pennsylvania's Four-Minute Men entered the war bond picture. Every state had such an organization of trained volunteer speakers. Their venue was diverse: industrial plants, churches, schools, theaters, movie houses. By war's end Pennsylvania had Four-Minute Men branches in sixty counties, with a roster of over four thousand speakers. Brumbaugh's commonwealth could boast having the largest and best organized corps of Loan spokesmen in the whole country.

With each loan, Brumbaugh, like his fellow governors, made an appropriate patriotic appeal. Pennsylvania's Third Liberty Loan was opened by a tremendous celebration in Philadelphia. Secretary of the Treasury William G. McAdoo, President Wilson's son-in-law, was there along with the governor. The central event was the unveiling of an immense replica of the Statue of Liberty at Broad Street and South Penn Square. The theme: "Liberty Enlightening the World." Brumbaugh was photographed in a high silk hat, his familiar headgear when reviewing Pennsylvania troops. Apparently, he had discarded the "democratic" Stetson derby he had worn on inauguration day—at least when involved in public ceremonies.

Pennsylvania also played a leading role in war-welfare work. Probably as much as seventy million to a hundred million dollars were raised between 1914 and 1918. The American Red Cross netted over twenty-seven million dollars in its two drives (10 percent of the country's total). (A one-dollar contribution from Fritz Brumbaugh was recorded for its Christmas Membership Campaign of 1917.) Two YMCA drives brought in more than six and a half million. Many millions of dollars more were also collected in "War Chest" drives and by many special organizations such as the Belgian Relief Commission, American-Jewish Relief Association, Armenian and Syrian Relief, and others. Churches and Sunday schools conducted their own campaigns for relief funds in behalf of members of their own denominations in countries of the Allies.

The Keystone State likewise furnished its fair share of young men to the armed forces—nearly 8 percent of the total. In all, about 350,000 Pennsylvanians entered military service either as draftees (226,000), volunteers (89,000), or Guardsmen (28,000). The Selective Service Law enacted by Congress on 18 May 1917, required each state to set up a vast administrative machine. Brumbaugh and his military staff established 282 local draft boards. Between the first registration day (5 June 1917) and the fourth and last one (12 September 1918), over two million males of draft age filled out "questionnaires," one-tenth of them getting a "greeting" from the president.

Brumbaugh's political antagonists carried their ongoing feud with him and his administration even to the point of urging a federal investigation into how the draft was being conducted in Pennsylvania. It seems that Major General Enoch H. Crowder, United States provost marshal and national director of the Selective Service Law, was not entirely satisfied with certain reports made to Washington by Adjutant General Beary. The problem involved the expenditure of money. Crowder asked for an explanation, and Beary went to Washington in April 1918 to give it. Nevertheless, the provost general decided to send an officer to go over vouchers filed in Harrisburg. Penrose lackeys tipped off newspapers that another administration scandal was about to be uncovered. The press thought these rumors newsworthy.

The rumors angered General Crowder. He ordered the inquiry to be dropped, saying he believed that "politics inspired the attacks" on Brumbaugh. The *Philadelphia Press* reported him as accusing the governor's enemies of "making an issue of a perfunctory matter" that would now be settled by mail or telephone. In no way, the general emphasized, was the integrity of Pennsylvania officials ever involved in the matter. That must have been why Brumbaugh made a special point of telling lawmakers in his outgoing Governor's Message that the "selective service duty and every other duty has been promptly met. Pennsylvania has not failed the nation at any point. Our record is clean and complete."

Pennsylvanians soldiered in several units: the National Guard's Twenty-Eighth ("Keystone") Division; the Seventy-Ninth ("Lorrain") Division; the Eightieth Division; the all-black Ninety-Second ("Buffalo") Division, composed of troops from several states; and the famous Forty-Second ("Rainbow") Division, which was made up of National Guard outfits from twenty-six different states. Brumbaugh, decked out in his Stetson-made stovepipe hat—and a side arm (a Colt .45 Automatic, Model 1911)—visited and reviewed the Twenty-Eighth at Camp Hancock and the Seventy-Ninth at Camp Meade, Maryland. During his time at Camp Hancock, he got in a few rounds of golf in Atlanta. His caddie was a fifteen-year-old youngster named Bobby Jones, who already the year before had played in an amateur national championship.

All five of the divisions in which a large number of Pennsylvanians served saw actual combat. About 20 percent of the frontline troops came from the Keystone State. Three of the divisions—the Twenty-Eighth, the Seventy-Ninth, and the Eightieth—took the brunt of the Meuse-Argonne offensive in September and October of 1918. This was the greatest battle ever fought by American troops prior to World War II. In all, more than 11,000 Pennsylvanians paid the supreme sacrifice—about 4,300 killed in action and almost an equal number by disease. This represented about 10 percent of total American military deaths. The number of wounded reached over 26,000—about 7 percent of the country's total.

Brumbaugh's date book for 11 November 1918, reads: "Peace at last. Thank God, it is over." The governor awoke at 3:30 A.M. that Monday, got up, and left the Executive Mansion to join a victory parade that made its way to Market Square. There he mounted a Bethlehem Steel Company truck and addressed the crowd. He told the people in the stillness of that morning hour: "I have the sacred and joyful duty of announcing to you that the Stars and Stripes now wave over Germany. The war is over and won. The German empire is dead forever." Then, waving a big flag, he led the crowd in cheers. Observed the *Huntingdon Globe* of the cheerleading governor: "He made a striking figure, standing as he did in the glare of the electric street lamp."

When Pennsylvania's much-decorated troops came marching home in late spring of 1919, Brumbaugh was no longer in office to greet them. But in his departing address to the General Assembly in January, he spoke of plans already completed to employ crippled soldiers in the various industries of the state. And he urged assemblymen to begin at once to plan "memorials of a patriotic character," both at home and in France and Belgium, in honor of "our citizen soldiers." Such steps were taken during the Sproul administration and eventually carried to completion in 1930 ("Memorial Bridge," at State Street).

The last months of the Brumbaugh governorship coincided with the disastrous worldwide influenza epidemic during the winter of 1918–19. Recent research places global mortality from the disease at 30 million people. Known as "Spanish" or "swine" flu, it killed 550,000 Americans. Pennsylvania lost 54,000 persons in the deadly pandemic. This exceeded by more than 16,000 the total number of American doughboys killed in battle. The virulent outbreak struck the Keystone State in September.

Panic soon broke out everywhere. Doctors and nurses still in civilian services were overworked and overwhelmed. In Philadelphia some physicians made as many as two hundred calls a day. Funeral supplies were exhausted and in some places it was impossible to recruit grave diggers. Servicemen with experience as undertakers were furloughed to help inter the dead in Philadelphia. The epidemic hit especially hard the anthracite and bituminous coal regions and the larger cities, some of which arrested and fined people who spit in public. The Department of Health divided the state into nineteen districts, each headed by medical and nursing officers, and designated sixty-four emergency hospitals. A statewide quarantine prohibited all public meetings and closed all schools, churches, colleges, theaters, and saloons the last two weeks of October. Schoolteachers became stopgap nurses in the emergency hospitals.

The governor, of course, made urgent appeals for volunteer personal service of all kinds during the emergency. The Red Cross and the Council of National Defense, through its Department of Medicine, Sanitation, and Hospitals, put as much of their physical and human resources as possible to easing the crisis. The Pennsylvania nurses who had gone to Massachusetts, where the epidemic hit earlier, now returned in the company of Bay State nurses paying back the favor. During the crisis the State Police were used in various ways; many members of the constabulary were felled by the virus and seven of them succumbed. As already noted, over one-third of the reserve militiamen answered their commander-in-chief's call for volunteer duty. Many caught the flu themselves and a number died. In Philadelphia they helped man hospitals, chauffeured doctors on their rounds, served with ambulance crews, and filled in as policemen. By Christmastide the lethal virus had pretty much played itself out in Pennsylvania and disappeared.

Political worries, war, and the epidemic did not keep the state's chief executive off Harrisburg's two golf links—the Country Club and the Colonial Club. And one day he played the course at Wernersville (near Reading) with a brilliant eighteen-year-old dancer who had made his debut on the New York stage in 1916: Fred Astaire. He also golfed at Pinehurst, North Carolina; the Tar Heel resort town, where the governor became famous as a clubhouse raconteur, prized the annual visits of the Brumbaughs. Their stay was always given appreciative notice in the *Pinehurst Outlook,* the local paper.

The Brumbaughs' February 1918 vacation there allowed the governor to bid Annie Oakley a good-bye in person. She was scheduled to leave in mid-March on a tour of army camps, where she and her adored costar, the setter Dave, would put on their modern version of William Tell's shooting stunts. "Little Sure Shot" had asked her "cousin," the governor, to be a character reference for her when she proposed the tour to the army's top brass. (Annie and Frank also put on money-raising shows for the Red Cross before civilian audiences.)

Nor did the pressures of being a wartime governor keep the Brumbaughs from high-summer stays at their Maine vacation home.

Like other patriotic Americans, Martin and Flora also gave some of their leisure hours to a victory garden during the two summers the nation was at war.
Theirs was planted in the backyard of the Germantown property. The government
promoted gardening as a way for citizens to feed America and its allies, as well as
starving Belgians. As Dr. Claude Flory humorously tells in his foreword, the
Brumbaugh's victory garden was the scene of their dog Fritz's urinary encounter
with the camera of a *Philadelphia Ledger* photographer.

No doubt, like their hoe-wielding fellow believer, many Brethren planted victory gardens, just as some of them bought Liberty Bonds or wore a uniform. At the
time of Brumbaugh's governorship, denominational leaders began rethinking and
redefining the denomination's concept of church-state relations. While Annual
Conference of 1916 reaffirmed the biblical basis of the Brethren opposition to war,
conference delegates in 1917 voted a resolution that called for "a constructive
patriotism and loyal citizenship of real service" now that America had taken up
arms. Though the resolution did not interpret the phrase in practical terms, it implied a radical shift in attitude toward the state.

It had been a basic tenet of the historically nonconformist religious body that
the state, because it relies upon coercion, is inherently evil. Still, Brethren doctrine
had paradoxically conceded, the New Testament enjoined Christians to obey civil
authority. Church writings cited scripture that says governments are ordained of
God to punish criminals and to protect the law-abiding. But when divine com-
mands and human laws conflict, then God must be served, not human rulers, despite the consequences. Before the Civil War the Brethren eschewed voting, holding public office, or bearing arms. After 1865, Annual Conferences began to waffle
on the first two bans—in 1866 on voting and in 1893 and 1912 on office-holding.
The nebulous resolution of 1917 seemed another equivocation to many draft-age
Brethren men and created denomination-wide confusion about the canonicity of
absolute pacifism.

Patriotism, in the dictionary definition of the word—loving, supporting, and
defending one's country—had rarely cropped up in Brethren vocabulary. For Martin Brumbaugh, of course, it was an obligatory virtue. He believed implicitly in
democracy and that America, more than any other nation in the world, was blessed
of God.

He once gave an offbeat lecture, for a Dunker, at the University of Pennsylvania entitled "The Patriotism of Jesus Christ." It was his only public stab at synthe-
sizing religion and patriotism as a personal philosophy. His argument was that
Jesus can be viewed not only as "the great Teacher" but also as "the great Patriot."
A citizen of three realms, he lived a perfectly law-abiding life under the most
trying conditions. As a Jew, he lived under "the banners of the Jewish nation"; as a
Roman subject, he persevered under "the imperial flag"; as the Son of God, he was
"a citizen of heaven." Yet he was loyal to the institutions of all three dominions: to
those of his people ("He said He came not to destroy, but to fulfill, the law"), to

those of Rome ("its chief representative in His land was forced at last to declare that he found no fault in Him"), and "to the eternal laws of His Father" ("This is my beloved Son in whom I am well pleased"). Jesus Christ, therefore, embodied "the source of every high and patriotic sentiment," Brumbaugh thus inferred.

"Love of country is love of its institutions," he said in defining patriotism for his Penn audience. Thus "That man is the noblest American who believes in universal education, Christian religion, and the sovereignty of the individual, and who puts the whole force and pressure of his life to working out these institutions." A person's loyalty to these ideals—to an "American Christian civilization"—was the measure of that person's patriotism. The high purpose of Memorial Day, collegians were told that 30 May, was to pay tribute to those patriots who lived and died to establish and protect our democratic, constitutional way of life. But even more important, the professor proclaimed, when we lay wreaths on the graves of those that died for the American republic, we are also doing honor to Jesus Christ who "came into the world and labored and died" for the very principles and qualities that have characterized the history and people of the United States.

That kind of theology was probably too heady for early twentieth-century Brethren (and obviously ignored the contribution of non-Christians to the nation's history). But he never backed away from preaching a responsible, participatory citizenship. Two decades later he even put this slant on the founding and mission of Juniata College. In 1926, on the occasion of his alma mater's Jubilee Anniversary, he said:

> This college founded in prayer and faith, fifty years ago today, has always taught reverent submission to the Divine Law and a hearty support of constitutional government. It has steadily sought to make good citizens for the Kingdom of Heaven and for the Republic of men. Its aim has been to charter its pupils for lofty service; to send forth young men and women sound in loyalty to God and to government.

Back in 1917, however, the Brethren faced the question: Did "constructive patriotism and loyal citizenship" imply military service? The draft law that spring, unlike the one in the Civil War, made no provision for commutation tax or hiring a substitute in the case of conscientious objectors. But it did exempt members of the historic peace churches from combat duty. Unfortunately, the Wilson administration tarried well into 1918 before defining noncombatant service (medical corps, quartermaster corps, engineering corps). Meanwhile, many peace-church draftees refused to wear the uniform and drill. So did a significant number of Christian social reformers, who viewed conscription as a violation of an individual's rights. For months, therefore, both sets of COs—biblical literalists and liberal pacifists—were left at the mercy of army officers.

The Church of the Brethren proved as dilatory about ruling on noncombatant service as the president. Not until January 1918 did its spokesmen reach a verdict of sorts: Obey the government as far as conscientiously possible. Most Brethren draftees interpreted this to mean they could put on the uniform but not fight, and so marched off intending to be rifleless doughboys.

As Pennsylvania's only pacifist governor since colonial times, Brumbaugh helped scores of those called to the colors to get noncombatant status. He considered this kind of soldiering an honorable alternative to being a gun-toting warrior or a rebellious dissenter. But he must have often been bemused by the fate history marked off for him. That is suggested by a comment he once made to Galen B. Royer, a prominent Brethren minister, writer, and Juniata College alumnus. He said, "Galen, it is mighty strange that the war-governor of Pennsylvania had to be a Dunkard." He sincerely felt that he had not compromised his peace convictions. While in office, he never missed a Love Feast at First Church, Philadelphia, solemnly kneeling to wash the feet of factory workers and coal miners or whomever chance put in the chair before him. And when he preached in Brethren churches—prior to 1917, at least—he conformingly denounced war as wrong, and prayed that the United States would not be drawn into the European conflict.

But once America became a belligerent, the governor had two options, according to Charles Ellis, whom seminarian Harold Statler once interviewed for a term paper on Brumbaugh. Ellis said, "He could have resigned his position or do what he actually did—go through with the obligation he had assumed as governor. So far as I know he never felt that he was in a position to do less than this."

In this connection, Statler also quotes a remark made by Juniata degree-holder Albert C. Wieand in 1939, when a second world war seemed impending. Wieand, who had just retired from the presidency of the Brethren's Bethany Theological Seminary, was one of the speakers at a denominational forum on what the church's peace testimony should be in the event of war. The seminary head stated, "I heard M. G. Brumbaugh say that he believed a magistrate was not personally responsible for any act he performed as a magistrate." Brumbaugh never formulated in writing a political philosophy expounding this essentially Lutheran view of magisterial authority and individual responsibility. But if he really held this belief about the dichotomy of official duties and personal conviction, perhaps that explains why he did not resign. Also, he thought of himself as an honorable man, a person of his word. To resign would have betrayed his oath of office.

No matter what logic Brumbaugh used to justify his actions as "War Governor," one fact seems indisputable: he was so intensely American that he could not divide his allegiance between country and church, between patriotism and pacifism. He heartily concurred with what Teddy Roosevelt once said, "To bear the name of American is to bear the most honored of titles." In the historical context of 1917 and 1918, then, he preferred this title to that of Brother, so to speak.

Yet, as he wanted Brethren to understand, he had not forsaken their cause of peace. After he left office, his public addresses frequently dealt with the horror of war and the peril of militarism. War, he emphasized, leaves people "morally bankrupt" and in need of "spiritual reconstruction." He pleaded for "the spirit of Christ" in attacking the problem of war. He said, "The problem will be solved when all the nations come in the spirit of Christ to do justice to one another."

Brumbaugh's public career, as it turned out, roughly coexisted with the emergence of the Brethren from a self-imposed cultural quarantine into an increasing identification with the wider society. Traditional taboos against voting, holding office, and social activism became passé. To what extent the church's most famous public figure served as a role model for this sociological change is ambiguous. As governor, he got a mixed review of plaudits and faultfinding from Brethren. Henry C. Early, who seven times would be moderator of Annual Conference, wrote to a friend in 1916:

> The feeling of the general brotherhood as to Brother Brumbaugh serving his state as governor is much divided. There is dissatisfaction and there is pleasure among the members with his position, some of the conservative members and congregations are displeased with his being governor.

That same year the *Gospel Messenger*'s Daniel Miller, although originally a Brumbaugh booster, voiced displeasure in a letter to a western Pennsylvania Dunker when the governor sent National Guardsmen to Pittsburgh to quell a labor riot. He wrote, "This is a clear violation of the teaching of the Gospel." He also complained: "The clipping you sent me shows that the Governor is busy even on the Lord's day. If he uses that holy day for political work he is clearly in the wrong."

While conservative Brethren thought the governor had fallen from grace— because of his political activities, his hobnobbing with generals, his personal lifestyle, and his marriage to Flora—college-educated members of the denomination tended to hold him, at least as an educator, in high respect. This was particularly true of the staff people at the church's headquarters in Elgin, Illinois.

But when M. G. died, Charles Ellis scolded the Brethren for having neglected to honor its widely renowned "Brother" during his lifetime. He wrote in the *Gospel Messenger* that the man who probably dedicated more new church houses than any other Brethren preacher of the past—many of them while governor—was never named to any important position in the denomination. That was a terrible disuse of his "great ability," Ellis charged, and undeserving of the church's pioneering historian and the most brilliant interpreter of its genius to the non-Brethren world. The Juniata professor was probably most perturbed that M. G. had never been elected moderator of Annual Conference, then the denomination's highest honor.

If Martin Brumbaugh felt unappreciated by the church he loved, he would have felt just as let down by Keystone State historians. They have attributed to his governorship a very skimpy scrapbook of accomplishments. Take the three most popular general histories of Pennsylvania written since Brumbaugh's death, all by Penn State professors. Philip Klein and Ari Hoogenboom, in their 1973 textbook, write that Brumbaugh "had little sympathy with the idea of legislating progressivism" and "vetoed many reform bills." They go on to say that William Sproul, his successor, "proved far more progressive" than he did.

Sylvester K. Stevens, in an earlier work (1956), sees it the same way. Then holding the title of state historian as well as professor, he writes, "Brumbaugh was a well-meaning man and certainly an outstanding educator, but his political talents were less sure. . . . [He] was the last Pennsylvania governor who publicly espoused the idea that government should not concern itself with the social and general welfare of the people." Sproul, claims Stevens, was clearly a progressive by contrast. The university scholar sums up Brumbaugh's term by saying the "major happening" in the years 1915–18 was "the participation of Pennsylvania in winning World War I.".

The third historian, William F. Dunaway, damns with faint praise. His 1935 textbook, published just five years after the "War Governor's" death, says of him that "he retired from office highly respected for his character and services." But, writes Dunaway, his administration, though "successful" was "not outstanding."

The *Encyclopaedia Britannica*'s columns on "Pennsylvania" (1971 edition), does not even deign to praise faintly. It was authored by Donald H. Kent, then state archivist. Kent skips over the Brumbaugh governorship by name—noting only that a department of labor and industry was organized in 1915. Sproul, however, is cited for his term's legislation on the public-school system, highways, and a department of welfare.

Other people, nonhistorians, have left a different, more subjective version of Brumbaugh's shift at the Executive Mansion. They were his friends, of course, or political appointees. The testimony of four of them will suffice to counterbalance what historians have had to say. In 1917, midway through Brumbaugh's term before it was sidetracked by the war, Michael J. Ryan, spoke to a group of Philadelphia industrialists. A public service commissioner, Ryan said of the man who had appointed him to a subcabinet post:

> Governor Brumbaugh [is a] much misunderstood and maligned public official, [but] his name will stand through the years as one of Pennsylvania's greatest governors. . . . [He] has been at the helm of the State during the time that has been marked by as constructive legislation as ever has been passed by any State.

He declared, "Pennsylvania legislation has kept pace in every way with the advance of civilization."

Edward J. Stackpole, president and editor-in-chief of the *Harrisburg Telegraph,* editorialized in much the same vein two years later, when his friend's term had run out. Soon to be drawn into the Juniata family as a patron and honorary-degree recipient, Stackpole wrote:

> Governor Brumbaugh was the center of political controversy from the moment he was inaugurated, and before, and in the light of what has transpired the wonder is not

that more was not accomplished along constructive and progressive lines, but that so much was done.

The "cold facts" show, the editorial asserted, that "the constructive accomplishments [of the Brumbaugh regime] will stand forth clearly as great influences for good on the life of the Commonwealth."

Stackpole, incidentally, also rated the governor's oratorical and literary ability as high-quality. A 1925 retrospect of his acclaimed Brumbaugh as having been the "most eloquent" chief executive in recent memory and added, "It has been said that no other occupant of the Governor's chair has left among his records finer specimens of English."

Two of M. G.'s closest political friends, Harry Mackey and William Vare, also had no doubts about his exalted niche in the pantheon of Pennsylvania governors. Mackey, an early touter of the Brumbaugh-for-president boom and first head of the Workman's Compensation Bureau, had a ready quotation for the press when told, in 1930, of the former chief executive's fatal heart attack. He said, "I hope that some clear-visioned historian will now accurately assess the great humanitarian value of Governor Brumbaugh's term of office." Mackey, then mayor of Philadelphia, went on to credit the deceased as "alone" being responsible for the "portfolio of laws" protecting Pennsylvania's workforce. Workers, women as well as men, he declared roundly, ought forever to "revere" the late governor's name as the "champion of labor."

Bill Vare paid *his* homage three years after Brumbaugh's death. In his autobiography, the sixty-seven-year-old former Quaker City lawmaker, in poor health and no longer the local GOP heavyweight, writes of the only man he ever personally recruited for a gubernatorial race:

> Brumbaugh was one of the greatest of Pennsylvania Governors and few administrations have approached his in terms of achievements in the way of humanitarian legislation. I feel sanguine that the future will render the full justice to him to which he is entitled. He was a man of broad vision and well in advance of his times.

That "clear-visioned" historian, doing "full justice" to a "humanitarian" administration never came forth in the six decades since Mackey and Vare first called for one. The closest any historian came to fulfilling the two Philadelphia wheelhorses' hopes was in the eight-volumed *Pennsylvania: A History.* It was edited by George P. Donehoo, who had once been state librarian, and published between 1926 and 1931. The section on Brumbaugh's governorship (vol. 3) is concise in style and almost falls into the Dunaway faint-praise mode. But then, oddly, in a lengthy biographical sketch of him (vol. 8), an anonymous chronicler is lavish in praise of his administration, though mentioning no specific legislation. Of his term, the writer says it was notable for "many and important" achievements. Of Brumbaugh, it is said, he constantly gave proof that the public welfare was at all times uppermost in his mind and, in spite of the fact that at various times he had to face strong political opposition, his administration is a fine record of progressive legislation and honest public service.

He got high marks for the war years, too: "Faced by many emergencies and the heavy responsibilities of this difficult period, Governor Brumbaugh proved himself a man of unwavering patriotism, untiring energy and great ability for organization and leadership."

It is somewhat puzzling that, almost to a man, the Pennsylvania fraternity of historians has dismissed Martin Brumbaugh as having been all but a dead loss as governor: a rather colorless, ultraconservative, veto-mad, laissez-faire Old Guard Republican. To describe him as a right-wing stand-patter does not comport with the actions of someone who fervently nominated Teddy Roosevelt at the 1916 Republican Convention and, in 1922, published a little acclamatory biography of the old Bull Mooser, then three years in his grave. Nor does their portrayal of him take into account his admiration for California's governor Hiram W. Johnson, T. R.'s running mate on the Bull Moose ticket in 1912. In the late 1920s Brumbaugh would try to lure the famous Progressive, by then a senator from the Golden State, to Juniata College for an honorary degree. Much more than given credit for, he shared the Roosevelt-Johnson passion for direct democracy and making the sociopolitical system more fair and reasonable.

True, Brumbaugh always spoke of himself as a party "regular," but never as a "conservative." Even as a GOP loyalist he could show an independent streak. And never did he flinch when anybody called him progressive-minded. Indeed, the peroration of his inaugural address hardly comes across as a call for retrenchment. Lawmakers were told: "That [the people] may be safeguarded in their health, their recreation, their education, their homes, their property, their regulated freedom, their toil, should be our constant endeavor." Even earlier, as a gubernatorial campaigner, he had said he thought that the Republican Party had been justly "chastened for its conservatism" in 1912 when the Democrats took over the White House. The lesson for Pennsylvania, according to the candidate: give the people "a large social program of legislative reform."

Martin Brumbaugh's term as governor has been recounted at considerable length in these pages. Yet much of what he had in mind for reinvigorating the Republican Party in Pennsylvania by means of a progressive legislative agenda has been left untold—such as his concern for public health and the need for health-protection regulations; his appointment of a commission to codify and revise banking laws, giving greater protection to depositors and investors; his outspoken interest in the "great problem" of unsanitary housing conditions, in prison reform, and in improving the Philadelphia harbor; his support for the Mothers' Pension Law, to enable widows to keep their children at home and in school; his advocacy of increased provisions for the care and education of the blind; his stand for pure food and drugs and truth-in-marketing; his commitment to increasing the number of game preserves and adding to state-owned forest lands; his fight for coal-mine safety; his call for legislation to enable returning war veterans to complete, tuition-free, their interrupted college education; his anticipatory program to provide employment for the thousands of soldiers, sailors, and marines crippled or disabled as a result of war service; and his dream of a state art gallery ("the finest in America"), publicly funded, to collect and exhibit the works of Pennsylvania's artists.

How explain, then, his Inaugural Day declaration that Pennsylvanians were "over-lawed," and that, too much, lawmaking was presumed the cure-all for societal pockmarks? Also, how account for his record-setting 409 vetoes?

First of all, his "over-lawed" comment must be examined in context. He goes on in the inaugural speech to say, "A government that enriches life and widens the people's vision will endure." Therefore, he argues, "Our laws should be not only regulators of procedure, but educators of the public conscience." He said, "It is the business of government to make it easy to do right and difficult to do wrong." That was the "holy experiment" lawmakers ought to address themselves to.

But he accused legislators of "actually making legal criminals" by multiplying laws "when, as a matter of duty, we should have addressed ourselves to the vastly worthy task of educating our people into an increasing love for liberty, respect for law and devotion to our American civilization." As he told members of the Reading Chamber of Commerce, speaking on this theme of an overregulated state a month later, "the whole mess of nonsense that crept upon our statute books . . . is more honored today in its breach than in its observance." Why not, he asked, "let us see whether we can't depend on old-fashioned common sense and fundamental honesty in the people of this Commonwealth to behave seemly under the old common law for awhile." As a philosophy of government, such ideas seem to suggest, if anything, a libertarian and not a reactionary stance. Nor, by the same token, do they necessarily conflict with a progressive outlook.

But there was another reason Brumbaugh deplored "loose legislation," a term he used in an interview for the *Outlook* in December 1915. It was a "scandal," he told the reporter, that state courts so repeatedly had to strike down bad laws. He said his administration was dedicated to stopping "that waste of energy." The first thing he did as governor, therefore, was to instruct the attorney general to go over every bill coming before the legislature to make sure that, if passed, it would be upheld by the courts. Otherwise, suspect bills ended up "meat-axed."

A scrutiny of bills vetoed by Brumbaugh shows that not a single one of them could be considered a substantive "progressive" measure. A great number fell into the pork-barrel category. Perhaps in decrying excessive laws Brumbaugh meant to serve subtle notice on the Republican machine: self-serving legislation could no longer be taken for granted, as it had been since the days of Boss Quay. As he said in his inaugural address, "We should never make a law that in operation will work

... good only to the selfish or potential few." Brumbaugh also vetoed scores of appropriation bills—in part or wholly—that the General Assembly smugly passed but irresponsibly declined to fund. By constitutional law, Pennsylvania could not then incur indebtedness except by a plebiscite. In his post-Harrisburg years, Brumbaugh liked to recall how he left office with every state debt paid, but the law dictated he had to.

Finally, to regard his bounteous vetoes as prima facie evidence of a holding-the-line administration fails to recognize how much he had been victimized by the vindictiveness of the Penrose pack on Harrisburg's Capitol Hill. Many of Martin's friends thought it a certainty that he would have been elected president of the United States had he been governor of any other state at that time than machine-tyrannized Pennsylvania. That era's frequent moderator of the Church of the Brethren, Henry C. Early, voiced the same opinion, according to Bethany Seminary professor Floyd E. Mallott in a 1951 interview by Harold Statler.

Brumbaugh's ideal of public service, as he emphasized in his inaugural address, was "the unselfish leadership of clean men." As a school superintendent and then as governor, he liked to hand out little cards with upbeat mottoes on them and always displayed a Teddy Roosevelt-like saying on his desk about "playing hard but fair." Boies Penrose taught him that the political game is often played by another code. Probably no other chief executive of the state ever had to cope with a legislature as recalcitrant, obstructionist, and rancorous as the Penrose-policed one of 1917. Said his private secretary, William Ball, of Brumbaugh's troublous tenure: "We prayed ourselves through many difficult times."

Nor has any Pennsylvania governor proved so confrontational vis-à-vis a machine boss, especially Penrose, as the Dunker schoolman. Certainly not William Sproul. Ironically, virtually every popular measure passed during Sproul's Penrose-blessed administration had been initiated and agitated by his beleaguered and checkmated predecessor: the Eighteenth and Nineteenth Amendments to the Constitution of the United States; bond loans for a great highway-building program; enlarging the State Police force; construction of the Delaware River Bridge; further reform of the public-school system; and rehabilitation and relief work among returning war veterans.

The day after he left office, Brumbaugh, in a rare display of gasconading, told reporters:

> What ever you or others might think, I tell you that I have been the best Governor this State has had in many years and, perhaps, ever had. I had integrity and vision, and I believe that is why party leaders could not endure me.

His last words to the press about his watch at the state helm, according to LeRoy Greene, were, "I rather enjoyed it."

Then he and Flora headed south to Pinehurst, for several weeks of post-gubernatorial recuperation.

15

Juniata College:
Presidential Encore

IN January 1919 Martin Brumbaugh, nearing his fifty-seventh birthday, found himself an ex-governor without a job or, in those days, a pension. At first it looked as though he had a choice between two temporary income-earning situations. To his great disappointment, however, both fell through.

During the last month of his administration, the War History Commission announced that, when his term was up, he would be appointed state war historian. The position was to carry a salary of ten thousand dollars a year. The commission, created in June 1918, collected everything relating to Pennsylvania in the war: from military records to legal, constitutional, and political affairs; to economic, industrial, and financial activities; to social, educational, and religious aspects. It was expected that the commission would edit and publish this vast store of materials when peace came. To its members, the departing chief executive seemed the ideal person to handle the project for them. But a Penrose ally filed for an injunction to stop the appointment, and Martin put out public word he would not fight it. So the mass of wartime documents and reports, collected at great expense, ended up in the state library and at the state arsenal, unclassified and unpublished.

At the time Martin declined the prospect of becoming war historian, he told newsmen that he would instead "accept a position as one of three educational commissioners to be sent by the United States to France." He said, "Large numbers of American troops are to remain abroad some time and the government plans to look after their education while they are abroad." His statement to the press left no doubts: "I am going to be one of the commissioners." His overseas duty would allow him "to learn as well as teach," newsmen were told. After one or two years he would return to this country and "lecture on his experiences."

There is nothing in his private papers to suggest that an assignment to this kind of postwar civilian duty in Europe came from Uncle Sam. Rather, it seems that he was angling for it through the National War Work Council (NWWC) of the YMCA. And at the time he talked to reporters nothing was certain in his case. Martin's date book for 10 January reads: "To N.Y. Y.M.C.A. to Europe?"

The NWWC, as Martin knew, came into existence when the United States declared war. It did religious work with soldiers and POWs, eventually enlisting twenty-six thousand men and women. He wrote to a cast of friends—among them Congressman Simeon Fess, Francis Brown, Nathan Schaeffer, Edgar Fahs Smith, United States Commissioner of Education Philander P. Claston, and Russell Conwell—asking each man to intercede for him with the NWWC. He said,

> I have a great desire to further serve our boys by going over to help in the great Educational work now organizing for the Army of Occupation. There is an opening and a call to me for important Executive and administrative work.

These hopes were soon dashed, however. John R. Mott, world-famous YMCA organizer and leader and, in 1919, head of the NWWC, replied that there were no such openings. Why Martin gave reporters the impression he was all but on the boat for France is strange indeed.*

The pages of his date book for the spring and summer are blank except for a half-dozen or so notations of speaking engagements in Ohio, New York, and Pennsylvania. On 23 June the University of Maine conferred upon him his seventh and last honorary degree, an LL.D.

Three days later, his daughter Mabel, at age thirty-three, married Ralph P. Lewars, a widower with a son. The wedding took place at the Brumbaugh Germantown home. In a couple of years the Lewars would present Martin with his only Brumbaugh-blooded grandchild—Kenneth B. Lewars.

Then on the 28th Martin got word of the death of eighty-three-year-old Henry B. Brumbaugh, the senior member and chairman of the Juniata College board of trustees. The trustees immediately elected M. G. their presiding officer. Of the three Brumbaugh founders, only Henry's brother, John, survived, and he would be gone in another three years.

Flora and M. G. spent the rest of the summer at Wayne, during which he taught at Bates College at Lewiston. By the time they returned home the last week of September, he had lined up months of lectures and appearances at educational functions. It was like the old days, when his professional life was wrapped up in teachers' institutes and he was forever on the run. With 1920, the tempo of his platform schedule became even more allegro, leaving Flora—as his jet-speed pace had once left Anna—a virtual grass widow. His date book shows that during the last months of 1921 he spoke in at least twenty-eight states.

For two years his was a stellar name for the traveling Chautauquas. In 1921 it was estimated that thirty-five million Americans attended these small-town Chautauquas, held in huge canvas tents. Ida Grove, Iowa, hyped ticket sales for

---

*In July 1921 Brumbaugh, still in search of a permanent job, contacted President Penniman about a possible deanship at Penn. Penniman was receptive to the idea, and a vacancy did occur, but the board of trustees opted for someone at the university.

Brumbaugh's lectures by calling him "one of the greatest men in the country"—a "fine speaker and a great story teller." He has "the statesmanship of a great mind," proclaimed the promotional spiel.

He was deemed enough of a drawing card to be scheduled at Lake Chautauqua, New York, itself in the summer of 1922. Among those sharing the billing with him was William Jennings Bryan. Now a Miamian, Bryan used a palm-frond fan—as he would a few years later during the Scopes "monkey trial"—for relief from the heat. Charmed by Flora Brumbaugh, he gave her a battery-powered minifan, which was quite a curiosity in those days, to carry around for cooling comfort.

Among other topics, Chautauquans heard Brumbaugh address the problem of illiteracy in postwar America. The recent draft revealed shocking evidence of widespread illiteracy among native-born Americans. But a greater threat to the American way came from illiterate immigrants, in Brumbaugh's thinking. Like Teddy Roosevelt, he despaired at how slowly the more recent foreigners from southern and eastern Europe were blending into the "melting pot." And like Teddy, he could talk tough about what ought to be done. If he had his way, he said, "I'd say to immigrants, if at the end of five years you haven't learned the English language then get out and stay out. . . . If there'd be more stiffening up of our backbone there'd be less of this red flag menace, of which we have had more than you know." Unpleasant as it may seem, he thundered, "speedy deportation is the only national safeguard."

This was a very popular view in that era of the Red Scare, when nativists were crying for Congress to stem the foreign flood by imposing strict nationality quotas. The so-called "Americanization" crisis also allowed him to accentuate some of his pet themes: public education as the crucible of American democracy, love of American institutions, and teaching as a moral function in creating worthy citizens.

Two years earlier, in October 1920, the Republican National Committee made use of his platform powers, for pay, in behalf of the Harding-Coolidge presidential ticket. Republicans regained control of Congress, and would not relinquish it for another decade. Martin juggled his stumping for the party with his Chautauqua itinerary. It took him to the Southwest, the Plains states, the Midwest, New York, and New England. In November the tobacco-chewing, poker-playing, whiskey-drinking, roving-eyed Harding won by a thundering margin (60.3 percent), the greatest majority in an American presidential election up to that date.

But the Ohio senator's White House days were numbered; he died on 2 August 1923, in San Francisco, while returning from a speechmaking tour across the country that took him all the way to Alaska. Just before his death he had received news— sent him in a ciphered message—of impending scandals involving cabinet members. Some people said he died of a broken heart.

Brumbaugh sadly noted the president's death that Thursday in his date book; he was in Wayne. He spoke at a memorial service there on Sunday and twice more the following Friday, at nearby Livermore Falls and Wilton. Later that year, he became a fund-raiser for the Harding Memorial Association. Speaking in behalf of the association to a gathering of Philadelphia Republicans in December, he said:

> It may be truly said that his untimely death was due to the war. He was soon tired in high office. Those to whom he confidently turned in an earnest endeavor to help arouse in the American people, as speedily as possible, a realization of the critical situations, domestic and foreign, facing the nation, were not infrequently hostile [*sic*] or at least indifferent to, the tragedies of the times. *It was this that saddened his official life and, it may be safely declared, led to his death.* [Italics added]

Again in 1924 the Republican National Committee would come after him, this time to politick for "Silent Cal" Coolidge, who had moved into the White House after Harding's death. In the fall, then, he pitched in like "a good soldier" to help return the famously laconic New Englander to the Oval Office. He made this commitment even though he knew, prior to the Grand Old Party's June convention in Cleveland, that he had been elected president of his alma mater.

Politics, however, never seriously engaged him after he left the governor's mansion. But two other causes did: recreation and physical fitness. In the first instance, he worked with Community Service (he may have been one of its founders), an organization established in 1920 with national headquarters in New York City. Community Service, which was allied with the Playground and Recreation Association of America, promoted the idea of neighborhood centers as municipal agencies to foster diversified recreational use of leisure time.

Brumbaugh became Community Service's major epistolary contact with mayors of large cities throughout the country and also a much-traveled speaker in its behalf. He spoke at the Recreation Congress held in Atlantic City in October 1922; his address later appeared in the February 1923 issue of the *Playground,* organ of the Playground and Recreation Association of America. That year, 680 cities had playgrounds and community centers. This represented remarkable progress, but what kept Brumbaugh energized in his cause was the knowledge that as many as 1280 cities with a population of five thousand or more had neither playgrounds nor community recreation of any kind.

His prominence as a spokesman for Community Service brought him an invitation to participate in the National Conference on Outdoor Recreation, called by President Coolidge. Chaired by Theodore Roosevelt, Jr., assistant secretary of the navy, the conference was held in Washington, D.C., on 22–24 May 1924. The program was wide-ranging, covering national parks and forests, hunting, fishing, wild flowers, Scouting, camping, playgrounds, and other alfresco topics. Roosevelt appointed Martin to the General Resolutions Committee, whose work, wrote Teddy's son, would be "extremely important and arduous" and the bases of "action by the conference." He was also asked to be a featured speaker.

There were 309 delegates—from 128 organizations—in attendance. They heard

Brumbaugh speak on Friday afternoon, the 23rd, on the subject, "Citizenship Values of Outdoor Recreation." His thesis was that leisure time is double-barreled: it can be "full of menace" or it can be "full of blessing." According to his argument, America, in an age of increasing leisure, must make free time count for the intellectual, social, and physical betterment of its people. Only in this way can the nation "stem the tide of crime and physical decay." In Puerto Rico, Brumbaugh said, he found that "the ideals of American life were more quickly acquired through play than through education." Puerto Rican children at play more quickly learned the English language and the American spirit of going by the rules of the game, he maintained. The speech was published in the July 1924 edition of the *Playground*.

The conference produced a long list of resolutions, one of which recommended the formation of a permanent national organization on outdoor recreation that would convene annually. An advisory council of seventy members, each to serve one year, would work with a presidential committee in planning future conferences. Martin Brumbaugh was elected to this initiatory council—but representing the National Physical Education Service, not Community Service.

In the years between 1919 and 1924, he gave even more time to the National Physical Education Service (NPES) than to the cause of playgrounds and outdoor recreation. The NPES, another spawn of the Playground and Recreation Association of America, was formed in 1918 and set up its head office in Washington, D.C. It devoted its efforts to securing national and state legislation for physical education in the public schools.

It had field representatives—Brumbaugh became one in late 1919—lobbying at all political levels, furnishing drafts of bills, giving speeches, and turning out articles for popular, professional, and religious magazines. Martin himself wangled frequent appearances before state legislatures. In 1919 only eleven states, including Pennsylvania, had laws that in some degree promoted public-school physical education. By 1922 the count had been raised to twenty-eight states.

As a speechifier for the NPES, he roamed as far south as Louisiana, his first visit to Cajun Country since his teachers' institute summers. Colonel Thomas Boyd, who had brought Martin as a young man to the Pelican State to help build the foundation of a public-school system there, heard his sales pitch and said he "made a killin'." Another prominent Louisiana educator and Brumbaugh fan since those summer institute days, Edwin Stephens, thought so, too. He later wrote a letter to "Dear Old 'Brumy'," rejoicing in the "re-flaming of the sacred fires of old friendship." The letter included a poetic tribute:

> With blessed consciousness of duty done
> Thru shock of war, with vict'ry cónsummate,
> Takes now his holiday from helm of State
> The big-brow'd, great-soul'd son of Huntingdon
> And comes he first to the realm of Southern Sun

Where erst in early manhood's prime estate
His eloquence in lecture and debate
From Lethargy the teacher's cult had won.

Meanwhile a mighty harvest gathered is
From seeds he then had helpt select and sow,
Of free instruction unto ev'ry child
With fear of God and love of Truth and Law:
Wherefore 'tis meet that midst his honors piled
Be laid a Sheaf of Southern Memories.

—E.L.S.

Lafayette, Louisiana,
November 27, 1919

Stephens had a daughter, whom Brumbaugh never met, but as a girl she regularly wrote to "Uncle Brumy," who faithfully answered each letter.

The National Physical Education Service took its rise at a time of growing pressure on Congress to pass a law dictating compulsory military training for all males between the ages of eighteen and twenty-one. Many Foggy Bottom lawmakers tended to like that idea. The reason was twofold: to buttress a downsized standing army and to address a serious national health problem.

The nation had been shocked to learn in 1917 that 37 percent of the first-round draftees were rejected as physically unfit for military duty. Curiously, rural conscripts flunked their medical examinations in greater numbers than those from the city. Then one year later the National Committee of Health and Education reported that more than three-fourths of American schoolchildren suffered from some sort of serious physical defect. In Pennsylvania the incidence of juvenile infirmity was found to be much lower but still alarming—46.67 percent.

This pitiful showing spurred educators to demand federal funds to promote universal physical education in the nation's schools, nurse and dentist visitation, and basic instruction in hygiene and sanitation. A weak body, the argument went, impairs the mind, which in turn distorts one's view of life. Healthy citizens, by contrast, are disposed to productive, law-abiding lives—as crucial in times of peace as in times of war.

As early as 1918 President Emeritus Charles W. Eliot of Harvard began raising this cry. The National Education Association rallied behind him and formed the Commission on the National Emergency in Education, pushing as well for a Department of Education at Washington. A veritable modern health crusade was thus set afoot, with a dozen or so national agencies, like the National Physical Education Service, springing up to champion the Eliot-NEA agenda. All of them deplored the fact that the United States was doing far less for the physical fettle of its youth than many other nations of the world.

In late 1919, the NPES, with the endorsement of such notables as Major General William C. Gorgas of yellow-fever fame and clinic cofounder Dr. Charles H. Mayo, made its move in the chambers of Capitol Hill. The organization found sponsors for a bill in two mid-Westerners: Representative Simeon Fess, the longtime friend of Brumbaugh, and Senator Arthur Capper, newspaper publisher and former Kansas governor. The NPES-drafted measure they introduced provided for federal aid ($10,000,000) to the states on a matching-grant basis. The funds would go for the training of physical-education teachers. Meanwhile, the National Education Association submitted to Congress a companion measure broader in scope.

Educators tend to be antimilitary in peacetime, and the two bills before Congress registered their constructive opposition to universal military training (UMT). Schoolroom partisans argued that UMT did not guarantee physical fitness. They cited the example of New York State's National Guardsmen: 30 percent failed their "physicals" for induction into the army. Nor did military training include females, it was also emphasized.

Meanwhile, as the late Charles DeBenedetti writes in his *Peace Reform in American History,* many postwar Americans—and especially educators—were of the conviction that UMT was "by definition subversive of democratic principles." They believed, according to the peace historian, that UMT's compulsory nature "would override the sovereignty of the individual conscience," and "by drilling young men in obedience and death-dealing" would undermine "the first values of a free Christian society."

Martin Brumbaugh strongly shared that view. In a letter to Galen B. Royer, then teaching missions at Juniata College, he defined the agitation behind the Fess-Capper Bill as "a vast and truly religious movement. It is in harmony with the teachings of Jesus and ought to enlist the active support of all Christian people." The letter, which Royer had published in the 3 January 1920 issue of the *Gospel Messenger,* went on to say:

> It happens by reasons of my public service, I am able to gain audience and give important assistance to this humane and Christian work, and you may be assured that I do it all the more gladly because of my love for our church and its honored principles.

Brumbaugh urged the Brethren to get involved in fighting compulsory military training. A year later, he made a direct appeal to all Brethren ministers through the church paper to "see" or "write" their home congressmen in support of the Fess-Capper Bill and to prod their congregants to do the same thing. He wrote:

> In this way you can do a tremendously important service for our country and our church. This Bill is so vital to the future welfare of America and to the cause of the Lord, that we can well afford to work heartily for its immediate passage.

Both presidential candidates in the campaign of 1920—Ohio Republican Senator Warren Harding and Ohio Democratic Governor James M. Cox—had come out for some kind of federal "encouragement" of universal physical education. So had the GOP platform, promising to take effective action. Along with E. Dana Caulkins, head of the National Physical Education Association, Martin Brumbaugh became a key lobbyist for the Fess-Capper Bill. The two men were also its chief spokesmen when the House Committee on Education, chaired by Simeon Fess, held hearings on it in January and February 1921.

On Friday, 27 February, Brumbaugh and Fess met with President Harding in the Oval Office about the possibility of a national conference on the educational rationale for physical training. Harding asked Brumbaugh to prepare a rough draft of what might go into a presidential proclamation calling for such a gathering. Martin promptly did this and was promised he would hear very soon what the plans were for a conference. Hearing nothing after a few months, Brumbaugh, vacationing at Wayne, wrote the president, asking whether or not he had made a decision. Harding replied that since Congress seemed to be foot-dragging on the Fess-Capper Bill, he did not want to go public in its behalf until there was stronger sentiment for it at the other end of Pennsylvania Avenue.

This was a great disappointment to NPESers, since the bill had now been before Congress for almost two years. Martin Brumbaugh himself turned to an acquaintance of recent years, Secretary of State Charles E. Hughes, in an effort to prod the administration. In December he wrote Hughes an appreciative letter apropos of his startling proposal, put forth at the current Washington Disarmament Conference, calling for the world's major naval powers to measurably scale down their battle fleets by scrapping ships and limiting future growth of their navies. Now that the United States had rejected the Treaty of Versailles and the League of Nations, Brumbaugh thought Hughes's globe-shaping initiative to be an imaginative stroke for international peace. But the real purpose of his letter was to urge Hughes to side publicly with the National Physical Education Service's crusade and endorse its bill.

Hughes chose to keep silent, but a year later, in the fall of 1922, President Harding did keep his word to Brumbaugh and Fess, despite Congress's inertia on the NPES's bill. Through Secretary of War John W. Weeks, he issued a call for a national conference on the mental and physical health of America's youth. It was held in the nation's capital on 16–18 November, with Martin Brumbaugh prominently among the delegates. Weeks, hobbled by a wrenched ankle suffered in a recent automobile accident, presided at the conference. Top military men, like Army Chief of Staff John J. Pershing, delivered jeremiads about the alarming subnormal physical condition of young Americans as evidenced by draftees in the late war. The delegates unanimously resolved that

a comprehensive, thoroughgoing program of universal physical training is of pressing and vital importance to the nation, particularly for all boys and all girls under the age of nineteen in all communities, rural and urban, in every state of the Union.

According to Brumbaugh, everybody left the conference in the high hope that Congress would now, at last, come to befriend what he called the most important educational reform then before the American people. They had seen education make giant strides by the 1920s, undergirded by laws that prolonged schooling. Most states by that decade required young people to remain in school until age sixteen. The number of high-school graduates was on a steady rise, to about one in four among all teenagers. And more and more states were legislating physical education into their curriculums. This last trend, which Brumbaugh and his fellow reformers cheered on, in the end worked against their cause at Washington. For, as time passed, an indifferent Congress saw no need for federal intervention; both the Fess-Capper Bill and the NEA's eventually died in committee.

Meanwhile, Brumbaugh found enough free time in 1922 to author a minibiography of Theodore Roosevelt. Printed in paperback by the F. A. Owen Publishing Company of Danville, Ohio, *The Story of Roosevelt* was designed for public-school use and pitched at the eighth-grade level. In its sixty-four pages, the biographer extolled the athletic preacher of virile virtues and fair play as the exemplar of American citizenship. Juvenile readers learned that young Teddy became "a sturdy, active strenuous leader of his fellows" by building up his spindly, asthmatic body through a daily regimen of exercise with bars and rings and weights. They read how he further developed his physique as a ranchman and cowboy in North Dakota. Taunted as "Four Eyes" by the local buckaroos because he wore spectacles, the tenderfoot from New York soon won their respect and admiration as a horseman and boxer, having hardened his body into "clear bone, muscle, and grit," wrote Brumbaugh.

To him, an ardent spokesman for the Fess-Capper Bill, Teddy's struggle for health served as a contemporary paradigm:

> His heroic example in gaining for himself the strength of body so necessary to a successful career is an inspiration to all young Americans. Physical fitness is the basis of intellectual and moral fitness. A nation that does not directly train for physical power in its people will never achieve leadership or accomplish larger services for mankind.

Thus in portraying Roosevelt as an American paragon, both as private citizen and public figure, the book's recurrent theme is his doctrine of the "strenuous life," a phrase the hyperkinetic Rough Rider himself coined. Brumbaugh's résumé of the character, genius, and ideals of the man he once nominated for president reads:

> He touched life in more ways than any other American of his time. He was a man of wide scholarship, an authority on natural history, a fine historian, a great political leader, a lover of the out-of-doors, a devoted friend of all oppressed people, an admirable husband and father, and a defender of the power and dignity of the country he loved. For the United States of America he lived, and for it, in a very real sense, he gave his life.

"His death," said the author, "brought profound sorrow to the entire nation." There followed a quote from a eulogy of Roosevelt by William Howard Taft: "The nation has lost the most commanding, the most original, the most interesting, the most brilliant personality in American public life since Lincoln." Brumbaugh thought these words were richly deserved by an incorruptible Progressive who "taught all Americans, save the office-seeking horde, that public office is a public trust, and that only those should hold office who honestly and capably serve the whole people."

A couple of much more scholarly biographies of T. R. had already been published, but his sister, Corrine Roosevelt Robinson, who had written one of her own, told Brumbaugh that his was the best to date.

Primarily, however, it was as a lecturer, not as a writer, that Brumbaugh made his living between 1919 and 1924. He crisscrossed the country on behalf of the teaching profession, public playgrounds and physical education, the Republican Party, and the traveling Chautauqua. In the meantime, he had invested his money wisely, especially in farm mortgages. All told, by 1924 he enjoyed a comfortable income of seventy-five hundred dollars a year. That provided the Brumbaughs with the amenities of an upper-middle-class life.

By middecade, as anyone could see, the Twenties had taken to "roaring"— both in terms of the nation's mass-consumption economy and the moral climate. A revolution in lifestyles and values was underway, creating social tensions that were partly generational. Victorian moral codes caved in to new and shocking behavior, symbolized by the cigarette-smoking, speakeasy-haunting, stockings-rolled-down, short-haired, short-skirted, rouge-cheeked and lipsticked "flapper" girl. Jazz-loving American youth championed Freudian sexual liberation and frankness, use of contraceptives, and equal rights for women. It was the era of Scarface Al Capone and bootleg liquor, the reborn Klu Klux Klan and its "one-hundred percent American" nativism, fundamentalism versus modernism and the Scopes "monkey" trial, the radio revolution, the first "talkie" movies, the Harlem Renaissance, and angry and frustrated writers critical of American society.

On many small college campuses students rebelled against *in loco parentis,* clamoring for less intramural social restraints. Martin Brumbaugh's alma mater was no exception. As trustee chairman he was well aware of unrest among postwar Juniatians. In 1919 their clamorings pressured the faculty into condoning a Council of Co-operation that gave the student body a voice on academic matters. Trumpeted the *Echo,* now student-edited: "This marks the beginning of a new era in the student life at Juniata. And why not? Co-operation is the advance word of progress; and the spirit of democracy dominates in the new order of things following the war."

Then in 1922 College Hill got a full-fledged student government. Two self-governing bodies—one for men and one for women—regulated dorm and campus life, administering penalties by a system of demerits. What was heralded as the

New Youth movement had at last brought democracy in full measure to Juniata, exulted the *Echo*, overstating the situation. In point of fact, social restrictions remained as tight as ever. Students were not at liberty to fix rules without faculty review; nor could they enforce penalties without approval from on high.

Nevertheless, from 1920 on some of the trustees became more and more upset about campus discipline, which they felt was "far below what it should be." These troubled trustees began to nag the faculty and the president to show "more concern." They still saw Juniata as an "institution of the church," dedicated to teaching "true Christian piety," despite the college's rewritten charter of 1908.

The reactionary element of the board had sought ever since then to reaffirm Juniata's historic ties with the church. They were unhappy that the new charter deleted Brethrenism as a condition for becoming a trustee, a clause that Martin Brumbaugh had urged upon the board. (The board's bylaws had been amended in 1918 to reinstate this criterion.) Then in 1923 the conservative faction got in another lick: effecting a rewrite of that section of the charter on the college's mission. Greater emphasis was placed upon Juniata's commitment "to perpetuate good and sound learning . . . imbued with Christian purpose."

By the mid-1920s, then, College Hill was beset by all sorts of tensions, but none more troubling than that of student life. On more than one occasion, President Harvey Brumbaugh had suggested bringing back his cousin M. G., the trustee head, to replace him and straighten things out. Perhaps the campus's longtime hero could awe the students into more respect for authority, he pointed out. All the clamor finally got the better of him, and in February 1924 he asked for a sabbatical. He was a tired administrator—twenty-eight years he had run the school in one capacity or another. The trustees honored his request for a leave unhesitatingly. But Vice-President Charles Ellis balked when told he would be the interim deputy while Harvey was gone.

Ellis had more than one reason to protest: he did not want to give up his teachers' institute work; he thought it an "unfortunate time" for Harvey to go away, what with the paramount problem of student ferment and the need for someone to keep a tight hand on things; and, as he wrote to M. G., just beyond the horizon—in 1926—loomed Juniata's semicentennial and all the dollar signs it conjured up. Thwarted, Harvey saw no way out except to resign.

The trustees feared the college was in crisis not only because of a leadership problem. The Middle States Association of Colleges and Secondary Schools told Juniata it would have to close the Academy in the spring if Juniata wished to gain accreditation. An Academy-less campus meant a frightful drop in enrollment and revenue. The only hope, the majority of board members felt, was to persuade their charismatic chairman to become the college president.

Prior to the 2 June board meeting they swamped him with mail, beseeching him to come to the "rescue of Juniata College," as Jennie Stouffer (Newcomer), a trustee since 1900, put it. She further exhorted, "You surely cannot close your mind to the fact that you are the man for the crisis." Frank Foster, a local non-Juniatian, said: "You are the one man that can bring harmony out of discord, order out of the confusion that exists at the college."

To the chorus of epistolary appeals, Charles Ellis, to whom New Youth gains were something of a scandal, added a refrain of his own. He said student leaders must be left "under no misapprehension as to the fact that all their authority is delegated to them from the trustees through the faculty." He mentioned the need of a "capable [night] watchman" and "more campus light." He abominated the many opportunities men and women had—or took—to be alone together.

As for fund-raising, he told Martin that he was "the only opportunity I see for *permanence*" in the "Greater Juniata" Campaign, an endowment drive of five hundred thousand dollars begun in 1918. Since then, the trustee chairman himself had come through with a bundle of war bonds worth ten thousand dollars. Although the drive had gone "over the top" by 1923, Ellis said that an M. G. presidency was "the only way to get a vigorous administration . . . that [would] command the largest enthusiasm for the 50th anniversary."

He went on, playing upon Martin's legacy of dedication to his alma mater:

> I feel that [the presidency] offers an opportunity greater by far than any political honor likely to open to you in this same period, and in addition it puts you back . . . in the field where you really belong by training, adaptation and successful achievement, namely the field of education.

Ellis hastened to say he did not mean to "discount your service in the governorship." But, he argued, politics was for a time "your avocation"; now "your real vocation is calling again"—"in the place where your real heart interest is."

The one-page letter was an eloquent cri du coeur from Martin's erstwhile protégé and no doubt helped persuade him to accept the presidency. His stated reason for finally accepting was because "Juniata is a church College. . . . I'd not go if it were not for that fact." That is what he wrote to his forty-one-year-old cousin, Norman J. (Jacob Brumbaugh's only offspring), whom he was trying to woo back to Huntingdon with a professorship. He told the sworn bachelor—who accepted, and whose quarter century of illustrious, and legendary, headship of the chemistry department would bring it national recognition—

> I firmly hold to the value of a sound religious education and I want to make not only worthy scholars but charactered people—and this is possible only through religious training.

M. G.'s was a routine election when the board convened on commencement morning, 2 June. But there remained the matter of compensation; the college could not hope to match his current income. It was proposed that he supplement his president's salary with lecture fees. Martin shook his head on that idea, as did Flora. She was tired of her husband's being away so much of the time. He finally agreed on a salary of five thousand dollars. Heretofore, the president earned only nominally more than the highest paid professors; now it would be twice as much.

Also, it was understood, his cigars and pipes were quarantined to his domicile. The campus was then still smoke-free—for moral reasons, not medical ones.

As president-elect, he immediately resigned his board chairmanship.

Two weeks later, Dr. Oscar J. Snyder, founder and trustee head of the Philadelphia College of Osteopathy, approached Brumbaugh about taking over that institution. He must not have known about Juniata's prior claim on his friend. Martin, very reluctant to leave the Philadelphia area, seems to have been intrigued by this proposition, despite what had happened at Huntingdon on the 2nd. Evidently, it can be inferred from a Snyder letter to him, he tried to back out of the Juniata presidency. On 26 June the osteopath wrote, "I am not surprised that they would not release you at Juniata. What is our loss will be their gain and in all probability the work there will be much more congenial."

While at Wayne that summer he put in another stint at Bates College, from 8 July to 8 August, for which he was paid four hundred and fifty dollars.

It had been agreed that he would not assume the presidency of Juniata until the first of December, so that he could honor his teachers' institute engagements already scheduled for the fall. Also, he wanted to be available to the Republican Party, whose message to voters that year was "Keep Cool with Coolidge."

On Wednesday, 1 October, he and Flora dined for the last time at their Germantown home. That same day Martin signed over the West Walnut Lane property for forty thousand dollars. He wasted no time investing the purchase price in the bullish stock market of the mid-Twenties—putting more than half of it in Pennsylvania Railroad shares.

The day before their last Walnut Lane repast, the Brumbaughs had shipped their furniture and other household things by van to Huntingdon. There they lived in cousin Harvey's house while he was away at Columbia. Then, upon his return, they moved into the second floor of the Mission Home, a just-completed brick, rectangular two-story building. Located two blocks west of the campus, the Mission Home had been erected, on a lot donated to the college, by the Brethren Sunday schools of the area as a retreat for missionaries on furlough. (It is a college dormitory today.)

The upstairs apartment must have seemed a great comedown to the Brumbaughs, whose spacious Germantown residence had been resplendent with rich, ornate woodwork and high, chandeliered ceilings, and a grand sweeping staircase. The Mission Home once elicited an embarrassing reaction from a distinguished visitor. The guest was former Secretary of the Navy Josephus Daniels (a teetotaler and near-pacifist), whom Martin got to know during the war. Daniels, whom Franklin D. Roosevelt would one day name as United States ambassador to Mexico, came to the campus to receive an honorary degree. When he saw the Mission Home, he burst out in astonishment, "Why, Governor, is *this* where you live?"

Obviously, the Mission Home put Juniata's president, although a consummate sophisticate, at a serious handicap in courting the patronage of his wealthy and politically high-placed friends. So he arranged overnight hotel lodging in downtown Huntingdon for men like William Woodin and Charles Schwab (who in the spring of 1926 showed up at College Hill on Founders Day in a chauffeur-driven, topless Stutz Bearcat), when they came for honorary degrees. Even before Martin began his encore as Juniata's helmsman, he had urged the trustees to do something about a college-owned president's home. But the board kept putting it off for four years.

Another thing bothered Juniata's repeat-president. He was not particularly pleased to learn that students saw him as their deliverer from the "screws"—a word they used—that had been put on them of late. An editorial in the *Echo*—which became a weekly in November 1924 and was renamed the *Juniatian*—voiced expectation that someone with the new president's background would "not long entertain some of the characteristic medieval narrowmindedness which has long been present [on campus]."

But M. G. himself was not fully sold on student government. As a matter of fact, he served notice on rambunctious New Youthers right from the beginning that he would run the college much the way his cousin Harvey had: as a "right little, tight little college." Juniata, he emphasized,

> is a Christian College—dedicated to the advancement of right living here and teaching that there is a hereafter of tremendous significance. This College teaches the Supremacy of God, the deity of Jesus, the power and presence of the Holy Spirit. It accepts without apology the inspiration of the Bible and teaches that it and it alone holds in its enfolding teachings the hope of immortal life through the resurrection of Christ of the World. From this ideal I pray we shall never depart. In this respect the College is not only conservative, it is immovable.

Therefore, he said, "We shall not only endeavor to teach right but we shall insist that our pupils shall do the right."

He deplored the fact that the student generation of the Twenties embodied a disturbing set of moral and cultural values. Spiritual ideals, he lamented, lay "shattered" and "broken" in the wake of war, the American way vitiated by an increasingly secularized society. This gave rise, in his view of things, to a set of problems more complex than college administrations had ever before faced. But during his presidency, he vowed, the values of Juniata would not change. He intended that it "be counted among those agencies that stand in a crisis for law, for country, for righteousness."

His presidency, he said, entertained "no ambitious dreams or plans for a college of many thousands." He thought it "essential" that Juniata remain a small college, optimally with an enrollment of five hundred. This would ensure a campus community in "close personal touch," he believed. Moreover, as he had written to his cousin Norman, "We cannot compete in any big way with great schools in imparting knowledge." Rather, he said, "It is in the range of educational by-products that we must excel. As I see it now—fine Christian character is the big, meaningful by-product we shall stress."

That meant, he went on to say, he wanted, as president, a faculty that was "as enthusiastic for conduct of a worthy sort as for knowledge of a high order." He said Juniata had had a few professors in the past who "in secret laughed at our religious concerns." He knew of none now, he said, but "If I find one, he goes." He envisioned an M. G.–fashioned college as being "sincere, genuine, frank, open about our goals." Therefore, wrote the incoming president:

> My great desire is to have Juniata measured in terms of its product. I want a family of
> loyal scholars—sound in knowledge, firm in teaching powers and decent and moral
> in soul. For such I shall search and for them I shall seek financial aid to make them
> comfortable and permanent. It can, it must be done.

M. G. had taken over a school of 327 students and 29 faculty members, of whom 7 held earned doctorates. Summer sessions swelled to a student body of 485. There were eighteen academic departments. Nine buildings stood on a nine-acre main campus (adjoining property added a little over fourteen more acres). Total costs for tuition, room, and board for the year ran to a little over four hundred dollars. The physical plant was worth a half-million dollars. The college's endowment amounted to a few thousand dollars more. Thanks to thrifty management, Juniata was solvent, and owed not a cent of mortgage indebtedness on its grounds and buildings. Administratively, M. G. retained Charles Ellis as vice-president and welcomed Harvey Brumbaugh back from his sabbatical at Columbia by naming him professor of classics and director of summer school.

Academically, Juniata was in sound condition. In the spring of 1922 it had gained accreditation by the Middle States Association of Colleges and Secondary Schools. This automatically qualified the college for recognition by the American Medical Association. The library ranked eleventh among the colleges and universities in the state, the legacy of Martin's personal interest over the years.

Brumbaugh's fabled sway over people soon had all segments of the campus in a much friendlier mood. Some skeptical trustees, however, questioned whether everything was really under control, especially after the president wrote in his first annual report to the board that he would much rather be an "adviser" to students than a "disciplinarian." Photographs in the *Alfarata,* the college yearbook, showed raised hemlines, though not to "flapper girl" heights. Bobbed hair was common. Only recently the basketball team had been hit by a poker-playing scandal that cost the coach his job and three starters their positions. And everybody knew that after-curfew (9:45 P.M.) trysting behind Ladies Hall was still a popular sport.

At this time more than a third of the student body was non-Brethren. Over 40 percent of the Hilltoppers came from the Keystone State.

M. G.'s prospectus of a "Greater Juniata" (his slogan) had more to do at first with fund-raising than with discipline or academics as such. The college of five hundred students he envisioned would require expanded facilities and greater endowment income. (Students at Juniata, as at other church-related colleges, paid only about a third of their educational costs.) So he and the trustees planned to exploit Juniata's jubilee year to the hilt. They set a campaign goal of $750,000 and engaged the oldest fund-raising firm in the country. The senior class, playfully labeling themselves "M. G.'s Sunbeams," canvassed the student body and netted some thirty-three thousand dollars, an average of almost a hundred dollars per undergraduate. The faculty came through with subscriptions in excess of fifteen thousand dollars, and the trustees nearly ten times that.

But the jubilee campaign turned out to be somewhat less than a rousing success. It fell short of its goal by more than just a few thousand dollars. This was the first in a series of disappointments for Martin, who wanted to show the larger world that Juniata was not a backwoods sectarian college. His dream was to make the school more visible to Pennsylvanians, to "firmly entrench" it, he once said, speaking with double meaning, "in the heart of the Commonwealth."

He had built the events of Founders Day weekend 1926 around the theme of "law and law observance." Robert von Moschzisker, chief justice of the Pennsylvania Supreme Court, gave the main address. In introducing Judge von Moschzisker, Brumbaugh hailed education, as he so often had, "as the means and safeguard of American Democracy." From "Jubilee to Jubilee," he adjured, the College must always honor "in an enlightened way the values of our country."

The college's president not only brought jurists and political and educator friends of his to the campus that Golden Jubilee weekend in April but also two others, both big names in the state's business and industrial world: "57 Varieties" Howard Heinz and Bethlehem Steel's Charles Schwab. Each received an honorary degree, but the payoff was practically nil. Heinz did make a modest gift; Schwab, however, proved closefisted. He felt insulted by someone's lack of tact in soliciting his philanthropic help. Instead, he became a benefactor of Penn State.

Brumbaugh, as Dr. Salvatore M. Messina notes in his unpublished Ph.D. dissertation, apparently disliked cadging monetary gifts from his friends. Mrs. Anna Shively, wife of the mathematics professor, once visited Flora Brumbaugh in the Mission Home apartment. According to Messina, she saw Martin lying on the couch, obviously disturbed. She asked what was wrong, and he said he was worried about "raising money for the College." He added that he "had some rich friends, [but] could not ask them for money because they were friends."

It soon became apparent—to a frustrated M. G.—that he lacked the Midas touch in cultivating big-money men. He could get nabobs to campus—besides Schwab and Heinz there came Bruce Barton, Josephus Daniels, Owen Roberts, and William Woodin—but never with their checkbooks. In the case of Woodin, the railroad-banking magnate and later Franklin Roosevelt's secretary of the treasury, the antics of silly students probably jinxed his 1929 Hilltop visit. Everybody knew why he was getting an honorary degree on Founders Day, and a gang of fellows stood outside the president's office chanting, "We want Woodin nickels."

Claude Flory remembers that day. A farm boy from eastern Pennsylvania, he became the Brumbaughs' chauffeur his freshman year, 1925. Years later, looking back at the Woodin affair, he said he had come to understand why the well-to-do friends of "Prexy," as students affectionately called him, proved so ungenerous toward Juniata: "I now realize that while the campus of those days looked all right to most of us country students it must have looked terribly unsophisticated—a hopeless educational investment—to men of national and international experience."

The only important academic gain from Brumbaugh's scenario for a "Greater Juniata" was membership in the Association of American Colleges (AAC). Founded in 1915, the AAC had become the patron saint of liberal arts institutions. Its blessing was bestowed on Juniata in January 1927.

There was always golf—at Huntingdon and Pinehurst—and summers fishing in Maine to take his mind off money-raising disappointments. In 1927 sophomore Claude Flory wrote a little story for the *Juniatian* facetiously titled: "WORLD'S RECORD FOR THE 'PREXY'—Fifty-three fish in ninety minutes." According to young Claude, an eyewitness, this hour and a half's catch of silver perch was interrupted now and then by the landing of a three- or four-pound bass.

When baiting the hook for white perch or pan fish, M. G. always named each individual worm. Each was given a girl's name, as meteorologists used to do for hurricanes. Several worms might be given the same moniker when the fishing was good. Always, of course, the piscatorial addict chain-smoked cigars—to keep mosquitoes away, he would explain.

By the time of M. G.'s "world record," America had gone almost mad with joyful pride over the feat of a homespun, bashful, but brave, lanky aviator named Charles Lindbergh, conqueror of the Atlantic by air. "Lucky Lindy" and his plane, the *Spirit of St. Louis*, were still the talk of the campus when the yearbook for 1927 went to press. Americans had come to speak exuberantly of the 1920s as the New Era, a phrase popular on the Juniata campus and everywhere heroically symbolized by the "Flyin' Fool's" New York to Paris nonstop solo flight. So the college's yearly pictorial for 1927 was called *The New Era Alfarata,* an expression of the students' enthusiastic expectations for Juniata under its new dynamic leader. M. G. wrote a page-long piece for this issue captioned "The Outlook in the New Era." One paragraph read:

Accepting the challenge of the times and the demands of every prophecy concerning the years ahead we shall enter upon a New Era of service to God and society, resolved to keep close the first things of the Soul and adjust ourselves as fully as may be to the needs of the age. We shall not give up God, the church, the Christocentral life. But we shall adjust our offerings to cover the needs of right ordered living in the years to be.

In 1927 Juniata's athletic teams now had a mascot. Pre-New Era varsity sports had no "fighting" nickname; they were simply the Blue and Gold. Then in the spring of 1925 the *Juniatian,* somehow, came up with the sobriquet Indians in headlining the opening game of the baseball season with Penn State. The JC nine were "Indians" the rest of the season. The name stuck in the fall for the football squad, and by 1927 was set in stone. Nobody remembers today who suggested "Indians" as the college mascot. In the spring of 1994, however, at the height of the political correctness debate on American campuses everywhere, the trustees voted to drop the name Indians and adopt that of Eagles. But there is every reason to believe that Juniata's president in the 1920s, a great admirer of the northeastern woodland tribes, would have regarded the nickname as a term of honor, not of ethnic disrespect.

In October he was elected president of the Pennsylvania German Society for the year 1927–28, at its annual meeting in York. In his 1928 presidential address Brumbaugh urged the society to prod the commonwealth into acquiring the site of the Ephrata Community, whose buildings were falling into decay. He said the buildings should be restored and "preserved as one our sacred historic shrines." (The state purchased the Ephrata site in 1941.)

At Juniata, New Era dreams produced few direct physical changes on the Hill, though, foresightedly, the trustees continued to purchase additional land adjacent to the campus, nearly doubling college-owned acreage since 1924. Thus the sole brick-and-mortar monument to New Era dreams was the Cloister, a men's dormitory, completed and occupied in the fall of 1928.

The architect was Edwin Brumbaugh, who became well known in Pennsylvania for his original interpretations of the German colonial style. Modeled on the famous Ephrata Cloister in Lancaster County but with a brick exterior, it cost $140,000 to build. M. G. proudly—and correctly—said of his son's campus masterpiece, "There is nothing like it in college architecture in America. It will be distinctive of Juniata."

The year 1928 brought Juniata and its president other kinds of publicity. In January M. G., at the invitation of Theodore Roosevelt Jr., accepted chairmanship of the Pennsylvania "American Forest Week" Committee. The celebration, which had been observed for the past five years, sought to focus public attention upon the importance of reforesting and protecting America's timberlands. In May the college gave an honorary degree to Governor John S. Fisher, a sometime schoolteacher whose administration would be renowned for its building of public highways. In 1928, and again in 1929, Juniata's chief headed the state's Christmas Seal drive.

By 1928 Brumbaugh's enthusiasm as president was waning. It seems that tension had developed between him and certain influential members of the faculty. Who they were or why they were unhappy with him is not at all clear. Nothing came out in the open. Perhaps the friction had to do with some administrative decisions he had made. Among other things, he introduced the college to the niceties of a budget, brought in a business manager, urged raising standards of admission, and terminated the popular annual Bible term. He also took a more or less laissez-faire attitude toward the faculty, allowing considerable academic freedom—which perhaps disturbed the old-timers but appealed to the new bloods. Some Hilltoppers blamed him for the suicide of a distinguished biology professor, the father of four children, whose ambitions to be dean at Juniata were stunted after 1924.

And then there was his lifestyle. In April 1928 he got a letter from an alumnus of the mid-1890s who wrote of the faculty's cast of mind:

> I know they howl like hyenas when you go fishing or golfing. They try to know how many cigars you smoke and it makes THEM sick. They consider themselves saints and every body else a sinner.

The letter-writer went on:

> [The] Juniata Company or official faculty are so set in their ways that it will be hard to tell them anything at all and I know something of what you are up against in your efforts to make a real school out of the place. I know the complaints, mutterings and cheap jealosies (pardon the spelling) of the place. I have been there several times, heard them, know them, realize the extreme narrow minded old fogies they are.

"I wonder," his correspondent wrote, "how you hold them to an even semi-modern program in the administration of the affairs. . . . It must require a big man to handle successfully such a bunch of good meaning cranks." These are strong words and perhaps overstate the professoriate's carping ways and cranky mood. At any rate, one story around this time has it that M. G., in a choleric moment, remarked to a golfing partner, "What we need is a few deaths on campus."

Pinehurst in the spring (where he won two tournament trophies in golf) and Wayne in the summer afforded weeks of escape from campus stress. There were church and alumni meetings, a few teachers' institutes, and the business of the Association of College Presidents of Pennsylvania (ACPP) to get him away from the Hill periodically. Early in 1929, upon being elected the ACPP's president, he drafted a bill intended to improve the quality of practice-teaching supervision given aspiring high-school teachers enrolled in the state's liberal arts colleges.

The Edmonds Act of 1921 had mandated that all institutions of higher education in Pennsylvania provide apprenticeships as part of their teacher-training programs. But this law put private colleges at a financial disadvantage. The state teachers colleges received appropriations that covered the costs of engaging public-school "critic" teachers as stipendiaries. Some independent colleges provided no compensation, and it soon became evident that their students often got indifferent supervision as a result. Other schools, like Juniata, did make recompense, but their students were penalized with an extra fee.

This whole matter became a great worry to heads of liberal arts colleges. For obvious reasons, they looked to the ex-governor for a legislative solution. His bill, if enacted, would subsidize apprentice teaching for all the state's accredited colleges. Backed by the Society of College Teachers of Education, it passed both houses of the General Assembly. But Governor John Fisher, his 1928 Juniata honorary doctorate notwithstanding, vetoed the bill, one of twenty-nine education bills he refused to sign. This put the issue permanently to rest, as it turned out.

Another situation that alarmed and surprised heads of liberal arts colleges developed in the fall of 1929. Trustees of the Pennsylvania State College that October adopted a graduate program in education leading to master's and doctor's degrees. In November Penn State worked out a graduate degree alliance with the state teachers colleges. (The teachers colleges in 1929 had an enrollment just under ten thousand.) Bachelor degree holders from the latter schools would automatically be eligible to enroll for advanced study in education at Penn State. So would those from "an institution of equally higher rank," said the agreement. Theoretically, this referred to accredited liberal arts colleges.

But the Association of College Presidents was disturbed to learn that the state department of public instruction, freezing out the ACPP, had established a permanent committee "to discuss and recommend further coordination of the teacher training facilities of the State." Such rhetoric only abetted the belief—and fear—that state-owned institutions in America were out to monopolize the education of public-school teachers. Martin Brumbaugh was pondering what strategy the ACPP should adopt in challenging the state board of public instruction as to its ultimate purpose and how best define the role of the ACPP's own institutions in Pennsylvania's teacher-training program when he was taken by death.

Meanwhile, the decade's "great bull market" had come crashing down during the "black" last days of October 1929. The golden Twenties closed with Wall Street in a panic. Neither Martin Brumbaugh's date book nor any of his letters makes mention of the catastrophic economic situation that had befallen the nation. Like countless other Americans, he seems not to have foreseen the tough times ahead heralded by the stock market collapse. And his imminent death would remove him from the constant worries of presiding over a college during the deepest and most prolonged depression the United States—and the world—ever knew.

By 1930 Juniata College, under M. G.'s guidance, had made significant advances. The regular-year enrollment had nearly doubled, to over five hundred. In fact, in the ten years since he had become trustee chairman and then president, the college had grown 500 percent, or four times the average growth for other liberal arts schools of Pennsylvania. Ranked twenty-second in the number of students among the fifty-three accredited Keystone State colleges, Juniata had a nearly equal mix of men and women.

The endowment, though quite modest by Harvard standards—or, in Pennsylvania, by those of Swarthmore and Haverford—had passed the million dollar mark, half of that coming in the last six years. It was largely through his efforts that Juniata gained recognition by the Association of American Colleges and the Home Economics Department had been accredited by the state. He constantly took steps towards beautifying and enlarging the campus and initiated the transplanting of many trees. College Hill now had a men's dormitory of architectural distinction. The library, thanks to his special interest and book donations, ranked among the best in the state. He had brought to the campus men of prominence in education, business, industry, law, politics, and religion, thereby widening the college's reputation.

For the faculty, the M. G. years brought salary increases and sabbaticals. The trustees also provided for retirement funds (Juniata did not join the Teachers Insurance and Annuity Association until 1938) and financial assistance for widows or "families of teachers dying in service."

Never once, however, did he betray the slightest desire to lead Juniata out of the Brethren fold. Indeed, in a 1929 letter to a brotherhood dignitary he emphatically declared: "We are trying here to build a school of the Church of the Brethren. We are certainly as loyal to its principles as I know how to make the school."

Even so, he could rankle at what to him looked like signs of undue church interference. He had not been happy at all when Juniata terminated its school of theology in 1925 in grudging deference to a strong sentiment among Brethren to make Bethany Bible School the church's official seminary. Now, in 1929, the denomination's General Education Board (of which he was a member) sought to keep Juniata from recruiting south of the Mason and Dixon Line. They wanted Maryland to be reserved for Bridgewater College in Virginia.

But M. G. wanted Maryland declared "open territory." He argued that Juniata had already been forced to reach out into "other fields" for students because it had grown faster than the church and other Brethren colleges. In strong words he let the people know at the denomination's headquarters in Elgin, Illinois, that he felt "keenly on this matter." He wrote that he "certainly [did] not want the church itself through any of its Boards or actions to cripple us in any way."

By this time Martin had been a grandfather for seven years and, for some reason, made note of that on 5 March 1929, Kenneth Lewars's birthday (Martin was never very close to the older Lewars step-grandson). Juniata's president could draw much better than average, and when Kenny was four years old used that talent to entertain and edify him. He drew a whole notebook full of cartoons about a creature he called *The Gubernocker. The Gubernocker* was a kind of huge dragon fly with a long tail, which enabled it to perform some quite magical feats. The gigantic insect, which lived on a diet of pine cones, was depicted as a playmate of Kenny's with very human traits. Kenny also liked to hear his grandfather Brumbaugh's auditory imitations of bullfrogs and steam locomotives.

Cartoon-drawing grandfather Martin, however, never showed much inclination toward music. He of course liked hymns—"O God, Our Help in Ages Past" was his favorite—and did join in the public singing of them. But Claude Flory, during the five years he chauffeured for the Brumbaughs, recalls never having heard M. G. sing, or even hum, on his own initiative.

But with the trustees there was one refrain he descanted upon over and over since returning to College Hill: the need for a president's house. The board was sympathetic enough, but the limited success of the Jubilee Fund made everybody hesitant to incur a mortgage debt. Finally, late in 1928, Martin decided to take matters into his own hands, in collaboration with board chairman Joseph Oller. He put up twenty-eight thousand dollars, and Oller doled out another twenty-thousand, both gifts in the form of low-interest annuities, toward construction costs. The college donated three lots on the corner of Mifflin and Eighteenth Streets, a block west of the campus. Edwin Brumbaugh drew the plans for a two-story Dutch colonial structure with two separate entrances, one for each street. The dwelling would revert to the college, it was agreed (but not in writing), after M. G. and Flora were both gone. Construction began early in 1929 and would cost in excess of forty thousand dollars.

Claude Flory remembers his surprise at learning that the president's house would not be a single-family residence. He was even more astounded to be told that the Brumbaughs were to have the upper floor (Professor Jack Oller, son of Joseph, and his wife were to occupy the lower-level). One day the Juniata senior summoned up the courage to say to M. G. that he expected the college, for the sake of dignity, to build a house intended for occupancy only by the president's family. M. G. responded that he intended to be away from campus a great deal in the near future, so he wanted Flora to have a safe place, with friendly company under the same roof, when he had to leave her at home.

The reason for his frequent absences, he revealed, would not be because of presidential duties. Rather, he contemplated stumping for "Frank" Brown, his administration's attorney general during World War I, who planned to seek the Republican nomination for governor in 1930. Then M. G. confided in his student employee a secret that would have panicked the trustees. Some board members knew of his intention to campaign for his old attorney general but not that Brown, if elected, had promised Juniata's president to appoint him state superintendent of public instruction. Brown, as Brumbaugh hoped, did become the organization-backed candidate, and in the primaries that spring ran against Gifford Pinchot, a party maverick, for the GOP slot on the final ballot. However, Pinchot, who had served one gubernatorial term in the early 1920s, bested Brown in May (and won against his Democratic opponent in November). All of this, of course, was irrelevant to Brumbaugh's life story; he died a month before the primaries.

He never had a chance to occupy the new president's home, which was finished by the first of March. On Wednesday the 5th, the Brumbaughs had left for Pinehurst, having delegated to Claude Flory the task of making all the moving arrangements while they were gone. Flory, having stayed on as an English instructor after graduating in 1929, recruited some of his well-muscled students as movers. The job was half done when the shocking news came from North Carolina. Martin is supposed to have remarked, while the president's house was being built, that he would never get to live in it, and later, in a freakish oversight, only one of the ordered twin beds was delivered.

Apparently, Juniata's president had been subjected to attacks of angina for some while, although few of his friends were aware of this. He had gone to Pinehurst upon the advice of his local physician, who recommended a rest because of his heart. He had a bad cold when he left Huntingdon that kept him "housed up" for two days at the golf resort. But otherwise he seemed in good health. The Brumbaughs had gone on their vacation in the company of the John B. Kunzes, their closest friends in Huntingdon. Kunz, one of his regulars for bridge, was a frequent golf partner of Martin's at the home country club and once or twice had gone fishing with him in Maine, a rare invitation.

Friday morning, 14 March, a foursome of M. G., Kunz, and two other Pennsylvanians had begun playing on Pinehurst's Number Four Course. At the eighth tee M. G. complained of feeling dizzy. After a brief rest, he played another stroke, and collapsed. His golfing partners carried him to the clubhouse, and from there he was transported by car to the Carolina Hotel, where the Brumbaughs always stayed.

Flora was on the links elsewhere and was hastily summoned to their hotel room. Meanwhile, Dr. Myron W. Marr, the resident physician, did all he could to save her husband. She arrived at Martin's side a few minutes before he died, at 1:30 P.M. He was conscious to the end, dying in his wife's arms. His last words to her were, "Flora Belle, I love you. I don't want to leave you." Flora's telephone call to Claude Flory passed the sad news on to a shocked campus. M. G. died exactly one month shy of his sixty-eighth birthday.

The Pinehurst people were badly shaken by the death of the popular Pennsylvanian, but none more so, according to a Henry Shoemaker anecdote, than a teenaged black caddie. The day before, he had been struck on the forehead by an errant golf ball and knocked senseless. Martin happened to see the accident and, although in the midst of a tournament, dropped everything and rushed to where the moaning boy lay. He then carried the lad, still woozy, to the hotel where he was kept overnight. The next afternoon, propped up in bed, the injured youth offhandedly asked a nurse, "Where's the big man who was so good to me?" She looked at him somberly and replied, "He died ten minutes ago." The caddie was quiet for a moment, as Shoemaker related the incident, and then said softly, "I can just see him teaching the angels how to putt."

M. G.'s body was brought to Huntingdon the next day. A small delegation of faculty and students met the train at two o'clock, after which the corpse was taken to Brown's Funeral Home. All college functions were suspended until after the funeral, Tuesday the 18th.

A funeral like it would never again be held in the quiet railroad town. On the morning of the 18th, the body, attended by a student guard of honor, lay in state in the college chapel. There, from 9:00 to 9:45, students, faculty, and other Hilltop employees passed before the bier. Then followed a simple memorial service for the "Juniata family" only. It included the president's favorite hymn. William Ball, the private secretary of M. G. when he was governor and a worshipful intimate of his ever after, was the only non-Juniatian to offer obsequies. The Philadelphia realtor said of the college's president, "No man meant more to me than he. I am a better man because of him. I loved him." Claude Flory also spoke, among other Juniatians, referring to his patron as having been to the Juniata family "a great father—understanding, loving, kind, never provoked and never impatient."

After the morning memorial service, the students and faculty formed a double line from the front entrance of the chapel to the Stone Church, on the southern edge of the campus. The body of the late president, his "mammoth bronze casket" draped with a large American flag, was carried between the two lines by a contingent of student pallbearers to the church sanctuary. There it lay in state again, until 2:30, when the public funeral began. Downtown stores and businesses closed for the afternoon service. (The capitol in Harrisburg shut down for the entire day.)

The church overflowed with mourners; several hundred had to stand outside in an intermittent rain. Most Pennsylvania colleges sent representatives to the funeral, among them Brumbaugh's old friend from the University of Pennsylvania, Provost Josiah Penniman. Also present was Felix Schelling, who had supervised his doctoral dissertation at Penn. Governor John Fisher and his staff were there, as was former governor John Tener. A number of prominent Republican politicians, especially from M. G.'s gubernatorial days, attended, including Mayor Harry Mackey of Philadelphia.

Following the church service, a long automobile cortege drove through a downpour to the Brumbaugh family cemetery in Marklesburg. To reach the graveyard, on a hillock, the funeral procession had to leave the improved highway and make its way up through an orchard. The cars almost mired getting up to the grave site. There, in a drizzle, he was lowered to rest beside his parents, his nameless infant brother, and his sister Amanda. Otto Mallery, who had risen to national prominence in the field of public recreation since that day a quarter of a century before when Brumbaugh had asked his help in establishing the Philadelphia Playgrounds Association, requested a special postinterment ritual. He arranged, in absentia, for a cluster of three dozen daffodils to be scattered over the grave. "They represent the sunshine of his life scattered everywhere," wrote Mallery.

Flora, of course, received a mountain of letters and telegrams offering condolences. Many of them came from state and national leaders in the fields of education, politics, business, law, and religion. But perhaps the tribute paid "my dear friend" by Charles Schwab best synopsized the eulogies that came by mail and wire. He said, "Martin G. Brumbaugh was gifted by a practical idealism that enabled him to serve his God, his country and his state in a measure that cannot be forgotten. . . . He was a great man and I loved him very much."

All the state newspapers had good things to say about him, and his death was given front-page coverage in large headlines. Henry Shoemaker's *Altoona Tribune*, to be sure, editorialized with lavish praise. One out-of-state newspaper, Augusta, Maine's *Kennebec Journal*, carried an equally eloquent editorial. It began, "The sudden death of Governor Brumbaugh is a great blow to this portion of Maine, as well as to the Nation." It spoke of him as a "stout friend" of the Pine Tree State and of his love for Wayne, where he lived in summers "like a commoner" despite his fame. Then the piece went on to say of him:

> Few men have had a greater power of expression, greater charm or a more magnetic presence. . . . Behind this was something solid. He was impressive personally. He had character. He had practical wisdom and also great learning. His life was grounded in honesty. He thought straight and from old-fashioned principles of justice.

The editorial, whose readers were wont to call their July-August residents "summer complaints," ended with the words: "Maine had assumed him to be its own citizen. We pay Gov. Brumbaugh no greater compliment than this—for we, the people of Maine, do not always adopt our summer visitors."

Countless Juniatians have testified to the impact their beloved "Prexy" had on their lives and careers. The late George Griffith, who became an acclaimed professor of medicine at the University of Southern California and an internationally renowned cardiologist, used to tell how Brumbaugh, when governor, had a diversionary influence on his life's work. Griffith had come to Juniata in 1917 planning to prepare for the ministry. One weekend the governor happened to be on campus when the aspiring preacher was scheduled for a Sunday sermon. M. G. made it a point to hear this very intelligent young collegian hold forth from the pulpit.

The governor's presence made young George nervous, and the sermon did not go well. M. G. could recognize in that day's stumbling preacher intellectual gifts that might better be put to use in a different profession. So after the service he shook hands with Griffith and asked him if he had ever thought about becoming a physician rather than a minister. Medicine, said M. G., afforded "greater opportunities" to teach and heal. Griffith would smile when telling this story of his ineptitude in the pulpit and the governor's response. But the advice he got that day would give the world one of its great twentieth-century medical educators and clinical researchers.

Another very successful physician and Juniatian, Samuel J. King, now deceased, also had fond memories of Martin Brumbaugh. King had stayed on after graduating in 1928 to teach chemistry before enrolling at the University of Chicago's medical school. Seventeen pages of his 7½" × 9½" diary tell in poignant language his own deep sorrow, and that of the campus, the "solemn weekend" of M. G.'s death. In a state of shock, he writes of the "gloom" that fell upon the chemistry laboratory and all College Hill that Ides of March. "I don't know what to think, say, or do," he records for Friday night the 14th. "The beloved President of this college, Martin Grove Brumbaugh—a great man, a personality of great inspiration to thousands (myself not least of these)—is dead. His career is over." On Saturday he chanced upon Claude Flory, who was going to get the Brumbaughs' Lincoln and meet the funeral party. "I walked a short distance with [him]," wrote King. "I didn't know what to say, so we walked in quietness most of the way."

On Sunday the sad chemist rode in the company of M. G.'s two cousins, Gaius and Norman, to Marklesburg to call on Frank Brumbaugh. Several pages of King's journal recount a number of the family's cherished anecdotes about Martin's childhood and youth told him on that visit. That afternoon all of them went to watch the gravediggers at work.

On Tuesday the 19th, the young diarist writes: "This is one of the saddest but most outstanding days in the history of Huntingdon." He summarizes the "fitting eulogies" at "the last chapel with Dr. M. G." He especially likes what Claude Flory had to say, writing:

> Claude has answered the question, "Where is Prexy?" many times. This time, he prefers to answer it: "Prexy is on a speaking engagement. He is gone beyond to speak with God in behalf of his Juniata family."

"This is wonderful," King exclaims, mentioning the "pat of approval" Charles Ellis gave the speaker when he sat down. There also follows a summation of the eulogistic speeches later given in the Stone Church. These pages of the diary record a sight that probably shocked some of the more traditional Brethren: two State Policemen standing watch, in the company of a college honor guard, over the casket.

The twenty-four-year-old future internist confided in his daily journal, "Once I made a New Year's resolution to the effect that I resolve to live true to the confidence which Dr. M. G. has in me." And to Flora he wrote:

> Inspiration truly has come to me from the great life of President Brumbaugh. The influence of his unselfish personality—always willing to pass on wise counsel for real achievement and right living—is one of the greatest intangible assets I ever hope to have.

Juniata's departed paterfamilias could not have phrased a fitter epitaph for himself than the one penned in "Sam" King's diary:

> I write all this about Martin Grove Brumbaugh because he is a true representation of the American ideal where a lad's initiative takes him from the humblest of circumstances through the help of Providence to real achievement and right living.

In July the trustees elected Vice-President Charles Ellis to succeed M. G. Ellis had been deeply devoted to his predecessor ever since his doctorate days under him at Penn two decades before. The vision of a small liberal arts college, strong in academics and Christian values, that the ex-governor had given his alma mater would continue on undimmed in the new administration. Juniata would survive the withering decade of the 1930s in sounder fiscal condition and with a healthier enrollment than most Keystone State colleges, private and public.

———*∿∿∿*———

When Martin Brumbaugh made his will he seemed to think that he was leaving an estate of about two-hundred thousand dollars, part of it in the form of various trusts for Flora, Edwin, and Mabel and her son Kenneth. His will made Juniata College the ultimate beneficiary of these trusts. Over and above these basic bequests, M. G. apparently thought he was leaving his wife a comfortable income. Unfortunately for her, the other Brumbaughs, and the college, the Great Depression shrank his actual legacy to many fewer dollars. Flora died in 1972 at Tallahassee, Florida, at the age of 97. She was buried beside her husband at Valley View Cemetery, Marklesburg.

On the campus of Juniata College the name of Martin Grove Brumbaugh is perpetuated today by an endowed chair in education, established in 1935 in his memory. That year the college also began a two-decade tradition (interrupted during World War II) of making an annual summer pilgrimage to Brumbaugh's grave. The first—and perennial—speaker was his great admirer Henry Shoemaker, the Altoona newspaper publisher and former Herbert Hoover-era diplomat. An authority on Pennsylvania folklore, Shoemaker, for years the state archivist, was a master raconteur, if a sometimes unreliable one. His graveside tributes were rich in biographical anecdotes about Brumbaugh's youth, his traits, and his notable achievements as an educator and a wartime governor. Usually an entourage of about two dozen Juniatians, Huntingdonians, and local relatives made the trek to the cemetery knoll above the Brumbaugh ancestral farmhouse. The last pilgrimage was in August 1957; Shoemaker had died in July of that year.

Soon after the Second World War (1947) the Pennsylvania Historical and Museum Commission placed a highway marker along Route 26 telling of the schoolman-governor's nearby birthplace and grave site. Brumbaugh's marker was supposed to be the first of its kind erected along the state's roads, but for some reason there was a delay and a few others went up before his. The governor's roadside sign, a half century later, still stands its memorial vigil along Route 26's farmland course through Woodcock Valley.

Frank Brumbaugh, *left,* **and State Highway Superintendent Ralph Volke stand by the Route 26 highway marker, erected in July 1943, near Marklesburg.**

Bibliographical Essay

As noted in the preface, there is no published biography of Martin G. Brumbaugh. But academia has produced a doctor's and two master's theses on his educational career: Salvatore M. Messina, "Martin Grove Brumbaugh, Educator" (Ph.D. thesis, University of Pennsylvania, 1965); Valentino A. Ciampa, "Martin Grove Brumbaugh, Educator" (M.A. thesis, Pennsylvania State College, 1937); and Naomi H. Warren, "Martin Brumbaugh and His Educational Philosophy" (M.A. thesis, Temple University, 1938). All three works were somewhat handicapped by what was, before the 1980s, a relatively meager collection of Brumbaughana in the archives of Juniata College. As their titles indicate, these studies focus on Brumbaugh the educator. But none of the three deals with his life in the context of his religious heritage—its formative influence on him and his role in helping to reshape Brethren attitudes toward civic duty and social and political activism. Nor do they tell the story of his enduring ties to Juniata College. While Messina and Ciampa do each include a chapter on Brumbaugh's work in Puerto Rico and another on his governorship, they do so in a very general way. His struggles with political bossism while governor, for example, go untold. Also, both theses only sketchily treat the years 1919–24. In aggregate, however, they are indispensable as guides to understanding the evolution of Brumbaugh's educational philosophy. For my purposes, they happily provided time-saving bibliographical leads, especially Messina's thesis. Curiously, his makes no reference, even in its bibliography, to the earlier studies by Ciampa and Warren.

I have not appended a list of works—articles, books, addresses, pamphlets, sermons, reports—authored by Martin Brumbaugh. Such a listing appears as part of the bibliographies in two of the theses cited above, those by Messina and Ciampa. Neither, however, is complete. The latest compilation (also incomplete), by Ira F. Lydic, appears under the title "A Bio-Bibliography of Martin Grove Brumbaugh," *Brethren Life and Thought* 13 (Winter 1968).

CHAPTER 1. FAMILY HERITAGE

An invaluable source for this biography was Gaius Marcus Brumbaugh, *Genealogy of the Brumbach Families* (New York: Frederick H. Hitchcock, 1913). Martin Brumbaugh was much intrigued by his Germanic roots and family pedigree. He encouraged his cousin Gaius—they were born within a week of each other—in the preparation of this voluminous, richly illustrated genealogical record, helped collect data, and wrote the introduction. Taken as a whole, it is a treasure mine of historical commentary as well as the registry of a remarkable bloodline. Three standard histories of Huntingdon County and south-central Pennsylvania that I used were J. Simpson Africa, *History of the Juniata Valley and Its People* (New York: H. Everts, 1883); Uriah J. Jones, *History of the Early Settlement of the Juniata Valley* (Harrisburg, Pa.: Telegraph Press, 1940); and John W. Jordan, *A History of the Juniata Valley and Its People*, vol. 1 (New York: Lewis Historical Publishing Co., 1913). But the most helpful of early area histories, because of attention given to public schooling, was William S. Lytle, *History of Huntingdon County* (Lancaster, Pa.: William H. Roy, 1879). I found the post-World War II articles written for the *Huntingdon Daily News* by Albert M. Rung very useful in researching the early life of Martin Brumbaugh. Some of them were published by the Huntingdon County Historical Society under the title *Rung's Chronicles of Pennsylvania History*. One volume was printed in 1977 and the other in 1984, both by the John S. Rodgers Company of Huntingdon, Pa. A constant source on Church of the Brethren history for me was *The Brethren Encyclopedia*, 3 vols. (Philadelphia, Pa., and Oak Brook, Ill.: Brethren Encyclopedia Inc., 1983). For the denomination's formative decades I also made use of Martin G. Brumbaugh, *A History of the German Baptist Brethren in Europe and America* (Mount Morris, Ill.: Brethren Publishing House, 1899); Floyd E. Mallott, *Studies in Brethren History* (Elgin, Ill.: Brethren Publishing House, 1954); and two sourcebooks by Donald F. Durnbaugh, editor and translator: *European Origins of the Brethren* (Elgin, Ill.: Brethren Press, 1958) and *The Brethren in Colonial America* (Elgin, Ill.: Brethren Press, 1967). On Brethren roots and history in south-central Pennsylvania, see Earl C. Kaylor, Jr., *Out of the Wilderness, 1780-1980* (New York and London: Cornwall Books, 1981). George Brumbaugh's land purchases can be traced through recorded deeds in the Huntingdon County courthouse.

Chapter 2. A Village Boyhood

The first years of Juniata College can be followed in the Brumbaugh brothers' church paper, the *Pilgrim*, and then in the *Primitive Christian*, after the Brumbaughs consolidated their paper with Quinter's in 1876. Art professor David Emmert's sprightly *Reminiscences of Juniata College* (Huntingdon, Pa.: Illustrated and published by the author, 1901), its pages adorned with charming pen sketches, describes with delightful humor and anecdote the first twenty-five years of Brumbaugh's alma mater. Later histories of the school are Charles C. Ellis, *Juniata College: The History of Seventy Years, 1876–1946* (Elgin, Ill.: Brethren Publishing House, 1947) and Earl C. Kaylor, Jr., *Truth Sets Free: A Centennial History of Juniata College, 1876-1976* (Cranbury, N.J.: A. S. Barnes and Co., 1977). For general histories of Brethren education there are Solomon Z. Sharp, *The Educational History of the Church of the Brethren* (Elgin, Ill.: Brethren Publishing House, 1923); W. Arthur Cable and Homer F. Sanger, eds., *Educational Blue Book and Directory of the Church of the Brethren* (Elgin, Ill.: General Educational Board of the Church of the Brethren, 1923); and Auburn A. Boyer, "Changing Conceptions of Education in the Church of the Brethren" (Ph.D. thesis, University of Pittsburgh, 1969). Anecdotal material came from a variety of sources—the *Juniata Echo*, the *Juniatian*, the *Sunday School Times*, various newspaper articles during Brumbaugh's gubernatorial race, interviews as reported in Messina and Ciampa, graveside addresses by Henry W. Shoemaker between 1935 and 1957, and my many interviews with Claude Flory. Some of the textbooks used by Brumbaugh as a schoolboy can be found in the Juniata College Museum. I found the mention of young Martin using dynamite to break logjams in Cornelius Weygandt, *The Dutch Country* (New York: D. Appleton-Century Company, 1939). The story of Cassel's buying matches is told in Kermon Thomasson, "Abraham Harley Cassel: Antiquarian From Indian Creek," *Messenger,* October 1978. To this tale Brumbaugh added the umbrella, according to Dr. Flory. See also Donald F. Durnbaugh, "Abraham Harley Cassel and His Collection," *Pennsylvania History* 26, no. 4 (October 1959).

CHAPTER 3. MAKING OF A SCHOOLMAN

The Pennsylvania School Journal was never far from my reach as I tried to place the educational career of Brumbaugh within the context of public schooling in Pennsylvania. Also, I relied heavily upon the annual reports of the Pennsylvania superintendent of public instruction in this and the following chapter. Reminiscences of his college days made good news copy during his gubernatorial campaign. In the Brumbaughana of Juniata College's archives can be found report cards, letters, the mail-order study guides Martin used as a teaching tenderfoot, and Huntingdon County teachers' institute brochures. The college catalog and trustee minutes also fill in the story. On comparative wages for this period see U.S. Bureau of the Census, "Average Annual Earnings in All Industries and in Selected Industries and Occupations: 1890-1926," *Historical Statistics of the United States, Colonial Times to 1957* (Washington, D.C.: Government Printing Office, 1960). Henry Shoemaker told the story of the Martin Brumbaugh-organized club at Sugar Run logging camp in one of his graveside speeches. Trustee chairman Henry B. Brumbaugh and William J. Swigart, an early professor-trustee at Juniata, were both faithful diarists whose entries sometimes provide anecdotal tidbits about Martin. His uncle Henry Brumbaugh, the farmer and mortgage-holder, also kept a diary. The story of the washed-away telephone poles and Martin's part in paying off his father's bankruptcy were oft-told ones in later years.

CHAPTER 4. COUNTY SUPERINTENDENT

For general histories of education I relied on two old standbys: John S. Brubacher, *A History of the Problems of Education* (New York: McGraw-Hill, 1947) and James Mulhern, *A History of Education* (New York: Ronald Press Co., 1959). For the national scene I turned to Adolphe E. Meyer, *An Educational History of the American People* (New York: McGraw-Hill, 1957); R. Freeman Butts and Lawrence A. Cremin, *A History of Education in American Culture* (New York: Henry Holt, 1953); and Newton Edwards and Herman C. Richey, *The School in the American Social Order* (New York: Houghton Mifflin, 1947). Especially useful for my purposes—summarizing the theories and methods of pioneering progressive-education theorists—was Daniel Tanner and Laurel N. Tanner, *Curriculum Development: Theory into Practice* (New York: Macmillan, 1975). For the Keystone State scene I diligently quarried the *Pennsylvania School Journal* and the annual reports of the state superintendent of public instruction. I also made much use of Louise G. Walsh and Matthew J. Walsh, *History and Organization of Education in Pennsylvania* (Indiana, Pa.: State Teachers College, 1928). Another excellent source was Saul Sack, *History of Higher Education in Pennsylvania*, 2 vols. (Harrisburg, Pa.: The Pennsylvania Historical Commission, 1963). So was his "The Higher Education of Women in Pennsylvania," *Pennsylvania Magazine of History and Biography* 133 (January 1959). Genealogical data on Anna Konigmacher can be found in "The Konigmacher Family of the Cocalico Valley," *Journal of the Historical Society of the Cocalico Valley* 14 (1989): 1–43.

CHAPTER 5. BAYOUS AND GRADUATE DEGREES

I have uncovered letters that give a fuller picture of Brumbaugh's contribution to the late-nineteenth-century revival of public education in Louisiana. For a biography of the man who was his principal correspondent, see Marcus M. Wilkerson, *Thomas Duckett Boyd* (Baton Rouge: Louisiana State University, 1935). Also useful to me in researching the period of Brumbaugh's Louisiana experience were T. H. Harris, *The Story of Public Education in Louisiana* (New Orleans: Printed by students of the Printing Department of Delgado Trades School, 1924); Faye M. Hutchinson, "The Louisiana Chautauqua: History and Program" (M.A. thesis, Louisiana State University and A & M College, 1976); and Kathleen DeCou Thain, *Professor J. E. Keeny* (New Orleans: Pelican Press, Inc., 1945). Articles in three issues of the *Louisiana School Review*, in 1897, 1907, and 1908, tell of Brumbaugh's contribution to public education of that state. So does Edwin L. Stephens, "Education in Louisiana in the Closing Decades of the Nineteenth Century" (reprint from the *Louisiana Historical Quarterly*, January 1933). Two works by Samuel Eliot Morison give biographical data on Brumbaugh's professors at Harvard. One of them he edited: *The Development of Harvard University, 1869-1929* (Cambridge: Harvard University Press, 1930). The other one is *Three Centuries of Harvard, 1636-1936* (Cambridge: Belknap Press of Harvard University, 1965). For his Penn professors there are Joshua L. Chamberlain, ed., *Universities and Their Sons: Alumni Register of the University of Pennsylvania*, 2 vols. (Boston: R. Herndon Company, 1902) and Edward P. Cheyney, *History of the University of Pennsylvania, 1740–1940* (Philadelphia: University of Pennsylvania Press, 1940). By the 1890s Brumbaugh had begun keeping a little date book each year, which enabled me to keep track of his growing reputation as a public figure. There are some pamphlets in Brumbaughana on his involvement with the university extension program. Booklets of his class notes at Penn are also among the Brumbaughana. Juniata has several copies of his doctoral dissertation on John Donne in its archives. To determine general scholarly interest in Donne over the years, I consulted two main works. One was Lawrence F. McNamee, ed., *Dissertations in English and American Literature: Theses Accepted by American, British, and German Universities, 1864–1964* (New York: Bowker, 1968). Two supplemental editions bring the data up to 1980. The other comprehensive index was John R. Roberts, *John Donne: An Annotated Bibliography of Modern Criticism, 1912–1967* (Columbia: University of Missouri Press, 1973). Another reference work is William White, *John Donne Since 1900*, a bibliography of periodical issues (Boston: F. W. Faxon Company, 1942). See also Wrightman F. Melton, "The Rhetoric of John Donne's Verse" (Ph.D. thesis, Johns Hopkins University, 1906). John L. Haney's account of his futile bibliographical work on Brumbaugh's thesis is given in "The Unwritten Magnum Opus," *General Magazine and Historical Chronicle*, published by the General Alumni Society of the University of Pennsylvania (Autumn–Winter 1955). For a biography of Brumbaugh's longtime friend and Pennsylvania's superintendent of public instruction from 1893 to 1919, Nathan C. Schaeffer, see Charles D. Koch, *Nathan C. Schaeffer* (Harrisburg, Pa.: Telegraph Press, 1951). A sourcebook on growing sociopolitical awareness and involvement by members of the Church of the Brethren in the half-century after the Civil War is Roger E. Sappington, comp., *The Brethren in Industrial America* (Elgin, Ill.: Brethren Press, 1985).

Chapter 6. Rise to Public-School Fame

Brumbaughana contains several family letters during these years, a couple from Martin's mother and some from his brother Frank. There are a number of works on the two Christopher Sauers, father and son. But see especially Brumbaugh's *History*; *The Brethren Encyclopedia*; Anna K. Oller, "Christopher Sauer, Colonial Printer" (Ph.D. thesis, University of Michigan, 1963); and two articles by Durnbaugh in the *Pennsylvania Magazine of History and Biography*: "Christopher Sauer," in vol. 72 (1958) and "Was Christopher Sauer a Dunker?" in vol. 93 (1969). The Juniata College archives are mandatory for researching Abraham H. Cassel's unique collection of books, magazines, newspapers, tracts, and letters, and his correspondence. The best biography of the famous antiquarian is by Marlin L. Heckman, "Abraham Harley Cassel: Nineteenth-Century Pennsylvania German Book Collector," *Pennsylvania German Society*, 1973. See also *The Brethren Encyclopedia*. Brumbaugh's popularity as a Penn professor is documented in the provost's annual reports to the university's board of trustees (1894–1906), Cheyney's history of the university, and a few letters from admirers of his. Brumbaughana contains the ongoing correspondence between him and the Juniata College board of trustees about his status as the school's president. It also includes some newspaper clippings and educational journals published during this period of his career that laud his work as an educator and textbook author.

Chapter 7. Caribbean Call

There are a number of letters related to Brumbaugh's appointment as commissioner of education to Puerto Rico in Juniata's archives. His reminiscences of how the invitation to be commissioner came about, his initial opposition to it, the nature of McKinley's appeal, and the reasons he accepted the appointment appear piecemeal in a variety of publications, from newspapers to printed speeches and articles to *Juniata Echo* columns. All these are in Juniata's archives. The secondary sources on Puerto Rico that best suited my purposes were Paul N. Chiles, "The Puerto Rican Press Reaction to the United States, 1888-1898" (Ph.D. thesis, University of Pennsylvania, 1944); Earl P. Hanson, *Transformation: The Story of Modern Puerto Rico* (New York: Simon and Schuster, 1955); Vincenzo Petrullo, *Puerto Rican Paradox* (Philadelphia: University of Pennsylvania Press, 1947); and Knowlton Mixer, *Porto Rico: History and Conditions* (New York: Macmillan, 1926).

Chapter 8. Commissioner of Education

For information on Victor Clark—as for many other lesser-known public figures in this book—I turned to the *New York Times Obituaries Index* (New York: The New York Times, 1970 and 1980). Biographical data on George Groff can be found in Lewis E. Theiss, *Centennial History of Bucknell University, 1846–1946* (Williamsport, Pa.: Grit Publishing

Co. Press, 1946). For original sources during Brumbaugh's years in Puerto Rico, I researched the following government documents: *First Annual Register of Puerto Rico,* prepared and compiled by the Honorable William H. Hunt, Secretary of Porto Rico (San Juan: Press of the San Juan News, 1901); *First Annual Report of Charles H. Allen, Governor of Porto Rico, From May 1, 1900 to May 1, 1901* (Washington, D.C.: Government Printing Office, 1901) and the second one, 1 May 1 1901 to 1 July 1902, printed in the latter year; *Report of Brigadier General George W. Davis, U.S.A. on Civil Affairs of Porto Rico, 1899* (Washington, D.C.: Government Printing Office, 1900); U.S. Department of Interior, *Miscellaneous Reports, Part II, 1900–1902* (Washington: Government Printing Office, 1902); *Annual Reports of the War Department for the Fiscal Year Ended June 30, 1900,* Part 13, Report of the Military Governor of Porto Rico on Civil Affairs (Washington, D.C.: Government Printing Office, 1902); *Report of the Commissioner of Education for Porto Rico to the Secretary of the Interior, U.S.A., 1900* (Washington, D.C.: Government Printing Office, 1900) and the report for 1901; *Insular Government of Puerto Rico with Roster of Employees*—revised to 15 November 1902 (San Juan: Press of the San Juan News, 1902); *Official Directory of the Civil Government of Porto Rico,* compiled by Arthur E. Parke (San Juan, 1901); *Address of His Excellency, Charles H. Allen, to the Two Branches of the Legislature of Porto Rico, December 4, 1902; The Acts and Resolves of the First Legislative Assembly of Porto Rico* (San Juan, 1901); *The School Laws of Porto Rico,* issued by the Department of Education, 9 April 1901; *Education in Porto Rico, Letter from the Secretary of War to the Senate of the First Session of the 56th Congress,* Document No. 363 (Washington: Government Printing Office, 1900); *Annual Report of the Auditor of Porto Rico to the Governor for the Fiscal Year Ending June 30, 1902,* Auditor's Office, 1 January 1903. On library-building by Andrew Carnegie prior to 1902, see *Year Book, Carnegie Institution of Washington* (Washington, D.C.: Carnegie Institution of Washington, 1902). Brumbaugh's own published views on the post-Spanish-American War educational scene in Puerto Rico are set forth in "An Educational Policy for Spanish-American Civilization," *Annals of the American Academy of Political and Social Sciences* 30 (July 1907); "Civil Administration in Porto Rico," *Juniata Echo* 10 (February 1901); "Porto Rico: The Pearl of the Antilles," *Juniata Echo* 9 (October 1900) and a follow-up article in the *Echo*'s November edition; "Education in Puerto Rico," *Journal of American Social Science Association* 40 (1902); "Problems in the Beginning of Education under Civil Law in Porto Rico, 1900–1902," *Proceedings of the Twenty-Second Annual Meeting of the Lake Mohonk Conference,* 1904; "Progress of Education in Porto Rico," National Education Association, *Proceedings and Addresses* 41 (1902); "Puerto Rico, What Has Been Done in Her Education and Development," Pennsylvania Commandery Military Order of Foreign Wars of the United States, *Proceedings of Annual Meeting and Banquet,* 10 January 1907. Brumbaugh's deep affection for Henry Houck is eloquently stated in his eulogy of Houck, one of three printed in *In Memoriam,* published by the Pennsylvania Department of Public Instruction, 1917).

CHAPTER 9. BACK TO ACADEME

For articles on the Sunday-school movement and the Religious Education Association, see *The New Schaff-Herzog Encyclopedia of Religious Knowledge,* 12 vols. (New York: Funk and Wagnalls, 1911). Two books on these topics were particularly helpful to me: Edwin W. Rice, *The Sunday-school Movement, 1780-1917, and the American Sunday-school Union,*

1817-1917 (Philadelphia: American Sunday-school Union, 1917) and Henry F. Cope, *Religious Education in the Church* (New York: Charles Scribner's Sons, 1918). Brumbaugh's role in Juniata's capital fund drive for a new library in these years is told in my *Truth Sets Free*. When I wrote the college's centennial history, however, I did not know that he had already solicited a financial gift from Andrew Carnegie for a library in San Juan. His interest in a Caribbean-located university is reflected in a petition to Congress he signed supporting a bill (HR 15233 and S 4810) to this effect. See the brochure *Pan-American University or Bureau of Education*, International Education Conference and New England Education League (Boston: W. Somerville Sta., 1908), which contains the text of the bill and a letter of endorsement by Brumbaugh stating his preference for Puerto Rico as the university's future site. Several addresses by Brumbaugh during this period of his academic life were printed in pamphlet form: "Educational Principles Applied to the Teaching of Literature," an address delivered before the National Educational Association, at Charleston, S.C., 13 July 1900 (Philadelphia: Christopher Sower Company); "Educational Setting of Stephen Girard's Benefaction," an address delivered in the chapel of Girard College on Founder's Day, 20 May 1902 (Philadelphia: Press of Allen, Lane and Scott, 1902); "Why Women Teach," an address to teachers (Philadelphia: Christopher Sower Company, 1903); "Progress of a Century," an address before Directors' Department of Pennsylvania State Educational Association, Harrisburg, 12 February 1903 (Printed by *The Pennsylvania School Journal*, 1903); "The Simplification of the Secondary School Curriculum," The Association of Colleges and Preparatory Schools of the Middle States and Maryland, *Proceedings and Addresses* 18 (25–26 November, 1904).

CHAPTER 10. FAREWELL TO PENN

A superb source on the first twenty-five years of the Philadelphia Public Education Association—its goals, accomplishments, and officers—is set forth in its booklet, *A Generation of Progress in Our Public Schools, 1881-1912* (Philadelphia: Philadelphia Public Education Association, 1914). Two exemplary muckraking exposés of the political scene per se in Philadelphia are: Lincoln Steffens, "Philadelphia: Corrupt and Contented," *McClure's Magazine* 21 (1903) which became a chapter in his book, *The Shame of the Cities*, published in 1904; and Gustavus Myers, "The Most Corrupt City in the World," *Living Age* 12 (20 February 1904). A revealing account of boss shenanigans and the administration of Philadelphia schools is Clinton R. Woodruff, "A Corrupt School System," *Educational Review* 26 (December 1903). Philadelphia politics in the early 1900s get extensive review by Samuel W. Pennypacker, Brumbaugh's fellow historian of the Pennsylvania Germans who was governor, 1903–7, in his *Autobiography of a Pennsylvanian* (Philadelphia: John C. Winston Company, 1918). From a different perspective, an excellent secondary source on the same period is J. C. Furnas, *The Americans: A Social History of the United States, 1587–1914* (New York: G. P. Putnam's Sons, 1969). For a historical background of Philadelphia and some of its prominent public figures, I relied mainly on Ellis P. Oberholtzer, *Philadelphia: A History of the City and Its People* (Philadelphia: S. J. Clarke Company, 1911) and *Distinguished Men of Philadelphia and Pennsylvania* (Philadelphia: The Press Co., 1913). Various Quaker City newspapers also spoke out against a school system tainted by the Republican machine. Juniata's archives contain a goodly number of letters and newspaper clippings related to the nomination and election of Brumbaugh as Philadelphia's superintendent of schools. For information on Brumbaugh's New England vacation town, see Jack Perkins, *Illustrated History of Wayne, Maine* (Wayne, Me.: Reprinted by the Perkins family, 1993).

Chapter 11. City Superintendent

For this chapter I made extensive use of Brumbaugh's annual reports to the Philadelphia board of education for the years 1906 to 1915. Also of aid in giving me an overall picture of Philadelphia's school system—school buildings, teaching personnel, student population, board bylaws, boards of school visitors, and other data—was *Hand Book of the Board of Public Education*, School District of Philadelphia, 1914. The Public Education Association's booklet was very helpful, as was one by Rabbi Joseph Krauskoff, *What Ails Our Schools?* (Philadelphia: S. W. Goodman, 1910). Another important resource was Jeannette B. Gutman, "The Parent-Teacher Association of the Philadelphia Public Schools (M.A. thesis, Temple University, 1936). On the early years of the city's playground movement, see City Club of Philadelphia, "The Playground Association," *Bulletin No. 3* (4 November 1909). An example of programmatic innovation to meet after-the-school-day needs of children is described in "Agnew Social Center," *Twenty-sixth Annual Report of the Public Education Association of Philadelphia* (Philadelphia: Philadelphia Public Education Association, 1906). See also "Home and School League," *Annual Report No. 7* (Philadelphia: Printed by the pupils of the Philadelphia Trades School, 1912) and "School Gardens," *Twenty-fifth Annual Report of the Public Education Association of Philadelphia* (Philadelphia: Philadelphia Public Education Association, 1906). I found in Brumbaughana two booklets that are seminal in tracing out the playground movement in the Quaker City: one is *Report of the Philadelphia Playground Association* (1910) and the other is *Report of the Board of Recreation on Playgrounds* (1914). Some articles and speeches by Brumbaugh that articulate his educational philosophy as an urban superintendent include "The Function of Education in a Democracy," *Journal of Education* 77 (29 October 1908); "The Teacher in a Republic," *Social Education Quarterly* 1 (March 1907); "A Definite Propaganda to Impress upon the American Mind . . . as Now Provided for Education for Study," National Education Association, *Proceedings and Addresses* (6–12 July 1912); *After Home and School—What?* (Philadelphia: Printed by the pupils of the Philadelphia Trades School, 1913); *Industrial Education and National Progress* (Philadelphia: Printed by the pupils of the Philadelphia Trades School, 1908); "Moral Training of the Young—Pedagogical Principles and Methods," *Ethical Addresses* 15, a lecture supplement to *Ethical Record*, February 1907; *Philanthropy and Public Education* (Philadelphia: Printed by the pupils of the Philadelphia Trades School, 1910); "Some Consideration in Arriving at a New Basis for Promotion and Transfer of Pupils," *Ohio Educational Monthly* 56 (April 1907); "The Relation of an Urban Community to Its Public School System," National Education Association, *Proceeding and Addresses* (6-12 July 1912). The following articles by John Dewey provide interesting resources for comparing his views on industrial education with those of Brumbaugh's: "A Policy of Industrial Education," *New Republic* 1 (19 December 1914); "Industrial Education and Democracy," *Survey* 29 (22 March 1913); "Learning to Earn," *School and Society* 5 (24 March 1917). On Brumbaugh's part in his denomination's bicentennial celebration, see *Two Centuries of the Church of the Brethren* (Elgin, Ill.: Brethren Publishing House, 1908). For Woodrow Wilson's opinion of Brumbaugh as an educator, see John Garber's letter (19 April 1931) in the Juniata College archives.

CHAPTER 12. GUBERNATORIAL CAMPAIGN

In the Juniata College archives there is a large, thick scrapbook of newspaper clippings on Brumbaugh's race for the governorship. Two favorable pieces, one on his nomination and another on his election, were written by noted historian and newspaper literary editor Ellis P. Oberholtzer. The article of his on Brumbaugh the candidate appeared in the *Public Ledger,* 22 March 1914 and was reprinted as a pamphlet. His "Governor Brumbaugh of Pennsylvania" was carried in the *Review of Reviews* 61 (January 1915). There is another scrapbook of press stories on Brumbaugh's condidacy but much smaller. William S. Vare, *My Forty Years in Politics* (Philadelphia: Ronald Swain Company, 1933) tells of his role in plumping the Philadelphia school superintendent for the Republican nomination. I also quote from a pamphlet that is a reprint of an article written by Harry A. Mackey, "The Man Brumbaugh: His Worth and Works" for the 2 November 1914 issue of the *Public Ledger*. For the political background of that era I made use of Robert D. Bowden, *Boies Penrose: Symbol of An Era* (New York: Greenberg, 1937); John T. Salter, *The People's Choice* (New York: Exposition Press, 1971); Robert G. Crist, ed., *Pennsylvania Kingmakers*, Pennsylvania History Studies No. 15, The Pennsylvania Historical Association of The Pennsylvania State University (Camp Hill, Pa.: Plank's Suburban Press, 1985); Ira V. Brown, *Pennsylvania Reformers: from Penn to Pinchot*, Pennsylvania Historical Studies No. 9, The Pennsylvania Historical Association of The Pennsylvania State University (Gettysburg, Pa.: Times and News Publishing Co., 1966); and LeRoy Greene, *Shelter for His Excellency* (Harrisburg, Pa.: Stackpole Books, 1951). There are all sorts of miscellaneous materials related to the campaign in Brumbaughana—promotional pamphlets, platform brochures, booklets of political statistics on each county, expense accounts, speeches, telegrams, and letters. Two anonymous sources I cite in this chapter are among a collection of pamphlets, under the general heading "Pennsylvania Politics, 1901–1915," at the Historical Society of Pennsylvania in Philadelphia: "The Ills of Pennsylvania" and "A Pennsylvania." The Annual Conference minutes of the Church of the Brethren for the years 1910–22 are in the Juniata College archives, hand-bound.

CHAPTER 13. GOVERNOR VERSUS GANG: 1915–16

There is a third scrapbook of newspaper clippings in the Juniata College archives, this one on Brumbaugh's governorship. The clippings peter out after the first legislative session. Some anecdotal material for these years I gleaned from press stories and from other sources such as Charles P. Cooper, "Progress and Reaction in Pennsylvania: Harrisburg's Vision," *Outlook* 111 (29 December 1915); "Penrose and Brumbaugh," *Outlook* 110 (12 May 1915); and reminiscences of Brumbaugh's governorship carried in the *Juniatian* or told in funeral eulogies upon his death or, later, in the memorial graveside talks of Henry Shoemaker. Central to my research, of course, for this—and the following chapter—were public documents such as Brumbaugh's inaugural and his final speeches to the General Assembly, *The Legislative Directory* for his term (containing names of heads of departments, senators and representatives, standing-committee personnel of both houses, and newspaper correspondents), *Vetoes by the Governor* (1915 and 1917), *Laws of the Commonwealth of Pennsylvania* (1915 and 1917); and the mass of Brumbaugh's public papers and letters. Brumbaugh's speech at Reading, in which he deplores the political-spoils system, is printed in a pamphlet by the city's chamber of commerce, dated 26 February 1915. His "Pennsylvania Day Address," on 4 September 1915 at the Panama-Pacific Exposition is printed in pamphlet form and was sent out by him as a Christmas greeting. Statistical data on vocational training in the nation's schools during Brumbaugh's term in office are given in *Biennial Survey of Education, 1916–1918*, Bureau of Education, Bulletin 1919, No. 88, vols. 1, 2, 3 (Washington, D.C.: Government Printing Office, 1921). Juniata's Brumbaughana put at my disposal a batch of pamphlets and booklets on the child-labor problem and proposed reform laws. Among the ones most relevant for this chapter were the following: "Stopping Child Labor By Use of the New Compulsory Education Law," provided for distribution by the Philadelphia Child Labor Committee (April 1908); "Laws Relating to Compulsory Education and Child Labor Affecting the City of Philadelphia On and After January 1, 1909" (Issued by the Board of Public Education, 1909); "Child Labor Laws and Compulsory Education Laws of Pennsylvania," summary prepared by the Pennsylvania Child Labor Association (Philadelphia: October 1911); Charles L. Chute, "The Glass Industry and Child Labor Legislation," reprinted from the *Proceedings of the Seventh Annual Conference on Child Labor*, held at Birmingham, Ala., under the auspices of the National Child Labor Committee, 6–12 March, as published by the American Academy of Political and Social Science, Philadelphia, in the Supplement to *The Annals* of the Academy, July 1911; "Some Facts Relating to the Child Labor Bill Now Before the Legislature of Pennsylvania, Pamphlet No. 33, published by the Pennsylvania Child Labor Association, 5 April 1913); "Your Problem As Well As Ours," published by the Pennsylvania Child Labor Association, n.d.); "A New Child Labor Law for Pennsylvania, 1913," published by the Pennsylvania Child Labor Association); "The Federal Government and Child Labor: A Brief for the Palmer-Owen Child Labor Bill," Pamphlet No. 216 (New York: The National Child Labor Committee, March 1914); "Industrial Education," *Report of the Committee on Industrial Education at the Twentieth Annual Convention of the National Association of Manufacturers*, New York City, 25 May 1915 (New York: Issued from the Secretary's Office, 30 Church Street); the section headed "Public Education and Child Labor Association of Pennsylvania" in the Philadelphia Public Education Association's historical booklet, cited as a source for chapter 10. See also Act No. 131, Section 2, in *Laws of the Commonwealth of Pennsylvania* (Harrisburg, Pa.: W. Stanley Roy, 1917). A pro-Brumbaugh, anti-Penrose "machine," article on child labor appears in "Child Labor," *Outlook* 110 (12 May 1915). A full account of the local-option issue during the Brumbaugh candidacy and governorship appears in my "The Prohibition Movement in Pennsylvania, 1865–1920" (Ph.D. thesis, Pennsylvania State University, 1963). A sixteen-page pamphlet in Brumbaughana, put out in 1914 by the Pennsylvania Motor Federation and promoting a pro-highway-bond vote, is titled "Why You Should Vote for the Fifty Million Dollar Constitutional Amendment for GOOD ROADS." Claude Flory's article, "Annie Oakley in the South," which appears in the *North Carolina Historical Review,* Summer 1966, refers to her sharpshooting exhibitions and gunmanship classes at Pinehurst, North Carolina.

CHAPTER 14. OUTGANGED GOVERNOR AND WORLD WAR I

A long pro-Brumbaugh editorial appears in the *North American* 6 December 1916 on the second speakership contest. LeRoy Greene's *Shelter for His Excellency* gives an insightful and balanced account of the controversy over Brumbaugh's expenses as governor. The

Church of the Brethren's stand on militarism and peace from its formative years to the Second World War is told in Rufus D. Bowman, *The Church of the Brethren and War, 1708-1941* (Elgin, Ill.: Brethren Publishing House, 1944). The official decisions by the denomination on service in the armed forces at the time of World War I can be found in its *Annual Meeting Minutes*. On how Brumbaugh, as a pacifist, rationalized carrying out his official wartime duties I am indebted to Harold B. Statler's "Martin Grove Brumbaugh: Brethren Educator and Statesman," a term paper written in 1951 for a course at Bethany Theological Seminary. See also "The Patriotism of Jesus," *Bible Record*. 3, no. 6 (June 1906), in which Brumbaugh gives a biblical justification for ardent love of one's country. The peace movement in the United States and it anti-universal conscription stand is treated in chapter 6 of Charles DeBenedetti's *Peace Reform in American History* (Bloomington: Indiana University Press, 1980). The secondary sources I researched on Pennsylvania's contribution to World War I included Sylvester K. Stevens, *Pennsylvania: Keystone State* (New York: American Historical Company, 1956); George P. Donehoo, editor-in-chief, *Pennsylvania: A History*, vol. 8 (New York and Chicago: Lewis Historical Publishing Company, 1926); Frederic A. Godcharles, *Pennsylvania: Political, Governmental, Military and Civil*, Military Volume (New York: The American Historical Society, 1933); and *Philadelphia in the World War, 1914–1919*, published by the Philadelphia War History Committee (New York: Wynkoop Hallenbeck Crawford Co., 1922). A good background source on western Pennsylvania for this period is *History of Pittsburgh and Environs*, 4 vols. (New York and Chicago: The American Historical Society, 1922). For representative evaluations of Brumbaugh the governor by professional historians, I drew upon Stevens, *Pennsylvania: Keystone State*; Philip S. Klein and Ari Hoogenboom, *A History of Pennsylvania* (University Park, Pa.: Pennsylvania State University Press, 1973); Wayland F. Dunaway, *A History of Pennsylvania* (New York: Prentice-Hall, 1935); and Donald H. Kent's article, "Pennsylvania," in volume 17 of the *Encyclopedia Britannica*'s 1971 edition. For Brumbaugh's declaration, before an NEA audience, that God was on America's side in the war, see his address "New World Standards of Educational Efficiency," National Education Association, *Journal* 3 (October 1918). His speech on the day of the National Arch presentation at Valley Forge, 19 June 1917, is printed in the *Congressional Record*, Sixty-fifth Congress, First Session, Friday, 22 June 1917.

CHAPTER 15. JUNIATA COLLEGE: PRESIDENTIAL ENCORE

On Brumbaugh's advocacy of outdoor recreation and physical training in the public schools, see the following articles of his: "Physical Fitness for America," *Playground* 16 (February 1923); "Citizenship Values of Outdoor Recreation," *Playground* 18 (July 1924); "Physical Training for All Children," *World's Work* 44 (May 1922); "Physical Education in the Schools," *Normal Instructor and Primary Plans,* March 1923. For his involvement at the national level see *Proceedings of the National Conference on Outdoor Recreation, Held in the Auditorium of the New National Museum, Washington, D.C., May 22, 23, and 24, 1924* (Washington, D.C.: Government Printing Office, 1924). He also published an article entitled "Moral Meanings in Education" in the foregoing journal (September 1923). Brumbaugh's "Harding Memorial Address," given at Wanamaker's Wood on 14 December 1923, is in manuscript form. His second presidential stint at Juniata is dealt with in my centennial history, though from an institutional point of view and thus in much greater detail on the academic program, student life, alumni outreach, athletics, and trustee involvement.

Brumbaughana is replete with records, letters, college publications, and other printed miscellany for the years covered in this chapter. Dr. Kenneth Lewars kindly sent me a photocopy of "The Book of the Guberknocker," the cartoon strip Brumbaugh drew for him in 1924. For eulogies of the deceased Brumbaugh, see the *Juniatian* 6 (19 March 1930); "Memorial Bulletin to Martin Grove Brumbaugh," *Juniata College Bulletin* 27 (May 1930); and a pamphlet put out by the college titled "Tributes to a Lost Leader Whose Vision of a Greater Juniata Must be Fulfilled." Dr. Claude Flory shared his memories of M. G.'s second presidency with me, and Mrs. Frances King graciously let me photocopy pages from her husband's personal journal, which poignantly describe his grief at Brumbaugh's death and the deep affection and respect Juniatians felt toward their departed president.

Index